The AFRICAN ROOTS OF

MARIJUANA

The AFRICAN ROOTS OF
MARIJUANA

CHRIS S. DUVALL

Duke University Press   *Durham and London*   2019

© 2019 DUKE UNIVERSITY PRESS
All rights reserved
Printed in the United States of America on acid-free paper ∞
Designed by Courtney Leigh Baker
Typeset in Garamond Premier Pro by Westchester Publishing Services

Library of Congress Cataloging-in-Publication Data
Names: Duvall, Chris S., [date] author.
Title: The African roots of marijuana / Chris S. Duvall.
Description: Durham : Duke University Press, 2019. |
Includes bibliographical references and index.
Identifiers: LCCN 2018044272 (print)
LCCN 2018053869 (ebook)
ISBN 9781478004530 (ebook)
ISBN 9781478003618 (hardcover : alk. paper)
ISBN 9781478003946 (pbk. : alk. paper)
Subjects: LCSH: Marijuana—Africa—History. | Marijuana—
Social aspects—Africa—History. | Marijuana—Economic aspects—
Africa—History. | Marijuana—Therapeutic use—Africa—History. | Cannabis—
Africa—History. | Cannabis—Social aspects—History. | Cannabis—
Economic aspects—Africa—History. | Medicinal plants—Africa—History.
Classification: LCC HV5822.M3 (ebook) | LCC HV5822.M3 D88 2019 (print) |
DDC 362.29/5096—dc23
LC record available at https://lccn.loc.gov/2018044272

Cover art: "Usage du tabac et du chanvre chez les Wadia," Maes expedition, Congo Basin. Photo postcard, ca. 1914, published by Ern Thill, Brussels. Courtesy of the author. Leaf illustration: "[D]akka, a plant, called Bangua by the Indians," engraving, in J. J. Schwabe, *Allgemeine Historie der Reisen zu Wasser und Lande* (Leipzig, Germany: Arkstee and Merkus, 1749).

To JHR

Contents

Pay Attention to African Cannabis

ONE

Cannabis and Africa

Marijuana does not cause trypanosomiasis. This is one fact I will offer.

I will not offer much information on other topics some readers might expect in a book about marijuana and Africa. I offer very little about Rastafarianism, for instance, and mention Bob Marley just once more. These examples are crucial in a history of cannabis broader than this one. My research period ends in approximately 1925, a few years before Rastafarianism arose in Jamaica. I have chosen 1925 because this was when cannabis was first listed in an international drug-control agreement, which initiated the now familiar condition of global cannabis prohibition. This book is about what preceded the familiar.

For the period before 1925, I touch on some characters that frequently appear in cannabis histories, including Scythians, Queen Victoria, and the Bena Riamba. Perhaps these characters are unfamiliar to you; their parts will unfold. Whatever your awareness of cannabis in the global past, I will touch on the unfamiliar, because I focus on Africa.

I make a simple argument: Africa has been neglected in popular and scholarly histories of cannabis, and this neglect undermines the capacity of global societies to manage the plant drug. There are no histories of psychoactive cannabis in any continental region, not just Africa. However, Africa is especially important. African knowledge is foundational to the now dominant global use of cannabis as a smoked drug. If you know *nothing* about cannabis except that it can be a smoked drug, your knowledge traces to Africa.

FIGURE 1.1. The imagery and content of Jamaican reggae music has shaped popular understanding of cannabis in Africa. Reggae lyrics that celebrate *ganja* and African heritage reflect views within Rastafarianism and Jamaican society, not an awareness of the plant's actual African past. Photograph by Sheila G. Duvall.

There is an enormous literature on cannabis. I do not cover it all. At points, I am quite critical of recent portrayals of the plant's history. I mention publications ranging in substance from *The Lancet* to *Playboy* magazine. My view is that histories of cannabis—whether book-length scholarly studies, vignettes in medical literature, or tidbits in popular media—are poorly researched and unjustifiably neglect Africa. My critiques may seem frivolous—it should be obvious that ads in *Playboy* may be misleading—only if you overlook the closeness of pop culture and academic discourse about cannabis. The same factual errors appear in high and low places, because the same conceptual errors are shared across society. The conditions of cannabis prohibition have warped ideas about the plant. The collective historical narrative about cannabis is built predominantly from pretentious, politically motivated factoids rather than documented evidence about the plant's past.

Africa is ignored in the collective historical narrative. The widely shared nonportrayal overlooks the fundamental importance of African knowledge to the global practice of cannabis smoking. More important, the nonportrayal of Africa intellectually justifies notions that drug use is a racially determined

In New York City, during 1997–2008,
53% of people
arrested for marijuana possession
were Black,

and 26% of the population was Black.

35% of the population was White,

and 12% of people
arrested for marijuana possession
were White.

In Chicago, during 2012–2014,
78% of people
arrested for marijuana possession
were Black,

and 33% of the population was Black.

45% of the population was White,

and 4% of people
arrested for marijuana possession
were White.

In the U.S. in 2010, among males aged 18-25,

17% of Blacks   and 20% of Whites
admitted to using marijuana in the past month.

FIGURE 1.2. Marijuana arrests and population by race in New York City and Chicago, 1997–2014. New York City decriminalized possession of small amounts of marijuana in 1977, as did Chicago in 2012. Sources for these data are given in n. 1. Graphic by Chris S. Duvall.

behavior. The collective narrative, being unconstrained by evidence of the plant's African past, enables anti-Black, racial stereotypes about cannabis drug use. In the United States, one outcome of these stereotypes is biased drug-law enforcement.[1]

Again, however, my focus is on Africa and the period before 1925. I do not offer much on current drug-law enforcement, primarily comments about its intellectual basis. My focus is on what preceded the familiar. To understand why cannabis appears in international drug laws at all, for instance, the intellectual pathway leads to colonial Africa.

Neglect of Africa in cannabis history has real-world consequences in and beyond the continent. African knowledge lies at the foundation of the dominant global culture of psychoactive cannabis use, even as Pan-African experiences are ignored in developing approaches to managing the plant as an economic, pharmacological, ecological, and political resource.[2] To understand cannabis in the modern world, the pathway leads to Africa.

CANNABIS IS AMONG the most widely recognized plants. Its leaf ☘ is globally iconic. This book is written for people who know that cannabis can supply psychoactive drugs, as well as industrial products such as fiber for rope or cloth. Many people know little else about the plant. Some people know brief anecdotes about its history; George Washington and Queen Victoria are sometimes mentioned. A few people with especial interests in the plant have published world histories of it.

World histories of cannabis comprise a distinct literary genre. Among the canon, *Cannabis: Evolution and Ethnobotany* (2013) is a new classic; *Smoke Signals: A Social History of Marijuana* (2012) and *Cannabis: A History* (2005) have both sold many copies for mass-market publishers; *Marihuana: The First Twelve Thousand Years* (1980) is foundational to many newer works.[3] The most influential of all is *The Emperor Wears No Clothes*, an anti-prohibition tale first published 1985 and now in its twelfth American English edition, with editions in other languages and countries.[4] *The Emperor* is as poorly researched as widely read. Many works offer shorter histories, ranging from the obscure to the current mainstream (such as in 2014's authoritative *Handbook of Cannabis*).[5] Many physicians have offered historical vignettes about cannabis to justify their scientific interest in medical marijuana (see chapter 10). George Washington somehow used cannabis, so why shouldn't we?[6] The vignettes of scholars blend with the sound bites of popular media to become common knowledge about the plant's history, a knowledge poorly rooted in facts.[7] It is not true, for instance, that "Cannabis has been used throughout the world for thousands of years and by all types of social classes, including Queen Victoria in the 1800s."[8]

Cannabis histories reflect the political-economic conditions of their authorship. Most have been written by authors interested in advancing political arguments for or against the drug plant's prohibition. Cannabis histories display political advocacy more than desire to build knowledge and test assumptions about the past.[9] The first serious history of *marihuana* in Mexico, of all places, was published in 2012, Isaac Campos's *Home Grown: Marijuana and the Origins of Mexico's War on Drugs*.[10] Other serious historians have investigated cannabis elsewhere. Some who have looked at the plant drug in African societies include Emmanuel Akyeampong, Johannes Fabian, Gernot Klantschnig, Liat Kozma,

James Mills, David Gordon, and Wolfgang Cremer. Academic histories are much less well circulated, though, than popular books like *The Emperor*.

Political debates about cannabis in current societies have shaped knowledge about the plant in past societies. Real historical events have been overlooked, or, if noticed, spun beyond recognition and never studied for insight on the people-plant relationship. An important example is the origins of global cannabis prohibition. Campos shows that a War-on-Drugs mentality originated within Mexico, well before the rise of harsh anti-marijuana rhetoric in the twentieth-century United States. Political-advocate histories have ignored the plant drug's past outside the United States, simplistically portraying global prohibition as a blight spread by U.S. political-economic dominance and tinged by racist attitudes within the United States.[11] Cannabis histories often target Harry Anslinger as the driving force behind global prohibition. Anslinger was the first commissioner of the Federal Bureau of Narcotics, a precursor to the Drug Enforcement Administration (DEA). He strictly enforced drug laws through his thirty-two-year commissionership (1930–62). His influential public discourse vilified marijuana and its growers, peddlers, and users.[12] Anslinger's classic paper, "Marijuana, Assassin of Youth" (1937), adapted a centuries-old Orientalist stereotype about drug-fueled violence to serve his purposes in twentieth-century America.[13]

Despite his real role in cannabis history, Anslinger has been made into a semifictional straw man, easy to topple as a stand-in for the idea of prohibition. *The Emperor Wears No Clothes* ostensibly paraphrased U.S. prohibitionists in Louisiana in the 1910s as saying marijuana "mak[es] the 'darkies' think they [are] as good as 'white men.'"[14] These unsavory words were written in 1985 by a pro-marijuana activist but now circulate without restraint as a direct quote from Anslinger in outlets that include *Rolling Stone* magazine (2016), the scholarly book *Race and the Black Male Subculture* (2016), and the academic periodical *Kansas Journal of Law and Public Policy* (2017).[15]

These false attributions serve to make cannabis control an outcome of "abhorrent hatred toward immigrants and racial minorities" in the United States.[16] This is not an accurate portrayal of prohibition. Initial U.S. cannabis-control laws were about controlling pharmacy practice and preventing use of a drug thought to produce individual and public-health problems.[17] Local anti-cannabis laws preceded federal prohibition, but these were widely preemptive bureaucratic initiatives passed before psychoactive cannabis gained any other local attention.[18] Anslinger was initially hesitant to bring marijuana under federal control but did so to favor domestic politicians; he always remained more concerned about morphine and heroin. Racial bias in all aspects of U.S. law enforcement was entrenched long before Anslinger, whose ideas about human difference surely reflected his time. However, none of his published writings display the racial virulence that pro-marijuana activists have placed in his mouth.

Legal controls on cannabis did not originate in the United States. Controls were in place globally before the U.S. federal government began worrying about marijuana in the 1930s.[19] The roots of global prohibition lay in early twentieth-century Africa, not in American bureaucrats. Cannabis first appeared in an international drug-control agreement, the International Opium Convention signed in Geneva in 1925, because South Africa and Egypt asked for it to be included, and the world went along. Both countries had had cannabis controls in place since 1870. Decades before Anslinger, most African colonies had banned cannabis, often in explicitly racist terms and principally to control the hard laborers who were the plant drug's principal users (see chapters 8 and 9). The world came into compliance with colonial African ideas about cannabis.[20]

Cannabis is a global crop. Over the past five centuries, the plant genus has colonized the world, expanding its outdoor range to encompass effectively all ecologically suitable territory between about 60 degrees north and south latitudes. Humans have been the primary dispersal vector for the plant. People have carried cannabis seeds into many landscapes, including colonists hoping to make rope in new lands, slaves saving seeds to plant somewhere someday, and marijuana growers trying to breed new varieties. The plant's biological dispersal was inevitably a political-economic process, because it was a human endeavor.

It's challenging to understand the plant's history because of its challenging nomenclature and its dichotomous material values. I discuss cannabis taxonomy in chapter 2. At this point I will simply adopt the view that there are two major genetic groups within the *Cannabis* genus: *indica*, which exhibits psychoactive chemistry, and *sativa*, which does not.[21] When italicized, *indica* and *sativa* refer to these groups, which are not the same as the groups of plants that marijuana aficionados call indica and sativa. Nonitalicized indica and sativa designate folk species—plant types that are recognized informally within a social group—and are unreliable indicators of genetic relationships between plants.[22]

The genetic lineages have their own histories of biological dispersal. The center of evolutionary origin for *Cannabis indica* was around the Hindu Kush mountains in highland South Asia, while *Cannabis sativa* originated in temperate Central Asia. The midlatitude population traveled westward to colonize Europe, where people valued it for fiber and hempseed. The psychoactive population colonized southern and eastern Asia and about a third of Africa, the

TABLE 1.1. Key Components of a Cannabis Vocabulary

Term	Definition as used in this book
Cannabis	The formal, scientific name of the botanical genus.
cannabis	An informal name for the botanical genus.
Cannabis indica	The genetic group of plants that displays psychoactive chemistry. This group originated in the southwestern Himalayas and has been grown globally up to about 35 degrees latitude (see chapter 2).
Cannabis sativa	The genetic group of plants that does not display psychoactive chemistry. This group originated in temperate Central Asia and has been grown globally between about 35 degrees and 60 degrees latitude (see chapter 2).
drug	A substance that is consumed or applied externally that alters bodily function through biochemical pathways beyond the digestion of calories or nutrients.
hemp	A use of *Cannabis* plants that generally entails fiber production (as for textiles and cordage) or hempseed production (as for food or oil).
indica	A psychoactive folk species recognized by marijuana aficionados. Although idealized as a short plant with wide leaflets, it is recognized by its pseudosedative effects, not its physical form (see chapter 3).
marijuana	A set of practices and knowledge that is associated with *Cannabis indica*, as developed in the United States since circa 1900. This is not a general term but has specific geographic, historical, and cultural relevance.
pharmaceutical cannabis indica	*Cannabis* herbal material that is used in Western pharmacy and some preparations made from this herbal material (see chapter 9).
sativa	A psychoactive folk species that is recognized by marijuana aficionados. Although idealized as a tall plant with narrow leaflets, it is recognized by its pseudostimulant effects, not its physical form (see chapter 3).

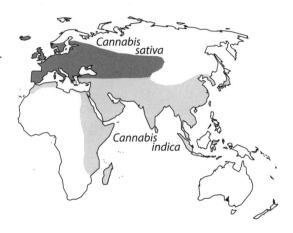

MAP I.I. Global distribution of cannabis, circa 1500. Map by Chris S. Duvall.

northeastern portion, by 1500. Three major subgroups exist within the psychoactive population. In eastern Asia, these plants were bred for fiber and hempseed production, not psychoactive products, although they retained psychoactive chemistry. In South Asia, people developed two major subgroups, one associated with the production of *charas* (cannabis resin), and one associated with *ganja* (female flowers or, more precisely, pistillate inflorescences).

Historical accounts of cannabis come principally from European observers, many of whom had strong opinions about how others interacted with the plant. During the Age of Sail, hemp fiber was crucial to European political-economic power. Each large ship required dozens of tons of maritime-quality rope and canvas that needed to be regularly replaced. Political-economic authorities sought continually to increase plant-fiber production, but farmers often did not want to grow the crop because of its heavy labor demands. An early impetus for economic botanical exploration of the world was to find fiber plants that were easier to process into high-quality rope and cloth.[23] Yet despite the problems of producing cannabis fiber, throughout the period before 1925, hemp represented agricultural bounty, industrial success, and maritime strength in European media. Psychoactive cannabis drug use was contrarily framed as a waste of a plant resource presumed to be more valuable if made into rope.

For European documentarians in colonial Africa, perceptions of cannabis drug use were entangled in ideas about class and race. Racial ideas coevolved with the historical epidemiology of drug use. The drug-use practices of people in social underclasses were stereotyped as deleterious to individual and public health. The social-ecological processes that produced marginality elevated the importance of subsistence therapeutic resources to these people, including cannabis. Racial categories commonly served to mark class differences so that the social-ecological conditions of wealth and poverty were considered the natural states of different racial groups. Notably, the racial category "Black" (and historical synonyms) arose as an intellectual justification for chattel slavery.[24] In colonial societies around the Atlantic, the conditions of Blackness, marginality, and psychoactive cannabis drug use became associated and were assigned negative meanings in European thought.

Drug use by White, social-ecological elites, by contrast, was sanctified as open-minded experimentation, free-thinking expression, or intrepid worldliness. The documents of cannabis history come almost entirely from Western travelers, few of whom claimed direct experience with the plant drug. Those who did could boast of cannabis consumption even while condemning it among others, because their status allowed them to dabble with low-class drugs without fear of social repercussions. Elite privilege has shaped the telling of cannabis history, too. Consider the twentieth-century American writer Paul Bowles, whose writings helped form current popular understanding of cannabis in Morocco. Public representations of Bowles's drug knowledge exuded worldly coolness, as when he told eager but naive *Rolling Stone* readers in 1974, "There's no good Moroccan hashish. It's not a product [Moroccans] ever used. The first ones who made it were mostly American blacks who brought presses and showed the Moroccans how to do it."[25] His worldliness alone backed up his anecdote: trust the expert, the bad drugs trace to Blacks. Yet Bowles's knowledge of Moroccan language and culture was superficial, despite his long residence in the country.[26] Narratives of cannabis history reflect the partial perspectives of privileged observers; race and class shaped both patterns and portrayals of drug use in past societies.

It's crucial to think about race and class in understanding cannabis history. For the world population of *Cannabis indica*, the main pathway to global dispersal passed from southern Asia across the Indian Ocean to sub-Saharan Africa and from there across the Atlantic. The political economy of its trans-African and transatlantic dispersal was the global expansion of capitalism after 1500. Cannabis was integral to exploitative labor relationships upon which capitalist endeavors and colonial expansion depended, including plantation economies in the New World connected to slave economies in the Old World. The psychoactive cannabis seeds that crossed the Atlantic accompanied disease, trauma, violence, and poverty. Cannabis histories have overlooked this people-plant relationship, mostly because Pan-African experiences have been ignored.

Common-knowledge history provides intellectual bases for decisions made about managing the drug plant in current societies. My pre-1925 focus limits my engagement with current debates. Cannabis decriminalization is a prominent issue in many countries and jurisdictions[27]—notably, in the United States, where I reside. Not until chapter 10, the last chapter, do I discuss current debates, and even there I consider only three topics: how global society manages cannabis as an agricultural resource, as a medicinal resource, and as an object of legal control. I conclude that wider understanding of cannabis history would improve how societies manage it today.

To start toward these conclusions, I begin by reviewing portrayals of Africa in cannabis histories. The documentary record for cannabis in Africa is rich but has been almost completely ignored by historians. This book summarizes what has been overlooked, and with what consequences.

MY BACKGROUND IS in the field of African studies. I am interested in historical geographies of Africans in the Atlantic World, by which I mean the many and varied connections that exist across and around the ocean basin.[28] I am trained as a geographer, focused on people-plant interactions. My thinking about Africans and plant geography has been shaped by Judith Carney, Andrew Sluyter, Robert Voeks, Londa Schiebinger, and others who have shown that Africans were fundamentally important in the transformation of landscapes around the Atlantic after 1492 and that long-standing biases have led scholars to overlook the creative contributions of Africans in historical societies.[29] Africans were not merely labor in Atlantic history, even if slavery sharply constrained how people could alter the conditions they experienced. Obviously, Africans were not alone. People from Europe, Asia, and the Americas shaped post-Columbian landscapes, too.

Biological and cultural diffusions of cannabis are historically and geographically traceable.[30] The minimal facts in cannabis histories show that Africa and Africans should not be overlooked. Here are the minimal facts: human-cannabis interactions originated in Central Asia more than twelve thousand years ago. The plant and knowledge of its uses diffused globally along several pathways. Perhaps one thousand years ago, cannabis arrived in East Africa from South Asia and in North Africa through connections around the Mediterranean Sea. The plant dispersed widely throughout the sub-Saharan region.

Within Africa, three cultural features are widely agreed on. First, many works have suggested that *dagga* is *the* African word for cannabis. This is the principal term for the plant drug in South Africa, ultimately from an unknown

Khoisan language. Many publications have applied the term widely, including a book that states *dagga* is "spoken widely across the continent, and sometimes applied to any psycho-active plant material."[31] Other cannabis histories use *dagga* in situations as diverse as historical South Sudan; among slaves in the southeastern United States; in reference to both Louis Armstrong and "Black Africans"; and as an "Arabic or Khoikhoi" term in Southern Africa.[32]

Second, all works emphasize "the most interesting anecdote concerning cannabis in Africa[,] . . . in which the drug transformed . . . a tribe of feuding miscreants to one dedicated to peace and goodwill."[33] This interesting anecdote refers to the Bena Riamba political-religious movement, which persisted around 1870–90 in what is now the southern Democratic Republic of the Congo (see chapter 6). In its normal telling, marijuana inspired tranquility and goodness in a group of people who previously had been prone to warmongering and cannibalism.

The third commonly (but quietly) repeated mention of Africa in cannabis histories is that slaves perhaps carried knowledge of the plant drug across the Atlantic to Brazil.

Only one work ostensibly covers *Cannabis in Africa*, the title of a 1980 book by the sociologist Brian du Toit.[34] This remains the state-of-the-art historical geography of the plant on the continent, although its geographic aspect was identified explicitly as a survey in the book's subtitle. The book instead was a sociological study of drug use in 1970s South Africa. It is valuable in both regards, even though its historical-geographic limitations are clear. For example, it reports "no evidence of cannabis in West Africa before the Second World War."[35] This statement has been widely repeated. Nonetheless, primary sources show that psychoactive cannabis was present in nineteenth-century Gambia, Liberia, Niger, Nigeria, Sierra Leone, Senegal, and, possibly, Guinea and Togo.[36] Du Toit did his research before the internet. I have benefited from digital repositories made available in the past decade, which allow unprecedented access to an enormous number of searchable historical documents.[37] This book is an outcome of investments global society has made that make printed knowledge widely available via the internet.

All histories agree that the drug plant's African dispersal pathway essentially ended at the continent's shores and had little consequence for world culture. All that departs Africa on global dispersal maps is a single, thin line vaguely toward Brazil that represents weak statements such as, "[Cannabis was] possibly . . . brought directly by slaves or traders from Africa to the New World."[38] This portrayal of Africa as globally unimportant except (perhaps) for Brazil reflects conventional wisdom, not the documentary record.

Cannabis histories are almost uniformly bad when it comes to representing African experiences. There is no shortage of outlandish statements that belie ignorance of historical context, if not of documented facts. A book from 2005 announced that it "has been conjectured" that African slaves brought cannabis seeds to Brazil in "magical talismanic dolls."[39] This is a ridiculous conjecture, given basic knowledge of transatlantic slaving. Enslaved people were not allowed to retain personhood, let alone dolls, particularly dolls that might have been related to indigenous spirituality. Uninformed embellishments such as magical dolls belittle the experiences of the millions who endured enslavement and obscure the real involvement psychoactive cannabis had in slavery.

The idea that a fantastically primitive spirituality underlies the plant drug's African past resonates with—or, rather, is sustained by—notions about African backwardness. Cannabis histories offer fantastic rumors of the primitive and exotic—*talismanic dolls!*—to supplement thin knowledge. A book from 2012 generalized with no apparent basis that cannabis was "a staple of African shamanism."[40] Another from 2016 says that "the savants of Zululand . . . burned cannabis flowers . . . and prophesized the future,"[41] although such prophesizing is not traceable in the book's cited sources. Poor research practice sustains nonsensical—or, at least, misleading—anecdotes. A book from 2013 gossiped that "a somewhat obscure sect in the Sudan [was led by] a strange woman [who promoted] the smoking of *Cannabis* (*dagga*)."[42] The basis for this factoid *is* obscure: the book cites no source but obviously borrowed from a 1980 book that inaccurately summarized and incompletely cited a 1927 paper by a colonial administrator, who started the rumor to suggest that cannabis made the natives hard to rule.[43] Cannabis histories have preserved an array of outdated ideas and plagiarized errors by failing to perform the basic research practice of checking and citing sources. Plagiarism in the cannabis literature has a proud history, going back to sixteenth-century European scientific botany and following more than a millennium of embellished, distorted, and inaccurate repetitions of the Greek physicians Dioscorides and Galen.[44]

More widespread than plagiarism is uncritical repetition. Scholarly reviews of cannabis books have included such praise as "highly incestuous" (1975) and "less . . . careful scholarship than a polemic" (2007).[45] Common-knowledge stories supplement thin knowledge about Africa even in high-end histories. Consider the book *Forces of Habit: Drugs and the Making of the Modern World* (2001), which remains foundational to studies of drugs in global history. Nearly everything that *Forces of Habit* includes on cannabis and Africa is the quote: "Angolan slaves . . . brought cannabis [to] northeastern Brazil . . . sometime after 1549. One story has it that the slaves carried the seeds in dolls. . . . The planters allowed the slaves to grow [cannabis] between the rows of cane, and to smoke and dream during periods of inactivity."[46] The entire passage is an unsourced rumor, presented as common knowledge. Its factoids can be traced alongside the errors they perpetuate. "Dolls" and "1549" come from a 1975 paper that has been widely repeated without citation, despite its critique of incestuous cannabis books.[47] The paper cites another paper from 1958 that no one seems to have read since 1975. The 1958 work introduced two errors. First, 1549 was when the Portuguese crown authorized sugarcane plantations in Brazil; the date is meaningless regarding cannabis for reasons related to labor history and because there is no evidence cannabis was present in western Africa until the 1700s. Second, it stated that Pio Corrêa, an author no one since 1958 has traced, wrote that slaves carried seeds in "dolls."[48] In 1926, the Brazilian botanist Manoel Pio Corrêa reported an oral history that was inaccurately summarized in 1958. Pio Corrêa wrote not about "dolls" but about captives who "tied [seeds] into the edges of their wraps and loincloths."[49] This anecdote is believable; slaves were sometimes allowed rags and at least occasionally succeeded in carrying valued seeds across the Atlantic.[50] The between-the-rows-and-smoke-and-dream factoid comes ultimately from a 1937 book that offers an impressionistic, idealized, and simplistic recollection of northeastern Brazil. It frames psychoactive cannabis as an unfortunate remnant of slavery and thus something to expunge from twentieth-century Brazil.[51] This factoid also betrays ignorance of historical context. A basic knowledge of Brazilian slavery suggests plantation bosses would not have tolerated slaves' planting anything in direct competition with a principal cash crop, especially not a drug plant that slave owners disdained (see chapter 7). The smoke-and-dream nonsense is contrary to documented uses of cannabis among laborers in Brazil and Central Africa, who valued the plant drug as a stimulant associated with work (see chapter 8).

Even the best academic works have treated Africa as an episode in cannabis history worth mentioning for its fantastic qualities—*between the rows and smoke and dream!*—but not worth examination. Unsourced, common-knowledge statements about cannabis history are mostly traceable rumors, errors, or omissions, whether about Africa or elsewhere.[52]

AFRICA HAS BEEN NEGLECTED in cannabis histories. The broader intellectual problem is the history of scholarship that neglects African contributions to world culture.

This problem has markedly affected knowledge of the sub-Saharan region and the African Atlantic Diaspora. Historically, Africans were portrayed as recipients of knowledge introduced from Europe or Asia rather than as producers of knowledge that shaped societies elsewhere. However, recent studies of agriculture, technology, and ethnobotany have shown that African knowledge was foundational to practices of plant use and management within societies across the Americas.[53]

One notion I challenge is that Africa is backward technologically, that useful inventions have gone to Africa but none have come out. I raise this challenge with regard to smoking paraphernalia in chapter 3. The technologies of plant use are crucial components of people-plant interactions. Smoking pipes were unequivocally invented in sub-Saharan Africa centuries before 1492—in some locations, as much as two millennia before Europeans encountered American Indian pipes packed with tobacco.[54] Dry pipes were invented on both sides of the Atlantic. Water pipes originated in Africa, where they were historically associated with cannabis. The earliest direct evidence of cannabis smoking anywhere is residue that archaeologists scraped from fourteenth-century water-pipe bowls unearthed in Ethiopia.[55] Earlier pipes have been recovered widely across sub-Saharan Africa, just without evidence of what was smoked.

Most cannabis histories make no mention of paraphernalia, despite the dominance of smoking in current people-cannabis interactions worldwide. Histories that do mention pipes and Africa rely on two outdated narratives: that smoking pipes arrived in the Old World only with Europeans coming back from the New World, and that cannabis smoking arrived in Africa only with "Arabs" or "Muslims."[56]

The unchallenged dominance of these narratives has forced researchers to fit their data to them rather than interpret data to understand the past. The field of archaeology has particularly struggled to overcome belief in African backwardness.[57] Archaeologists have considered pipes in ancient African sites not as evidence of ancient pipes, but as evidence of erroneous radiocarbon dates, site disturbance, or mysteriously rapid sediment accumulation. Archaeologists have struggled to develop regional chronologies because some have taken pipes as indubitable indicators of the post-Columbian period regardless their broader context, while sites without pipes have been dated based on interpretation of the entire context. Some archaeologists have maintained ignorance of readily available, published evidence of ancient smoking in Africa. For example, the few archaeologists who have examined the origin of water pipes in southwestern Asia—Iran and Yemen specifically—have puzzled over their regional appearance around 1600. Some of this literature completely omits Africa,[58] despite the evidence of ancient smoking on the landmass mere miles across the Red Sea from Yemen. Other works dismiss African pipes as not indigenous but "more likely to have . . . spread there . . . from the Middle East," with no justification offered for the presumption.[59] This statement from 1993 echoes a publication from 1930 that interpreted the mere presence of water pipes in Madagascar as proof that Portuguese ships had brought the technology there from Persia.[60] The 1993 statement neglects the best review of African pipe archaeology, published in 1983, which concludes that water pipes came to Persia from Ethiopia.[61]

Africans are portrayed as passive recipients of cannabis, too, not just of pipes. The stereotype that Arabic-speaking Muslims brought cannabis drug use into Africa has dominated interpretations of the plant for 150 years. In the 1860s, European visitors in Central Africa concluded that cannabis smoking "probably spread from the East—Egypt and her neighbours" and that "the negroes" were unable to resist the drug plant's "gradual but sure advances" across the continent.[62] Cannabis and tobacco came to symbolize colonialist belief in the fundamental character of western European versus Islamic culture. In 1886, one traveler concluded that cannabis had "penetrated a considerable distance westward [because] Islam, carrying its special cult from East to West by the instrumentality of fire and sword, accomplished its work far more speedily than the civilisation of Western peoples [has] advance[d]."[63] In 1932, the thesis was fully developed:

> [The] distribution [of cannabis smoking] is closely and curiously associated with the distribution of Islam. For some obscure reason—perhaps the prohibition of alcoholic beverages—it seems to be more attractive to Mohammedans than to others. Next to Mohammedans, African Negroes are the principal hemp smokers. [T]hey learned the habit from the Arabs . . . , though there may have been an earlier diffusion of it among the [South African] Bushmen.[64]

This stereotype has been updated—the terms "Mohammedan" and "Negro" are no longer used. The theme, characters, and narrative remained in 2005: "Under Arabic influence, cannabis use spread across North Africa and south into sub-Saharan eastern Africa, although even an approximate date for this expansion outside the Islamic sphere is uncertain."[65] The practice of attributing people-plant dispersal to some unknown, ancient moment discourages research.[66] Historical distancing makes the mythical drug trafficker and the passive smoker into characters whose existence is not worth questioning.

The only basis for the Arab/Muslim-influence narrative is its repeated publication. There is no evidence cannabis was used in the Arabian Peninsula at the time of Muhammad, and such use did not appear elsewhere in conjunction with the expansion of Islam in the late first millennium of the common era (CE). There are many examples in which psychoactive cannabis has been prominent in non-Muslim societies, most obviously in South Asia, where secular and religious use traces back at least four thousand years in at least four religious traditions.[67] Cannabis drug use has never been prominent in some Muslim areas, conspicuously including the Sahel region immediately south of the Sahara. The earliest hints of psychoactive cannabis in the Levant are about three thousand years old, but there is no clear, consistent evidence until about nine hundred years ago in Persia and eight hundred years ago in Egypt and Arabia. Smoking pipes existed widely in eastern and southern Africa by that time and held cannabis in fourteenth-century Ethiopia, where Christianity was practiced. There were few Arabic speakers or Muslims south of the Sahel until centuries later. The earliest documentation of cannabis from the sub-Saharan region came in the 1600s from locations far removed from the influence of Islam or Arabs, including southern Mozambique, Madagascar, and South Africa.[68] East African coastal entrepôts—most notably, Zanzibar—hosted Arabic- and Farsi-speaking merchants beginning in the first millennium CE, but they had essentially no presence on the continent beyond these towns. Instead, Swahili traders organized caravans to inland areas.

Nineteenth-century European travelers referred to "Arab" traders in East Africa and Central Africa and alleged that they spread cannabis smoking. However, the so-called Arabs were Swahili-speaking Africans who perhaps spoke Arabic, too, because it was useful in commerce. They also likely professed Islam, wrote Swahili with the Arabic script, and dressed in styles that Europeans considered stereotypically Muslim, with flowing robes and turbans. There is scant evidence that traders used cannabis themselves but abundant evidence that their employees—the porters who carried commercial goods—smoked the plant drug. Porters carried cannabis on their travels and acquired it en route, but they were definitely not Arab and mostly not Muslim. Commercial porters were predominantly younger men, poorly paid, poorly fed, and poorly sheltered for months-long hikes, made while carrying fifty or more pounds at the rate of twenty miles per day.[69] They were often forced into service by political leaders who found benefit in supplying labor to traders, colonial bureaucrats, or European travelers. (For more on porters, see chapters 5–8.) There was no sweeping Arab, or even Muslim, expansion through the continent's center, particularly one bearing cannabis. Africans at the very bottom of international commerce—those who carried the political economies of slavery and colonialism directly upon their backs—helped the plant cross Africa, not some mythical Arab overseer.

By 1800, water pipes and hashish had become stereotypical motifs in European images of the Orient. These motifs diversified and flourished with Orientalist thought. Cannabis smoking was rhetorically important in establishing an

FIGURE 1.3. Émile Bernard's painting situates hashish in Egypt's lowest social class. The woman's clothing, jewelry, and *gozeḥ*-type water pipe are symbols that would have indicated poverty to many European viewers and would also have suggested that she was a prostitute. These symbolic elements were common in contemporaneous postcards from exotic Egypt—indeed, the painting was reproduced abundantly as a postcard in the early 1900s. Yet Bernard simultaneously challenged customary Orientalist imagery. The woman is fully clothed and appears lucid, rather than drug-addled. Émile Bernard, *La fumeuse de haschisch* [The Hashish Smoker], oil on canvas, Cairo, 1900. See P. A. Conley, "Émile Bernard in Egypt," *Nineteenth-Century Art Worldwide* 5, no. 2 (2006): article 3.

exotic, non-European character for people and places worldwide, in situations as far-ranging as West Africa in the 1870s, Algeria in the 1890s, and Mexico in the 1910s, as well as in the works of Allen Ginsberg, The Beatles, Timothy Leary, and other marijuana aficionados of the 1960s.[70] In these imagined, Orientalist contexts, psychoactive cannabis evokes a dreamy, sensuous hedonism, an inversion of idealized Western pragmatism and industriousness. In 1873, a travel writer portrayed a fictional British physician in Sierra Leone as someone who "moderately smok[ed] the *liamba*, or African haschisch" and "possessed an Oriental temperament, and shunned the . . . social restrictions of the North [Europe]."[71] Europe imagined psychoactive cannabis as best typified in the Levant, where many travelers first encountered the plant drug.

The tales of European travelers have captivated readers for centuries. Their travelogues are key sources for cannabis history, and it's important to understand their perspectives, but this book is mainly about the anonymous people foreign travelers observed.

Travelers had varying views about drugs. On one extreme were people like Mary Kingsley (English, 1862–1900) and Henry Morton Stanley (American, 1841–1904) who found African drug use absolutely foul and a cause of the uselessness they perceived in many Africans. David Livingstone, the English missionary (1813–73), was more sympathetic, but he still got "a feeling of disgust" from cannabis smokers.[72] Most travelers were indifferent. The strange use of the familiar plant was notable but not particularly interesting to many observers, including João dos Santos (Portuguese, circa 1560–1622), Peter Kolbe (Dutch, 1675–1726), and Paul Du Chaillu (French American, 1831–1903). Their uninterested mentions of cannabis are among the best records of the plant's past. Some travelers discussed the plant drug more extensively, although extensiveness usually did not produce insightfulness. Alexandre Dumas (French, 1802–70) was less interested in understanding hashish than in using it to produce exotic literary atmospheres; Hermann von Wissmann (German, 1853–1905), was more concerned with political-economic machinations than ethnography in his accounts of the Bena Riamba movement (see chapter 6).

The British voyager Richard F. Burton (1821–90) was a particularly important source writer. He provided firsthand accounts of cannabis in India; Arabia; North, East, Central, and West Africa; and Brazil. His relationship with the plant drug was fraught. In 1851 he decided that Indian users were a "debauched . . . set of half savages."[73] Cannabis was a "poison" among slaves in Brazil in 1869.[74] But in 1876 he admitted smoking cannabis "for months together" in Central Africa,[75] and in 1857 he wrote, "Egypt surpasses all other nations in the variety of compounds into which this fascinating drug enters, and will one day probably supply the Western world with 'Indian hemp,' when its solid merits are duly appreciated."[76] Despite his global knowledge, he finished by portraying hashish as a "Mohammedan paradise" in his rendition of the Thousand-and-One Nights folk tales (1885–88).[77]

FIGURE 1.4. Like all European travelers, Hermann von Wissmann (standing, second from left) depended on Africans as guards and porters during his travels in the southern Congo Basin in the 1880s. Wissmann particularly relied on Chingenge, Sangula, and Mukenge (seated, left to right), who were leaders of the Bena Riamba political movement. Bena Riamba adherents used large, calabash-based water pipes, such as Mukenge holds between his legs in this engraving. "Am Kongo," engraving, in H. von Wissmann, L. Wolf, C. von François, and H. Mueller, *Im Innern Afrikas: Die Erforschung des Kassai während der Jahre 1883, 1884, und 1885*, 3d ed. (Leipzig: Brockhaus, 1891), facing page 414.

More important to me are the people whose names I don't know—the slaves, porters, prostitutes, soldiers, sailors, and laborers whom travelers saw smoking cannabis. Unfortunately, I can learn of these people only through past writers, who recorded scant information about them. I can name very few of the people this book is about, such as Nimo and Musulu. Nimo (Congo Basin, lived in the 1920s) was a teenage servant of an American traveler who smoked cannabis while working (see chapter 8). Musulu (Congo Basin, lived in the 1890s) was a young man abandoned into slavery by his fellow travelers after he suffered a foot injury (see chapters 6 and 9). Musulu was a subject of the cannabis-smoking Bena Riamba movement, which Wissmann found useful. He thus recorded much about the movement's leaders, particularly Mukenge, Chingenge, and Sangula (who were active from 1870 to 1890). Again, though, I am more concerned with those who were unnamed, including the people who emerged from slave ships in Sierra Leone in the 1840s "so deplorably emaciated that the skin appeared tensely stretched over, and tied down to the skeleton."[78] Forgotten people such as these carried cannabis seeds across Africa and the Atlantic, helping it become one of the world's most widespread drug plants. Many European travelers led fascinating lives, but their stories are not those to learn to understand cannabis, despite my repetition of their names in this book.

Islam was wound into Orientalist caricatures as the compelling force behind the drug plant's dispersal. This stereotype ignores a long history of Islamic prohibitions raised by political-religious authorities, earliest documented in Egypt in the thirteenth century CE.[79] The stereotype also neglects processes of historical change. Psychoactive cannabis initially arrived in Europe, for example, not with Muslims or outsiders in general, but with European sailors who began using the plant drug in India before 1540.[80] Early modern Europe had cultures of smoking herbs other than tobacco—including hallucinogens and perhaps psychoactive cannabis—that are scarcely remembered.[81] It's important to recognize this shadowy European past, because the small historical population of sailors on European ships carried knowledge of smoking and psychoactive cannabis to port cities worldwide, including many in Africa. This shadowy past extended into the early 1900s in the activities of drug runners such as the Frenchman Henri de Monfried, a sailor turned smuggler turned best-selling author of dozens of semifictional adventures.[82]

Accounts of cannabis in Africa were important in forming European ideas about the plant drug. Explicitly fictional and ostensibly nonfictional portrayals of cannabis overlapped to produce a common knowledge of its cultural geography. Stereotypes are often inextricable from portrayals of cannabis use.[83] Historical European observers purposefully blurred real observations with fictional embellishments, because their accounts served simultaneously to produce an imagined geography of their travels and to impart authenticity to their writing. The Englishman Winwood Reade, who in 1873 created the *liamba*-smoking European doctor in Sierra Leone, had earlier created the image of *Savage Africa* (1864) in a travel account. His fiction was poorly researched, despite his traveler's credentials. In 1864, he showed scant knowledge of cannabis among the savages: "In Angola, [they have] a kind of narghileh or water-pipe. The narghileh is generally used to soften the niamba [*sic*], a kind of haschisch which they smoke. . . . So powerful is this drug that one whiff will make these inveterate smokers cough."[84] Reade at best watched non-European smoking practices from afar and betrayed no particular interest in them. Reade's word choices were dismissive of Angolan cannabis. *Ḥashīsh* and *nargīleḥ* were Levantine Arabic terms for a drug product and a type of water pipe, respectively; the product, the pipe, and the terms were not used in Angola. Orientalist thought created holes in the historical record because it offered easy rhetorical shortcuts to conceal ignorance of unfamiliar smoking practices.

African practices were overlooked partly because European writers framed the Levant as where psychoactive cannabis reached its cultural pinnacle. Cannabis consumption in the eastern Mediterranean region included sweet, hashish-based confections with lengthy recipes, such as *majūn* (an Arabic word).[85] Edible cannabis concoctions that existed south of the Sahara were overlooked and uncommon anyway. Historical sub-Saharan societies were satisfied with smoking cannabis. Smoking transforms the plant drug as a pharmacological agent; its effects are felt quickly after inhaling, compared with a half-hour or more after eating cannabis-laced food. It is easy for smokers to control dosage but difficult for hashish eaters. Nonetheless, Europeans perceived this preference for smoking as backwardness. "Orientals use refined preparations of cannabis resin," reported a French traveler in 1889, but Central Africans only smoked "the rustic form" of mixed flowers, leaves, and seeds.[86] A paper from 1972 stated, "None of the more elaborate techniques of using *Cannabis* in the Mediterranean or the Near East accompanied the plant into Africa, and practices in the central part of the continent in the thirteenth century were very simple."[87] (Evidence describing uses of *any* plant in thirteenth-century Central Africa would be unprecedented; it is unfortunate this evidence was not cited. It is likewise unfortunate that the 1972 passage was repeated uncritically in 2013.[88]) The very presence of the plant in African landscapes has been taken as evidence of prehistoric visits from more civilized peoples. One traveler determined that ancient Phoenicians must have built the Great Zimbabwe ruins, because cannabis grew on the site in the 1890s.[89]

Cannabis smoking in Southern Africa troubled historical European observers because no Levantine influences were obvious in the region. Observers struggled to find evidence to fit the narrative. In the 1950s, a German missionary in what is now Namibia concluded that *dagga* came from the Arabic word *dukhān* (smoke). Indigenous Khoikhoi people must have adopted the foreign word, he thought, because there might be a similar-sounding Khoikhoi phrase meaning "drunkenness." His critics considered the Khoikhoi link "rather too tortuous" but accepted the proposed Arabic derivation, for which no historical, linguistic, or other evidence was supplied.[90] There was no historical presence of Arabic speakers in southwestern Africa, and no languages south of the Sahel have any Arabic loanwords related to cannabis or smoking in general.[91] Presumptions of Africa's backwardness have for decades necessitated that scholars seek outside influences to explain cannabis on the continent. Orientalist thought established the Muslim Levant as the only reasonable source of influence, and uncritical repetition has maintained this bias in cannabis histories.

Cannabis history must be rethought, especially in relation to Africa. Historians have overlooked considerable evidence while repeating rumors. The assumption that Africa is a cultural backwater must be rejected. The minimum facts of cannabis in Africa—the plant and smoking pipes existed on the continent centuries before 1492—necessitates paying attention to African cannabis. This book offers a cannabis history with Africa at the center, not the margins.

THIS BOOK HAS HISTORICAL and geographic limits. The time period I consider has an indefinite beginning and an approximate end in 1925, the date of the Geneva opium convention. The indefinite beginning encompasses prehistoric evidence for cannabis, stretching back to uncertain hints three thousand years old. The approximate end date reflects two considerations. First, the historical record on psychoactive cannabis shrank as antidrug sentiments arose; smokers hid their activities from observers. In most locations I touch on, the documentary record ends sometime before 1925, because many jurisdictions had already banned the plant drug. Second, in a few locations there are important accounts of psychoactive cannabis more recent than 1925, and I cite these newer studies as sometimes relevant for understanding earlier conditions. I want particularly to mention anthropological studies from the 1970s that examined why workers used cannabis and how it affected their performance, in Colombia, Costa Rica, Jamaica, Cuba, Trinidad, and South Africa.[92] The results of these studies are broadly generalizable and relevant for understanding past and present drug use among laborers (see chapter 8).

My main historical focus is the nineteenth century, partly because this was when Europeans began to notice and regularly document psychoactive cannabis worldwide. More important, the century was crucial in the plant's global dispersal, because the last and largest flows of captives in transatlantic slavery came from western Central Africa, where slavers supplied *mariamba* in their feeble efforts to manage slaves' health. During the last century of transatlantic shipping (approximately 1760–1860), this Central African captive migration grew to exceed all other geographic segments in the history of the transoceanic trade.[93] This group of people included about three million who entered the Middle Passage; many million more died during forced marches from inland towns to seaports. This migration by far surpassed in size and geographic extent that of all other groups of people who carried knowledge of psychoactive cannabis across the Atlantic. This book is about the broader histories and geographies that surrounded the unknowable experiences of these enslaved people.

My geographic focus is the continent of Africa, but my spatial scope is global. In organizing my thoughts, I will generalize about Africa as a continental region and about several other regions worldwide. My geographic scope and focus vary by chapter, but my broad limits reflect four historical processes. First, I outline conditions in southern Asia, where psychoactive cannabis originated evolutionarily and had a long history with humans before it came to Africa. Second, I sketch the global commerce in pharmaceutical cannabis indica that endured from about 1840 to 1925. This drug trade linked growers in British India to commercial traders in London, then to pharmacists worldwide. Third, I consider Africa as a whole, to identify social-ecological conditions that have existed widely, and to identify limits to generalization about people-cannabis relationships across the continent. Finally, my narrowest scope is western Central Africa and the diaspora of people taken from that region.

My work also has limitations due to my research methods. I have relied only on published data; I cite two unpublished, archival sources. There are untapped archives of cannabis in African history, but the published literature has been untapped, too. Scholarly histories have overlooked major episodes in the plant's history because they have overlooked published works that were not obscure in their day. An article that described cannabis drug use among slaves in Angola, for instance, appeared in 1850 in London's *Pharmaceutical Journal*

MAP I.2. African regions, countries, and territories mentioned in the text. The Cape Verde islands, which lie several hundred miles west of Senegal, are also mentioned once in the text. Map by Chris S. Duvall.

and Transactions,[94] which was widely read by nineteenth-century medical scientists. The journal's pharmaceutical content suggests that recent researchers reasonably should have encountered the article when studying the plant drug's history in medicine, a topic several authors have claimed.[95] None, however, have mentioned this documented use of cannabis in chattel slavery. Of course, some of the published primary sources I've read were obscure, such as trade records from secondary colonial ports. My review of the published literature is a necessary step toward locally or regionally focused archival studies. My broad geographic scope matches my reliance on the published record, which offers mostly sparse information about particular locations, though about many locations. I offer a spatially and topically broad overview that may help readers identify archives relevant to cannabis research in specific locations.

Further, unlike Thembela Kepe, Laurent Laniel, Franco Loja, Julian Bloomer, Ann Laudati, Brian du Toit, Pierre-Arnaud Chouvy, Kenza Afsahi, and others, I have not conducted field research on cannabis in Africa. My research trajectory began with historical documents, not field experience. In 2011, I found reference to psychoactive cannabis as "Angolan tobacco," but found no mention of this plant in recent works on Africans in transatlantic crop dispersal.[96] I then consulted the principal world histories of cannabis but became distrustful of what I read. I independently researched the plant's world history, which I published in the blandly titled book *Cannabis* (2015).[97] After that, I refocused on Africa. This is a broad focus; regional and national histories, including field research, are needed. I have studied overarching themes.

Published literature is heavily filtered through the writer's view of the world and choice of words, the editor's purview, and the publisher's willingness to put something in print. A frustrating aspect of the published, primary record is that European documentarians often just didn't care much about psychoactive cannabis drug use. I am saddened that Du Chaillu began his comments on *liamba* in 1850s Gabon with the disclaimer, "Hasheesh and the *Cannabis Indica* are so well known that it is not necessary to say anything about them here."[98] He went on to describe a slave who was keeping cannabis seeds—the only known observation of seed saving by a slave in Africa of any plant. I am saddened that the British botanist William Daniell concluded his comments about Angolan cannabis in 1850, "It would be unnecessary here to enter into any further details connected with this subject, as it has been fully treated of in the works of several able writers, who have given ample descriptions of this plant."[99] He had just described how slavers gave *liamba* to their captives, who were loaded with commercial cannabis drug shipments while themselves bound for sale. These were among the most detailed accounts of African cannabis; most observers were succinctly dismissive. "What is iamba?" asked a Frenchman in 1883 after having lived four years on the Lower Congo. "I do not know, and, to my great regret, I neglected to collect it; but, if it is necessary to believe certain travelers, it will be the leaves of hemp or flax."[100] The majority of travelers didn't mention it at all. I take the minority view, as expressed in 1853 regarding North Africa: "The mention of hashish leads me to speak about this plant, on which much has been written for several years now and on which there remains much to say."[101]

There are no historical accounts of cannabis from drug users other than tales from a handful of European experimenters, people such as the writers and artists who formed the Parisian Club des Haschichins in the 1840s. Other than these men, who sampled hashish because they wanted to sample an imagined Oriental experience,[102] I do not know why historical people used psychoactive cannabis. Some European observers ostensibly recounted what users said about the plant drug. The attributed statements are informative, though filtered. In one example from 1843, freed slaves from Angola allegedly considered *diamba* "a sovereign remedy against all complaints," according to a colonial surgeon.[103]

To evaluate such claims, I assume that the past pharmacology of cannabis can be estimated from current medical science. Cannabis is chemically complex. All plants in the genus produce chemicals called cannabinoids, of which about 110 are known to occur naturally. I mention just three: Δ9-tetrahydrocannabinol (THC), the psychoactive one; cannabidiol (CBD), which affects pain sensations, appetite, and immune response; and tetrahydrocannabivarin (THCV), an appetite suppressant. Plant cannabinoids interface with the mammalian endocannabinoid system, made up of nerve receptors and endogenous chemicals, such as the neurotransmitter anandamide. The endocannabinoid system has roles in motor learning, sensing appetite and pain, recalling memories, and modulating mood.[104] Plant cannabinoids can chemically mimic endocannabinoids, as THC mimics anandamide.

Present knowledge of cannabis pharmacology is strong, with thousands of articles published annually in the medical sciences and major summaries in books such as *The Handbook of Cannabis* (2014), *Marijuana and Madness* (2011), and *The Health Effects of Cannabis and Cannabinoids* (2017).[105] The medical consequences of consuming any drug are categorized as objective effects (physiological responses with biochemical explanations) and subjective effects (the individual experiences of users). I assume that objective effects of cannabis drug use that are known in current medical science existed for past users. Thus, Algerian hunters who smoked before going out in the 1840s perhaps valued the plant drug for enhancing their night vision, a pharmacologically verified effect among current Moroccan fishermen.[106]

An important, objective aspect of cannabis pharmacology is its toxicity, which is very low. Nonetheless, cannabis overdoses are unpleasant, if not debilitating, and can cause fatal cardiovascular events.[107] Historical accounts of cannabis smoking that led to unconsciousness and death (see chapters 5 and 6) are medically believable. Further, current medical science robustly links cannabis drug use to increased risk of psychosis, schizophrenia, and other mental illnesses.[108] Not all past reports of mental health crises—of smokers running amok or going mad—came from ethnocentric, racist, or anti-cannabis biases.[109]

Unlike objective effects, subjective effects are context-dependent. People have widely varying experiences from taking psychoactive cannabis, partly because genetic variation among people affects cannabinoid uptake and metabolism.[110]

Further, subjective effects depend upon the mind-set of the user and the social setting of drug use.[111] By *thinking* psychoactive cannabis will produce an effect, the user's expectations help produce that effect, aided by plant biochemistry. Thus, context determined whether cannabis stimulated boldness and bravery or relaxation and sociability among Zulu men (in South Africa) in the 1890s, one of several examples I mention in chapters 4 and 5.

An important form of subjective experience with cannabis is nowadays called "addiction," or, more formally, cannabis use disorder. In current societies, approximately 10 percent of regular users develop behavioral dependence on psychoactive cannabis.[112] Historical users also sometimes developed attractions to the plant drug that are analogous to the current diagnosis of cannabis use disorder. In South Africa in 1913, a physician reported symptoms from smokers that modern physicians have associated with dependence: fixation on the plant drug, irritability when deprived of it, and continued use despite negative health effects.[113] Users sometimes had strained relationships with cannabis. An extreme example is the Ḥeddawa brotherhood in Morocco, a group of mendicant Islamic monks who considered *kif* a sacrament and a curse.[114] Some Ḥeddawa adherents found their drug use beyond control and a self-diagnosed cause of mental illness.[115] Those afflicted in this way made a pilgrimage to the tomb of the sect's founder to seek release from the plant drug. This ambivalence—of psychoactive cannabis being both good and bad to its users—extends widely in its global history.

It is necessary to restrain estimates of the plant drug's past importance. First, cannabis consumption was not uniform within or between societies, although there are almost no quantitative data. Perhaps one in twenty adult male Egyptians used *hashīsh* in 1893, or perhaps one in one hundred adults.[116] Perhaps one in thirty or forty adults smoked in the southern Congo Basin in 1913;[117] more generally in Central Africa, during the 1850s–1910s, scattered observers had impressions that cannabis was not heavily consumed.[118] Rates of consumption at the population level varied between societies. The two estimates I can make are for 1891 for British Guiana (42.8 grams of *ganja* per capita), just one-ninth the consumption estimated in 1899 for a town in northern Morocco (360 grams of *kif* per person—a gram per day, on average, for every townsperson).[119] Rates of consumption varied between individuals, of course. Some who tried cannabis didn't like it and didn't adopt it, as documented in South Africa in 1913.[120] I have found only one quantitative estimate of what a European observer considered heavy use. A physician in British Guiana recorded that a patient in a mental hospital—an indentured Indian laborer—had been spending 3–4 shillings per week on *ganja* in 1893, at a time when indentured workers could be fined a shilling per week for absenteeism.[121] In 1895, *ganja* cost 16 shillings per pound, which suggests that the man was smoking 12–16 grams *per day*.[122]

Such heavy use was exceptional. Most historical users received low doses of THC and other cannabinoids. There were no robust tests of psychoactive potency until THC was identified in 1964,[123] and, anyway, there were no earlier efforts to test plants outside the Western pharmaceutical industry. Since 1964, researchers have chemically assayed cannabis worldwide, primarily material seized by police. In the 1970s, plants tested around the tropical Atlantic exhibited low THC concentrations, in the range of 0–10.5 percent.[124] People were not smoking flowers with 20–30 percent THC, as are now sold in open markets in the United States. Historical accounts similarly suggest weakly psychoactive material. "Our *maconha* [is] weak in active principles," reported a Brazilian in 1937, "and often it is smoked without giving any strong sign of intoxication."[125] There is little historical evidence on other cannabinoids, mainly tests for CBD since the 1970s. Historically, people preferentially smoked inflorescences, where THC is concentrated, but sometimes also burned leaves mixed with flowers. Prices limited individual intake based on income, while shared pipes in group settings limited how much each person could inhale. Some people, of course, took high doses via intense smoking bouts, and some smoked constantly for years on end.

It is unnecessary to characterize instances of drug use as "medicinal" or "recreational" (to employ current language). People who consider cannabis simply a good-time intoxicant receive the same chemicals that cause others to consider it therapeutic. Regardless of the contexts of consumption, the plant drug has objective effects for all users, although the strength of an effect can depend on individual health factors. Notably, malnutrition can produce endocannabinoid deficiency, which means that small doses can produce marked therapeutic effects in users with extremely poor diets.[126] Good-time feelings may arise from generalized if unrecognized therapeutic benefits, magnified by euphoriant objective effects and enjoyable social contexts. For people facing physical and emotional challenges, cannabinoids can be beneficial even in small doses, and even if the plant drug is not explicitly considered therapeutic.

People-plant relationships bear health meanings, for humans and the environment, and are products of entangled social, cultural, and ecological conditions.[127] In Trinidad, the anthropologist Ainsley Hamid studied the social-ecological conditions of psychoactive cannabis farming, distribution, sales, and use, calling this "the ganja complex."[128] I examine many such complexes in varying detail. I provide names for psychoactive cannabis in many languages and regard these names as representing unique people-plant relationships, often similar to others but nonetheless historically distinct. Several names are the principal foci: *dagga, ḥashīsh, maconha, marihuana, cangonha, kif, takrūri, soruma, ganja,* and the cognate word groups *bhang/bang/bangue/bangi* and *diamba/riamba/liamba/iamba*. Each people-plant relationship combines human cultures of practice and knowledge, genetic lineages of both people and plants, environmental conditions necessary for human and plant survival, and the political-economic conditions that enable the system's reproduction.

I emphasize context because I am influenced by ideas in the scholarly field of political ecology, in which human-environment interactions are thought of as simultaneously social and natural events.[129] Three threads of thought I will mention. First, I am convinced of the value of understanding health as a product of political-economic and environmental processes.[130] Wellness and illness are not simply characteristics of individuals; they are aspects of more-than-human ecosystems. Social structures differentially expose people to health risks, to knowledge about risks, and to resources for managing illness and injury. Drugs can be risks and resources for individuals, but their use can also be more broadly symptomatic of health vulnerabilities produced by human activities and ecological change.[131] In terms of public health, I take the perspective of descriptive epidemiology.[132] I identify and describe social-ecological conditions associated with historical cannabis drug use (especially in chapter 8). Although I suggest causal linkages between cannabis use and individual and public health conditions, the historical data are insufficient for an analytical epidemiological study. I argue that the plant drug has been symptomatic of trauma produced on the social and ecological margins of capitalist political economies, but I do not identify particular processes that lead to drug use.

The second thread I follow is to use political-economic approaches to evaluate human-environment interactions.[133] This I do mostly in chapters 6–9. I argue that cannabis has helped social elites extract value from workers by enhancing the capacity of people to endure risky environments while caught in exploitative labor relationships—chattel slavery, indentured servitude, coerced labor, wage slavery, and so on. Cannabis must be included among the drugs that were "labor enhancers" in colonial Africa, functioning to draw people into labor relationships and to improve their endurance while working.[134] At the same time, though, cannabis drug use enhanced the capacity of these workers to resist their exploitation by aiding purposeful inefficiencies, mental escapes, conspiracies against bosses, and so on.[135] Understanding psychoactive cannabis as an element of capitalist political economies helps clarify the historical epidemiology of drug use. Historical precedent has strongly shaped current opinion in medical science, yet past epidemiologies of psychoactive cannabis use have been mostly overlooked—in part because medical scientists have completely overlooked Pan-African experiences with the drug plant (see chapter 10).

The final political-ecological thread I take is to analyze environmental knowledge as expressions of social and cultural power.[136] Knowledge of people-cannabis relationships is rooted deeply in the colonial past, although these roots mostly have been forgotten. Common ways to think about cannabis nowadays commonly reflect outdated assumptions first made by people with arrogant faith in the objectiveness, accuracy, and completeness of their worldviews, and with disdain for the worldviews of others. Colonial scientists, travelers, and bureaucrats who observed cannabis in faraway lands presumed to know better than the natives how the plant should be used. During the past half-century, pro-marijuana activists and anti-cannabis prohibitionists have exchanged presumptions about the faultiness of the other side's knowledge. In interpreting the cannabis literature, I have been inspired by political-ecological studies showing that conventional wisdom about environmental problems in Africa—such as deforestation, desertification, and erosion—often reflect antiquated presumptions and political-economic machinations rather than actual observations.[137] I am ambivalent toward all accounts of cannabis, reading each as objective description and subjective portrayal alloyed in varying ratios. Cannabis histories should not be accepted uncritically, because the same politically motivated errors have been repeated for decades, in both high-end research and low-end pulp.

The greatest error has been to overlook African cannabis.

TWO

Race and Plant Evolution

How does a history begin? For plants, histories begin in the arcane world of botanical taxonomy.

All cultures classify plants on the basis of subjective ideas about what makes different plants different. Taxonomies specify the plants that are perceived in a culture.[1] In Western science, professional taxonomists have classified the world's plants for centuries, mostly by studying dried specimens in herbaria. Scientific taxonomies provide the conceptual building blocks of natural history. There is no thinking about evolution, biodiversity, or ecology without species to think about. Likewise, only if a plant is perceived to exist can it have a distinct, traceable history.[2]

When a plant is given a branch in a taxonomic tree, this suggests how it relates to other plants—in terms of use, appearance, habitat, or some other way. Western natural science focuses on biological relatedness, because evolutionary theory is a powerful means of understanding how the biosphere acquired its current form. In technical terms, a "species" is a population of organisms with a shared ancestral lineage.[3] Species are often physically, behaviorally, or ecologically distinct, but the key characteristic, again, is that each species is a separate lineage that began at some point, for some reason. Species are crucial to studying the biological past because they are simultaneously historical objects (things with histories) and analytical tools (events that provide evidence of historic processes). Once a species is placed in a taxonomy, scientists speculate on how it became distinct—the event biologists call speciation. Numerous processes can cause speciation. Ecological interactions, such as competition, can cause groups of organisms to become different within a single landscape, while geological processes such as continental drift can divide a population geographically, giving rise to distinct species. When change happens, natural selection favors the genes that give individuals a survival advantage. With sufficient time, surviving individuals become a self-reproducing lineage. By identifying a species and a cause of speciation a scientist is stating a hypothesis about how current biodiversity patterns reflect evolutionary history.[4] Every plant history begins with both a species and a hypothesis of how that species became distinct.

Identifying species is not always straightforward. Scientific taxonomy has been a mostly visual activity. Taxonomists have spent numberless hours examining the visible forms of plant specimens to distinguish species. Form is generally a good indicator of evolutionary and ecological differences among groups of organisms.[5] In many cases, however, groups of similar plants are less obviously distinct. These taxonomically difficult organisms have defied scientists by failing to exhibit clearly and consistently distinct physical appearances. Taxonomic proposals for these organisms are debated, revised, rejected, and scorned until taxonomists reach consensus and formally name the species under specialized naming rules. Yet even formal naming does not end the debates about some taxonomically difficult organisms, particularly *Cannabis*.[6]

In recent decades, taxonomy has experienced transformation. Molecular genetics have allowed botanists to perceive previously unrecognized, cryptic species and to hypothesize origins for these genetically distinct but physically indistinguishable organisms.[7] Biodiversity is hidden in essentially invisible molecules. Physical features still matter, but hypotheses about species and speciation are increasingly tested with molecular data that indicate biological relatedness.

Historians have also provided data for testing ideas about the biological past—not evolutionary hypotheses per se but instead ideas about how humans have shaped the biosphere. Historical data are most important for domesticated plants. In particular, scholars have shown that Africans had important roles in transforming New World environments after 1492. Their findings have challenged long-standing belief that enslaved Africans were nothing but passive labor in European-led initiatives.[8] The geographer Judith Carney, for example, has shown that slave plantations in the southeastern United States first grew West African rice, *Oryza glaberrima*, and not the more familiar Asian species *Oryza sativa*, as had been assumed.[9] The slaves' foundational contribution to the plantation economy is recognizable, in part, by recognizing two species of rice.

SCIENTISTS HAVE DEBATED *Cannabis* taxonomy since the 1700s.[10] Dozens of species have been proposed and rejected. The defining characters of the putative species have been ostensibly visual: leaf shape, plant height, floral structure, seed size, stem fiber, and so on. However, in most cases these visual characters have been conceptually secondary to how humans use particular cannabis populations, because human behaviors have seemed more distinctive than the plants themselves.[11] Most importantly, not all cannabis individuals are psychoactive. The plants farmed in Enlightenment Europe for fiber and oilseeds (and non-psychoactive drugs) were not. The plants grown elsewhere, especially in India, where Europeans first began to study mind-altering cannabis, were farmed to produce drugs (and fiber and seed, but these uses were often overlooked). In 1783, the French naturalist Jean-Baptiste Lamarck was the first to name psychoactive *Cannabis indica* separately from non-psychoactive *Cannabis sativa*. He said the two were distinct because *indica*'s leaves occur singly along the stem while *sativa*'s leaves come in pairs. Other naturalists were not convinced the types were so distinct. In fact, Lamarck was more focused on what people did with the plants. He did not really know what the putative *indica* plants looked like, having seen only "some [dried] morsels brought from India."[12] Lamarck's comments about *Cannabis* use were, in contrast, substantial. He considered *sativa* "an extremely interesting plant because of its usefulness." This species was "planted abundantly in Europe, for the great utility we have for the filaments from its stem, and for its seed." In contrast, *indica* "[is] incapable of furnishing filaments similar to that [of] the former species.... The principal virtue of [*indica* is] to provide [the brain] a type of drunkenness that makes chagrin forgotten and provides a sort of gaiety."[13] Lamarck's selection of European hemp as the archetypical *Cannabis* remains prominent in botanical literature.

Cannabis has been a contentious taxonomic subject because it is highly variable in physical form, and people have not found physical characters that reliably correlate with the psychoactive-versus-non-psychoactive distinction. The appearance of individual plants depends on environmental conditions, especially soil fertility. The plant's capacity for long-distance pollination and seed dispersal facilitates genetic exchange among distant populations. Layered on this inherent variability are the distorting effects of millennia of human selection. People have harvested cannabis seed, fiber, leaves, and flowers from one end of Eurasia to the other for at least twelve thousand years and have farmed it for eight thousand years in China, four thousand years in South Asia, and two thousand years in Europe.[14] For centuries botanists have acknowledged the lack of reliable, visible characters to distinguish cannabis types.[15] The current, formal taxonomy deals with the morphological challenge by describing cannabis as "a single, highly variable species" distorted through millennia of artificial selection.[16] Morphological data are poor for identifying cannabis lineages.

Chemical and molecular data provide a better foundation for cannabis history. Since the 1970s, botanists have found several consistent combinations of cannabinoids among cannabis types. Taxonomically, the most important are THC and CBD. Psychoactive plants produce more THC than non-psychoactive ones. However, the total quantity of THC or CBD a plant produces is less important taxonomically than the THC-to-CBD ratio. People can alter the total quantity of cannabinoids that plants in a particular lineage produce, but not the ratio (which can be manipulated only by crossing different lineages).[17] Altogether, phytochemical evidence suggests two major cannabis lineages: one that produces mostly THC, another that makes mostly CBD.

Molecular data similarly suggest two major lineages that correspond to the chemical types. Researchers have identified several genetic traits that consistently differ between the types.[18] The botanist Karl Hillig's analyses of cannabis allozymes are particularly important because they suggest how the two types originated.[19] Allozymes are genetically determined chemical variants of a single enzyme. Agricultural selection does not affect the occurrence of different allozymes, because the chemical variants of an enzyme all perform the same biological function. People might select plants with traits linked to one enzyme, but this will equally affect all of that enzyme's variant forms. Hillig's analyses show that two genetic types of cannabis arose independently of human selection of plant traits.[20] Cannabis biodiversity has been degraded in many landscapes because the two types are cross-fertile (like many pairs of related plant species) and have mixed for millennia in many locations across south-central Eurasia.[21] Nonetheless, distinct, cryptic species underlie outcomes of artificial selection.[22] For instance, despite millennia of agricultural selection for fiber and seed characters, East Asian cannabis cultivars maintain THC-dominant phytochemistry.[23] Cannabis history encompasses at least two narratives, of two distinct plants separately colonizing the world.

Possible narratives of cannabis history are constrained by the plant's biogeography. There is consensus that the genus originated in Central Asia. The two types have—or, at least, historically had—broadly distinct distributions characterized by latitude.[24] The non-psychoactive *Cannabis sativa* has dispersed globally between about 35 degrees and 60 degrees latitude, north and south of the equator. This type was the sole cannabis in Europe from prehistory into the 1800s.[25] *Cannabis indica* grows primarily below 35 degrees latitude, with several exceptions.[26] Plants grown for fiber and seed in Japan, Korea, and northeastern China grow beyond this latitude. European and North American hemp farmers began widely planting East Asian seed in the 1840s, thereby germinating persistent feral populations that people would harvest for drug use in the twentieth century.[27] Drug plants in the Afghanistan-Pakistan-Tajikistan borderlands also grow north of 35 degrees. There are two strains of plants from this area, not fully separate lineages but associated historically with different farming practices. One strain was selected to produce cannabis resin (i.e., hashish), the other to produce cannabis flowers (or *ganja*).[28] The latter strain has colonized the low latitudes starting with lowland South Asia about 3,500 years ago.[29] Both strains have been grown with patchy success in warmer mid-latitude locations, principally since the 1960s. Despite these exceptions, the underlying biogeography is clear: psychoactive plants grow at lower latitudes, non-psychoactive ones grow nearer the poles.

Based on this pattern alone, botanists have recognized the need for two narratives of cannabis history at least since the 1850s.[30] Nonetheless, virtually all nontaxonomic publications have adopted a one-species concept of cannabis, considering every plant to represent *sativa*.[31] *Cannabis indica* has been a secondary plot. Some taxonomists still champion a one-species concept,[32] while others have adopted a two-species idea reflecting genetic evidence.[33] Whatever taxonomical consensus might emerge, it is necessary to recognize that botany is not apolitical and that the one-species idea has long borne political ideologies.[34] Taxonomists adopted a one-species concept in the 1970s, for instance, because it was useful in drug-law enforcement.[35] A more deeply historical example is that the one-species idea has coevolved with a plant history that depends on, and seemingly substantiates, racial stereotypes of drug use.

THE DOMINANT THEORY of cannabis speciation is that the types became different because people bred one plant population for psychoactive potential and another population to produce fiber and hempseed.[36] For example, a textbook from 2013 specifies, "THC content is not of great natural adaptive significance [to the plant]. From evolutionary and ethnobotanical points of view, THC is to a large extent a human artifact."[37] This hypothesis of anthropogenic (or human-caused) speciation recognizes that "nature" had some role in producing diversity within the genus, but a secondary one: "Natural environment and culture work hand-in-hand[, but] human intervention has been the major force in the evolution of *Cannabis*."[38] The anthropogenic speciation hypothesis means that historians must examine the human past to understand the plant rather than analyze the plant itself. The central historical question becomes identifying the farmers who chose drug over hemp or hemp over drug, a pair of uses that bear powerful meanings in Western thought.[39] And like Lamarck, historians have taken European hemp to be the archetypal cannabis. The drug type, it is assumed, was derived from hemp, turning the analytical lens directly toward any people who presumably chose drugs.

However, no biological process has been observed through which non-psychoactive *Cannabis* can become psychoactive. Humans have bred plants with elevated levels of THC, but this truism provides entry into circular reasoning. Artificial selection is taken as the cause of cannabis diversity because the conditions necessary for artificial selection—natural variability in, and human use of, the plant—have existed for millennia. The circular logic enables scholars to insert humans into cannabis prehistory and cannabis into the human past, notwithstanding absences of evidence: "[*Cannabis*] may have been introduced to [Scandinavia] during Mesolithic times. *Cannabis* would have been a very useful plant and . . . may have been one of the first plants to be consciously managed."[40] The circular reasoning is reinforced through a process that science studies scholars call coproduction, when two sets of ideas are mutually supportive.[41] Cannabis taxonomies include human use as the basic character for distinguishing the two types,[42] paradoxically making their chemical difference the cause of their chemical difference.

The logical problem is apparent in attempts to explain the appearance of psychoactive cannabis in locations where morphological, molecular, and historical evidence is absent or inconclusive. Published historical evidence for the dispersal of *Cannabis indica* is psychoactive or lacking for many locations around the Atlantic, including Central America. To explain the eighteenth- to nineteenth-century appearance of psychoactive cannabis in Mexico, a historian concludes that European cannabis "strains imported for fiber eventually became drug-producing plants," even though his consulting botanist found it "unlikely."[43] Even botanists have only unlikely explanations for how one type might be transformed into the other. Again, the chemical/genetic types are cross-fertile, and there is environmentally driven variability in physical and chemical traits. But both natural and artificial selection act on genes, and there is no evidence that a non-psychoactive population can gain mind-altering chemistry, except by crossing it with a psychoactive lineage.[44]

Other than such hybridization, the only proposed process through which non-psychoactive cannabis might become psychoactive is a combination of founder effects (when a small range of genetic diversity occurs in an initial population), genetic drift (random change in genetic diversity), and atavism (the reappearance of primitive characters through chance genetic recombination).[45] Past founder effects and genetic drift are unknowable, but neither would produce a consistent, widespread pattern of non-psychoactive plants becoming psychoactive. Atavism in relation to cannabinoid production has not been observed.[46] Atavism is a fraught idea, having had its widest usage in nineteenth-century European attempts to explain the purportedly primitive and degenerate characters of certain races and of criminals, anarchists, and other social groups. The concept of atavism arose in botany in the mid-1700s and was used to explain any unexpected outcome of plant and animal breeding.[47] The concept was obsolete by the 1920s, when botanists could understand change between plant generations through knowledge of genetic inheritance.[48] Current evidence (from animal biology) suggests that atavism is rare and should be hypothesized only if it is the most parsimonious and plausible explanation for observed phenomena.[49]

In any case, even if a cannabis population can revert to having the potential to become either psychoactive or non-psychoactive, this transformation becomes evident only if someone decides to try a plant as a drug. Thus, even hypotheses about natural, biological change within plants frame the drug as a product of human behavior. If cannabis psychoactivity is understood as fundamentally a human choice, characterizations of people can substitute for data about, or even consideration of, the biological past. Simultaneously and circularly, this condition means that plant psychoactivity can substantiate generalizations about people and drug use. Indeed, the dominant historical narrative for cannabis relies on generalizations about people at least as much as on data about the biological past.

Inserting Humans in *Cannabis* Evolution

Historical neglect of *indica* is not just rooted in biological theory. It also reflects outdated ways of thinking about Europeans and non-Europeans. Cannabis histories have generalized about past people in terms of race, assigning positive, active roles to Whites, with various non-White groups cast as foils. The character contrast is highlighted in two major episodes: the prehistoric origins of cannabis drug use and the introduction of the drug plant to the Americas. The normal telling of these episodes relies on racial ideologies, which are not perpetuated through the willful intentions of cannabis historians. Instead, racial ideas permeate the plant's scientific canon and have not been identified and challenged as such. Race is a social construct, not a feature of any human being. Cannabis has been part of social constructions of race that follow a general pattern: non-Whites seemingly prefer drugs over hemp, while Whites choose hemp over drugs, at least in historical contexts.

RACIAL HISTORY, PART I: THE ARYANS. The earliest racially stereo-typed episode is not directly related to Africa but is the bedrock of cannabis historiography. Cannabis histories normally portray proto-Europeans as the people who first discovered the plant's multifaceted utility and conveyed this knowledge across ancient Eurasia. Languages from Bangladesh to Britain are undoubtedly related, constituting what linguists now call the Indo-European language family. Nineteenth-century European scholars saw this linguistic pattern as proof of a common origin of civilization across western Eurasia. More perniciously, the language map was read as racial history. The spread of Indo-European languages represented proof of the ancient spread of the mythical Aryan race, which supposedly overran western Eurasia beginning 1,500 years before the common era (BCE). Of course, colonial-era Europe could only imagine the supposed founders of Western civilization as light-skinned people from temperate climates.[50]

Colonial scholars further determined that the light-skinned Aryan prototype had degenerated in locations distant from Europe, diluted by the blood of earlier, darker, less industrious peoples. A further problem for South Asia was that the basal branches of the Aryan race had been unequal at the start. The first Aryans in Europe were active, combative founders of nations, while the southern Aryans were passive, meditative lovers of philosophy and religion.[51] The two branches were doers versus dreamers. Given these conditions, British (i.e., European Aryan) colonial rule was justified, despite the relative advancement of South Asian cultures compared with true non-Aryans elsewhere in the colonized world. Colonialism represented a new Aryan invasion that doubtless would prove as civilizing as the ancient one. (Aryan racial theory has also bolstered nationalist, fascist, and racist ideologies in Europe, South Asia, and beyond.)

Modern scholars have debunked the tale of the ancient Aryan invasion of South Asia.[52] Aryan warriors did not sweep across the subcontinent, despite the persistence of the colonial idea.

Cannabis has been placed directly into the Aryan tale. Nineteenth-century scholars read the common names for cannabis across western Eurasia as evidence that the Aryan race introduced the plant across the vast region, to the benefit of other races. In this tale, non-psychoactive hemp in Europe and psychoactive *bhang* in South Asia were both Aryan inheritances.[53] Twentieth-century cannabis experts embraced this story, increasingly writing "Indo-European" instead of "Aryan," a word that has become uncomfortable in polite society because of its prominence in Nazi and neo-Nazi rants. A cannabis history from 1980 tells that the "light-skinned and blue-eyed" Aryans invaded India and culturally supplanted the "dark-skinned and dark-eyed" aborigines. The lighter ones created "the first marihuana-oriented culture" by using psychoactive cannabis as a sacramental beverage,[54] a widely celebrated episode in the plant's past. A history from 2013 clarifies that invading "Aryans" brought not just cannabis culture but also the plant itself to South Asia and further says that "warriors speaking Indo-European languages" helped initiate "Chinese civilization" by introducing new uses of the plant.[55]

Placing cannabis in the Aryan narrative implies that the plant's two lineages arose because southern Aryans preferred the plant as a drug, while the northern race chose to use it as hemp. The plant has no historical role other than being present; it has no heritage itself, but its character depends entirely on human behavior. The concept and language of the Aryan model resonate deeply in the cannabis literature, even when they are not explicit. The current, formal taxonomy confirms that "the northern races" of the plant are distinct from its "southern, intoxicant races," and that this variation "is due in large part . . . to selection by man."[56]

Purported proof of the plant's Aryan past does not bear scrutiny.[57] The most widely repeated evidence supposedly shows that ancient Indo-European people carried knowledge of psychoactive cannabis drug use to Europe, where it was subsequently forgotten. The Greek historian Herodotus recorded in the fifth century BCE that Scythians—nomads who occupied what is now Ukraine—burned hempseeds at funerals and showed emotion after breathing the smoke.[58] Since 1870, scholars have assumed Herodotus documented psychoactive cannabis drug use, with patently unqualified certainty: "without a doubt . . . hashish was used as a narcotic" by the Scythians.[59] This conclusion is unsupportable.[60] Archaeological sites confirm the Scythians burned hempseeds (which are not psychoactive) but provide no evidence of any potentially psychoactive plant parts (leaves or flowers). The Scythian story does not show that ancient nomads carried knowledge of mind-altering cannabis drug use across Eurasia.

Psychoactive cannabis drug use originated in South Asia. Archaeologists have unearthed in Pakistan's Indus Valley cannabis seeds from about 2000 BCE,[61] centuries before the supposed Aryan invasion. These seeds were among the remains of the Indus Valley civilization, whose material culture included a ritualistic beverage that seemingly included cannabis.[62] The Indus Valley culture was similar to roughly contemporaneous cultures in present-day Turkmenistan and in western China's Xinjiang Province. These groups also made presumably psychoactive beverages that included cannabis. None of the three ancient groups seems to have been particularly invasive, but all certainly participated in long-distance trade. Cannabis spread widely along commercial routes across southern Asia centuries before the purported Aryan expansion, whether as a weed, a crop, or a commodity.[63] Probable speakers of Indo-European languages—we don't know what people spoke in the ancient Indus Valley, Turkmenistan, and Xinjiang cultures—were no more likely to be initiators of exchange than other peoples. In China, the eastern Han culture learned about psychoactive cannabis because they established commercial and diplomatic contacts in Xinjiang and beyond, probably in the second century BCE.[64]

Perhaps the plant's South Asian and European names originated in Central Asia,[65] but scholars continue to debate how the Indo-European language family became so widespread and how cultures developed in antiquity.[66] Perhaps the so-called Aryan expansion began in South Asia and eventually encompassed Europe. More likely, language was part of a widespread set of social changes that did not stem from the biological expansion of any human group. Whatever the case, placing cannabis in the Aryan narrative makes anthropogenic speciation inherently racial, based more on social constructions of human difference than on knowledge of the plant itself.

RACIAL HISTORY, PART 2: THE COLUMBIAN EXCHANGE. The transatlantic transfer of plants and animals is one of the globally most important environmental processes since 1492. Historians study the so-called Columbian Exchange to understand relationships between social systems and ecosystems.[67] Nearly all organisms that have crossed the Atlantic undoubtedly came on European ships. Historians, as a result, have focused on understanding the environmental consequences of European commercial economies and colonizing efforts, neglecting the subsistence economies and migrations of non-European peoples.[68] Europeans have been characterized as the sole—or, at least, the only significant—source of initiative in carrying useful plants across the ocean. Africans in particular have been overlooked, under the belief that slavery prevented the enslaved from having any active role in shaping the environments in which they lived. Slavery posed extraordinary constraints, and most slaves had almost no opportunity to act except as they were forced to act. Nonetheless, the idea is simply wrong that Africans did not carry plant seeds across the Atlantic or help create new environments in the Americas.[69] Assuming that Africans in the Americas were only passive and powerless reflects a Eurocentric view of history and a deep-seated practice of denying African contributions to global culture.

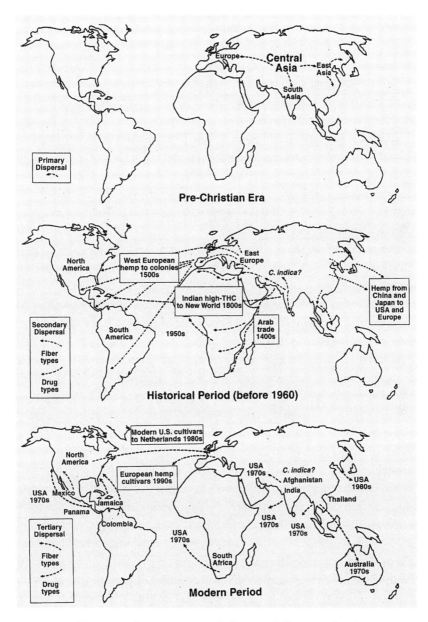

Pre-Christian Era

Primary Dispersal

Europe← Central Asia ⟶East Asia

South Asia

Historical Period (before 1960)

North America

West European hemp to colonies 1500s

East Europe

C. indica?

Hemp from China and Japan to USA and Europe

Indian high-THC to New World 1800s

Secondary Dispersal

Fiber types

Drug types

South America

1950s

Arab trade 1400s

Modern Period

Modern U.S. cultivars to Netherlands 1980s

North America

European hemp cultivars 1990s

USA 1970s

C. indica?

Afghanistan

India

USA 1980s

USA Mexico 1970s

Jamaica

Panama

Thailand

Tertiary Dispersal

Fiber types

Drug types

Colombia

USA 1970s

USA 1970s

USA 1970s

South Africa

Australia 1970s

FIGURE 2.1. This series of maps represents the history of all types within the genus. From R. C. Clarke, "Botany of the Genus *Cannabis*," in *Advances in Hemp Research*, ed. P. Ranalli (New York: Food Products, 1999), 9.

Eurocentrism is obvious in maps depicting how cannabis crossed the Atlantic. The narrative is that cannabis in the Americas came almost exclusively from Europe, where non-psychoactive *sativa* hemp was valued long before 1492. Africans are given almost no role in this Eurocentric history, other than initiating a non-European use of *sativa* in the Americas. For example, to explain the undocumented origin of marijuana in the United States, a history from 2005 concludes, "Hemp had been grown in the USA for a long time but this had not led to an awareness of its psycho-active potential, at least in the white population. Black slaves, however, knew of it from their experience of *dagga* back in Africa."[70] This statement bears layers of errors that expose recourse to race as an explanation for the plant's psychoactivity. There is no evidence of psychoactive cannabis plants in the United States until 1895,[71] thirty years after abolition. And essentially no slaves in the United States came from South Africa, as is suggested by the irrelevant term *dagga*.

Portrayals of drug use as a Black racial behavior are widespread in the cannabis literature—in histories, sociologies, botanies, and elsewhere. In 1965, an international expert on crime stated that "different races of people vary in their susceptibility to marihuana," but his list of cannabis-induced crimes carried just one racial identifier: "Negro."[72] Race-based histories seem to validate race-based generalizations about the present. Indeed, the sociologist Júlio César Adiala argues that the dominant history of cannabis in Brazil—that slaves brought the plant from Angola—is an untested tale that portrays drug use as a Black behavior, thereby validating racially biased law enforcement.[73] Like the Aryan version, the Black version of anthropogenic speciation relies on current racial stereotypes while seemingly substantiating these stereotypes as historical facts.

The Black version of anthropogenic speciation has benefited from poor research on the plant's post-Columbian history. Eurocentric maps reflect bias within the historical record and in how historians have analyzed the record. European maritime expansion required great quantities of plant fiber, and there is abundant documentation of European desires and efforts to grow *Cannabis sativa* worldwide. Historians have assumed that cannabis flourished in the colonies because imperial authorities wanted it to flourish. Yet historical records clearly document the widespread failure of hempseed plantings, especially in the low-latitude Americas. This failure is generally overlooked or misrepresented. A book from 2013 says that "hemp cultivation in Cuba was common as early as 1793," even though the book's cited source states only that Cuban agriculturalists wondered whether cannabis could be grown on the island.[74] By 1795, the Cubans had identified just two farmers trying to grow the plant. *Cannabis sativa* plantings failed widely for political, economic, and ecological reasons.

At low latitudes, plant introductions failed because *sativa* needs the long days of mid-latitude summers to grow the long, fibrous stems that humans desire.[75] Low-latitude plantings yield poor fiber, if any, and no usable seeds, because the plants flower too early, before they are fully developed. In Cuba and elsewhere, the crop also failed because it was not necessary to colonists, even if authorities wanted it. Various indigenous plants readily yielded good fiber, and high-quality, imported hemp—mostly from Russia—was inexpensive.[76] Even in mid-latitude North America, *sativa* did not spread rapidly from its points of introduction,[77] for similar reasons. European cannabis did not sweep across American landscapes to await non-European drug users.

In contrast, few historical sources document human migrations that certainly carried *Cannabis indica* into the Atlantic. Many maps show an *indica* vector coming from western Africa toward Brazil at an uncertain date. An African heritage seems obvious in Brazil, where common names for psychoactive cannabis include *maconha* and *diamba*, both attributed to Angola's Kimbundu language.[78] Histories cite no evidence indicating how this pattern might have emerged; they just associate it generally with transatlantic slaving. The plant's African past is so poorly researched that, even in Brazil, people dismiss the conventional wisdom that slaves carried the plant as no more than a racial myth.[79]

One other non-European vector appears on most maps, representing indentured South Asian laborers. (The fact that European sailors carried the plant widely from the 1500s to 1900s is overlooked in all maps.) South Asian laborers were shipped worldwide from British India between 1819 and 1920 and carried *Cannabis indica* with them.[80] (More commonly, though, British pharmacists supplied the plant drug to them [see chapter 9].) In the Americas, South Asian laborers were brought to British Caribbean colonies specifically to replace slaves, most numerously in Trinidad, Guyana, and Jamaica. Caribbean authorities knew of drug use among these people because of experience in colonial India, and in the late 1800s the authorities adopted the Hindi term *ganja* in initial drug-control laws. The legal vocabulary established *ganja* as the primary regional name for the plant drug and ultimately made the South Asian connection apparent to historians.[81]

This situation—a salient European introduction that did not produce teeming *Cannabis* populations and obscure Asian and African vectors that seemingly affected few locations—produces problems of historical explanation. A textbook's map entitled "Dispersal of *Cannabis* to the New World" indicates that *indica* arrived in Colombia, Cuba, Mexico, and Panama with South Asian laborers, and the accompanying text further names Guatemala and Brazil.[82] However, no workers arrived in these countries,[83] a fact that seemingly falsifies any hypothesis that South Asians introduced psychoactive cannabis. In addition, European attempts to farm hemp in these countries failed,[84] which would prevent hypothesized Asian immigrants (or African arrivals) from somehow breeding European hemp into *ganja*. Similarly, the failure of European plantings challenges any hypothesis that THC-rich cannabis appeared—and suddenly flourished—through atavism or some other biological process. The same problem exists widely; the dominant historical narrative fails to account for known, historical patterns of *indica* distribution. Initial instances of psychoactive cannabis in the historical record are attributed either to anthropogenic speciation or to hypothesized hybridization events that depend on human migrations for which there is no evidence.

Inserting cannabis into the dominant narrative of the Columbian Exchange is inherently Eurocentric. Europeans certainly planted *sativa* widely, but this did not widely produce American cannabis populations. Other people carried *indica* across the Atlantic and didn't simply use *sativa* in a novel way. Failures of the Eurocentric model have been masked with untenable biological assumptions, inaccurate human geographies, and racial stereotypes about how people interact with cannabis. A more parsimonious and plausible explanation is that Africans were more important in cannabis history than normally acknowledged.

Recentering *Cannabis* History

The anthropogenic speciation concept is human-centered and coexists with Europe-centered racial ideas that fail to explain the historic dispersal of cannabis. The plant's past can be better understood by centering the historical narrative on the plant, which obviously has been long entwined with humans but nonetheless exists as a distinct evolutionary lineage. Like other domesticated plants, cannabis shaped its own past, as well as human history.[85]

A plant-centered consideration of cannabis suggests that its two types became distinct because of geological change rather than agricultural selection. The two types probably arose through natural selection centered on water and sunlight. *Cannabis* requires a moist climate or abundant soil moisture. Feral plants in Central Asia seem best adapted to sunny patches in woodland valleys.[86] Around eleven million years ago, the Indian subcontinent drifted into the rest of Asia, transforming the broad region where cannabis likely existed at the time. The continental collision changed Central Asia's climate by reducing the ocean's influence on the now distantly landlocked region. A wide swath of land, from western China to the Caspian Sea, became dry and likely split the cannabis population in two. Suitably moist habitat remained north of the dry band (in central Siberia) and to the south (in mid elevations in the southwestern Himalaya region).[87] *Cannabis sativa* likely originated in central Siberia, while *indica* probably arose in the Hindu Kush, in the Afghanistan-Pakistan-Tajikistan borderlands.[88]

Cannabis is highly sensitive to light. The two types succeed best under day-length conditions characteristic of different latitudinal zones.[89] The non-psychoactive population thrives in the long days of mid-latitude growing seasons, while the psychoactive population prefers the more consistent day length of lower latitudes. Light conditions also affect cannabinoid production.[90] Particularly, *indica* plants produce more THC with greater exposure to ultraviolet-B (UV-B) radiation and grow more inflorescences and young leaves (the plant parts with the greatest THC concentration) when exposed to high-intensity light.[91] *Cannabis sativa* does not produce greater amounts of THC in relation to light conditions, because it lacks THC-dominant molecular chemistry.[92] THC protects plant tissues from damage caused by UV-B radiation, so perhaps the phytochemical serves as a sunscreen[93]—if, indeed, it has an ecological role and is not simply a by-product of plant metabolism. Whatever the case, the collision of India into Asia caused rapid geological uplift in the Hindu Kush—about 2,700 meters (or 9,000 feet) over the past three million years.[94] The sunlight-filtering effect of the atmosphere is reduced at higher elevations, where there is strong natural selection for UV-B tolerance. Additionally, the Hindu Kush's lower latitude means that it receives higher-intensity sunlight than mid-latitude Siberia, where *Cannabis sativa* originated at lower elevations with much lower UV-B exposure. Exposure to UV-B in the Himalayas is unequaled worldwide, except in the high-elevation, low-latitude Andes.[95] Other plants in the Hindu Kush are adapted to high levels of ambient radiation.[96] Natural selection favored THC production in the Hindu Kush cannabis plants.

For cannabis, humans are dispersal agents. So are birds and, probably, rodents, insects, and flowing water.[97] The plant has coevolutionary relationships with all of its animal dispersers. Cannabis, like other domesticates, shares a mutually advantageous relationship with people that carries costs on each side. The plant provides materials—stems, leaves, flowers, hempseeds, THC-bearing resin—that humans value. In exchange, humans help the plant colonize new locations (by carrying seeds during travels), help provide suitable habitat for it (if not in fields or gardens, then in the disturbed soil around settlements), and help reestablish populations each year (through seed saving and planting). The cost for the plant is that it must conform to human needs, channeling its growth into the products people desire; humans must expend labor to care for the plant. Humans have enabled cannabis to travel far and wide, but its survival has been best only when both sides accept the costs of the domestication relationship. Unlike most domesticated plants, though, cannabis can tolerate a wide range of conditions. Its variability and adaptability has enabled it to thrive widely as a feral escapee of fields and to colonize new locations independently of humans. Indeed, the central threads of cannabis history are how the plant found ways to travel broadly and how it either survived or failed in new locations.

Importantly, plant-centered historical analysis clarifies the social processes that have sustained the numerous traditions of human-cannabis interaction. Each of these traditions has persisted or disappeared depending on whether the necessary social, cultural, and ecological conditions have persisted. A plant-centered history shows that past instances of mind-altering cannabis drug use accompanied particular biological dispersals of the plant, as well as particular human conditions. *Cannabis indica* entered and circulated around the Atlantic primarily as a subsistence plant resource for underclasses in exploitative labor regimes. Populations of *indica* in the Americas mostly descend from seeds from Africa, because enslaved Central Africans were by far the most numerous and widespread group of migrants to carry the plant in their travels. A plant-centered analysis challenges a Eurocentric narrative for *indica* even while confirming a Europe-centered history for *sativa*. *Cannabis sativa* traveled far and wide with European ships. Although the European plant did not sweep across new landscapes to await drug users (and did not have psychoactive potential to begin with), its global history is unequivocally centered in Europe.

The cannabis literature is rife with racial ideologies that must be identified and challenged as such. Racial ideologies are deeply embedded because European scholars first gained knowledge of *indica* in southern Asia and Africa and understood the plant as characteristic of "the tropics," "the Orient," and other imagined geographic regions.[98] For centuries, drug use has represented cultural and racial difference rather than biological dispersal of a genetically distinct plant. The language of race has been explicit in cannabis science, even when anthropogenic speciation has not been called on to explain the plant's evolutionary history. An important paper on ultraviolet radiation and cannabis ecology, for example, began with "the casual observation that the sun-drenched areas growing the most potent Cannabis [are] populated by native peoples of the darkest complexions."[99] This observation is flatly inaccurate. It reflects thinking about race as environmentally determined and offers a basis for thinking about cannabis drug use as a coproduct of race and natural environment. Cannabis science has too frequently relied on, and simultaneously validated, racial discourse in its portrayal of people-plant relationships.

Race-based generalizations, both blatant and subtle, have distorted cannabis histories. Preoccupation with commercial economies and European hemp has obscured the human subsistence–oriented dispersals of the drug plant. European, African, and Asian laborers carried psychoactive cannabis across the Atlantic,[100] even if Africans demographically dominated historic underclasses. Further, subsistence drug use of cannabis was, emphatically, not a generic African (or European or Asian) thing. Cannabis drug use can be traced initially to specific groups of people who were the plant's transatlantic dispersal agents. When these people entered New World societies, other laborers of all geographic, linguistic, ethnic, and cultural origins came to value their plant knowledge. Cannabis drug use diffused socially within labor underclasses and did not remain associated with any particular cultural or geographic group. The plant's dispersal depended on social-ecological conditions produced within globalized capitalist economies. These conditions—of ecological disruption that provided habitat for the weedy plant, and of human marginalization that caused people to seek subsistence medicinal plants—represent a uniquely effective dispersal relationship a unique plant has developed with people.

How Cannabis Came to Africa, What Happened to It There, and How It Crossed the Atlantic

THREE

Roots of African Cannabis Cultures

Marijuana's deepest roots lie in South Asia, where people have used the plant drug for four thousand years. South Asian knowledge of cannabis accompanied the plant when it arrived in East Africa, as early as two thousand years ago. Before cannabis crossed the Atlantic, it crossed Africa, where people transformed it as a plant and as a drug. African knowledge and experiences represent a second set of roots underlying the cannabis cultures that exist today. Most importantly, in Africa cannabis entered ethnobotanies that already included the practice of pipe smoking. In Asia, the plant drug had been consumed orally. This chapter outlines these two sets of roots, while chapter 4 traces the dispersal of cannabis to and within the continent.

It's necessary to begin with some information about research methods. Scholars can reconstruct past plant dispersals by studying ancient plant remains and human-centered evidence including language, artifacts, and written observations. Humans are a dominant factor in the biological dispersal of domesticated plants, so human-centered evidence is crucial for understanding crops like cannabis.

Direct evidence that a plant was present in a past landscape is rare because organic material decomposes. Archaeologists have widely found hempseeds in temperate Eurasia, but none have been reported in Africa.[1] Pollen can persist in lake-bottom sediments and other contexts, but this form of evidence can be difficult to interpret. Cannabis produces abundant, wind-borne pollen that can cover long distances and make landfall far from parent plants. Further, cannabis pollen grains look like those from related plants—particularly *Humulus* (hops) and some trees in the genus *Celtis*—so that experts identify "*Cannabis*-type" grains rather than assigning pollen particularly to the genus. Human-centered evidence can be abundant for domesticated plants. People recorded many observations of plants in historical landscapes, although written accounts do not exist for most species in most locations and most time periods. Technological artifacts can indirectly show past people-plant interactions. Archaeologists have recovered many pipes in Africa, which provide evidence of prehistoric smoking. With one fourteenth-century exception, however, no pipes can be directly linked to cannabis.

The words people use for plants and associated technologies can suggest dispersal pathways if words are viewed as geographic and linguistic data. I have collected many words for cannabis, tobacco, and smoking pipes in African languages to analyze the plant's history. My language data are imperfect.[2] I have used only published material. This reliance has allowed me to gain information for many languages, but it has made me dependent upon researchers who mostly were not linguists and whose research questions differed from mine. Many sources are pre-1930 dictionaries, which aligns with my historical interests but means that the data are methodologically outdated. Other sources are recent ethnobotanical studies, although current words were not necessarily spoken decades or centuries ago. Orthography in published sources is variable and mostly nontechnical,[3] and information on grammar and syntax is uncommon. The scientists, missionaries, travelers, military officers, colonial administrators, and others who compiled wordlists generally published only approximate pronunciations and imprecise, single-word definitions for words they encountered.

The mostly pre-1930 age of my data reflects that smoking practices changed worldwide gradually after 1890, when machine-rolled cigarettes became increasingly widespread and popular.[4] In Africa, pipe smoking declined over the following decades, with published pipe vocabularies similarly declining. Also, cannabis smoking was outlawed across most of Africa before 1925. Cannabis knowledge was pushed underground and has been widely replaced or modified since the 1960s by global popular culture. People in Africa nowadays use global words like "marijuana," "hashish," "ganja," and "weed," although many indigenous words are still spoken.

Despite these limitations, language data are valuable for understanding historical plant geographies.[5] Since 1867, scholars have reconstructed the travels of psychoactive cannabis from language geography.[6] Current understanding of the plant's dispersal to and within Africa is based primarily on linguistic evidence.[7] I have compiled cannabis words in 164 languages, as well as tobacco terms in 301 and pipe names in 175 languages. For reference, between 1,500 and 2,000 languages are indigenous to Africa. For comparison, the most thorough studies of cannabis language geography have considered fifteen or fewer languages.[8]

In addition, all studies have assumed that the Hindi word *bhang* is the ultimate root of all sub-Saharan terms, on the assumption that the plant came to the region from South Asia only under this name. Scholars have designed etymologies to link African words back to *bhang* rather than analyzing words independently of presumptions about their origins. I have found no reasonable connections between *bhang* and most of the cannabis words I have located. Finally, I have also considered pipe and tobacco words in my analysis. These words provide evidence of relationships between the practice of smoking and the histories of the two smokable herbs. I discuss pipe terms further in the next chapter and mention tobacco words at several points. I have detailed my data and analyses elsewhere,[9] and just summarize them here.

South Asian Cultural Foundations

Bhang is an important word for understanding the plant's past in Africa, even if it is not at the root of most of the continent's cannabis names. A Hindi word, *bhang* has three overlapping meanings. It is the name of the cannabis plant; it refers to dried herbal material; and it is the name of a psychoactive drink made of the herbal material. *Bhang* is the most basic psychoactive cannabis product: a mix of dried leaves, flowers, seeds, and stems used to make edible and smoked products.

Two other Hindi terms are also important. *Charas* and *ganja* are concentrated forms of the plant drug. THC is most densely accumulated in pistillate inflorescences, and more specifically in the resinous hairs that cover inflorescences. *Ganja* means "pistillate inflorescences of cannabis" in Hindi, while *charas* is "cannabis resin." Marijuana aficionados associate *charas* and *ganja* with the folk species indica and sativa, respectively. The ideal images of the folk species are that indica plants were originally hashish cultivars, bred to be short so that people could collect resin by rubbing bodies against standing plants. Idealized sativa plants are tall-growing *ganja* cultivars. These ideal types correspond to the wide-leaflet and narrow-leaflet drug varieties botanists have named.[10] Yet despite the idealized forms, aficionados identify the folk species based on subjective effects, not appearance.[11] The folk species indica yields sedative-like effects, while sativa yields stimulant-like highs. Marijuana aficionados consider sub-Saharan cannabis cultivars to belong to the pseudostimulant sativa folk species, as with *ganja* plants in India.[12]

These three basic psychoactive products have very long histories and distinct geographies in southern Asia. In India, *bhang* was historically most prominent in the central lowlands and coast facing westward toward the Arabian Sea.[13] The word was recorded about 1000 BCE in the Hindu text Atharvaveda, and cognate words occurred anciently in several languages across southern Asia, although the specific meanings of these words are often uncertain. For instance, in Old Arabic (before 700 CE), *banj* referred generically to any psychoactive plant, though especially to cannabis, datura (*Datura stramonium*), and henbane (*Hyoscyamus niger*).[14] In ancient times, knowledge of *bhang* circulated prominently in the western Indian Ocean; there is slim evidence that people in Europe or Southeast Asia gained this knowledge.[15] In the first millennium CE, people began sailing across the Arabian Sea on seasonal monsoon winds, from western India toward southern Arabia, the Red Sea, and East Africa's Swahili Coast. Sailors were likely important in *bhang*'s ancient Arabian Sea crossing, although there is no evidence of this until the 1600s, when shipmasters supplied tobacco, opium, and cannabis to sailors, along with rice and copper coins.[16] A shipwreck off Egypt's northern Red Sea coast from 1765 yielded both dry pipes and water pipes.[17] The dry pipes were likely for tobacco; the water pipes, for cannabis or opium. *Bhang* cognates occur around the Red Sea. Arabic *bango*, which means "psychoactive cannabis herbal material," is spoken in Sudan, Yemen, and Egypt.[18]

Charas was produced principally in the mid-elevation Hindu Kush and neighboring ranges in the present-day borderlands of Nepal, India, Pakistan, Afghanistan, Tajikistan, and China.[19] *Charas* probably arose as a by-product of harvesting cannabis for other uses. Cannabis is a sticky, resinous plant; the most basic technique of hash production is to collect resin accumulated on the hands.[20] Both *charas* and *ganja* have been produced for two millennia or more, but their histories are vaguely known before 1500 CE.[21] Plant genetics offer evidence for their antiquity. These products entail different approaches to agricultural selection. *Ganja* farmers saved seeds on the basis of the characteristics of individual plants, which were known from harvested inflorescences. *Charas* farmers selected seeds at the field level, because masses of resin were collected from many plants, not individuals. Ancient application of these selection practices produced two genetically distinct varieties of *Cannabis indica*, with genetic markers linked to individual-level versus field-level selection.[22]

The plant and knowledge of *charas* production traveled along the ridge of mountain ranges stretching from the Himalaya to Turkey. In the Mediterranean basin, cannabis resin would become best known as Turkish *esrar* and as Levantine Arabic *ḥashīsh* and *shīra*. Turkey, Syria, and Greece were principal commercial producers of *ḥashīsh* in the eighteenth- through nineteenth-century Mediterranean, supplemented with *charas* carried from South Asia through the Red Sea and Suez Canal.

Ganja strains are adapted to hot subtropical and tropical growing conditions.[23] During the 1300s and 1400s CE, books from the eastern and western Ganges Valley listed *gañjá* as a synonym for *bhang*.[24] This form of the plant drug became associated with the eastern end of the valley, in the area of present-day Bangladesh and India's Bengal State, and in the southern third of Indian subcontinent. Knowledge of *ganja* had crossed the Bay of Bengal to Southeast Asia by the seventeenth century, probably via trade. In the late 1600s, an English sailor reported that "*Bangha*... groweth in many places of this coast [central eastern India]; but Gangah is brought from the Island Sumatra."[25] From Southeast Asia to southern India, historical common names for cannabis were mostly *ganja* cognates, including Bahasa Malay *ganja* (first recorded in Indonesia in the late 1600s), Sinhala *comsa* (documented in Ceylon in 1689), and Malayalam *ganscho* (used in southwestern India in 1747).[26]

In chapter 4 I sketch how these Asian geographies suggest cultural linkages across the Indian Ocean to Africa. Here I will simply remark that *bhang* cognates link northeastern Africa with South Asia. The word *charas* was supplanted by other words in the Mediterranean basin, but the practice of hashish consumption links parts of North Africa to the highlands between Turkey and Nepal. Finally, *ganja* faintly echoes across the Indian Ocean, in cannabis names recorded in Madagascar and Mozambique. Faint echoes also appear in the smoking paraphernalia characteristic of Southeast Asia and southeastern Africa.

African Technological Foundations

If you are aware of cannabis smoking in the United States, you are probably familiar with the bong. This technology has a global past.

The bong traces most directly to U.S. Patent 4,216,785, "Water Pipe or Bong," registered in 1980.[27] The patent embellished on the bamboo-based water pipes that Vietnam-era U.S. soldiers encountered in Southeast Asia. The word "bong" entered the American vocabulary around 1972 and comes from words like Khmer *babong* (bamboo water pipe).[28] The history of Southeast Asian bamboo-based water pipes is unknown,[29] but the bamboo tradition differs from clay pot, glass jar, and coconut husk pipe traditions evident in South Asia.

The global center of bamboo-pipe diversity is across the Indian Ocean, in southeastern Africa. The earliest documentation of a bamboo water pipe is from the Comoro Islands, in 1626; identical pipes were smoked in South Africa, around 1790.[30] In Madagascar around 1720, people used bamboo-based dry pipes.[31] Other bamboo-based pipes were documented during the nineteenth century in Mozambique, South Africa, Zambia, Tanzania, and elsewhere.[32] Bamboo was integral to other early water pipes, connecting pipe bowl to water container. Water pipes with cattle horns as the water container were described in Madagascar (1638), South Africa (1775), and Mozambique (1795).[33] I don't know how knowledge of bamboo-based pipes came to exist on opposite shores of the Indian Ocean, but all evidence indicates that the bong is ultimately from Africa, despite its recent history in Southeast Asia.

Africans invented many variations of two basic technologies: water pipes and dry pipes. These technologies are designed to deliver a controlled stream of smoke to the pipe user. Smoke is generated via combustion in the pipe bowl, then enters the pipe stem due to suction by the smoker. In water pipes, the stem enters water held in the pipe chamber. The user draws smoke through the water into the airspace within the chamber, then into the mouth. The water cools and filters the smoke. Dry pipes are simply tubes, usually with an upturned bowl at the end of the stem, which the smoker holds in his or her mouth. These technologies are simple enough to fabricate from almost any tube, almost any watertight container, and some form of a pipe bowl.[34]

Archaeological evidence shows that smoking is indigenous to Africa, as it is indigenous to the Americas. Pre-Columbian pipes have been recovered widely in sub-Saharan Africa, from Chad to Ethiopia and South Africa.[35] Near Lake Chad and in the lower Niger Delta, pipes as old as 600 BCE have been found,[36] predating both tobacco and cannabis by two thousand years. In Botswana, a dry pipe made from bone dates to around 700 CE,[37] one thousand years before the local written record for either plant. There is no evidence of what Africans smoked before cannabis, but there are many candidate plants.[38] *Datura*, a genus that includes several species, was the most widespread. *Datura* smoke allegedly produces subjective effects similar to those of cannabis, but it is pharmacologically very different: it is highly toxic, and overdoses cause permanent injury or death.

Most pre-Columbian pipes postdate 1000 CE, and most come from eastern Africa.[39] This apparent pattern—increased regional appearances of pipes during a specific period—perhaps tenuously suggests the arrival of cannabis. Earlier pipe bowls generally had smaller capacity than later ones, implying conservative use of an uncommon substance.[40] Pipe bowls expanded over time. The first certain evidence of cannabis smoking comes from pipes unearthed in Ethiopia that retained residue from about 1325 CE.[41] Chemical evidence has not been found elsewhere.[42]

Historical geographies of African smoking pipes are poorly known. Archaeological evidence is important but rather incomplete. Clay or stone pipe bowls are nearly all that survive in archaeological sites. Bowl shapes and ornamental designs suggest technological traditions. The angle between pipe stem and bowl is usually straight in water pipes and angled in dry pipes. Biodegradable components indicate different water-pipe traditions, but these have not been reported from archaeological sites. Historical water-pipe containers were mostly biodegradable, made of bamboo, calabash, coconut, horn, or wood. Some pipes were entirely biodegradable, such as dry pipes made from banana leaves. Earth pipes—formed entirely in the ground—had no manufactured components.

Language geography suggests multiple inventions of smoking, although no pipe-related words have been recorded for most African languages, and published translations are generally poor and not helpful for identifying specific technologies. Nonetheless, three broad categories of pipe terms are evident: indigenous African words, others derived from Farsi or Turkish, and those borrowed from English *pipe* (or its cognates in other European languages). This language pattern correlates to the distribution of distinct sets of paraphernalia and to histories of tobacco diffusion in Africa.

Pipe vocabularies for the widespread Bantu language family are well documented. These many languages (and some unrelated ones) share several root words. The shared vocabulary suggests that a distinct smoking-pipe tradition originated among proto–Bantu-speaking peoples, perhaps associated with pre-Columbian pipes unearthed in eastern Central Africa. Distinctly different vocabularies exist in non-Bantu languages and suggest separate inventions of smoking, perhaps in the Ethiopian Highlands and the Lake Chad basin.[43] Pre-Columbian pipes are known from both areas. Importantly, indigenous pipe vocabularies do not correspond to tobacco vocabularies or to the historical biogeographies of the tobacco species *Nicotiana tabacum* and *Nicotiana rustica*, both introduced from the Americas after 1492. In most of the sub-Saharan region, tobacco and smoking have separate origins.

The earliest pipes were probably the simplest: earth pipes that were a tube and bowl formed in the ground. Earth pipes were widespread in the southern

TABLE 3.1. Many pipe words have been recorded in African languages. At least three major sets are recognizable. Representative examples have been selected to suggest variation between recorded words and generalized forms.

Major Groups of Pipe Terms in African Languages

Linguistic and geographic distribution	Generalized word form	Apparent, generalized meaning	Representative examples: Language pipe word (generalized location)
Bantu languages, Central, East, and Southern Africa	central syllable like -un-	water pipe	Nyankore *enyungu* (Uganda), Herero *onyungu* (Namibia), Lingala *potongo* (Republic of Congo), Asu *pundé* (Tanzania), Xhosa *igudu* (South Africa), Vili *nkondo* (Angola), Yao *ndundu* (Malawi), Hemba *mutonga* (Democratic Republic of the Congo [DRC])
	ending in -tete	pipe bowl or stem	Sena *n'téte* (Mozambique), Luba *mutete* (DRC), Hehe *mdete* (Tanzania), Rundi *umutete* (Burundi)
Multiple language families, Lake Chad basin	leading syllable like *lof-*	smoking pipe	Dazaga *lof* (Niger), Hausa *lofe* (Nigeria), Manga Kanuri *lófè* (Niger), Adamawa Fulfulde *lopé* (Nigeria)
	paired syllables like *kolo*	smoking pipe	Central Kanuri *kólo* (Niger), Tupuri *kolong* (Chad), Wuzlam *kwelá* (Cameroon), Mofo-Gudur *kwala* (Nigeria)
Cushitic languages, Abyssinian highlands	*gaayya*	smoking pipe	Amharic *gayya*, Burji *gaayá*, Hadiyya *gaawwa*, Kambaata *gaayyata* (all languages in Ethiopia)

half of the continent into the early 1900s. Other early pipes were probably made of hollow bones. An eighth-century example has been recovered in Botswana. In historical times, bone pipes were documented in Ethiopia and South Africa, where they were abandoned once manufactured, European-style pipes became commercially available.[44] Stone and clay pipe bowls are clearly and widely ancient because they persist in archaeological contexts. Stone pipes remained in use in the 1800s in South Africa and into the 1950s in Tanzania.[45] Clay pipe bowls are still made widely, though uncommonly. Historically, in most locations people used multiple technologies. In South Africa, for instance, in 1790 people made pipe bowls from baked clay and carved soapstone, with dry-pipe stems made of reeds or bamboo and water-pipe containers made of bamboo or horn.[46] Bamboo- and horn-based pipes were documented primarily in the southeast. The earliest account of cannabis smoking was from Madagascar about 1720, with bamboo-based dry pipes.[47] Such pipes remained in use with cannabis into the 1930s. Similar dry pipes were documented near Cape Town, South Africa, about 1790.[48] Liberated slaves from Angola and Mozambique made a bamboo-based pipe on mid-Atlantic St. Helena island in 1843.[49] Most water pipes in South Africa were made of horns. Other types of water pipe were more prominent elsewhere. Coconut-based pipes were recorded being used with cannabis from Tanzania to Egypt and Algeria.[50] Calabash-based water pipes were most prominent in western Africa. They were documented earliest in Angola in 1832 and their use was widespread, from Sierra Leone to South Africa, in the late 1800s.[51] People also carved water-pipe containers from wood, and by 1900 were fashioning pipes from bottles and cans.[52]

The second group of pipe words are Farsi or Turkish loanwords used in North Africa—most notably, in Arabic. The historical meanings of most words are best known from nineteenth-century Egypt. *Shīsheh* ("shisha" in English) were water pipes based on ornate glass jars, with long, flexible hoses for inhaling smoke.[53] The name came from the Farsi word for glass.[54] *Nargīleh* ("narguilé" in English) also had flexible drawing tubes but used conical ceramic water containers held in metal floor stands.[55] Although the Farsi root of "narguilé" means coconut, Egyptian pipes truly made of husks were called *gozeh*,[56] the Arabic word for coconut.[57] *Gozeh* did not have floor stands and had reeds or wooden pipes, not hoses, as drawing tubes.[58] Finally, dry pipes, called *shibūk* (a Turkish word written as "chibouk" in English), were for tobacco. These ornate pipes had four-foot-long stems wrapped and tasseled with silk thread and tipped with mouthpieces of semiprecious stone.[59]

Based on the root meanings of *nargīleh* and *gozeh*, ceramic and glass water pipes were innovations on coconut-based water pipes. There is not enough evidence to pinpoint where coconut-based pipes originated, but it seems that ceramic and glass pipes were first produced in the Levant, probably during the 1500s.[60] Coconut-based water pipes were never prominent in southwestern Asia; they were documented later than glass-jar and clay-pot pipes in that region.[61] Portuguese sailors had encountered coconut-based pipes somewhere in

FIGURE 3.1. This engraving, published in 1800 and representing southernmost Mozambique, is the earliest portrayal of an African water pipe in sub-Saharan Africa. The same pipe form was described in Madagascar in 1638 and widely used in South Africa into the early 1900s. "Natives of the South Side of the River Mafumo, One of Them Smoking Bang," engraving, in W. White, *Journal of a Voyage Performed in the Lion Extra Indiaman* (London: John Stockdale, 1800), following page 34. James Ford Bell Library, University of Minnesota, Minneapolis.

the Indian Ocean by the mid-1600s because they appeared in the Portuguese Atlantic soon afterward. Indeed, the earliest description of a coconut-based water pipe is, quite remarkably, from the Cape Verde islands in the central Atlantic Ocean in 1672.[62] These islands were nodes along Portugal's primary shipping route into the Indian Ocean, where traders were active especially in East Africa—Mozambique, Madagascar, and the Comoros—and India.

Coconut palms dispersed with people along two pathways in the Indian Ocean, from the Indonesian islands to Madagascar and the Comoros, then to mainland East Africa, and, second, from Indonesia to India then southern Arabia.[63] Along the northern pathway, the plant was likely domesticated in India two thousand to three thousand years ago. Coconut fruits were known in Persia during the first millennium CE as imported items.[64] The country's climate is too cold and dry for the plant, which reaches its distribution limit south of the Persian Gulf, in Oman.[65] Coconut palms grew in Yemen and Oman by the 1300s; genetic evidence suggests that the current population came from the south, from

FIGURE 3.2. Chuma, a teenager, and Susi, an adult, were David Livingstone's servants, who famously accompanied his body back to England. Bamboo-based water pipes like the one Chuma holds in this engraving were called *ndundu* in his native language, Yao. "Chuma and Susi," engraving, in H. Waller, *The Last Journals of David Livingstone, in Central Africa* (New York: Harper Brothers, 1875), following page 318. Huntington Library, San Marino, CA.

CHUMA AND SUSI.

the Comoros, Madagascar, or mainland East Africa. Along the southern path-way, coconut was probably among the plants Madagascar's Indonesian settlers brought with them, around 800 CE.[66] Firm evidence of coconut palms in East Africa comes from the 1400s, though contextual evidence suggests an earlier date.[67]

In East Africa, few terms have been published with meanings given specifi-cally as "coconut-based water pipe." The published terms, though, differ from plant names, such as Swahili *kiko* and Kigiryama *bororo* versus *mnazi*,[68] mean-ing coconut palm in both languages.[69] This pattern suggests separate origins for the plant and the technology, reasonably that the plant arrived after pipes

FIGURE 3.3. These men, portrayed in Angola in 1832, are sharing a calabash-based water pipe while drinking maize beer. In the background, women are grinding maize. "Blacks of Tamba," drawing, in J.-B. Douville, *Atlas du Voyage au Congo et dans l'intérieur de l'Afrique équinoxiale* (Paris: Jules Renouard, 1832), plate 9. Special Collections Library, University of Michigan, Ann Arbor.

were known, and coconut husks were adapted to serve as water-pipe containers. In southwestern Asia, pipes and plants share names similar to either *gozeḥ* or *nargīleḥ*—the technology was associated specifically with the plant.

Altogether, evidence suggests an undocumented arrival in the Levant of a package of knowledge and technology centered on smoking cannabis in coconut-based water pipes. Perhaps this happened around 1500. Ceramic and glass water-pipe containers were Levantine innovations that emerged later, about when tobacco arrived. The new plant and the technological innovation became more prestigious than the older cannabis-coconut combination. In India in the 1750s, Algeria in the 1780s, Syria in the 1790s, and Egypt in the 1830s, coconut-based water pipes were associated with *ḥashīsh* and poor smokers, while glass and ceramic pipes were associated with tobacco and upper-class people.[70]

The last major pattern in pipe-language geography is that derivatives of the English word *pipe* ring the continent. (French *pipe*, Spanish *pipa*, German *Pfeife*, and similar European words derive from English.) These terms are most prominent in West Africa, where smoking was absent before pipes and tobacco arrived on European ships in the 1500s. The pipe types Europeans brought are traceable to specific parts of the New World.[71] European-made pipes quickly

FIGURE 3.4. In 1950, a South African tobacco company ran an advertisement titled "Africa Smokes" in national magazines. The caption for the advertisement framed the history of tobacco and cannabis in terms of commerce and colonialism: "In 1652 a small Dutch Colony is struggling to maintain itself on the edge of Africa. The Hottentots have ivory, ostriches, cattle. The Dutch have copper, brass wire . . . and tobacco. It was largely on the bartering power of tobacco that the first Cape Colony was built, for the Hottentots were weaned to it from their insidious drug, 'dagga,' which they had been accustomed to smoke in the curious way shown in our drawing." Author's collection.

قهوة بمصر الحشيش

N.º 79 - Egypte - Au Café de Hachiche

FIGURE 3.5. As the sign advertises, ḥashīsh, ṭabaq (tobacco), and qahwa (coffee) complemented one another across North Africa. The woman is smoking a *gozeh* pipe, its water container made of a coconut husk. "No. 79—Egypte—Au café de hachiche," postcard, Egypt, postmarked 1904, published by H. K., no location given. Author's collection.

became widespread trade items. Just as quickly, African artisans began reproducing and embellishing imported designs, establishing distinctive industries. Imported and derivative designs were widely associated with tobacco. In 1798, for instance, an Englishman in Mozambique observed men and women smoking tobacco from locally made "iron pipes, [having] the shape of a common tobacco pipe." However, men smoked cannabis in horn-based water pipes that were novel to the Englishman.[72]

Pipe knowledge is diverse and deeply embedded in African languages and cultures, just as it is in American Indian languages and cultures. There is no parallel in Eurasia, where claims of pre-Columbian pipes are at best dubious, with two exceptions. First, unexplained containers recovered from Persia and Arabia from as early as the 1300s are shaped like historical narguilé containers.[73] There are hints, too, in Persian documents that smoking was known in the late 1400s.[74] However, the earliest known pipe bowls in the Levant postdate tobacco. If the mysterious earlier containers were water pipes, they reasonably derived from African precedents. Second, in highland Southeast Asia, archaeologists have unearthed a bare handful of ceramic pipes that may date to the eleventh century.[75] These remarkable dry pipes were not obviously part of any enduring tradition. Unequivocally, people purposefully inhaled smoke in ancient Eurasia, but via inefficient technologies, such as fumigated tents and face-size chimneys.[76] Pipes allow efficient smoke inhalation and enable users to control drug dosage closely. For cannabis, this is particularly significant, because dosages are difficult to manage via oral ingestion. Smoked cannabis also acts much faster within bodies. For these reasons, smoking has become the globally dominant form of cannabis ingestion. Cannabis smoking is ultimately an African innovation and contribution to world culture.

More generally, many people worldwide first encountered smoking via African technologies. This includes, most sweepingly, all water pipes. African dry pipes have been important too, although the American Indian technologies that sixteenth-century Englishmen called "pipe" were more widely adopted, along with tobacco. Indeed, I do not wish to diminish the global importance of American Indian paraphernalia. Consider, however, that words for smoking pipe in nearly all European languages derive obviously from "pipe." The Portuguese word *cachimbo* does not. People don't seem to have used pipes in northeastern Brazil when Portuguese ships first arrived in the New World, in 1500.[77] *Cachimbo* has no traceable roots in Brazilian languages.[78] Instead, Portuguese sailors likely learned to smoke in the lower Zambezi Valley, where several languages share words for "dry pipe" similar to Chichewa *kachimbo*. By 1514, Portuguese adventurers had traveled several hundred miles up the Zambezi looking for gold.[79] These men probably spoke languages learned along the way but left no written record of their experiences because they were illiterate.[80]

The Portuguese term *cachimbo* circulated widely in the Atlantic, entering Spanish, French, and Occitan (France) initially to label the pipes of sailors.[81] The original form of *kachimbo*-type pipes along the Zambezi is unknown, but the pipes of historical Portuguese sailors differed from other European pipes.[82] Beginning in the 1600s, most Europeans used white clay pipes with integrated clay stems, derived from a technology British travelers encountered in Virginia. Portuguese pipes generally had a narrower stem angle, shorter stem, and smaller bowl and were often made of red clay with separate stems made of reeds. White clay pipes were manufactured primarily in Britain and the Netherlands, while red clay pipes were widely manufactured with local materials. By 1800, Europeans regarded red clay pipes and the word *cachimbo* as marking "Negro" smoking practices.[83] Nonetheless, *cachimbo* remains the Portuguese word for all smoking pipes. The Portuguese term entered other languages, principally in Atlantic Central Africa and the Americas. Words such as Tupi-Guarani *catimbau* (Brazil), Zinacantán Tzotzil *kachimpa* (Mexico), and Q'eqchi' *kachimp* (Guatemala) trace to the Zambezi Valley.[84] African languages in which *cachimbo* is a Portuguese loanword have other pipe terms, particularly for water pipes. For instance, in northern Angola the Vili term for calabash-based water pipe, *nkondo*, exemplifies a widespread Bantu root, while dry pipes were historically called *timba* (from *cachimbo*). The two pipes were associated with different plants. A Vili proverb counseled appropriate behavior: put tobacco in the *timba*, cannabis in the *nkondo*.[85]

Smoking was a crucial fellow traveler for many Africans. Historically known water pipes were mostly—but not always—small and lightweight, unlike cumbersome shishas and narguilés of the Levant. A German traveler in what is now Zambia generalized that men in the area "always take along their pipes on a trip as well as while working in the fields, carrying them in their hands together with a spear."[86] Travelers often carried dry pipes instead,[87] which were smaller and did not require water. Some carried only pipe bowls to attach to expedient pipe stems. Expedient bowls of fresh clay meant carrying even less. Pipes made of banana petioles were easily made and disposable, useful for people on the move.[88] Baobab-shell water pipes, made from the fruit of a widespread wild tree, were reported from Zambia to the lower Congo.[89] Most mobile of all were earth pipes made entirely in the soil. Westerners ridiculed this technology as absurdly primitive from its earliest description in South Africa in 1848.[90] Its genius, though, is simplicity. Earth pipes allowed smoking anywhere herbs, fire, and dirt were available.

Their simplicity, efficiency, and mobility have allowed African pipes to remain valuable as contexts of consumption have changed. Into the 1900s, from the Cape to the Congo, people lightened their loads with earth pipes, perhaps the most ancient technology. Laborers, including porters and miners, made earth pipes to avoid carrying anything extra.[91] Surreptitious smokers made them to dispense with incriminating paraphernalia.[92] The compact form of *cachimbo*-type pipes made them suitable for carrying discreetly when necessary. Cannabis-specific dry pipes remain small.

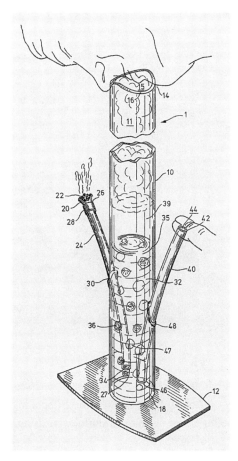

FIGURE 3.6. This is figure 1 from U.S. Patent 4,216,785, "Water Pipe or Bong" (1980). The claimed innovation of the patent is the second stem, part 40, which allows the user to draw ambient air into the pipe chamber, thereby controlling smoke flow through the pipe stem, part 24. W. V. Erickson, P. K. Jarvie, and F. L. Miller, "Water Pipe or Bong," U.S. Patent 4,216,785, issued 12 August 1980, assignee: F. L. Miller.

And, of course, the bong is a water pipe. The patented bong uses plastic pipe to mimic bamboo. The patent acknowledges prior art in the form of "Persian hookahs and narghiles" and "the oriental bong" but makes no mention of African technologies.[93] Ostensibly, U.S. Patent 4,216,785 solves the problem that "all current art of water pipes provide inadequate control" over the smoke. The claimed innovation of the patented bong is a second stem, without a pipe bowl, that enters the water. To draw smoke from the bowl, the user must close the second stem with a fingertip. By opening the second stem while continuing to draw from the pipe, the user brings ambient air into the chamber, to dilute the smoke if desired. Drawing air also enables the user to clear smoke from the chamber more efficiently than in pipes without a second stem.

African prior art is documented and is more efficient than the patented bong. In 1832 in central Angola, people made calabash-based water pipes with a

FIGURE 3.7. Calabash-based water pipes have been widely used in sub-Saharan Africa and were first described in Angola in 1832. In this engraving of an Angolan *mutopa* pipe from 1890, the carb hole is visible at the base of the calabash neck, above the pipe stem. "Mutopa," engraving, in H. A. Dias de Carvalho, *Expedição portugueza ao Muatiânvua: Ethnographia e historia tradicional dos povos da Lunda* (Lisbon: Imprensa Nacional, 1890), 293. Biblioteca Nacional de Portugal, Lisbon.

feature that current smokers call a carb hole, a small opening in the pipe chamber's airspace. When smoking, historical Angolans "put a finger on the opening made in the side, and . . . let [the smoke] escape [into the mouth by releasing] the little hole on which they have the thumb."[94]

This design remains better than the patented one. First, placing the carb hole above the water line eliminates the need to fashion a second stem and another watertight entry into the pipe chamber. Second, it is easier to clear smoke from the chamber without needing to draw ambient air through the water. Third, since air flows unimpeded through an open, above-water carb, no air is pulled through the pipe bowl, through which water impedes airflow. If the second stem and the pipe stem are sized equally, as in the patent, the two passages will draw air nearly equally, causing continued, albeit diminished, smoke flow. The Central African above-water carb hole clears smoke more easily and effectively than the second stem of the patented bong. In 1890, a Portuguese traveler in Angola recognized the genius of the Central African design and concluded, "So one sees that the custom of narcotizing with smoke is ancient in Africa."[95]

Most people outside Africa came to know water pipes through Asian technologies such as the hookah and the bong, but African knowledge is foundational to all water pipes. Historical commentary helped produce current ignorance of African pipes. Orientalist fixation on cannabis in the Levant caused shishas and narguilés to become the prototypical water pipes in European thought. Racist dismissiveness of African technological capabilities caused European observers to perceive African pipes as poor, primitive imitations of more familiar Levantine designs. "These pipes have no good characteristics," assured a Belgian ethnographer in Congo in 1913.[96] Yet the technology used to smoke cannabis in Ethiopia seven hundred years ago remains in use today. I agree with Richard Burton, despite his word choice in Central Africa in 1876: "'Progress' seems unknown to the pipe; the most advanced nations are somewhat behind the barbarians."[97]

Africans long ago had technologies that surpassed U.S. Patent 4,216,785. African technologies lie at the root of the world's now dominant mode of cannabis use as a smoked drug.

FOUR

Cannabis Colonizes the Continent

Cannabis came to Africa from southern Asia, where it emerged evolutionarily. The plant arrived alongside human knowledge of its use as a psychoactive drug. However, the techniques of cannabis processing and consumption known in southern Asia fared poorly in Africa. People discovered that their preexisting technologies of smoking transformed the plant drug, changing it from a slow-acting edible drug into a fast-acting, easily dosed pharmacological agent.

Cannabis cultures were not uniform within southern Asia or within Africa; they varied culturally, socially, and environmentally. The plant followed multiple dispersal pathways into Africa and traveled several routes across the continent. This chapter outlines these geographies of dispersal.

Cannabis Arrives

Two broad pathways into Africa are evident. In North Africa, cannabis arrived through oversea and overland connections in the eastern Mediterranean region. South of the Sahara it came across the Indian Ocean to eastern Africa.

Yet the earliest cannabis-type pollen recovered in Africa does not easily fit either pathway. In northwestern Botswana, researchers have recovered pollen deposited around 1800 BCE.[1] We know of no human connections between Asia and Southern Africa at that time. The nearest, broadly contemporaneous evidence of the plant is from Egypt, although this evidence is weak—a few pollen grains from the Nile Delta. The nearest strong proof comes from the plant's

MAP 4.1. Major African geographic features mentioned in the text.
Map by Chris S. Duvall.

evolutionary homeland, southern Central Asia.[2] In Southern Africa, the next
evidence of cannabis is a Portuguese account of Mozambique from the 1580s CE.[3]
There are no records from Botswana until the late 1800s. Speakers of Khoisan
and proto-Khoisan languages have probably always occupied the area where
the pollen was found, although the arrival of Bantu peoples altered Southern
African cultural geography during 1000–1600 CE. Smoking seems ancient in
Botswana, where archaeologists have uncovered a simple dry pipe—a tube
made of bone—from 700 CE.[4] Slightly younger pipes are known from Zambia,
but they were likely associated with early Bantu peoples.

Another faint suggestion of an early cannabis culture is that Khoisan cannabis vocabularies are not obviously related to words in other language families. The
most famous word is *dagga*, from an unknown, and probably extinct, Western

Cape Khoisan language. This term has been the dominant one in South Africa for centuries. Since 1900, linguists have recorded morphologically similar terms in several living Khoisan languages. Yet *dagga* is not the only distinctive cannabis word south of the Sahara. Other plant names not obviously related to widespread ones include Tswana *matokwane* (Botswana), Xhosa *umya* (South Africa), and, far from Southern Africa, Rwanda *urumogi* (Rwanda). These distinctive words are more parsimoniously explained as relatively recent—the plant has acquired many nicknames worldwide—than as remnants of three-thousand-year-old traditions.

Madagascar is a more certain font of cannabis culture. Sites near the island's center have yielded pollen as old as 300 BCE, associated with unknown settlers.[5] Cannabis pollen became abundant there about 800 CE, approximately when the ancestors of today's Malagasy arrived from Indonesia.[6] The Malagasy language historically had a diverse vocabulary for cannabis and smoking. The plant drug was first documented on Madagascar in 1661; it was mentioned again around 1720 and abundantly documented after 1880.[7] The most informative Malagasy plant names are *ahetsmanga*, *jamala*, *jía*, and *soróma* because they suggest connections between cannabis cultures on the island and elsewhere.

The oldest forms of Malagasy are spoken in the island's southeast, where *ahetsmanga* was recorded.[8] Perhaps this word echoes one that early settlers carried across the Indian Ocean. No words for cannabis have been published for the Indonesian languages closest to Malagasy. The earliest known name for the plant in Indonesia is *ganja*, which had been borrowed from Hindi into Bahasa Malay by 1747.[9] *Ganja* remained the most common word in Southeast Asia into the 1900s. In 1870, though, *bang* was recorded as an uncommon Malay word for psychoactive cannabis leaves.[10] This term was borrowed from Hindi *bhang* (which anciently was also written as *bhanga*), a word that is at least two thousand years old. In Malagasy, *ahets* means "plant." If *bhang* was spoken in the Indonesian islands before 800 CE—this is a stretch—perhaps *ahetsmanga* means "*bhanga* plant."[11] Other plant words persist that crossed the ocean with the island's first settlers.[12]

It is another stretch to suggest that *ganja* is somehow related to the Malagasy words *jamala* or *jía*. Doing so would imply knowledge sharing between the Bay of Bengal and Madagascar at an early date, parallel to the faint suggestion of cultural connections given by the distribution of bamboo-based pipes.[13]

What can be said more certainly about the Malagasy vocabulary is that it shows cultural connections between Madagascar and mainland Africa. No cannabis histories have considered that cannabis cultures might be related across the Mozambique Channel, 260 miles wide at its narrowest point. Similar

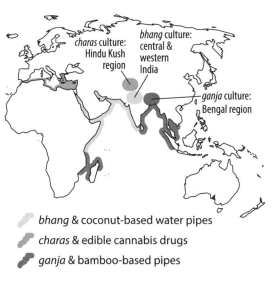

MAP 4.2. Transoceanic cannabis cultural connections before circa 1500. Evidence for the *ganja* and bamboo-based water pipe connection is weak, as described in the text. Map by Chris S. Duvall.

charas culture: Hindu Kush region

bhang culture: central & western India

ganja culture: Bengal region

bhang & coconut-based water pipes

charas & edible cannabis drugs

ganja & bamboo-based pipes

cannabis names and pipe technologies exist on each side of the channel, in Madagascar and Mozambique. People have traveled between the landmasses continuously for a millennium. An important group of migrants were slaves, particularly those who were transported from the mainland and called Mosambiky in the Malagasy language. The number of people who experienced captive migration increased after 1500. Tens of thousands were shipped from Mozambique to the Comoro Islands, Madagascar, Réunion, and Mauritius.[14] Slaves did not necessarily establish linkages between mainland and Malagasy cannabis cultures, but they certainly strengthened them. Slaves did carry terminology eastward from Madagascar. In Réunion island Creole, cannabis is *zamal*, from *jamala*, the word that captives spoke in the 1700s.[15] Knowledge exchange with the mainland would have been much earlier.

Among the Malagasy cannabis words, *soróma* is distinctive because it lacks a *j* sound. The word was first published in 1883; in 1895 it was spoken in an unknown language at Quelimane, a port in central Mozambique, and simultaneously one thousand miles north, in the Mochi language (northern Tanzania).[16] The plant drug was called *suruma* in colonial Mozambique's 1914 law that banned it.[17] In 2005, Ndau speakers used the term near the Zimbabwe-Mozambique border.[18] I don't know when or how these connections came to be.

Jamala and *jía* exemplify the most widespread phonetic feature of African words for cannabis: the *j* sound. Words in many languages share this sound, which writers have spelled in many ways, depending on orthographic conventions in European alphabets, variations in pronunciation among native speakers, and differences in the ability of listeners to hear and portray unfamiliar sounds. The *j* terms fall into two categories: those with a medial *m* sound (e.g., *jamala*) and those without (e.g., *jía*). The mainland terms without an *m* are clustered around Uganda, in many unrelated languages. The *m* words are widely dispersed, most notably in a linear cluster across the continent from Mozambique to Gabon and in an isolated cluster centered on Sierra Leone. Many *m* terms also include a *b* sound, such as Yao *chamba* (Malawi).

The distribution of putative cognates of *jamala*, *jía*, and *soróma* shows knowledge exchange between Madagascar and the mainland. It's most likely that knowledge went initially from Madagascar to the mainland, before Mosambiky slaves began traveling east. Madagascar lies on a human migration pathway between the mainland and the plant's southern Asian area of origin, and cannabis has had an apparently continuous presence on the island for at least 1,200 years. Somehow cannabis crossed the ocean to Madagascar, but there are only faint echoes—if any at all—to suggest where the transoceanic seeds might have originated.

Assuming that knowledge crossed the Mozambique Channel from island to mainland, it passed generally northward and westward from its landfall. Unfortunately, there are few historical accounts of cannabis from East African areas where the putative cognates of *jamala*, *jía*, and *soróma* are spoken, and no evidence for dispersal processes in that region. Sediments from one location in Kenya have yielded cannabis pollen from about 1500 CE, although associated plants—cereal grasses and various weeds—first appeared around 600 BCE.[19] Cannabis seems more ancient in East Africa than 1500, but there is only circumstantial evidence of this. Pipe bowls recovered in southern Zambia were radiocarbon-dated to 1200 CE; sites in Zimbabwe and Kenya have yielded bowls that seem roughly contemporaneous, though dated only in relative terms, on the basis of archaeological stratigraphy.[20] Pipes—including one with cannabis residue—have been recovered from fourteenth-century Ethiopia.[21]

Eastern African cannabis cultures seem deeply rooted. In Kenya in the 1980s, Luo speakers associated *njaga* with their ancestors.[22] This association says nothing about how or when the plant or knowledge of its use arrived. Diverse cannabis vocabularies were documented before 1915 in several southeastern African languages.[23] In Malagasy, there were at least four named varieties of cannabis, seven words (including three figurative terms) for cannabis farmed for smoking, and more than a dozen terms to discuss the processing of cannabis fiber. Speakers of Chichewa (Malawi) could discuss several cannabis varieties, including one grown for oilseed; different grades of cannabis inflorescences harvested for smoking; and various plant parts, including staminate and

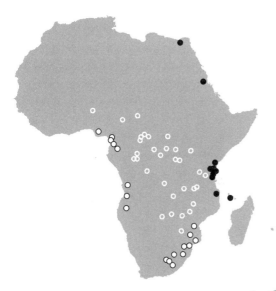

Left: Cognates of Hindi *bhang* are widespread in Africa. Those shown as black circles trace most directly to maritime trading in the Indian Ocean. Those portrayed as white rings likely originated via overland trading. The white circles represent words that probably arrived on European ships.

Right: The largest set of cannabis words can be divided into two groups. Those shown as black circles begin with *ja-* or *jam-*, and lack a *b* sound, such as Malagasy *jamala* (Madagascar), Nyamwezi *djemu* (Tanzania), and Nyankore *enjaya* (Uganda). Others, represented with white circles, usually start *jam-*, and have a *b* sound, as in Yao *chamba* (Malawi), Kanyok *diamba* (DRC), and Krio *jamba* (Sierra Leone).

Left: There are many other cannabis words in Africa. Some widespread cognate groups include *maconha* (**c**), *dagga* (**d**), *hashīsh* (**h**), *kif* (**k**), *urumogi* (**mg**), *matokwani* (**mk**), *qannab* (**q**), *soruma* (**s**), and *takrūri* (**t**).

MAP 4.3. Major sets of cannabis words in African languages. Map by Chris S. Duvall.

pistillate flowers. Zulu speakers (South Africa) could name at least four grades of cannabis harvested for smoking. The Nyamwezi language (Tanzania) had terms for several aspects of cannabis use, including the "cough of the hemp smoker." The plant and its use seemingly have long histories in southeastern Africa, but these histories are essentially unknown.

THE OBVIOUS LINGUISTIC indication that cannabis came to the continent from southern Asia are the many African cognates of Hindi *bhang*—most notably, Swahili *bangi*. For 150 years, historians and geographers have identified maritime trade across the Arabian Sea as the pathway cannabis followed to Africa. Some knowledge of the plant indubitably came from Asia. However, evidence for the *bhang*-to-Africa dispersal is imprecise and limited.

First, although maritime commerce between South Asia and East Africa began early in the first millennium CE, the only known record of *bhang* commerce is from 1872.[24] The plant may have been a fellow traveler, if not a trade good, but the earliest known mention of *bhang* in Swahili sources is from 1722. And this source tells us only that a member of a prominent trading family used *bhang* in Oman (on the southeastern corner of the Arabian Peninsula) when the family was active in Zanzibar.[25]

Second, *bhang* cognates cannot provide certain evidence of cultural linkages. Many languages share morphologically similar names for the plant, as well as for products harvested from it.[26] Cannabis traveled as Hindi *bhang*, as well as Farsi *bang*, Arabic *banj* (which generically meant plant intoxicant), and Arabic *bango* (more narrowly meaning herbal, psychoactive cannabis). The Swahili word *bangi* is borrowed from Hindi, Farsi, or Arabic.[27] Further, Europeans in South Asia consumed cannabis before 1540. The archaic Portuguese plant names *banga* and *bangue* (pronounced like *bangi*) were borrowed from Hindi or Swahili. Another complication is that Portuguese *bangue* and Hindi *bhang* entered into English by 1700. Many *bangi* cognates in East African languages came through direct contact with Swahili speakers, while others came via indirect contact as knowledge passed overland from one group to another. Direct Swahili influence remained closely limited to the coast until the 1800s, when traders began to travel with westward caravans. Some cognates reflect language shift, in which *bangi* supplanted earlier names in locations where the plant drug was already known. Language shift is suggested in several East African languages that historically retained *bangi* alongside unrelated words.

Other than cognate words, southern Asian inheritances are not obvious. Cannabis has supplied edible drugs in South Asia for four thousand years; it has been smoked in eastern Africa since at least the 1300s. The first sub-Saharan documentation of cannabis is a Portuguese account of *bangue* at the mouth of the Zambezi (central Mozambique) in the 1580s.[28] Arabs, Persians, and Swahilis had traded there since the 700s CE, the Portuguese since 1498. The document records oral consumption of cannabis in a manner similar to what the English sailor Robert Knox learned in Ceylon in the 1660s, when he washed down "dried leaves" with water.[29] (The leaves were probably mixed with flowers and roasted, not simply dried.) There are few other records of edible cannabis in sub-Saharan Africa, and published only around 1900.[30] *Bhang* cognates circulated widely, but South Asian knowledge of *bhang* uses did not. The singular location where Asian connections persisted was Zanzibar island (Tanzania), where drug consumption remained characteristic of the Arabian Sea region generally. In 1872, Richard Burton contrasted Zanzibaris and mainlanders, writing that "the Arab" on Zanzibar appreciated opium, imported alcohol, and "Bhang in its several [edible] forms . . . imported from Bombay and Cutch [western India]."[31] Otherwise, the plant drug's southern Asian cultural roots were almost completely lost in sub-Saharan Africa.

HISTORICAL CANNABIS CULTURES in North Africa maintained clear links to Levantine Asia. Perhaps the pharaohs oversaw Africa's first cannabis culture. Trade connected Egyptians to places far to the northeast, where cannabis grew millennia before the pharaohs. Evidence of cannabis from ancient Egypt is very thin.[32] A few pollen grains have survived from between 1200 and 2500 BCE.[33] The sparsity of pollen suggests it blew to the Lower Nile from across the Mediterranean. The tomb of Akhenaten, from about 1300 BCE, yielded a wad of plant fiber that archaeologists have identified as cannabis.[34] No other fibers have been identified in any tomb, including hempen textiles. The pharaohs mostly wore linen made from flax. Advocates of Pharaonic cannabis argue that the hieroglyphic medicinal plant *šmšmt* is cannabis, primarily because *šmšmt* was described as "a plant from which ropes are made."[35] The Egyptians made rope from many plants, but not, to anyone's knowledge, cannabis.[36] The prominence of cannabis in historical European ropemaking has led to biased scholarly interpretations of ancient cordage.[37] The list of medicinal uses for *šmšmt* is literally and figuratively hieroglyphic.[38] *Šmšmt* could reasonably mean many plants other than cannabis.

Whatever the case, any ancient Egyptian cannabis culture had no enduring impact. No known words derive from *šmšmt*, and uses for the hieroglyphic plant had no obvious echoes in Greek or Arabic medicine. In Coptic, the language descended from ancient Egyptian, cannabis was called *erbici* in the 1700s CE.[39] The Kingdom of Kush, centered in what is now Sudan, overtook pharaonic Egypt around 700 BCE. Meroitic, the extinct language of Kush, probably belonged to the Nilo-Saharan language family.[40] Words for cannabis in extant Nilo-Saharan languages are examples of *j*-type, sub-Saharan terms, such as Luwo *njaga* and Lugbara *ndzàài* (South Sudan).[41]

The earliest firm evidence of cannabis in North Africa is from the Maghreb— the continent's northwestern region, where indigenous Berber languages are spoken. The Maghreb also hosts North Africa's most distinctive cannabis cultures. Cannabis-type pollen from 300 CE has been recovered in northern Morocco's Rif Mountains, although it became abundant there only after 1000 CE.[42]

Cannabis meaningfully arrived in the Mediterranean via Greece in the 400s BCE.[43] The Greeks had not earlier known the plant they called *kánnabis* and valued for hemp fiber. Evidence of its medicinal use among Greeks dates to the first century CE, in the works of Dioscorides and Galen. Greek medicinal preparations of cannabis were non-psychoactive, although the Greeks vaguely knew of psychoactive uses in the Levant.[44] During the Islamic Golden Age (800s–1400s), cannabis was called *qinnab* in Arabic and grown widely, primarily to supply non-psychoactive medicines.[45] Names for the plant across Mediterranean Europe derive from the Greek, and Arabic *qinnab* probably does, too: Islamic medicine initially drew on Greek sources.[46] North African *qinnab* did not have obviously psychoactive applications.[47] Islamic medical texts began describing psychoactive uses in the twelfth century, under the name "Indian *qinnab*."[48] By the 1800s, *qinnab* meant "cannabis grown for fiber" across North Africa, though this was never more than a marginal crop. It persisted meekly into the 1900s in Morocco.[49] European seed was probably tried there; the French certainly planted their hempseed in Algeria by 1866, and perhaps also in Tunisia.[50] In the early 1700s, Morocco's small industry showed European influence: the complicated process of preparing hemp fiber paralleled European techniques developed millennia before.[51] Maghrebi *Cannabis* is genetically distinctive among African varieties because it is a cross between non-psychoactive *sativa* and psychoactive *indica*.[52]

North African knowledge of psychoactive uses traces to the Levant, where cannabis supplied mind-altering drugs by 1000 BCE.[53] The earliest documentary evidence is Galen's description, from 100 CE, of edible drugs in what is now Syria or Turkey.[54] There are many stories in the cannabis literature about Persia as a font of global cannabis culture.[55] Psychoactive cannabis was earliest evinced in Persia in the Zoroastrian text *Denkārd* (compiled in the 900s CE), which ascribed religious meaning to a hallucinogenic beverage, *bang*, made from cannabis, datura, and/or henbane.[56] The *Denkārd* traditions predate its compilation by one thousand years or more.

The most familiar name for cannabis in Arabic has become *ḥashīsh*,[57] which initially meant "herbage" but became a nickname for cannabis meaning "*the* herb." This name was used in Egypt by the 1200s, when people ate psychoactive concoctions in public gardens.[58] *Ḥashīsh* referred to the plant and to masses of cannabis resin. Other words were sometimes used to name masses of resin in Mediterranean commerce, particularly Turkish *esrar*, Arabic *shīra*, and Hindi *charas*. Although *ḥashīsh* was spoken wherever people spoke Arabic, in most of North Africa this was not the drug plant's primary name. Europeans widely wrote "hashish" in travelogues, but *ḥashīsh* was its main local name only in Egypt.

There is no known record of cannabis in the Horn of Africa before 1899, when colonial laws in Italian Eritrea prohibited "hasheesh" imports.[59] In Amharic— the dominant language of Abyssinia, or historical Ethiopia—cannabis was historically *esha faris* (plant of the Persians). It had the secondary name *esha tenbit* (prophecy plant), and may have had an earlier name (*seṭaṭirā*).[60] Archaeologists in Ethiopia have found chemical traces of cannabis in pipe bowls from around 1325 CE,[61] but smoking was stigmatized in Ethiopian Christianity by 1700.[62] European travelers rarely recorded smoking, whether cannabis or tobacco, but a German traveler observed hashish-based edibles on the northern Abyssinian frontier in 1866.[63] In the 1920s, cannabis seemed sufficiently unknown in Abyssinia, and Abyssinians sufficiently abstemious, that the French trafficker Henri de Monfried considered it an ideal location to start growing his own instead of smuggling supplies to western Europe out of Greece or British India.[64]

In the Maghreb, *ḥashīsh* referred to cannabis resin, as it did in Mediterranean Arabic broadly. The term wasn't particularly prominent, though, and resin was not significantly produced in the Maghreb until after 1950. Indeed, the use of cannabis resin in the Maghreb was first faintly evident only in 1884, when the Ottoman Tunisian government banned imports of *chīra*.[65] This term, meaning cannabis resin, was earliest documented as *shīra* in Syrian Arabic in the 1790s.[66] In the Maghreb, the proper names for the drug plant were *kif* and *takrūri*, terms that also referred to herbal material prepared for smoking. The earliest Maghrebian documentation of psychoactive cannabis is from Morocco from 1735; marabouts likely began using cannabis around the same time, calling it *kif*.[67] *Kif* was a widely used Arabic term for a state of deep mental and spiritual awareness. In the 1800s, Muslims around the Mediterranean "made *kif*" as a euphemism for using cannabis, tobacco, or other substances. (Notably, the earliest certain appearance of psychoactive cannabis farming within the United States came in 1895, when "Arabs[,] Armenians[, and] Turks" grew "kiff" in California

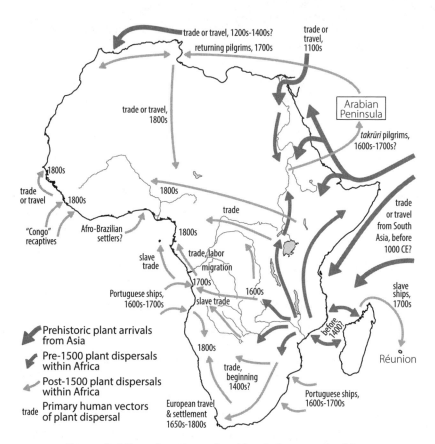

MAP 4.4. Dispersal of *Cannabis indica* within Africa before 1900. In addition to what is represented on the map, cannabis probably came to Mauritius after 1819, with indentured Indian laborers. Map by Chris S. Duvall.

to supply fellow immigrants in San Francisco.[68]) In Morocco and Algeria, *kif* became a nickname for cannabis, meaning roughly "*the* high." In Algeria and Tunisia, the drug plant was called *takrūri*.[69] This word originated with a transcontinental dispersal from south of the Sahara, and not from connections across the Mediterranean.

Cannabis Crosses the Continent

By 1500, cannabis was growing widely in North Africa, and in the sub-Saharan region north of the Zambezi River and east of the Great Lakes. The plant was not omnipresent in these areas. Its range expanded in subsequent centuries through overland dispersals, whether traveling as a trade item, a useful plant, or an opportunistic weed. I can sketch the plant's movement along four broad pathways after 1500. As these overland dispersals progressed, the plant arrived at new points along the coast, too, on European ships.

TRANS-SAHARAN EXPANSION. The Nile River is the easiest pathway through the Sahara. Cannabis certainly traveled along the valley via fields and weedy patches ever since it arrived in the river basin. However, this trans-Saharan passage does not seem to have shaped cannabis distribution significantly. The term *ḥashīsh* was not documented south of what is now the country of Sudan, except as written by European travelers. Conversely, cannabis terms documented in what is now South Sudan, like Luwo *njaga* and Zande *bangi*, did not travel north along the river. *Bango*, meaning herbal cannabis in Egypt and Sudan, likely came from Red Sea sailors, not up the Nile.

The only clear instance of a trans-desert dispersal comes from the Algerian and Tunisian plant name *takrūri*. In Arabic, the base meaning of *takrūri* is "from *Takrūr*." The imprecise geographic term *Takrūr* could refer to the entire Sudan region from Senegal to Ethiopia, or to specific areas within that region.[70] Most relevantly, it could name an area centered on the Darfur region in the present-day country of Sudan. The term *takrūri* was commonly used at Mecca, where it referred to pilgrims from across the Sudan region.[71] As a name for cannabis, *takrūri* was first published in the late 1700s in Algeria, where it named the plant as well as smoked cannabis.[72] The plant name *takrūri* was not documented in the country of Sudan, where the earliest evidence of cannabis came in 1799 when an Englishman reported "hashish" farming in Darfur.[73] Importantly, in 1903 the plant name *takrūri* was recorded south of the Sahara but far from Darfur, near Zinder, Niger, just west of Lake Chad.[74] It was spoken there in the unrelated languages Hausa, Tamasheq, and Chadian Arabic.

From this limited evidence I hazard to guess a dispersal history. There was a group of Muslim pilgrims from Darfur who, after visiting Mecca in 1504, went forth to settle an area at the northern edge of Abyssinia.[75] These pilgrims traveled in well-armed and wealthy masses. The settlers seized control of trade between Abyssinia and Ottoman Egypt and established the Fung Kingdom. They were called *takrūri*, referring to their Darfurian origins. Their new land straddled the confluence of the White Nile and the Blue Nile, a strategic location that likely led them to discover psychoactive cannabis via contacts in the uppermost Nile Valley. In the 1700s, some of their number carried the plant drug toward Mecca, where fellow pilgrims learned about the plant from people they called *takrūri*. Knowledge and probably seeds returned to various societies, but the name persisted only in Algeria and Tunisia. The plant was already known in these countries as elsewhere along the Mediterranean seaboard; perhaps cannabis smoking was previously unknown. In the late 1700s in Algeria, the plant was called both *takrūri* and *qinnab*,[76] the latter name recalling more ancient understandings of the plant.

Subsequently, the plant traveled overland from the Maghreb toward Lake Chad. A northward crossing is unlikely.[77] There is no evidence of cannabis in northern Central Africa before 1903. The town of Zinder had lain within the Kanem-Bornu Empire, which had controlled trans-Saharan trade from Central Africa from about 1000 CE to 1850 and had maintained embassies from Egypt to Algeria. Cannabis perhaps crossed the Sahara through Kanem-Bornu's commercial networks, but if so, this was only in the last decades of the empire's existence. The crossing may have happened only at the end of the nineteenth century, when *takrūri* was a commercial commodity in Tunisia. There are no other examples of Arabic words used south of the Sahara for cannabis, even if Europeans commonly wrote the familiar term "hashish."[78] Further, cannabis has never been common in the Lake Chad basin. Auguste Chevalier, a well-traveled French botanist, did not observe it during fifteen years of activities in the basin during the early twentieth century.[79] The plant has been common in the Maghreb for centuries and more reasonably dispersed from an area of abundance to one of rarity. Smoking is ancient in the Lake Chad basin—at least in its southern portion, where archaeologists have recovered pipes as old as 600 BCE—but oral histories indicate that people smoked datura before cannabis.[80]

The plant's trans-Saharan travels are intriguing, but late and minor events in cannabis history. Its main movements were south of the Sahara.

WESTWARD FROM EAST AFRICA. Cannabis arrived in northern Central Africa primarily from the south and east rather than across the Sahara. This expansion probably occurred mostly after 1800, when cannabis accompanied commercial caravans under the Swahili name *bangi*.

There is scant historic evidence from the region north of the Congo Basin, where the plant has never seemed abundant. In the early 1900s, in what is now the Central African Republic (CAR), the botanist Chevalier considered the plant's northern limit to lie just beyond the dense equatorial forests. He doubtless overlooked some occurrences of the plant, which was already frowned on by colonial authorities, years before it was formally outlawed. In French Congo in 1902, Chevalier found that smokers avoided using in front of European travelers and generally grew only "a few stems . . . in concealed places [that are] difficult to observe."[81] Nonetheless, north of the forest the plant was uncommon, not just hidden. The only other published observations were among Zande speakers in what is now South Sudan. Documents from 1906, 1926, and 1956 describe well-established, and discreet, cannabis farming and use.[82] The plant was supposed to have come to Zande lands from the southeast, the direction from which Swahili trade would have arrived. Indeed, in Zande the plant is called *bangi*. In other South Sudanese languages it is called something like *njaga* (as in Luwo), the northernmost known example of a cluster of similar *nja-* names centered on Uganda. Perhaps the plant traveled the northern margins of the equatorial forest under such a name. More certainly, by 1925 cannabis had gone westward to Nigeria under some derivative of the Swahili *bangi*, as evident in names such as C'Lela *v'bàzgnà* (northern Nigeria). It seemingly grew even farther west, in Togo, although its name there was not historically published.[83]

European colonial observers recorded this westward expansion, though only via generalizations. "The stupefying or maddening hemp . . . entered Congoland from the far Muhammadan north-east," announced an English administrator in the Belgian Congo in 1908.[84] The notion that "Arabs" enabled the plant's westward dispersal is common but unsubstantiated; Arabic words did not accompany the plant or its drug use. Instead, the plant traveled with trade caravans, its range expanding with Swahili commerce in the 1800s. The people who carried *bangi* were porters, not the merchants who employed them. The merchants favored tobacco, especially imported from Persia. Only Burton suggests they smoked cannabis too. In 1857, he generalized about *bangi* in East Africa: "The Arabs [i.e., caravan leaders] smoke the sun-dried leaf with, and the Africans [i.e., caravan porters] without tobacco."[85] Burton was attentive to drugs; other travelers may have overlooked cannabis among traders, especially if it was mixed with tobacco. In contrast, the plant drug was widely and consistently noted with commercial porters and paddlers. These men certainly called it *bangi*, among other names, because Swahili was the language of commerce. *Bangi* cognates occurred up and down the eastern Congo Basin and in other widespread trade languages, such as Sango (spoken in the northern basin) and Lingala (in the western basin).

Bangi cognates also occur beyond Swahili areas along Africa's coastline from southern Mozambique to Nigeria. These coastal cognates likely trace to the Portuguese word *bangue*. Sailors on European ships—whether Europeans, South Asians, or Africans—carried the plant name, if not seeds, to the coast. Portuguese ships began visiting southeastern Africa in 1498; Portuguese in India had tried edible cannabis concoctions by 1540.[86] Psychoactive cannabis is not documented on Portuguese ships. For comparison, though, seventeenth- and eighteenth-century British sailors in South Asia and Madagascar used the plant drug, including one who encountered it in Ceylon and knew only its Portuguese name.[87] He valued it as an edible to treat stomach ills. South Asian lascars carried it on British ships,[88] and some European sailors likely did, too. In English, the Portuguese name was borrowed as *bangue* by 1689, although by 1800, as British presence in India increased, the English word became "bang" and was considered a Hindi loanword.[89] In areas of Portuguese influence in the Atlantic, historical names for cannabis clearly derived from *bangue* and show that the plant drug circulated in Portugal's global trade networks. African cognates of *bhang* trace ultimately to South Asia but through a host of cultural intermediaries who cannot be certainly identified.

CANNABIS COMES TO THE CAPE. South and west of the Zambezi, most plant names do not trace back to *bhang*. *Matokwane* is a clear example, spoken in the related languages Lozi (Zambia, Zimbabwe), Tswana (Botswana), and Southern Sotho (Lesotho, South Africa). Cannabis, like other crops introduced from the north, first came to southeastern Africa as seeds passed between farmers. I would guess that it circulated within the expansive Kingdom of Zimbabwe (which persisted from the 1200s to the 1400s), and certainly within the successor Kingdom of the Monomotapa (1400s–1700s). Both kingdoms were roughly centered on modern Zimbabwe; pipes estimated to date from the 1200s have been recovered from sites that once lay within these kingdoms. The earliest pipes recovered in northern South Africa date to the 1400s.[90] A Tonga oral history from southern Mozambique, published in 1910, included "hemp pipes" among the things legendary ancestors brought from the north.[91] Whatever the plant's Southern African prehistory might have been, when the documentary record began in the 1600s, its dispersal trajectory was not southward but generally westward toward the Cape of Good Hope and northward from there.[92]

The written record for cannabis in Southern African is tied to *dagga*, the dominant word for cannabis in South Africa since 1700.[93] Its meaning has been geographically and botanically inexact, which hampers interpretation of historical sources. *Dagga* probably originated in a Western Cape Khoisan language, most of which have disappeared since Dutch settlers arrived in 1652. It was borrowed into Dutch-derived Afrikaans in Cape Town by 1658.[94] Many European travelers initially encountered the unfamiliar drug use of cannabis at the Cape and transported the word with them. Consequently, Europeans wrote *dagga* in Southern African locations where people almost certainly used different terms.[95] Outside this region, Europeans mentioned *dagga* in contexts where it was irrelevant, just as those familiar with the eastern Mediterranean wrote *hashīsh* more widely than warranted.

In Khoisan languages, *dagga* probably originally had a fluid meaning somewhere between "drunkenness," "green," and "to smoke."[96] It was perhaps related to the word *canna*, which refers to the plant genus *Mesembryanthum*, whose hallucinogenic roots were chewed straight or brewed into fermented drinks. European observers sometimes confused these (and other) plant names and often did not know which plants the names labeled. There are no accounts of oral cannabis consumption from Southern Africa, yet two seventeenth-century documents describe oral consumption of *dagga*, seemingly because they meant *Mesembryanthum*. In 1686, a Swedish slaver decided that Khoisan people misbehaved only when "drunk, for having eaten some *Dacha* root, or drank some water where it was infused."[97] Yet in 1713, *dagga* was clearly cannabis.[98] Subsequent works consistently agreed. A further complication is that "wild *dagga*" has labeled the mildly psychoactive plant *Leonotis*. A botanist first made this identification in 1785. He also identified "hemp, which is cultivated both by the Hottentots and the colonists merely for . . . replenishing the pipes of the former with it instead of tobacco," but he didn't supply its local name.[99] The dominant idea in recent cannabis literature is that people smoked *Leonotis* earlier than cannabis or tobacco and that *dagga* originally referred to *Leonotis*. This idea traces to a poorly founded botany from 1857.[100] Instead, *Leonotis*—as well as elephant and rhinoceros dung—was a desperate substitute for cannabis or tobacco in the late 1700s.[101]

What is clear about Southern African cannabis is that people had extensive knowledge of its production and use. The best growing conditions for the plant were in the cool, moist climates in the coastal belt from eastern Cape Province to Natal and in the highlands from there north to Zimbabwe.[102] Farmers across Africa transformed cannabis by selecting plants that provided desired products, but there is sufficient evidence to understand practices and consequences of seed selection only in Southern Africa. Across the continent, Europeans observed smokers saving seeds from cannabis flowers that were intended for smoking.[103] In Mozambique in the 1790s, people harvested inflorescences for smoking, leaves for non-psychoactive poultices, and stems for fiber.[104] This condition represents agricultural selection toward the preferences of smokers. If a plant had excellent stem-fiber characteristics but unfavorable floral characters—such as late or poorly developed flowers—the genes that yielded its excellent stem would not pass on with seeds from inflorescences headed toward pipes. Smokers' preferences over time would yield locally distinctive gene pools showing local preferences for pharmacological effects. Traveling smokers would help produce regional populations by scattering seeds between local areas. Overarching the human activities was natural selection, which favored individual plants that could survive drought, poor soil, competing plants, pests, and other ecological challenges.

Generalized in this manner, prehistoric and historic seed selection produced a genetically distinct plant population in Southern Africa. These plants produce greater amounts of the cannabinoid THCV, an appetite suppressant, than other populations worldwide.[105] Past seed savers produced this distinctive strain by favoring plants whose biochemistry mitigated hunger.[106] Cannabis has been valued as an appetite suppressant in southeastern Africa since at least the 1580s, when *bangue* was taken orally in Mozambique. Into the twenty-first century, South African laborers have smoked *dagga* to reduce their feelings of hunger. When growers saved seeds, they probably considered plant growth, too. Growers did not save seeds from plants that displeased them, or that could not survive the gardening. Southern African cannabis agriculture was well developed. In the late 1800s, the plant was grown in irrigated fields in eastern South Africa, and was the only irrigated crop in contemporaneous Botswana.[107] European settlers began growing the drug crop by 1713 and produced substantial quantities into the late 1800s for paying laborers. In the 1820s, Afrikaner farmers stored cannabis in the form of dried inflorescences, suggesting their seed-selection practices also centered on drug effects.[108] The sum of regional agricultural history is the THCV-rich cannabis lineage that current marijuana aficionados value for its energizing and appetite-suppressing qualities.[109]

By the 1680s, and probably much earlier, cannabis circulated in a Southern African exchange network between Bantu farmers and Khoisan hunter-gatherers. By the 1800s this network stretched from eastern South Africa to southern Angola.[110] Exchange relationships changed as European ships increasingly visited the coast, especially after 1652, when Dutch settlers and merchants colonized the Cape. Africans in eastern South Africa specialized in cannabis trading by 1668, including sales to European merchants who bought *dagga* to barter with locals at Cape Town.[111] In the 1680s, Dutch ships similarly bought cannabis in Natal to sell at the Cape.[112]

European settlers participated in cannabis commerce in the following centuries by furnishing *dagga*, alcohol, and tobacco to Khoisan peoples in exchange for labor. Cannabis was generally of lower value than alcohol, tobacco, and *Mesembryanthum* (which Europeans did not traffic). By 1657, settlers were growing tobacco to pay workers, and by 1713, they were growing *dagga*,[113] which was widespread and openly planted on settler farms. One account from the 1810s describes *dagga* in fenced, irrigated gardens alongside tobacco.[114]

African farmers continued growing as well, especially in river valleys, where it was planted separately or interplanted with food crops.[115] Cannabis was weedy in many locations, persisting in abandoned home sites and colonizing disturbed ground. Into the 1880s European travelers carried *dagga* to give to people they encountered while traveling,[116] a practice that carried cannabis north into present-day Namibia. The plant came to Namibia also from the east (in exchange networks that extended toward southeastern Africa) and from the north (from Angola, via contacts where Ovambo-speakers introduced cannabis, tobacco, and pipes to Herero-speakers).[117]

Finally, Europeans frequently bemoaned that Southern Africans did not value cannabis as a fiber source, and many desired to establish hemp production. They tried planting European hempseeds in 1657,[118] but the trial failed. European hemp, *Cannabis sativa*, did not colonize South Africa. Afrikaners experimented with hemp production again in the 1880s and found that local cannabis plants outperformed European cultivars.[119] There was no commercially successful cannabis hemp production in South Africa. At best, in 1908 farmers in Natal produced small amounts of fiber by crossing European *sativa* with African *indica*.[120]

WESTWARD TO THE ATLANTIC. The most important dispersal within Africa was from eastern to western Central Africa. Initial stages in this transcontinental journey can be inferred from language geography and historical circumstances. Nineteenth-century European travelers documented later stages that ultimately carried cannabis across the Atlantic.

Language geography suggests that western African cannabis traces to the Lake Tanganyika basin and the adjacent lower Zambezi Valley, the borderlands of modern Malawi, Zambia, and Mozambique. Several Bantu languages in this area, including Yao, Chichewa, Sena, Makonde, and Lala-Bisa, have plant names like *chamba*.[121] These are putative cognates of Malagasy *jamala*, but their *mb* sound is distinctive. Morphologically similar terms occur westward to Angola, then north through the western Congo Basin and along the coast to Nigeria, and in a patch from Côte d'Ivoire to Senegal. From Nigeria to Senegal, cognates occur in non-Bantu languages. In much of western Africa, these terms maintained the initial *j* sound, commonly written as *diamba* in French and Portuguese. However, published spellings vary, mostly among *riamba*, *liamba*, and *iamba*. Europeans had difficulty in perceiving and representing the word's initial sound,[122] made with the tongue against the roof of the mouth.[123] Switching between these sounds had no apparent semantic effect in regional Bantu languages, in which sound switching was common.[124] For instance, one Portuguese author wrote the same Lunda phrase, a title that meant "master of cannabis smoking," as *Xa Maliamba*, *Xa Madiamba*, and *Cha Mariamba*.[125] The word was sometimes perceived as including a glottal stop (as begins each syllable in the English word "uh-oh"), as these variant spellings suggest: *li-amba*, *lihamba*, *deïamba*, and *d'amba*. People who were not native speakers of Bantu languages had difficulty in perceiving and representing this word's sound. The difficulties non-native speakers had with the word are evident in derivative words spoken across the Atlantic—the distribution of *chamba* cognates tracks a specific migration within the transatlantic slave trade.

Many crop plants crossed Africa over the past two millennia. Dispersals between eastern and western Central Africa followed three broad pathways: along the Zambezi River and along the northern and southern edges of its basin.[126] The Zambezi stretches from the Indian Ocean to eastern Angola. Along the arid southern edge of its basin, people and plants crossed the watershed to Botswana's Okavango Delta, thence up that river, called Cubango in southern Angola. People and plants also followed the northern Zambezi watershed, through the woodlands and riverine forests at the southern margin of the Congo Basin.

Linguistic and archaeological data help identify domesticates that traveled along these pathways.[127] The earliest dispersals came to the south in the early first millennium CE—including sheep, cattle, sorghum, and millet—but this passage was inactive between 1100 and the 1750s. The Zambezi passage was relatively weak until the 1700s, though several Asian domesticates traveled it beforehand, including chicken, plantain, sugarcane, and cotton. The northernmost pathway was the most active one between the 1000s and 1700s, a period in which sugarcane, plantain, cotton, eggplant, and water yam (*Dioscorea alata*) crossed the continent. Although these various crops arrived in eastern Angola as early as 1100 CE, seemingly none made it to the coast until the 1400s. European trade along the lower Congo strengthened westward plant dispersal after 1500. Trade from inland to the Angolan coast and from there northward to the Lower Congo was first documented in 1546.[128]

Cannabis probably traveled all three of these pathways to some extent but primarily the central and northern ones. Documentary sources from 1850 onward describe the plant's westward trajectory within Angola, where it came to the coast in slave-trading networks. Slave exports from western Central Africa began in the early 1500s. Over subsequent centuries, the geographic origins of enslaved people shipped from the region continually shifted.[129] The trading system required an ever-expanding catchment area to supply the slaves demanded at the coast, because African societies could produce captives for only a genera-tion or so. Political, economic, and environmental changes—events from war to drought—transformed different areas into new sources of slaves, pushing the slaving frontier generally eastward. Simultaneously, African traders increas-ingly looked westward, to seek goods arriving on European ships. By the 1680s, Ruund traders from the area between the Kwango and Lualaba rivers, in what is now the south-central Democratic Republic of the Congo, had entered At-lantic commercial networks through contacts in central Angola.[130]

In the following decades, the Lunda Empire arose in the Kwango-to-Lualaba area, and expanded to encompass lands from eastern Angola to Zambia during the 1700s.[131] At the same time, Angolan traders increasingly sought direct com-mercial contacts by sending caravans and emissaries farther east. The Lunda routed trade along the northern Zambezi watershed, which Angolan traders followed in 1805 in the earliest documented crossing to Mozambique.[132] Yet Angolan traders also sought to bypass the Lunda, in collaboration with Afri-cans who competed with the Lunda for trade. The search for alternative trade routes fully opened the Zambezi River as a conduit across Central Africa dur-ing the early 1700s. Before, it had been the weakest transcontinental connec-tion; after, it became the most traveled. Altogether, economic change meant that enslaved people from the upper Zambezi Valley and areas just north in the Congo Basin began entering Atlantic commerce by 1700. Trickles of people came from even farther east, including the middle and lower Zambezi, to join the westward flow to the Atlantic.[133]

The drug plant entered the Kwango-to-Lualaba area as *chamba* from some-where toward Lake Tanganyika and the lower Zambezi. This probably began at the end of the 1600s, with the rise and expansion of the Lunda Empire. The plant's documentary record in eastern Central Africa began only in the 1870s, when it was commonly farmed along the middle Zambezi and uppermost Congo valleys.[134] All published cannabis names from the Kwango-to-Lualaba area are *diamba*, in the Salampasu, Kanyok, Kete, Luba-Kasai, Luba-Katanga, and Lunda languages. To the west of this area, published cannabis names more commonly showed the *liamba* and *riamba* spellings. People from the Kwango-to-Lualaba area entered the Middle Passage during the 1600s and 1700s, but historians can estimate numbers only for the 1800s. Between 1811 and 1848, about 21 percent of enslaved people who embarked from Angola originated between the Kwango and Lualaba rivers.[135]

The Kwango-to-Lualaba area was a stepping-stone toward the Atlantic. Angola was the stepping-off point. Cannabis probably began arriving in Angola by the mid-1700s. Its documented history in western Central Africa began in 1803, when Portuguese administrators lamented that Africans in Angola cultivated cannabis for smoking rather than fiber.[136] Many Portuguese observers before and after likely saw but did not recognize the plant, which was scarcely grown in Portugal.[137] Around 1848, the English botanist William Daniell found that slaves were made to carry cannabis from the east to Luanda, Angola's main port, partly because slavers valued it in their feeble attempts to manage slaves' health.[138] The plant drug was prominently associated with slaves in nineteenth-century Angola.[139] From 1845 onward, Europeans in multiple locations across the ocean reported that slaves from western Central Africa carried knowledge of cannabis with them.[140] Sometime during 1856–59, the French-American traveler Paul Du Chaillu observed a slave in Gabon saving *liamba* seeds to plant wherever fate took him.[141] His is the only known account of seed saving of any plant by a slave in Africa. Slave caravans continued carrying cannabis to the coast into the 1880s; in 1903, one plantation grew rows of cannabis to supply its slave laborers.[142]

Cannabis traveled north from Angola into the western Congo Basin and coastal areas as far as Gabon, primarily via trade. The earliest account of cannabis in the lower Congo is perhaps from 1818, when an English botanist gave a garbled description of "leimba," seemingly a plant drug.[143] Cannabis remained unfamiliar to Europeans there for thirty more years, when a brief note in a French pharmacological journal described "*Deïamba*, or Congo tobacco," as a "new narcotic," without identifying the botanical species.[144] This note circulated widely in academic periodicals, which inspired Daniell to correct the record that "d'amba" was neither tobacco nor exclusive to the Congo, but the same sort of cannabis that supplied "dakka" in South Africa.[145] Supplies came from inland to the port cities of Benguela (southern Angola), Luanda (northern Angola), and Cabinda (just north of the mouth of the Congo). From these ports, the plant drug was shipped commercially to Gabon and São Tomé in the late 1800s.

The plant spread slowly into the continent's center. Cannabis dispersed northward from the Congo-Zambezi watershed along larger rivers,[146] which were commercial thoroughfares for people and provided suitable growing conditions for the plant. Canoe-based traders in the central basin carried cannabis for personal consumption and presumably bartered it, too;[147] fishermen on the lower Congo smoked it;[148] European travelers complained about cannabis smoking among their hired rowers. Cannabis thrived in clearings around riverside villages from Gabon to the central Congo basin.[149] The plant is not shade-tolerant, so it needed clearings to thrive in forested landscapes.

In the early 1900s, cannabis seemed to be a recent arrival to some travelers in the Congo Basin,[150] where it was prominent only along its southern, eastern, and western edges. Cannabis was farmed in southern French Congo by 1886, but rare.[151] That area was still supplied mostly from the lower Congo in 1911,[152] when *diamba* was already illegal in Belgian Congo. Even at the mouth of the Congo cannabis seemed uncommon in 1904 and was mostly imported from Luanda.[153] Cannabis grew in Gabon in the 1850s—it needed "a soil humid, rich, and near the summit of a hill, in a sunny exposure"[154]—but it remained uncommon there into the 1890s.[155] Angolan imports are documented during 1870–99, but by 1910 production in Gabon was sufficient to supply European-owned stores in the colony.[156]

Language features further suggest the relative newness of cannabis in the southern and western Congo Basin. In these areas, published cannabis vocabularies are not diverse, as in southeastern Africa. There are no historically documented varietal names, no terms for specific uses. Further, plant names in western Central Africa are rather uniform. South of Gabon to Angola, and from there east to Zambia, nearly all published names are *diamba*, *liamba*, *riamba*, or *iamba*. Strong variation from these core terms occurs only north and west of Gabon, where non-Bantu languages predominate.

As cannabis traveled, it was taken into preexisting farming practices. Historical cannabis horticulture is best documented in Angola. Cannabis was farmed somewhere near Luanda in 1803, and in 1832, a Frenchman found it common around an inland slave-market town.[157] It was part of a cropping system that farmers continually adapted to deal with periodic drought, warfare, population shifts, and other challenges.[158] The drug plant persisted because it provided valued products and thrived in diverse ecological conditions. It was planted as widely as the dietary and economic staples manioc, maize, calabash, melons, tomatoes, and tobacco, though rarely in abundance.[159] In northern Angola in the 1880s, for instance, a Portuguese observer generalized that the average family farmed a quarter-hectare to a half-hectare of manioc, maize, various vegetables, and "four tomato plants and two of *liamba*."[160] Cannabis was a hardy crop that yielded valued products even with limited horticultural care. By the time Europeans started writing about it, cannabis was thriving widely. Climate, soil, and people pleased the plant. "Everywhere in the villages the *diamba* is growing, and grows, like most bad things, in the rain and in the drought," wrote an American missionary in the Kwango-to-Lualaba area in 1890.[161]

In much of Africa, cannabis and pipe smoking were ancient before Europeans arrived and began publishing travel accounts that mentioned the plant drug. Distinctive practices of cannabis use existed across the continent. Most significant for the plant's biological dispersal, cannabis smoking was a highly mobile practice. Many people carried seeds, pipes, and herb. This mobility carried the plant from Africa's eastern to western shores and, ultimately, into the broad Atlantic World.

FIVE

A Convenient Crop

Cannabis crossed Africa slowly, over centuries. As the plant colonized the continent, traditions of cannabis use traveled alongside it, though people continually developed new relationships with it.

African knowledge of the plant is globally important. Africans initiated cannabis smoking at least seven hundred years ago; this has become the dominant way humans interact with the plant. Beyond this global significance, cannabis shaped societies and landscapes across the continent. However, the historical literature is limited for all African locations and mostly dates to the period after 1840, when Europeans began regularly noting psychoactive cannabis use worldwide. Cannabis cultures predate their first documentation by years to centuries.

Despite the limitations of the written record, the historical geography of African cannabis cultures is evident. In broad terms, cannabis cultures north of the Sahara and along the Red Sea coast were representative of a wider set of people-plant relationships that arose in the Levant. South of the Sahara, cannabis cultures were diverse and distinct from traditions that existed elsewhere.

Cannabis in North Africa

North African cannabis cultures mostly derive from Levantine precedents that originated before smoking pipes were known. Cannabis has been an edible drug in South Asia since at least 2000 BCE.[1] People in the Levant knew how to make cannabis-laced electuaries by the first century CE.[2] They made many types of edibles, including beverages, sweetmeats, and seasoned chew made from roasted inflorescences.[3] Sweets such as *majūn* and *dawamesk* became particularly popular and widespread.[4] Specific recipes varied over space and time, but all used butter or oil in which cannabis had been cooked. Smoking was undocumented in the eastern Mediterranean until about 1590, when tobacco arrived.[5] The earliest known record of cannabis smoking in North Africa is from Morocco in 1735,[6] though people across the region doubtless had tried it during the prior century.

Islamic thought shaped cannabis cultures throughout the Levant and North Africa. The Quran does not mention cannabis, but Muslims began debating whether *hashīsh* was *harām* (prohibited) by the 1200s, when the Egyptian Mamluk Sultan determined it unacceptable and forbade its sale and use.[7] Yet *hashīsh* persisted. Another sultan prohibited it in 1515, along with alcohol, "But no one paid any attention to this order, and things went on just as before."[8] Edible *hashīsh* was abundantly apparent at the time of the first European account of Egyptian cannabis, in 1591.[9] Napoleon banned *hashīsh* among his troops during his brief occupation (1798–1801); the Ottoman Egyptian government outlawed it in 1868; many laws and policies have proved unsuccessful since then.[10]

Despite mainstream theological concerns, Islamic mystics—called Sufis—considered *hashīsh* an acceptable means of enhancing spirituality.[11] Spiritual use of cannabis predated Muhammad by millennia in South Asia. Sufis began using during the 1100s CE, in the Ḥaidariyya brotherhood in northeastern Persia.[12] Tradition is that their knowledge spread quickly in Levantine societies. Medieval Arabic literature commonly portrayed fakir mendicants—a subset of Sufis—as *hashīsh* users.[13] The only clearly documented cannabis use among African mystics is from the Atlas Mountains in the Maghreb region (Morocco, Algeria, and Tunisia).[14] Most notably, the Ḥeddawa brotherhood was prominent in Morocco's Rif Mountains, an important center of cannabis culture in the country's north.[15]

Ḥeddawa, Heritage, and *Hashīsh* in Morocco

Nowadays, Morocco is renowned for its *hashīsh*, but Moroccans didn't start making hash until perhaps 1921.[16] Even in 1961, the American expatriate Paul Bowles found that *hashīsh* was rarely sold in Morocco.[17]

Production didn't rise until the '70s, tied to rising hash consumption in Europe. Demand and supply have continually increased since then; Morocco is now the world's leading producer.[18]

Morocco's pre-*ḥashīsh* history is strongly distinctive but poorly known. Most important is the Ḥeddawa religious brotherhood, which has had a global, though inconspicuous, impact on cannabis history.[19] The roots of the Ḥeddawa lie in the early 1700s, when marabouts in the Maghreb first began trying cannabis as a means of attaining *kif* (blessed repose). The practice spread slowly through the Atlas Mountains. Near the end of the century, it encountered a skeptical marabout in northern Morocco's Rif Mountains, Sidi Ḥeddi, who in the end agreed to try *kif* with another marabout whom he had earlier chided for drug use.

With his first puff, Ḥeddi lost his mind; second puff, even worse; with the third puff, he was swept with an unimagined, true knowledge of being and began his own monastic order.[20] He died around 1805,

53. OUDJDA (Maroc) - Un groupe de Hcha chia (fumeurs d'opium)
à l'intérieur d'un fondouk (remise)

FIGURE 5.1. These men, generically labeled "Hcha chia" (hashish smokers), were perhaps devotees of a *kif*-smoking marabout. The man seated in the center holds a *sebsi*, the type of dry pipe associated with cannabis in Morocco. As for the postcard's caption, "Opium smokers," Europeans regularly confused cannabis and opium into the mid-1900s. "53. Oujda (Maroc)—Un groupe de Hcha chia (fumeurs d'opium) à l'interieur d'un fondouk (remise)," postcard, Morocco, dated 1911, published by Boumendil, Sidi Bel-Abbès, Morocco. Author's collection.

becoming the patron saint of *kif* smokers.[21] His tomb, near Tétouan, remains a pilgrimage site. His monastery is maintained but unoccupied.[22]

Sidi Ḥeddi is legendary but was real. Perhaps he wandered penniless for forty years before showing miraculous powers that gained him a following.[23] Perhaps "he distributed *ḥachich* like manna" to his followers daily.[24] Whatever the case, people followed him. A century after his death, the Ḥeddawa was Morocco's tenth-largest Islamic sect.[25] Other *kif*-smoking brotherhoods seemingly existed in nineteenth-century Algeria and Tunisia, where uninterested European travelers said that men joined formal groups centered on drug consumption.[26] In northern Morocco in 1849, for instance, Alexandre Dumas described "an association" whose members "smoke all day, defy danger, abstain from women, and make a vow of poverty."[27] These were Ḥeddawa brethren, cloaked by the generic name *ḥashḥashīa* (hashish smokers), chosen by Dumas.

The brotherhood was not identified as such in Western documents until 1899. The Ḥeddawa were nonconformists within Islam, sometimes considered heretics. They embraced poverty, celibacy, and drug use, defying social norms and secular and religious authorities. According to a disapproving French observer, their

> members pass their existence in the drunkenness of haschich, and make a furious proselytism to expand use of this plant. "When *kif* no longer exists on earth, you'll find it amongst the Heddaoua" is a popular saying. . . .
>
> Of an extreme uncleanliness, [Heddaoua] roam the streets completely nude or barely clothed, armed with a lance and asking alms of *kif*. . . . Very lazy, they live off the work of others and do not hesitate to rob isolated people who do not give [alms] quickly enough. In their meetings, it is with an enormous pipe that they pass from mouth to mouth that the Heddaoua get drunk, all while chanting a monotone prayer.[28]

A Ḥeddawa chant—powerful music—was recorded in 1972.[29] Elsewhere they were described as shepherds, not robbers, who feared nothing.[30] Some were persistent beggars ("If he dines, he demands breakfast; if he breakfasts, he demands dinner"), while others sustained penury ("Ḥeddawa can endure hunger, but they can't endure a lack of *kif*").[31] In their formal practices, adherents consumed cannabis in the mornings and evenings to enhance the trances they provoked through chanting and rhythmic movement.[32]

The brethren smoked enormous amounts of *kif* and influenced people outside the order to try the drug.[33] Consequently, they shaped Moroccan agriculture. Cannabis became an acceptable crop as Ḥeddi and other marabouts made it an acceptable drug.[34] The Ḥeddawa preferred cannabis from Ketama, a small town in the Rif Mountains. "Our brothers in Ketama are intelligent people," they said. "They clear the forest to plant *kif* and tobacco for [us] devotees."[35] As consumption increased nationwide over the 1800s—due mostly to secular use—the Ḥeddawa's Rif homeland became the preeminent *kif*-farming area. In the late 1800s, Rifian towns supported the Ḥeddawa by donating several hundred kilograms of *kif* to the monastery annually, even though it sold for high prices in cities.[36] The patron saint of *kif* growers, Sidi Moḥamed Jamhoun, is celebrated near Ketama.[37]

Moroccan Muslims more commonly discouraged cannabis use or condemned it outright. *Kif*'s place in religious life was fraught: cannabis was sold in markets not with medicinal herbs or spices, but with the checkered substances brandy, wine, tobacco, coffee, tea, and sugar.[38] Sultan Hassan I (r. 1873–94) was particularly concerned about *kif*, although his government profited from its monopoly control of the market (see chapter 9). In 1888, he narrowed *kif*'s legality by allowing farming only in the Rif, which helped him build political support there.[39] Subsequent elites accepted *kif* grudgingly, for convenience. In the 1920s, the French resident-general expanded the farming privilege only to prevent a religious order—the Ouazzanie brotherhood—from joining an anticolonial rebellion in the Rif.[40] In the following decades, *kif* farmers continued to defend the crop as authorities tried to prohibit it, which finally happened in 1954. The conflict of opinions about *kif* pushed the Rif into Morocco's political-economic periphery, a status expressed and accentuated by the postcolonial government's violent repression of revolt there in 1958–59.

Despite prohibition, *kif* continued to offer a reliable if risky source of income in the marginalized Rif. As European demand for *hashīsh* grew, the Rif remained Morocco's principal production region. The crop's illegality solidified the area's marginality, which in turn deepened Rifian dependence on cannabis for income. Residents embrace the term *"kif* boondocks" to describe their place within the country; the plant is simultaneously a source of and solution to their economic problems.[41]

The geography of cannabis in Morocco traces to Sidi Ḥeddi, a nearly forgotten figure. He first made the crop valuable for Rifian farmers. Yet within a century of his death his followers were already ambivalent toward cannabis, foreshadowing how people think of the *kif* boondocks. In 1905, the brethren recognized the worldly cost of their devotion:

Oh hachich seller, I blame you before God,
    You have fatigued me and you have gotten into my head.
I no longer do anything and [my] work is for God,
    You have taken two gold réals from me, and I have no silver.[42]

This complicated heritage is passing. Dependence on *hashīsh* markets has endangered the *kif* heritage; local cannabis varieties have been lost because farmers have adopted Asian varieties bred specifically to produce resin, not inflorescences.[43]

The roots of current cannabis markets—including the massive, illegal *hashīsh* trade from Morocco to Europe—lay deeply within place-specific political ecologies. Ignorance of these roots impedes drug-control efforts by favoring one-size-fits-all approaches over geographically attentive interventions. The millions of dollars spent annually, and fruitlessly, to suppress cannabis in northern Morocco is merely the most recent episode of efforts to shape activities at a margin of governmental control. These efforts are contrary to the flow of two centuries of cultural and agricultural development, two centuries whose cannabis histories have been neglected. The Ḥeddawa, for instance, are previously undocumented in English.[44]

The world needs better knowledge of African cannabis cultures.

Cannabis and coffee were common companions across North Africa (except in Morocco, where tea was preferred).[45] Coffee on its own was entrancing. In Egypt in the 1830s, fakirs drank it to propel all-night prayer; the only record they took cannabis is a rumor.[46] Coffee arrived in North Africa from Yemen around 1500. Coffeehouses became important social institutions that hosted musicians, storytellers, and endless conversation. In 1800, Cairo alone had more than 1,200 establishments.[47] To some European travelers, cannabis seemed comparable to alcoholic beverages back home, a substance used to facilitate socialization.[48] Some visitors acknowledged that "the number of Egyptians addicted to this vice is certainly not nearly so great, in proportion to the whole population, as is the relative number of persons in our own country [Great Britain] who indulge in habitual drunkenness."[49] By the 1830s, coffeehouses offered coffee, tea, tobacco, cannabis-laced confections, and smokable *ḥashīsh*, providing water pipes to patrons.[50] Shops (*maḥshīsheḥs*) that specially sold *ḥashīsh* were also abundant.[51] Different pipe types carried different social meanings. *Gozeḥ* (coconut-based water pipes) were associated with *ḥashīsh* and with "men of the lowest class."[52] In contrast, ornate shisha and narguilé evoked Persian tobacco—a specific plant variety prepared in a distinctive way—and were "most commonly used by persons of the higher classes."[53] Fancy pipes doubtless held *ḥashīsh* on occasion, and, further, Persian tobacco was often spiked with other substances.[54] Cannabis was widely mixed with tobacco, opium, and spices for effect and flavor.[55]

Europeans in Egypt associated cannabis with lower social classes—although often with the contradictory qualification that all segments of society consumed it. An Englishman in Cairo in 1829 reported that *ḥashīsh* was appreciated "especially among the peasants," yet he also discovered that "many persons of the first rank use."[56] European observers were unaware of many aspects of North African societies, partly because they avoided the unfamiliar. Nineteenth-century travel guides informed tourists that "Arab cafés" in Egypt and Sudan sold coffee, tobacco, and *ḥashīsh*, but dissuaded visits because the establishments were "small and uninviting" and "frequented only by Arabs of the low[er] classes."[57] *Maḥshīsheḥs* were more secluded than coffeehouses,[58] and wealthier people commonly partook in private rather than in public.[59] (Of course, the wealthy could also afford more expensive substances, such as opium and fine alcohol.[60]) Egyptians mostly consumed cannabis resin imported from Turkey and Syria, although peasant farmers (*fellaḥin*) grew the plant and smoked inflorescences rather than buying imported hashish.[61]

Cannabis culture was distinctive in the Maghreb. The plant drug was most commonly called *kif* or *takrūri* rather than *ḥashīsh*. People used water pipes less commonly than dry pipes, particularly the type called *sebsi*, which has a long stem and a small red clay bowl. People primarily consumed locally grown inflorescences and mixed cannabis with tobacco, which was generally less favored.[62] People in the Maghreb undoubtedly knew something about resin production via contacts across the Mediterranean. The earliest evidence of cannabis resin in the region dates to 1884, when Ottoman Tunisia banned imports of *shīra*,[63] a Syrian name for the substance. The earliest account of locally made *shīra* is from 1921, in the area around Constantine, Algeria.[64] Moroccan production probably started about the same time but remained minimal for decades.

People of all classes appreciated the plant drug in the Maghreb. Precolonial leaders smoked while in power, as did their soldiers and slaves.[65] The Ḥeddawa brethren purposefully adopted poverty, alongside religious obsession with *kif.* To most people, though, the plant drug offered just secular benefits. *Kif* defied simple categorical meaning in Maghrebian societies. It could serve to mark a social group in some contexts, but the habit of using it did not confine a person to a particular group. Consider a Moroccan folk story published 1905: a sultan's wife and legitimate sons detested his illegitimate son Moḥammed, who seemed indolent and smoked *kif* "like a Ḥeddawi."[66] Yet in the end, the *kif*-smoking bastard was the hero: he killed a demon, captured a genie and his treasure, saved six beautiful maidens (keeping the youngest for himself and giving the eldest to his father), exposed his brothers' betrayal of their father (and killed them for it), and became his father's trusted lieutenant. The plant drug had a distinctive identity in the Maghreb; *kif* and *takrūri* were far removed from their distant Levantine roots.

Sub-Saharan Cannabis

The documentary record for cannabis is thin or absent for most locations south of the Sahara. Local cannabis cultures were diverse, but few were documented in any detail.

The plant had multiple uses, although people valued it primarily as a smoked drug. Cannabis fiber was significantly harvested only in Madagascar, where in the late 1800s people made hemp fabric and had an extensive vocabulary for fiber processing and textile production.[67] The Malagasy plant name *rongony* referred generally to the plant, and specifically to plants grown for fiber. Cannabis fiber was not highly valued elsewhere. In Mozambique in the 1790s, people made cordage from stems but more prominently smoked cannabis inflorescences.[68] A century later, a Frenchman in southern Tanzania "only rarely [saw] hemp employed in making cordage."[69] It makes sense that Africans did not significantly harvest cannabis fiber. Cannabis fiber production was labor-intensive worldwide if high-quality products were produced.[70] Many African wild plants provided strong and easily processed fiber.[71] Fields of cannabis are necessary to supply much rope or cloth, but just a few plants can supply abundant smokable material, even with scant horticultural attention. The plant prioritizes inflorescences if grown in resource-limited conditions.

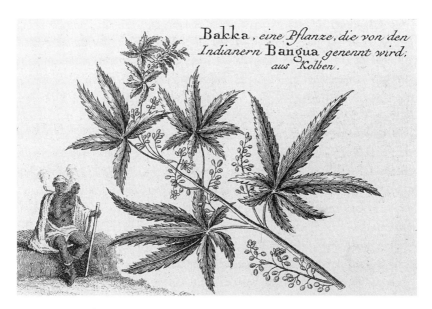

Bakka, *eine Pflanze, die von den Indianern* Bangua *genennt wird; aus* Kolben.

FIGURE 5.2. Before 1800, most European accounts of cannabis drug use in Africa beyond the Mediterranean region came from South Africa. Some observers compared African uses of the plant with those known from India, but most observers showed no knowledge of cannabis smoking anywhere and scant interest in unfamiliar African activities. "[D]akka, a plant, called Bangua by the Indians," engraving, in J. J. Schwabe, *Allgemeine Historie der Reisen zu Wasser und Lande* (Leipzig, Germany: Arkstee and Merkus, 1749). James Ford Bell Library, University of Minnesota, Minneapolis.

The plant was valued principally to supply psychoactive drugs. There are a handful of reports that it was taken orally. In Mozambique in the 1580s, people ate cannabis in a manner similar to contemporaneous accounts from India. There are no further records of edible preparations until around 1900, when Malagasy speakers had a word for a confection made of cannabis, sugar, and spices.[72] Zanzibari Swahili included one Arabic loanword, *majūn*, and two other words for edible preparations.[73] Cannabis chewing was once rumored to be a Swahili pastime; Lega speakers in the central Congo Basin reportedly chewed dried, powdered plant material; Portuguese Angola's first cannabis-control law (1913) called chewing an "older practice [that] might persist" in some areas.[74] Nothing else is known of sub-Saharan cannabis edibles.

Overwhelmingly, the plant drug was smoked. Descriptions of cannabis processing are few. Inflorescences were dried, quickly before a fire or slowly under the sun.[75] Dried inflorescences were hung indoors for storage. Few special preparations were documented. In the southern Congo basin, Songye women pounded cannabis herbal material in a mortar with salt, potash, cooking oil, and sometimes tobacco, then shaped the mixture into cakes that were dried and stored for later.[76] Such cakes were perhaps sold as "little balls" of cannabis along the lower Congo around 1880,[77] although these balls may have been simply plant material compressed in shipment. In Angola, commercial shipments were packed in leaf-wrapped packets.[78] People carried cannabis in banana leaves in western Tanzania and in cornhusks in Southern Africa.[79] Compressed packaging may have also represented a curing technique, as described for South African *dagga* in 1913: "For smoking purposes they select plants just before they burst into bloom and pick off the small leaves with the flower buds. These parts are put in a damp place for about twelve hours, then they are rolled into a mass, tied round with grass and left for about a week. This causes 'caking' and a slight fermentation. Next the dagga is unrolled, thoroughly dried in the sun and after being rubbed fine between the hands is smoked."[80] This preparation suggests a rich knowledge of horticulture, ecology, pharmacology, and drug manufacturing, fields of knowledge that must have existed elsewhere, too. Currently, people in the lower Zambezi valley ferment cannabis in cornhusk packets to produce "black Malawi," a product that has different pharmacological effects from unfermented material.[81]

The most consistent context of use in the historical record is that cannabis participated in labor relationships. Smoking on the job was widespread. It was rarely a form of payment, except in the earliest documented work-drug relationship, where Dutch settlers in South Africa began paying Khoisan laborers with drugs in the 1650s. *Dagga* wages were paid into the twentieth century.[82] I discuss relationships among *dagga*, African workers, and European settlers in more detail in chapter 8, which examines political ecologies of cannabis and labor. Broadly, the plant drug served as a stimulant, appetite suppressant, and euphoriant for workers across sub-Saharan Africa. Probably the most widely generalizable description of historic psychoactive cannabis use is "a large pipe is passed round, and each man takes a pull or two at it. This is the usual method of refreshment, when halting for a short time on a journey. [Alongside tobacco, people] smoke the intoxicating hemp (*chamba* or *dakha*), which they say is 'instead of food and drink' to them when they are tired."[83] This description from 1906 refers to the *chamba* heartland, among Chichewa speakers in present-day Malawi. Of course, this description might serve to generalize only about documented uses of cannabis; the written record is skewed. European male observers were not privy to many contexts of consumption. Travelers probably overlooked non-psychoactive uses—including fiber, oilseed, and veterinary applications—because they focused on unfamiliar smokable products. The historical record presents young men as the most prominent users, partly because many accounts were written by employers observing their employees. Similarly, many accounts refer to people smoking while traveling, because Europeans constantly observed their fellow travelers. Their most common companions were young men employed as porters to carry their stuff. Cannabis drug use was documented in many groups of laborers, not just porters. Across the continent, people with onerous occupations shared a pipe with co-workers when they were given a break. Tobacco was taken alongside cannabis, but distinct if overlapping practices of use accompanied the two drugs.

Cannabis was not simply an accompaniment to drudgery. Workers smoked after work, at the end of the day, passing around pipes while talking and laughing. People had good times with cannabis, what Kimbundu-speakers (Angola) might have called *úiji* (pipe fun).[84] Social smoking was the norm. Musicians and dancers smoked while performing.[85] Among Lunda-speakers in the Kwango-to-Lualaba area in the 1880s, men cradled water pipes between their legs while playing thumb pianos, and men and women sang call-and-response while taking turns smoking. "Their song [was] filled with interruptions" due to coughing, criticized a Portuguese observer.[86] Nyamwezi men in western Tanzania smoked after dinner, in communal huts where they spent "their nights, gambling, eating, drinking [beer], smoking bhang and tobacco, chatting, and sleeping."[87] Smokers played games of strategy in eastern South Africa, documented in Swazi, Tonga, and Zulu societies. In these games, players made mock fences of frothy saliva bubbles blown through long reeds, while also trying to deposit lines of bubbles through gaps in opponents' fences.[88] These games simulated the movement of people and animals across landscapes.[89] Perhaps objective effects of cannabis that elevate perceptual clarity facilitated understanding of livestock trajectories across landscapes. Whatever the case, livestock herders certainly smoked to relieve boredom and enhance their endurance.[90]

Cannabis was not stigmatized as a laborers' drug. Prosperous merchants smoked in the central Congo Basin in the 1880s.[91] People gave cannabis as gifts, in cases ranging from presents between boyfriend and girlfriend to tributes to and between leaders and prominent visitors.[92] Across Central Africa and Southern Africa, political leaders smoked during councils, and as a pastime.[93] The leader of the Lunda Empire in the 1880s was nicknamed Xa Mariamba, or "master of smoking riamba."[94] Of course, many nineteenth-century leaders, at least in western Central Africa, heavily consumed all available substances, including tobacco and especially imported liquor acquired in exchange for slaves.[95] Big men distributed substances as largesse to help retain followers and build patronage networks.

FIGURE 5.3. These men are playing a spit-bubble game while smoking, a practice characteristic of eastern South Africa. Their clothing suggests they are Zulu. Horn-based water pipes like theirs were called *igudu* in the Zulu language, and the spit-bubble pattern was called *sogerre*: A. T. Bryant, *A Zulu-English Dictionary* (Pinetown, South Africa: Mariannhill Mission Press, 1905). "Smokers," postcard, South Africa, postmarked 1905, published by Stewart and Schaefer, Cape Town. Author's collection.

Coughing is amusingly prominent in historical accounts. A Frenchman visiting the Nyamwezi (Tanzania) reported that "nothing is more annoying than the coughing fits provoked by this unhealthy intoxication: each minute, the smoker lets loose . . . savage explosions of the voice . . . as if he was going to give up the ghost[;] this endures sometimes for entire nights."[96] Other Frenchmen in Zambia complained, "Each night the hemp smokers keep us awake an hour or two" with their coughing and antics.[97] Cannabis "makes them cough and expectorate as if their lungs were coming out of their mouths," wrote a bothered traveler in Angola.[98] Richard Burton in Tanzania stated, "These grotesque sounds are probably not wholly natural . . . ; they appear to be a fashion of 're-nowning it;' . . . an announcement to the public that the fast youths are smoking *bhang*."[99] Coughing probably was sometimes performance. "It's an extremely comic spectacle to see an entire group squatting on the ground and coughing," wrote a Belgian. "The more the white laughs, the more the black's cough grows."[100] The cough seemed distinctive to Africans, too. Nyamwezi speakers had specific terms for cannabis coughing, while an oral history recorded at Lake Malawi before 1922 tells that people discovered that an island was inhabited by "hearing the cough of a man who was smoking hemp."[101] Some accounts hint that coughing was an appreciated component of smoking. In the late 1800s, Zulus sang praise songs between coughs.[102] A century earlier a traveler in South Africa concluded that "fit[s] of coughing, hawking, and rattling" were for San smokers "probably . . . a very desirable consequence [of the] delicious horn."[103]

Burton again heard coughing on the lower Congo in 1874 and clarified, "I have used it for months together, and my conclusion is, that mostly the cough is an affectation."[104] (Years earlier, Burton had enjoyed eating ḥāshīsh in Arabia while disguised as a Muslim pilgrim.[105]) Another Englishman with Indian experience smoked "bang" as an evening pastime while hunting in Mozambique in the 1860s.[106] Few other Europeans admitted smoking, although several alleged that "Portuguese" residents in western Africa appreciated cannabis as a "luxury"—that is, as a recreational drug.[107] Many of these residents were not Portuguese in a narrow sense but were born on the continent to African mothers and bore names that reflected their fathers' European heritage. Historians call this cross-cultural, multilingual group "Luso-African"; their syncretic customs were foreign to Portuguese arrivals and African residents alike.[108] They spoke Portuguese but also Kimbundu, a Bantu language from northern Angola that was used in commerce across the South Atlantic in the 1600s and 1700s. Although Luso-Africans self-identified as Portuguese, this identity served to distinguish them within Angolan society and did not indicate that they had come from Europe or shared a worldview with European Portuguese. Luso-Africans in Angola were familiar with *diamba*. The European Portuguese traveler Henrique Dias de Carvalho admitted smoking cannabis in Angola in 1894 for want of tobacco. His supplier was the translator he had hired in Luanda. A "Portuguese" resident of Luanda had predicted Dias de Carvalho would enjoy the experience, as he indeed did. Nonetheless, he swore off it, at least in his published journal; he continued to smoke a water pipe, implicitly packed with tobacco, alongside his porters on chilly mornings.[109] In South Africa, writers hinted coyly at *dagga* experiments among Whites, who smoked only in the interest of science, of course.[110] Government reports corroborated these hints beginning in the 1880s by identifying "*Hemp Smoking* by Natives, Indians, Europeans, or others" as a problem to monitor.[111] In the early 1900s, South African elites criticized "poor whites" for smoking.[112]

The other major settler group in South Africa, indentured laborers from India, arrived in the late 1800s with knowledge of cannabis as a Hindu sacrament and a secular stimulant. They came to work sugarcane in Natal. Historical records document only secular use and none of the edible forms known in South Asia. The migrants quickly entered the generalized South African cannabis culture they found on arrival.[113] By 1887, African farmers were supplying Indian laborers and White shopkeepers, who sold *dagga* over the counter.[114] The Indian laborers, though, were the explicit target of South Africa's first anti-cannabis law, in 1870.[115]

Europeans were less observant of the plant drug's medicinal applications. The best historical documentation pertains to Southern Africa; recent publications from Uganda and Mozambique report several medicinal and veterinary uses.[116] Most medicinal uses were not psychoactive. Cannabis-leaf poultices were reported in Mozambique in the 1790s. A century later, in eastern South Africa, Zulus and Fengus used poultices to treat snakebites and various ailments, as well as skin infections on horses.[117] Around 1917, Sotho women fed children hempseed as a nutritional supplement while weaning.[118] Prescriptions of smoked cannabis would have been psychoactive, but explicitly medicinal smoking was rarely recorded. Sotho women smoked to relieve pain during childbirth.[119] Zulu herbalists and people in Sierra Leone prescribed the smoke to treat chest complaints.[120] Pipe resin and bong water had external medicinal and veterinary applications, too.[121]

Afrikaners developed practices of cannabis use built on European, Bantu, and Khoisan precedents.[122] Afrikaners used cannabis medicinally by 1835, when a farmer recommended water-based cannabis tea—which would have been non-psychoactive—to treat "illness" in slaves.[123] At the end of the century, farmers gave such tea to sick poultry.[124] The only Afrikaner medicinal application that would have been psychoactive was documented in 1907, when healers treated stroke victims via smoke inhalation, including pipe smoking, if the patient could do so.[125]

Many smokers found cannabis generally therapeutic without having specific medical indications. Liberated slaves from Angola held by the British on St. Helena considered *diamba* useful against "all complaints" in 1843.[126] In colonial South Africa, a public-health study from 1913 quoted a "native" as saying, "It[']s the best medicine in the world."[127] At that time, many laborers valued cannabis to self-manage mental health. Among the range of experiences users may have had, some doubtless found introspective awareness under the influence, which was likely sometimes therapeutic. A Sotho smoking song, published in 1913, suggests this subjective effect: "We smoke it, and it reminds us of different things. We remember the miracles of the world. We remember those far and near. We remember."[128]

Such subjective effects merge into spirituality, yet there is scant evidence that cannabis had any formal, sacramental roles in African belief systems. The clearest exception is Khoisan groups, who used psychoactive substances to intensify trances that allowed spiritual communication.[129] However, this use of cannabis was not documented until 1892.[130] In the twentieth century, non-Khoisan peoples considered Khoisan expert herbalists and major cannabis consumers.[131] Khoisan still consume numerous psychoactive plants; cannabis often serves to accentuate the effects of other plants.[132]

Khoisan ideas about cannabis are poorly documented. Indications that the plant drug had spiritual uses among other peoples are dubious as well as poorly documented. All reports came from European missionaries, travelers, and colonial administrators, whose ethnographic observations blended into ethnocentric judgments. Portrayals of cannabis often sustained colonialist discourse about African primitiveness. Tales of "witch doctors" or "fetishers" with cannabis perhaps reflected some degree of sacramental value, but more certainly reflected stereotypes. Examples with subtler language remain suspect. In Malawi, a novice missionary reported in 1882 that "prophetess[es]" appeared fantastically at ceremonies wearing cannabis laurels and fresh scarification.[133] This anecdote contributed to the missionary's literary goal of showing that "Heathen Africa"—the "dark land"—was "left entirely to the light of nature." He further reported that people burned cannabis at funerals to "neutralise the smell" of bodies in "advanced state[s] of decomposition." More likely, cannabis was a grave offering, not a fumigant. Thirty years later, a British traveler in Zambia reported that wandering seers, who channeled spirits among Bemba-speakers, were "usually addicted to *bhang*" and looked "wild."[134] He also thought cannabis triggered insanity and violence, and that it was one of the four major impediments to colonial governance, alongside beer, witchcraft, and men's lust for finicky women.

The least dubious evidence suggests cannabis had three widespread religious roles. First, people included pipes and smokable herbs as grave goods.[135] Most accounts refer to the middle Zambezi Valley. In present-day Zambia in 1868, David Livingstone found that people offered cannabis, tobacco, beer, and flour to statuettes that represented deceased parents, and left fires burning for the dead to light their pipes.[136] It's uncertain whether such practices showed smoking had value in the afterlife or simply in life. Pipes and herbs served sometimes to show power, and respect for power, among the living. In the 1850s, for instance, people in Zambia sent cannabis as tribute to rulers and to Livingstone's entourage.[137]

Second, herbalists prescribed and consumed cannabis in contexts that bridged medicine, jurisprudence, and spirituality. In these cases, cannabis was not a sacramental pathway to greater awareness. Instead, it enhanced the performance of people involved in ceremonies. Only one example has a reasonably known history. The sole historical account of cannabis smoking in Ethiopia, from 1905, says that "thief-catchers" could divine the guilty after partaking,[138] which suggests the plant's secondary name, *esha tenbit* (prophecy plant).[139] This practice was probably established in the 1500s but remained mostly underground until around 1900.[140] Thief catchers smoked cannabis alongside datura and possibly opium.

In western Central Africa, examples of spiritual applications of cannabis relate to *nganga*, a category of plant experts shared in many Bantu cultures.[141] At the mouth of the Congo in 1850, *nganga* prescribed a tea of cannabis, tree barks, and the medicinal vine *Abrus precatorius* to treat gonorrhea.[142] One hundred and thirty years later, *nganga* in the Republic of Congo smoked cannabis to overcome fear of powerful, malevolent spirits.[143] The historical rootedness of this practice is questionable, since the plant did not arrive in the central Congo basin until the late 1800s. In western Central Africa generally, spiritualistic use of cannabis and other plant drugs was seemingly a nineteenth-century phenomenon.[144]

In some cases, cannabis served to influence not practitioners but their subjects. Historically documented cases were decidedly nontherapeutic; they involved punitive jurisprudence. In the eastern Congo Basin in the 1890s, *nganga* forced accused murderers to smoke massive amounts of cannabis during judicial ordeals.[145] The first among the accused to faint from cannabis intoxication was determined guilty and executed.[146] Contemporaneously among Fang-speakers in Gabon, cannabis was mixed into a beverage with the toxic sap of *Erythrophleum* (a tree genus), which stunned prisoners before their execution.[147] These were simultaneously religious sacrifices and punitive killings of captives seized from neighboring groups.

Finally, cannabis had roles in three political-religious movements.[148] Formal theologies that included sacramental cannabis arose in the African Diaspora, most famously Rastafarianism in Jamaica, but historical examples from the continent were esoteric and at least as political as religious. The least political was the Lemba cult, which arose along the Lower Congo in response to social upheaval caused by commercial slave trading.[149] It centered on beliefs about spiritual and physical healing. Evidence for cannabis use among Lemba adherents is weak. It consists only of water pipes that Europeans collected just before 1900, some two hundred years after the cult's origin.[150] Their smoking may simply have reflected drug use characteristic of broader society rather than anything specific to Lemba practice. In fact, one Lemba parable suggested that *diamba* was a shortcut to a shallow spirituality for undisciplined people.[151]

The second example is barely known but clearly political.[152] Exactly one primary source, written by a British administrator, mentions this movement. Around 1912 in present-day South Sudan, a "woman calling herself the Sirdar" organized resistance to traditional authority and made cannabis smoking an element of her movement's ideology. The only hint that this movement had a religious element is the administrator's allegation that it had "magic" connected to it. He complained that the movement caused "considerable trouble" in governing the natives. Indeed, the woman directly challenged colonial authority. The title she took—"the Sirdar"—was that of the British commander-in-chief of the Egyptian army.[153]

The Sirdar movement is no more than a rumor from one colonial officer. Yet it is worth mentioning as a parallel to the Bena Riamba political-religious movement, the most famous tale of cannabis in Africa.

SIX

Society Overturned: The Bena Riamba

The Bena Riamba movement existed between 1870 and 1890 in the Lulua River valley, at the center of the Kwango-to-Lualaba area.[1] Cannabis histories represent the Bena Riamba in a manner that supports current political views that the plant drug poses limited risk—and perhaps unacknowledged benefits—to individuals and societies. In the dominant telling, Bena Riamba adherents abandoned warfare because cannabis inspired universal friendship within them.

This romantic narrative obscures the best documented instance anywhere of the drug plant successfully entering a historical landscape and society. The Bena Riamba episode shows that cannabis was integral to the expansion of commerce and colonialism in Central Africa's Congo Basin. The episode does not show that cannabis produces peace, goodwill, friendship, or any other sort of contentedness; the plant drug's subjective effects are context-dependent. The Bena Riamba context was political, not spiritual. Cannabis aided the exercise of authoritarian power and violence while also becoming a therapeutic resource for people exposed to trauma produced by political-economic upheaval. Far beyond the Bena Riamba, people used the plant drug to prepare for and recover from trauma. This role helped carry it into new landscapes around the Atlantic.

FIGURE 6.1. These men were Angolan commercial porters, and are holding wrapped, new rifles. In the southern Congo Basin in the 1880s, the number of visible rifles would have traded for about twenty-five slaves. "Bailundo Porters," postcard, Angola, c. 1885 (postmarked 1913), published by Collecção Moraes, Luanda. Author's collection.

Rifles, rubber, ivory, slaves, and greed transformed the Congo Basin in the late 1800s. Greedy pursuit of the first four spread violence across a previously blank spot on European maps, which was also a power vacuum among African empires. The Bena Riamba briefly thrived in the turmoil because its leaders were quick to seize power in the vacuum through alliances with outsiders seeking to claim unmapped terrain.

Three factors generated political-economic opportunity in the Kwango-to-Lualaba area in the late 1800s. First, long-standing African powers were in decline. Most important were the Lunda Empire (1680s–1887) and the Luba Empire (1580s–1889). Their histories of expansion meant that Luba and Lunda speakers lived throughout the southern Congo Basin. By 1850, the areas under their control had shrunk, and previously subordinate groups increasingly challenged their authority. Both empires sought to maintain power by opening their heartlands to outsiders; more accurately, neither empire could continue to keep powerful outsiders out. Slavers extended their raiding and trading toward the imperial core areas, and European adventurers arrived intent on colonial expansion. The Bena Riamba arose in a minor valley between fading empires by collaborating with slavers and adventurers.

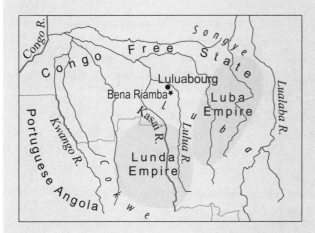

MAP 6.1. Kwango-to-Lualaba area, Central Africa, in the 1880s. Luluabourg was renamed Kananga in 1966. Map by Chris S. Duvall.

The second factor was sociocultural change within African communities. The Bena Riamba was an uprising against traditional authorities, among Luba speakers outside the control of the Luba Empire. Regionally, other social groups also sought new forms of governance, too, and forged new identities to build cohesiveness around their political movements. These were not "tribes" or any natural, preexisting groups. They were people who shared political-economic desires and enacted their desires on others. Two examples are relevant here. The Cokwe (or Chokwe) originated as a clan within the Lunda Empire but after 1850 rejected Lunda authority to pursue their own commercial interests. The group known as Zappo Zap began around 1883, when a Songye-speaking potentate named Nsapu Nsapu had amassed enough followers to seize independence from other potentates and to seek power through convenient alliances with anyone willing to pay. The Zappo Zap were mercenaries who amassed wealth through military prowess.

At last, European empires engaged in a geopolitical competition for formal colonies. In diplomatic circles, this scramble for Africa yielded the Berlin Conference of 1884–85, which divided Africa into spheres of control and regulated relations among the European countries that claimed territory in Africa. On the ground, their competition yielded shifting alliances among African leaders seeking power and European interlopers seeking to gain control over new lands, thereby extending their countries' colonial empires. On the ground, the colonial project was fundamentally economic, at least in the Congo, where colonialists sought wealth through primitive accumulation—the initial taking of land and resources into capitalist control. The Congo Free State (1885–1908) epitomized greed-driven colonialism. It was the personal property of King Leopold II of Belgium and operated through private concessionaires with near-absolute power. Employees of the Free State committed atrocities in pursuit of wealth, as portrayed in Joseph Conrad's *The Heart of Darkness* (1899) and described in the book *King Leopold's Ghost* (1998).[2]

The Bena Riamba belongs in this violent past, which, unfortunately, persists. As this book goes to press, war occupies the Kwango-to-Lualaba area. In late 2016, the government of the Democratic Republic of the Congo refused to recognize Kamuina Nsapu as the head of a Luba clan. He encouraged his supporters to rise against the state. The so-called Kamuina Nsapu rebellion intensified after government forces killed him in August 2016. Since then, the conflict has devolved into fighting between Luba-speaking Kamuina Nsapu supporters and the Bana Mura group, which is a government-backed militia dominated by Cokwe speakers. In 2017, at least three thousand people were killed in an area centered on Kananga (which was called Luluabourg during the Bena Riamba period). By mid-2018, the violence had displaced nearly 1.5 million people. Kamuina Nsapu fighters and Bana Mura fighters occupy the same lands as the Bena Riamba. Other commonalities include quasi-religious ideology, identity-based violence, and drug use.[3] The Bena Riamba established a precedent in the colonial Congo that has been followed since.

The Bena Riamba movement was unequivocally a political-economic event, and all documentarians had interests in the broader political-economic context in which the movement was embedded. Cannabis histories have blindly relied on just two observers, thereby transforming their particular interests into an ostensibly objective history of the Bena Riamba. Paul Pogge was a German explorer who sought and found a fabled "tribe" of exotic natives. Hermann von Wissmann was a German military officer and employee of the Congo Free State who praised the movement because it supplied porters and guards to him in his travels among peoples hostile to European interlopers.[4] Overlooked have been Portuguese and Belgian observers who diametrically opposed the Germans' opinions of the movement. Henrique Dias de Carvalho traveled among those who traded with the Bena Riamba, and several Belgian missionaries observed the decline and aftermath of the movement.[5] All accounts show that the movement was fundamentally political, not religious.[6]

The roots of the Bena Riamba movement trace to about 1864, when an elephant hunter named Mukwajanga, a Cokwe man from northeastern Angola employed by a Portuguese trader, shared cannabis with Chishimbi, a Luba-speaking potentate along the Lulua River.[7] Cokwe influence was expanding regionally as the Lunda Empire declined. Initially few in number, the group grew through commercial acquisitions of women and children.[8] Cokwe men reportedly carried cannabis seeds, herb, and water pipes whenever they were away from home, because they were unsure if political violence or commercial opportunity would keep them from returning.[9] People in the Lulua and neighboring valleys were isolated and decentralized and lived in relative peace prior to Chishimbi's rise.[10] Some groups refused contact with outsiders; the Lunda and Luba empires sought to exclude outsiders, despite their waning power. Chishimbi's group had been closed to trade, but he received Mukwajanga because he wanted firearms, cloth, and other goods and was curious to learn about Europeans. Conveniently, Mukwajanga sought to expand trade.[11] The two smoked together; Chishimbi learned to shoot a rifle; they became friends. Chishimbi planted *riamba* in his garden the morning after trying it.[12] He also presented Mukwajanga to his townspeople as his reincarnated father.[13]

Afterward, Mukwajanga came regularly to barter. When he failed to show for several years, Chishimbi organized an expedition to find his friend in around 1871. Wary of crossing unfamiliar territory, Chishimbi decided to distribute ivory and girls along the way, because that was what Mukwajanga had sought.[14] Chishimbi found his friend, who had been sick, in a market town in north-central Angola. Despite a gift of tusks and girls, Mukwajanga was disappointed by Chishimbi's arrival because it wrecked his trade monopoly in the Lulua Valley.[15] Nonetheless, he introduced Chishimbi to a key Luso-African trader (whose connections later enabled Pogge's travel to the Lulua Valley).[16] The trader and the potentate struck a deal to exchange ivory for firearms and other goods; the Cokwe middlemen would continue to acquire captives.

Chishimbi traced his success to "the goodness of the plant" he had encountered through Mukwajanga.[17] Upon returning home, he summoned elders of neighboring villages, displayed the goods (i.e., firearms) he had acquired, and declared that "he would henceforth only recognize as his friends smokers of liamba [who] would constitute a society of friendship [that] would seek to make happiness [among] the Balubas and [to open their lands] to foreigners who

FIGURE 6.2. "Dance [of the Bashilange]," engraving, in J. von Wissmann, *Unter deutscher Flagge quer durch Afrika von West nach Ost* (Berlin: Walther and Apolant, 1889), 71.

would like to maintain . . . relations of friendship and commerce."[18] Chishimbi called this society of friendship *lubuku*, which properly designates his movement even if the name Bena Riamba is firmly established.[19] Adherents greeted one another by saying "*moyo*," which meant either "oath" or "life," signifying commitment to Chishimbi's ideology.[20] To one another they were *bena moyo* (people of the oath/life) or *bena riamba* (people of the *riamba*).[21] Pogge and Wissmann called them "Bashilenge," even though the Germans knew explicitly that the people in question did not like the name.[22] These people self-identified as "Baluba" (Luba-speaking people). "Bashilenge" was a Cokwe word, probably referring to a creek labeled "Shilange" on a Belgian missionary's map of the Lulua Valley.[23] The Germans invented historical, physiognomic, and racial distinctions between "Bashilenge" and other purported groups.[24] Subsequent writers took "Bashilenge" as the name of a distinct, natural group, repeated and embellished Pogge's and Wissmann's notions, and thereby produced a "tribe" that did not exist beforehand yet persists in cannabis histories. Under the Congo Free State, "Bashilenge" became "Bena-Lulua," a label counterpoised with "Luba," another invented tribe.[25] These labels arose from warfare in the 1870s and 1880s: Bena Riamba adherents seized the Lulua valley—hence, "Bena-Lulua." The evictees became "Luba." All spoke the Luba language.

In any case, Chishimbi initiated many customs alongside the *moyo* greeting. Most obvious was sacramental cannabis smoking, but Bena Riamba religious practices cannot be disentangled from political events. Chishimbi's new religion espoused friendship, peace, and social unity on *his* terms, an ideology to support a political revolution against commercial isolationism and for centralized power. Primarily younger people supported Chishimbi's radicalism. His supporters became privileged individuals called *mukelenge*. This term was translated in 1906 as "chief, lord, king, master, nobleman, governor, prince, ruler."[26] The old guard who did not support Chishimbi's changes were called *mpelumba*, after a type of monkey.[27] The Bena Riamba killed many *mpelumba* while evicting them from the Lulua Valley.

The political nature of the movement intensified because Chishimbi died around 1873 without a clear successor. Dias de Carvalho says that Mukwajanga tried to install Chishimbi's young son, but his brother-in-law Chingenge seized power, purportedly with popular support.[28] Wissmann says Chishimbi's brother Mukenge came into power in 1874, only to be challenged later when his rival Chingenge had obtained firearms through the Cokwe.[29] Wissmann was not disinterested: "It had been my tactic . . . to keep the Natives separated in two parties, in order to play one against the other. I had made Mukenge and Tschingenge heads of the two parties."[30] In the end, he favored Mukenge. However, these men were potentates of different towns and likely did not see themselves as two parties within a group. Indeed, Mukenge may have been unrelated to Chishimbi but established a *lubuku* separate from Chingenge's, as a means of acquiring power.[31]

All primary sources came years after Chishimbi died, and all promoted one claimant over the other. Dias de Carvalho favored Chingenge, seemingly because both disfavored the Congo Free State.[32] His is the only Portuguese account. Mukenge's claim seems stronger simply because the most prominent sources took his side; the Germans found Mukenge useful and passed their preference on to the Free State—which quickly discarded him. Mukenge's crew is the only Bena Riamba represented in cannabis histories. His European allies crowed that Mukenge "would, among any people, be a remarkable, and, indeed, in many respects, a magnificent man."[33] Mukenge in turn claimed that Pogge, Wissmann, and another German traveler were past potentates returned from the dead.[34] Neither Mukenge nor Chingenge was a spiritual leader. Chishimbi's theology fell to a woman called Sangula Meta, probably Mukenge's sister.[35] She was a zealot in support of the new regime.[36] Mukenge's allies considered her "a woman of great intellectual power and force of character."[37] Her power and force were well documented. She once caned a group of reluctant guards/porters into

FIGURE 6.3. "Sangula Meta," engraving, in H. von Wissmann, L. Wolf, C. von François, and H. Mueller, *Im Innern Afrikas: Die Erforschung des Kassai während der Jahre 1883, 1884, und 1885,* 3d ed. (Leipzig: Brockhaus, 1891), 162.

action for Wissmann and invented a punishment for second-degree murder: the juice of *Capsicum* chili pepper seeds dripped into the eyes.[38]

Regardless of European praise, other potentates had no interest in the self-centered unity Mukenge sought. War inhabited the Lulua Valley during the 1870s and 1880s.[39] The Bena Riamba rhetoric of peace and friendship applied to conquered areas. The renewal the movement achieved was less spiritual than military. Old-fashioned weapons such as bows, arrows, and spears were banned, but rifles—the new weapon—were not.[40] By 1878, Cokwe middlemen had sold so many guns that they feared the consequences and tried unsuccessfully to halt sales.[41] Mukenge gained European backing against his rivals and found refuge when necessary at the Congo Free State outpost of Luluabourg (now Kananga). Self-interested missionaries there cheered the movement because "they threw their fetishes in the [river so that] now there are several million natives who are delivered from the degrading cult."[42] The missionaries saw opportunity in the Bena Riamba's perceived spiritual availability, as well as their hierarchical ideology. The American proselytizer, for example, who in

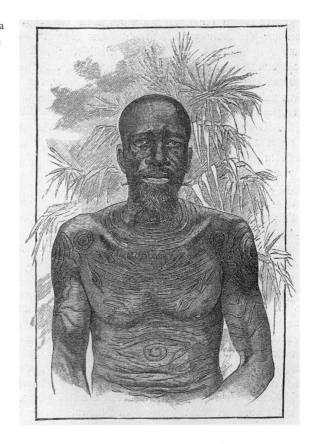

FIGURE 6.4. Kalamba Mukenge. The designs on his chest and arms are decorative scarification, which was common among Luba speakers in the late 1800s. "Kalamba Mukenge," engraving, in H. von Wissmann, L. Wolf, C. von François, and H. Mueller, *Im Innern Afrikas: Die Erforschung des Kassai während der Jahre 1883, 1884, und 1885*, 3d ed. (Leipzig: Brockhaus, 1891), 165.

1906 translated *mukelenge* as "chief, lord, king, master," and so on, also conveniently translated "missionary" as *mukelenge*.[43] Mukenge saw opportunity in the missionaries, too. He sought Catholic baptism in 1887, when his relationship with the Free State was deteriorating and his movement was falling apart.[44] Mukenge was an ineffective leader, called a "despot and tyrant" by a Belgian missionary.[45] His people were sometimes so strained by fighting that he could spare nobody even to serve Wissmann.[46]

Conflict intensified as the Congo Free State, founded in 1885, asserted itself. After 1887, the Free State became reliant on Songye mercenaries called Zappo Zap to supply armed force. Mukenge had done this for Wissmann, but the Bena Riamba were overextended and discarded by Wissmann once he concluded his travels (and got a job with the Free State) in 1887.[47] Overhunting meant that by the mid-1880s Mukenge could scarcely supply ivory and had little to barter except rubber.[48] In 1891, Mukenge refused to submit to the Free State; he allegedly threw chili oil in the face of a Belgian administrator.[49] In the 1890s, the Kasai Valley descended into anarchy.[50] As Mukenge faded, "Bena-Lulua" lost favor with the Free State, which preferred "Luba." Official favoritism continued under the Belgian Congo. Anticolonial and anti-"Luba" politicians in the 1950s called on Mukenge's memory to promote "Lulua" pride, helping to precipitate the Luba-Lulua War of 1959–62.[51] A Congolese historian concludes, "There is no better example of the invention of ethnicity" than the Lulua-Luba division.[52] Cannabis marked a social group—Bena Riamba adherents—to whom it brought war, a curse passed on to following generations.

Cannabis was unequivocally central to Bena Riamba ideology. It was simultaneously sacrament, medicine, recreation, and punishment, in the form of extremely high doses. Men and women smoked, but men's use was salient to male Europeans. The Bena Riamba forbade existing religious practices and destroyed "fetishes"—icons that embodied spirits—because opposing parties could call on them for support. At least one icon remained in use, though. It somehow represented gratitude for successful commercial transactions.[53] The movement allegedly claimed that ancestors could return from the afterlife, although such belief was documented only when Mukwajanga and the Germans were presented as reincarnated leaders—politically useful miracles for the Bena Riamba's headmen. All firsthand accounts of religious ceremonies are partial, ethnocentric, and sensationalized. Followers shaved their heads, marked themselves with white clay, and gathered in town squares to smoke communally. They sang, danced, and shared meals around hearth fires, like people across Central Africa. Other regional drug-use norms were present. Wissmann's guards/porters, for instance, smoked when they were tired or hungry and returned to their marches with greater vigor.[54] Followers employed cannabis in judicial ordeals, as in other societies, but for all manner of sins, large and small.[55] Ordeals were inescapably unpleasant, because they ended only when one participant had smoked into unconsciousness. When proposed, ordeals were likely unavoidable; participation was necessary to show adherence to the new order.[56] Gaining entry into the new order was an ordeal. When vanquished chiefs paid tributary visits to Mukenge, they were subjected to two nights spent outdoors in the nude, two baths in the open, a body painting with white clay, and an interrogation—in the nude and with chili-pepper juice dripped in the eyes (as if they had committed second-degree murder)—about past sins and religious beliefs.[57] The Germans were not subjected to this welcome, but on occasion they had to smoke to prove their trustworthiness.[58] Farmers grew "forestlike" *riamba* gardens around Bena Riamba towns, obscuring other crops.[59] Mukenge further reshaped agriculture by forbidding domesticates he associated with the old order. Banana and pineapple were disallowed; dogs, goats, and chickens were supposed to be slaughtered.[60] *Riamba* was the only medicinal plant allowed, though it was ineffective.[61] Palm wine was forbidden, and palm trees were felled. Instead, a new fermentation was allowed: sorghum beer, a Cokwe recipe.[62] Cokwe influence was evident throughout Bena Riamba life. Religious ideas perhaps reflected Cokwe theology.[63] Cokwe traders gained formal positions of power under Mukenge and his rivals.[64]

The religious and political-economic aspects of the movement cannot be disentangled. The historian Johannes Fabian calls Bena Riamba a cargo cult with Mukenge its charismatic head.[65] The only recorded act of devotion was to visit their singular icon after concluding a deal and leave food for the poor.[66] Mukwajanga and cannabis arrived in pursuit of commerce. The plant drug became special because Chishimbi credited it for a trade agreement. Chishimbi's initial support came from young people who were disgruntled because elders had forbidden them from purchasing and wearing trade fabrics.[67] The movement's success depended upon firearms and gunpowder, acquired in exchange for ivory, rubber, and people. Rifles became status symbols. Poor men kept but hid their bows, arrows, and spears, openly carrying only cudgels to avoid repercussions from bearing prohibited arms.[68] Bena Riamba adherents seized any opportunity to trade. Free State proponents alleged that Cokwe traders swindled Bena Riamba followers,[69] perhaps because Cokwe business came through colonial rival Angola. In any case, followers made deals that clearly profited their trade partners more than themselves. In 1883, for example, men under Mukenge and Chingenge sold women and children to Cokwe traders for one rifle or sixteen yards of fabric each.[70] Pogge estimated that for every seventy men who arrived in a caravan, eighty women and children left; his interpreter guessed that three hundred people had been taken from an area of about twenty-five square miles in the previous ten months.[71] Pogge believed that men sometimes smoked *riamba* to assuage seller's remorse. Friendship and unity applied only to those not traded away.

The Bena Riamba was remarkable because it gave cannabis formal importance. Its adherents provided amusing historical moments. Wissmann's guards/porters, for instance, once confronted hostile bowmen while armed with cudgels, laughter, and calabash water pipes.[72] Of course, many carried rifles, too, and marched in front of a well-armed, domineering European colonialist. Bena Riamba adherents initially led the nineteenth-century firearms race in the southern Congo. For a time, Chishimbi, Mukenge, and Chingenge manipulated powerful parties to their advantage, including European and African empires. They were not particularly malignant or benign in their regional context.

The last report of the Bena Riamba was in 1893, when a Belgian traveler told the story of Musulu, one of Mukenge's subjects whose comrades abandoned him into slavery.[73] (For more on Musulu, see chapter 9.) Mukenge last appeared in the record in 1895, when he reportedly forced a conciliatory rival to smoke *riamba* "until death followed" and received as a trophy the severed ear of a killed Belgian officer.[74] Of course, these lurid reports came from Belgians who vilified him. As with many aspects of the Bena Riamba, it is impossible to delineate what the movement's members did from what observers thought of them. No account, however, exhibits that cannabis necessarily generates spirituality, friendship, peacefulness, or other such sentiments, in Africa or anywhere. The plant drug's meanings and subjective effects are context-dependent. Any attitudes toward cannabis that Bena Riamba adherents expressed, and any effects it seemed to have had on them, were inextricable from the regional upheaval to which the movement contributed. The plant drug declined with Mukenge's crew. In 1913, an ethnographer estimated that just one in thirty or forty Luba-speaking adults smoked *riamba*.[75] The movement's legacy was war, not drugs.

CENTRAL AFRICA WAS TUMULTUOUS at the turn of the twentieth century. The illegal persistence of commercial slavery, the expansion of colonial control and monetary economies, and the disruption of agricultural and wild ecologies led to social disintegrations and profound cultural transformations. Cannabis participated widely in this upheaval. In 1899, the Congo Free State ordered Zappo Zap mercenaries to collect taxes from towns near former Bena Riamba territory. When townspeople would not or could not pay, the Zappo Zap massacred at least eighty-one, based on the number of severed hands found at the scene; about forty bodies had been eaten.[76] News of the massacre ultimately brought down the Free State. The news also included cannabis: when the reporter asked what had happened to the head of a decapitated body, he was told, "[The killers] have made a bowl of his forehead to [mix] tobacco and *diamba* in."[77] Cannabis may have been peripheral to political-economic chaos, but it is important to locate it in violent contexts like this because people valued the plant drug in war.[78]

Colonial-era war makers beyond the Bena Riamba and Zappo Zap used cannabis before, during, and after fighting. In northern Angola in the 1900s, the only obvious supplies indigenous troops carried to battle were manioc and *liamba*.[79] Outside western Central Africa, accounts of drugged-out warriors are dubitable.[80] Soldiers in South Africa, for instance, supposedly were made to smoke *dagga* because "part of the witch doctor's duties is the doctoring of armies [so that they] may become invincible."[81] There are three apparently firsthand reports of cannabis-smoking warriors in East Africa and Southern Africa (and one generalization that Nilotic peoples in eastern Uganda forbade warriors from smoking[82]). In 1857, Livingstone, in Zambia, determined that cannabis "causes a species of frenzy" and reported that in one battle Makololo soldiers "sat down and smoked it, in order that they might make an effective onslaught."[83] In what is now Tanzania, Ruga-ruga mercenaries (who fought for both African leaders and colonial governments) smoked cannabis and drank heavily.[84] Colonial authorities tolerated cannabis among allied fighters, but several early drug-control laws were directed against regular colonial troops, in German East Africa (1891), German Southwest Africa (1912), and Portuguese Angola (1913).[85]

It is impossible to know why these men smoked or how they might have described their drug use. None recorded their experiences. Sometimes soldiers probably smoked just to kill time.[86] In other contexts, cannabis was not a mere pastime, because it directly altered the perceptions of people engaged in organized violence. Depending on social meanings assigned to the plant drug, it may have served to elevate aggressiveness, improve perceptual clarity, dull emotions, or treat symptoms of physical and mental injury. The drug had different subjective effects depending on context. A Zulu oral tradition recorded in the 1970s told that cannabis made historical lion hunters brave and bold,[87] while in other contexts smokers relaxed and played games.

Cannabis for centuries has been complexly entangled in social and cultural transformations within Africa, during and before colonialism. In Central Africa, the plant traveled with slaves, porters, and soldiers, but many of the elites who provoked slaving, commerce, and warfare smoked it as well. Current medical practice considers cannabis potentially useful in managing psychological trauma, physical pain, appetite, and other sensations. While it is impossible to determine why historical people valued cannabis, its pharmacology suggests that cannabis enhanced at least some individuals' capacities for coping with traumatic realities. If so, this function helped carry it across the Atlantic.

SEVEN

Cannabis Crosses the Atlantic

Cannabis crossed the continent within the slave trade. It crossed the Atlantic, too, with enslaved people, who carried *Cannabis indica* to more locations and for a longer period of time than any other group of migrants.

The tale of the plant's slave-led dispersal is normally mentioned in cannabis histories, quietly and without supporting evidence. The Brazilian sociologist Júlio César Adiala has challenged the tale as unfounded conventional wisdom, whose repetition helps justify racially biased drug-law enforcement.[1] I partly agree with Adiala: evidence-free presentations can sustain racial stereotypes about drug use, because without evidence, there are few limits to generalizations about people-plant relationships. The conventional wisdom that sustains folklore, jokes, and common knowledge are the seemingly innocuous words that perpetuate structural and individual racism, in Brazil and elsewhere.[2]

I want to challenge conventional wisdom about cannabis history, and in so doing I partly disagree with Adiala: there is strong evidence that enslaved Africans carried cannabis across the Atlantic to many locations, including Brazil. The evidence is as robust as for any plant that slaves brought across the ocean and shows that cannabis contributed to geographically specific components of the transatlantic slave-trading system.[3] This evidence sharply constrains possible generalizations about historical drug use. Enslaved Africans as a generic group did not carry cannabis across the Atlantic, nor did the generic group of enslaved people who landed in Brazil or elsewhere. Cannabis use by current African-descendant populations in the Americas has no connection to an

FIGURE 7.1. It is common knowledge in Brazil that psychoactive cannabis participated in chattel slavery. In this comic from the cartoonist Arnaldo Branco, the narrator (top) continues telling his history of cannabis: "Speaking of sails, the world diffusion of *maconha* was the result of the Age of Sail. Slaves brought the habit of smoking to various corners of the globe." Below, slaves smoke and talk: "Gee, I had a heavy day of slavery today"; "It's good we can relax after 19 hours of work"; "I call it happy hour." The narrator comments at the bottom: "Thank God it's Friday, huh, playboy?" Obviously, this comic history is not meant to be authoritative. Yet by placing familiar, modern imagery in ostensibly past settings—the slaves are smoking joints, but *maconha* cigarettes appeared in Brazil only in the 1960s—popular portrayals efface the documented past and allow stereotypes of drug use to stand unchallenged. Slaves smoked to stimulate willingness to work, not to chill out afterward. A. Branco, *As aventuras do Capitão Presença* (São Paulo: Conrad, 2006), 85.

African past except the broad connections that all people share who smoke cannabis using African pipe technologies and call cannabis by certain names.

In criticizing how cannabis histories have portrayed slave-led dispersal, I must acknowledge that the available evidence poses challenges to my critique and argument. First, many cannabis histories do, indeed, provide evidence of slave-led dispersal in the form of plant names. Many writers have pointed out that some cannabis terms in Brazil match some spoken in Angola.[4] Notable examples are *maconha* and *diamba*, which linguists have attributed to Angola's Kimbundu language. This linguistic connection has been recognized since 1867,[5] but no one has analyzed language data beyond comparing Brazilian and Angolan drug slang. By looking at these countries in isolation and without detail, word historians have missed a broader pattern. African plant names, mostly from western Central Africa, occur widely around the Atlantic. This language geography agrees with documentary records of the slave trade and of subsequent population movements.

Second, I recognize that the written record is imperfect for understanding African roles in transatlantic cannabis history. The main problem is that published observations of psychoactive cannabis appeared late in the history of transatlantic slaving—after 1840 for most locations, whereas transoceanic shipping ended in 1865 and slave arrivals ended decades earlier in most countries.

The documentary record poorly reflects the plant's dispersal chronology. Primary sources show when and where documentarians noticed psychoactive cannabis rather than its first appearance in a location. Around the tropical Atlantic, botanically specific first records of *Cannabis indica* appeared widely in the middle 1800s. For several locations, though, earlier documents suggest cannabis and that European observers did not know what they were seeing. Importantly, many Portuguese probably had vague ideas about cannabis because their country grew essentially none, relying on imports of naval cordage and sailcloth from northern Europe. They used other plants for lower-end fiber products.[6] Stories about hashish circulated in nineteenth-century European Orientalist thought, but into the mid-twentieth century most Europeans knew effectively nothing about any cannabis drug other than pharmaceutical extracts and corn plasters (medicinal pastes for treating plantar warts). In the Americas, the historical record of psychoactive cannabis in many countries begins abruptly, and obviously well after the plant's arrival. In Panama, for instance, the first written notice of cannabis came in 1916, when Canal Zone police noticed U.S. soldiers smoking it.[7] The earliest botanical description, in 1925, stated, "the plant grows wild [in] Panama and is found quite widely distributed."[8] Soon after, U.S. Army researchers discovered that cannabis smoking seemed "to be not uncommon"

MAP 7.1. The low-latitude Americas. Map by Chris S. Duvall.

among regular Panamanians, and "the colored people [have] great faith in the [therapeutic] efficacy of [cannabis tea]."[9] This widespread, widely smoked plant, and its odd use as tea, did not arrive with World War I–era U.S. soldiers.

The plant's biological dispersal preceded its written record. Its arrival in a location must be estimated by backdating from the earliest published record. There are limits, of course, to how much backdating is justifiable. Slave trading ended at different times around the Atlantic, depending on the interaction of country-specific and global processes of change. In Angola, slavery continued into the 1900s, despite abolition in 1869; in Brazil, emancipation came in 1888 and the last transatlantic arrivals more than twenty years before; in Mexico, the last transatlantic arrivals came before 1800. The number of people taken from Africa increased after 1750; the overall annual rate peaked around 1810. More slaves left the continent during the last century of the trade (approximately 1760–1860) than during the previous centuries combined. The largest portion were from western Central Africa. Thus, the number of people taken from western Central Africa increased just as the plant was becoming common there. If late-documented cannabis knowledge is reasonably Central African, it traces back either to slave ships or to population movements within the New World.

In addition, Europeans recorded relatively little about medicinal plants among slaves but documented emancipated communities more fully. During the 1800s, various countries, particularly Great Britain, freed captives around the Atlantic through naval seizure of slave ships. These people were not truly freed, though; they were subject to their liberators' decisions about where they should live and what they should do. Scholars call these people recaptives, of whom 181,000 are documented—a small fraction of the people forced into the Middle Passage during the same years.[10] European observers published important accounts of their material circumstances. For example, a public health assessment of Portuguese São Tomé from 1869 detailed the foods and plant medicines of recaptives, including the first record of psychoactive cannabis on the island.[11] Historical records about captives and recaptives in Africa are highly relevant to understanding slave arrivals in the Americas. The greatest number of recaptives were disembarked in Sierra Leone, where 100,000 arrived between 1808 and 1863. Europeans shuttled recaptives widely around the Atlantic.[12] Many who landed in Sierra Leone, for instance, were transshipped to British Caribbean colonies. Records about cannabis among recaptives give evidence about people-plant relationships within specific human migrations and provide a sample of relationships that existed within the much larger migration of slaves from western Central Africa. The people who were not freed from slave ships disembarked in Brazil, Cuba, the United States, and other places that were late to outlaw slavery.

A key reason that Europeans transshipped recaptives is that societies around the Atlantic sought other sources of cheap labor after slavery declined. Many labor regimes arose—such as indenture, mandatory labor, and wage slavery—that supplied nominally free workers to replace chattel slaves. Chattel slaves and post-slave workers did not experience identical conditions of life or labor but faced analogous challenges of marginalization and exploitation that negatively affected individual health.[13] The social-ecological contexts of drug use documented after emancipation existed under slavery.

FIGURE 7.2. These men and woman were indentured servants, or *serviçais*, on São Tomé in the 1890s. They were almost certainly from Angola, and almost certainly enslaved before their "liberation" into indentured servitude. The men are carrying headloads of oil palm fruit. Palm oil was a minor export from São Tomé in the late 1800s. More commonly, laborers harvested oil palm fruit as food. "Serviçaes carregando andim para fabricação de azeite de palma," postcard, São Tomé, ca. 1890s, postmarked 1905[?], published by José Teixeira Barbosa, São Tomé. Author's collection.

Finally, the drug plant is relatively rare in the documentary record because people had many reasons to conceal their cannabis use. Authorities widely disapproved of the drug years before formal prohibitions began. Cannabis smoking was hidden from documentarians and thus absented from the record.

This chapter presents my argument that enslaved people from western Central Africa led the transatlantic dispersal of *Cannabis indica*. The evidence includes language geography, written accounts, and oral histories and underscores the importance of African inheritances in cannabis cultures around the Atlantic. Explicitly, other people carried *indica* across the ocean—European sailors, South Asian laborers, Levantine immigrants[14]—but their roles in the plant's historical dispersal were relatively minor. As a reminder of previous chapters, I estimate that *Cannabis indica* had first come to Atlantic Central Africa by 1730, when people from the Kwango-to-Lualaba region began moving westward in commercial captivity. Regional slave exports increased after 1730, not peaking until the 1820s. Seed dispersal grew over time as cannabis became increasingly associated with commercial slaving and more abundant in

Atlantic Central Africa. I conclude that African knowledge underlies practices of psychoactive cannabis use around the Atlantic, because in receiving societies people of all geographic and cultural backgrounds adopted the plant drug. Despite its African past, psychoactive cannabis has been an element of globalized society, not of specific cultural traditions, for centuries.

The Number of Enslaved People Shipped from Central Africa

From the 1500s to the 1800s, about 12.5 million people were forcibly taken from Africa on slave ships headed across the Atlantic. More than thirty-five thousand slave-ship voyages are documented. Millions died in captivity on the continent before their survivors were loaded onto ships; millions more died in the Middle Passage. From western Central Africa, 3.2 million people are known to have disembarked in the Americas, from 8,891 voyages.

These numbers come from the Trans-Atlantic Slave Trade Database (TSTD), a hugely important compilation of historical records started online in 1999.[15] I have relied on this database to understand the historical geography of captives who came from areas relevant to the biological dispersal of cannabis. Many researchers have used the database to analyze other captive migration streams.

It's necessary to recognize that the TSTD does not fully document the number of people who were forcibly migrated. First, many primary records were incomplete, and many have been lost since their creation. Some voyages were purposefully not documented. Trading that violated commercial laws happened for centuries, and illegal trading increased with abolition efforts after 1800. Many head of slaves were omitted from records to avoid per capita taxes or shipping load limits. Second, the database does not seem to include some records published elsewhere. For instance, several ships and voyages listed in the book *Human Cargoes: The British Slave Trade to Spanish America, 1700–1739* (1981) do not appear in the TSTD.[16] Third, the TSTD includes only transatlantic voyages and not movements of captives within the Americas. Slave trading within the Americas was active and profitable for centuries, although historians have only patchily quantified these trades.[17] Nothing is known of the individual origins of people trapped in this commerce other than the American port of embarkation. Finally, recaptives are not fully included in the TSTD; separately, however, historians have recently compiled data on their migrations.[18]

It's necessary to recognize these limitations because Central African captives seem to have carried cannabis relatively commonly, at least after 1800. In some receiving societies, small numbers of documented captives were sufficient to introduce the plant. As an example, cannabis was seemingly established in

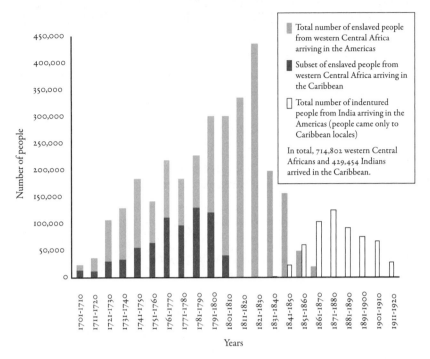

FIGURE 7.3. Transatlantic arrivals of enslaved people from western Central Africa and of indentured people from India. Graphic by Chris S. Duvall.

Liberia by about two thousand people arriving from western Central Africa over a period of forty years. The captives missing from the TSTD represent a potentially important if unknowable component of the plant's dispersal, even if the missing people were few relative to the transatlantic trade overall or in specific locations.

The captive migration from Central Africa dwarfed in size and extent all other migrations that *Cannabis indica* accompanied. Numberless merchant sailors circulated in the Indian and Atlantic oceans on European ships. Cannabis was a minor component of their material culture. The number and itineraries of people on these ships have not been estimated, although principal shipping routes are known. European shipping from the Indian Ocean was important in the drug plant's early post-Columbian dispersals but less important than later human migrations.

Many people left British India under indenture between 1819 and 1920,[19] including 429,000 disembarked around the Caribbean, primarily in the British colonies of Guiana (now Guyana), Trinidad and Tobago, and Jamaica, and in Dutch Guiana (now Suriname).[20] Indian workers were reputed to have carried cannabis with them, although their relationship with the plant drug has not been studied. Hindi words and practices became prominent in Guiana, Trinidad, and Jamaica,[21] partly because British officials in the Americas knew about cannabis from experience in India and wrote Hindi words—especially *ganja*— into initial drug-control laws.[22] In any case, all Indian laborers in the Atlantic entered societies that already bore strong Central African heritages. African arrivals greatly exceeded Indian arrivals before 1850, after which the pattern reversed. The total Indian migration, though, was smaller and less widespread than the Central African one. Indian influences likely obscured earlier, African influences.

Transatlantic Cannabis Words

Language geography provides important evidence for the plant's historical dispersal. Some common names for cannabis in Brazil are traceable to Africa. The Brazilian examples are important, but they are not the whole story.

In Brazil, several dozen cannabis names have been published since 1950.[23] Only a handful were recorded earlier. Most monikers are not analyzable as historical-geographic data because they have been published too few times and precise meanings are unknown. In 1869, for instance, Richard Burton reported that slaves in Minas Gerais called cannabis "Arirí,"[24] a name otherwise mentioned only in 1966, in the lower Amazon.[25] Other, better-documented names are not linguistically traceable. One example is *dirijo*, which meant "cannabis" in Amazonian caboclo villages in the mid-1900s.[26] (The caboclo social category represents rural smallholders of mixed Portuguese, Indigenous, and African heritage.) Perhaps this name comes from an Indigenous language; perhaps it is based on the Portuguese word *dirijo* ("I guide"). Untraceable names may evince unknown cultural connections or may be local nicknames.

Analyzable Brazilian names consistently come from Africa. They can't be associated with singular languages, but they do trace to specific areas. Two key examples are *soruma* and *cangonha*. *Soruma*, earliest documented in Brazil in 1958, is a term found in multiple languages in southeastern Africa.[27] In Brazil, *soruma* likely traces to Mozambique or Madagascar and to enslaved people who arrived between 1810 and 1840. Around 250,000 came to Brazil during this period; fewer than 30,000 came from southeastern Africa during other years.[28]

Cangonha was first recorded in several western Angolan languages in 1881 and in Brazil in 1899.[29] Brazilian usage of *cangonha* illustrates a challenge of the cannabis vocabulary. Knowledge about the plant has long been concealed for legal reasons—since 1830 in Brazil, when the city government of Rio de Janeiro

Cannabis words derived from African languages, with earliest publication date
Cannabis words derived from Portuguese, with earliest publication date
Cannabis words derived from Hindi, with earliest publication date

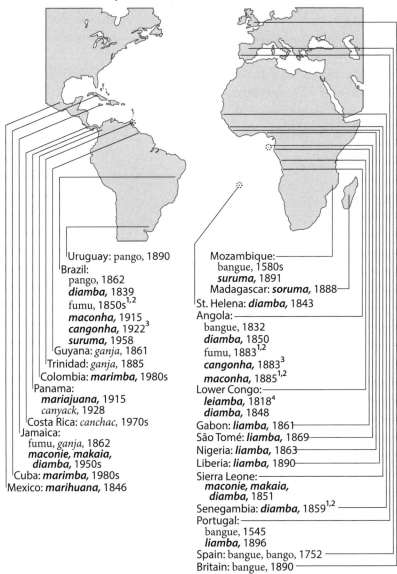

Uruguay: pango, 1890
Brazil:
  pango, 1862
  diamba, 1839
  fumu, 1850s[1,2]
  maconha, 1915
  cangonha, 1922[3]
  suruma, 1958
Guyana: *ganja,* 1861
Trinidad: *ganja,* 1885
Colombia: **marimba,** 1980s
Panama:
  mariajuana, 1915
  canyack, 1928
Costa Rica: *canchac,* 1970s
Jamaica:
  fumu, *ganja,* 1862
  **maconie, makaia,
  diamba,** 1950s
Cuba: **marimba,** 1980s
Mexico: **marihuana,** 1846

Mozambique:
  bangue, 1580s
  suruma, 1891
Madagascar: **soruma,** 1888
St. Helena: *diamba,* 1843
Angola:
  bangue, 1832
  diamba, 1850
  fumu, 1883[1,2]
  cangonha, 1883[3]
  maconha, 1885[1,2]
Lower Congo:
  leiamba, 1818[4]
  diamba, 1848
Gabon: *liamba,* 1861
São Tomé: *liamba,* 1869
Nigeria: *liamba,* 1863
Liberia: *liamba,* 1890
Sierra Leone:
  **maconie, makaia,
  diamba,** 1851
Senegambia: *diamba,* 1859[1,2]
Portugal:
  bangue, 1545
  liamba, 1896
Spain: bangue, bango, 1752
Britain: bangue, 1890

[1] Word was published earlier, but translated as "tobacco."
[2] Word was regionally translated as both "tobacco" and "cannabis."
[3] *Cangonha* may derive from Tupi (spoken in Brazil), meaning "plant used as tea."
[4] The 1818 document is too imprecise to identify *leiamba* certainly as cannabis.

MAP 7.2. Transatlantic cannabis words. Map by Chris S. Duvall.

banned the possession, sale, and use of cannabis.[30] Further, cannabis drug use has accompanied other behaviors that were criminalized. Users worldwide have engaged in linguistic subterfuge to hide their activities.[31] The name *cangonha* in Brazil probably served sometimes to conceal the plant drug by exploiting a near-homonym, spelled either *congonha* or *cangonha*,[32] which referred to plants used as tea, including the stimulant *Ilex paraguarensis* (yerba maté). The tea-plant term was recorded in the Tupi language in 1818,[33] but seventy years earlier, in a Portuguese poem, *congonha* was something that could be smelled on the breath of Rio de Janeiro residents; the city had strong slave-trading connections to southern Angola, where *cangonha* meant cannabis.[34] In central Brazil, slaves were given *congonha* tea to start the day in the mid-1800s,[35] and they probably said "tea" sometimes to imply "cannabis."

Cangonha was among several ambiguous words in the historical cannabis lexicon. It is unclear when dual meanings arose, and thus whether early uses referred to cannabis or something else. Consider the excerpted folk songs: the first (published in 1883) is ostensibly about tea; the second (published in 1922) is explicitly about cannabis:

Whoever wants me to sing well
Give me a tea of *cangonha*,
To cleanse this chest,
That is full of shame.
You call me ugly;
I am ugly but I am coy:
The green seasoning is also
Tasty in the eating.[36]

Maricas, my maricas,
Maricas of . . . *cangonha*:
I bit my lip
From so much *maconha* sucking. . . .
Maconha is a damned beast,
A damned beast is *maconha*;
[It's] of so much good to *maricas*
[That] we lose our shame.[37]

Maconha overtly means psychoactive cannabis. The mainstream meaning of Portuguese *maricas* had been "an effeminate fellow, a coward" since at least 1773.[38] Both passages suggest romance; the second, perhaps homosexuality. Yet the overt entendre of *maricas* in the 1922 song is "water pipe," a sense published in 1915 and consistently held in subsequent decades.[39] I have found no similar pipe words in African languages, although the water pipes first documented in Brazil in 1905 exhibited the Central African calabash-based design. The chorus of the second song celebrates that *maconha* "is from Congo," and in the 1880s cannabis was sometimes called "Congo."[40] Early twentieth-century authorities considered cannabis drug use, licentiousness, and other deviant behaviors to be mutually supporting threats to Brazilian civilization.[41] Shame is a theme that persisted in a popular saying published in 1975: "*Maconha* cigarettes make a shameless *negro*."[42] Attitudes toward the plant drug shaped language, which conversely shaped attitudes.[43] It is often impossible to know exactly what historical cannabis terms meant in context, and why.

The main Brazilian terms—*pango*, *maconha*, and *diamba*—were less ambiguous. *Pango* was printed first in 1828, when someone advertised "*pango d'Angolla*, good price" in a Rio de Janeiro newspaper.[44] In 1830, the city government prohibited stores from keeping and selling "*pito do pango*" and specified that "slaves, and other persons, who might use it, [will be punished with] eight days in jail."[45] A newspaper reader in 1832 was angry that stores were still selling.[46] *Pito* comes from the Indigenous Brazilian language Tupi and means "to smoke." *Pito do pango* meant "the act of smoking *pango*"; the associated verb *pitar* meant "to smoke [something in] a pipe."[47] *Pito* and *pitar* were both documented in 1749, seemingly in reference to cannabis.[48] In 1839, *pango* was defined as "*liamba* [or] *Cannabis indica*" and described as an African introduction to Brazil.[49] (This was the earliest that *liamba* appeared in print.) *Pito do pango* was recorded in 1890 in the Spanish spoken among "negroes" along the Río de la Plata (between Uruguay and Argentina).[50] Into the 1930s, *pango* remained the primary plant name in Rio and in Minas Gerais,[51] although *diamba* and *maconha* were more prominent nationally.

In Brazil, etymologists recently have classified *pango* as a generically "African" word, whereas *diamba* cognates are attributed specifically to Kimbundu.[52] Since 1880 linguists have been uncertain about *pango*; most have assumed it is from an African language, while others have questioned whether it has an African past.[53] Indeed, the evidence suggests that the Brazilian *pango* was ultimately a Portuguese loanword, tracing to sailors who first encountered Hindi *bhang* and Swahili *bangi* during the 1500s. They borrowed these similar names, with the loanword commonly spelled *bangue*. The first Portuguese published usage came in 1554.[54] In the Atlantic, *bangue* was the term used in 1689 in London, introduced by an English sailor who learned it as a Portuguese word in Ceylon.[55] In 1768, *bangue* was recorded in Galicia (the Spanish coastal region north of Portugal) when a Spanish writer observed cannabis sprung from bird droppings.[56] He did not try its psychoactive potential but recognized it as *bangue*, not *cañamo* (hemp); again, cannabis was scarcely grown in Portugal and neighboring parts of Spain. Early modern Iberian sailors seem to have had a distinct cannabis culture, but it is barely documented. In Spanish, the plant drug was historically called *bango*, and in French, *bangue*.[57] *Bangue* cognates that were recorded in western Central Africa all appeared in locations that experienced strong Portuguese influences. For instance, in southern Angola the term sounded like *epangue* or *pango* in Umbundu and Nyaneka.[58] Benguela, the principal port in southern Angola, had long-standing trade links to Rio de Janeiro and the Río de la Plata, the South American areas where the term *pango* was commonly used.[59]

In northern Angola, the primary word for cannabis was the cognate group *diamba, liamba, riamba*, and *iamba*. This word was spelled many ways because pronunciation varied, and Europeans had difficulty perceiving and representing its sound. *Diamba* was documented in Africa at the mouth of the Congo in 1848,[60] although five years earlier an English doctor had heard it on St. Helena island among people liberated from Angolan slave ships.[61] It is still spoken in many western Central African languages. It can be assigned to the 5/6 grammatical class of nouns generalized for the Narrow Bantu language family.[62] Like other nouns in this class, *riamba* refers to a plant product, and its plural form begins with the prefix ma-, as in *mariamba*. The word *maconha* similarly is the plural of *riconha* (leaf).[63] In contrast, *bangue*-type words do not fit any Bantu-family noun class and have no published plural forms. These are Portuguese loanwords. The plant drug's early, globalized sailor's past has been forgotten.

Liamba was initially published in 1839, in Brazil. Since 1867, the word has been read as evidence that cannabis crossed the Atlantic from Africa. Historically, *liamba* was considered a Kimbundu word while *pango* was generically "Angolan."[64] However, *liamba* should not be attributed uniquely to Kimbundu. Central African captives spoke many languages that included a similar plant name. Further, Kimbundu was a trade language, so that *liamba* was not just a slave's word but belonged to merchants, too. In 1883, an Angolan businessman advertised *diamba*, not *pango*, for export in a Brazilian magazine.[65] In Brazil before 1900, *liamba* was less commonly published than *pango*, but it was widespread and most commonly noted in the northeast and the lower Amazon basin.[66] In 1905, Indigenous peoples there said *diamba*, and cognates persist in Amazonian languages, including Krahô *iamhô*.[67] Indigenous peoples probably encountered the plant decades earlier. A book from 1855 rumored, without citing a source, that "the native Indians of Brazil know its value, and delight in its use."[68]

Beyond Brazil, *liamba* cognates occurred in locations that received enslaved people from Central Africa.[69] Some of these locations are not far from the African mainland, but nonetheless are overseas. The recaptives who said *diamba* on St. Helena in 1843 were in the Middle Passage when the British Navy landed them on the mid-Atlantic island. Even closer to the continent, captives carried cannabis knowledge to São Tomé island, which was unoccupied when

Portuguese ships arrived around 1470. Most slaves on the island came from ports from Angola to Gabon. Psychoactive cannabis was growing on São Tomé by 1869, when a Portuguese official noted that recaptives "smoke tobacco and leaves of a vegetable that they call *liamba*."[70] The official did not introduce this term, which was not taken into São Toméan Portuguese. Instead, writers wrote "*bangue*" and "Indian hemp," and exhibited no awareness that *liamba* was spoken on the mainland.[71]

Even locations in mainland Africa provide evidence about knowledge that came to the Americas. Cannabis was absent in West Africa until the 1800s, when it arrived with Central African recaptives. By mid-century, the term *diamba* was used in Sierra Leone, Liberia, and Senegambia. European travelers recorded that it came to Sierra Leone and Liberia with freed "Congo" slaves.[72] "Congo" was a label slavers applied to captives embarked from western Central African ports; it did not label a preexisting cultural, linguistic, or ethnic group. *Diamba* entered languages from Senegal to Côte d'Ivoire, although Europeans translated many cognates as "tobacco"—probably because they did not know or care what Africans were smoking.[73] Europeans widely called cannabis "African tobacco," "Angolan tobacco," and "Congo tobacco" to distance their own smoking practices from African ones. Accounts that Africans smoked "tobacco of poisonous-smelling qualities"—the words of an Englishwoman in Sierra Leone in 1847[74]—suggest that pipes held something other than the true tobacco that Europeans knew. In addition, Africans widely used generic and ambiguous terms. In Jamaica in 1862, "Congo Africans" called cannabis *fumo*,[75] Portuguese for "smoke." Afro-Brazilians also said *fumo*, which could mean any smokable herb, while *tabaco* more specifically meant the plant *Nicotiana* (tobacco).[76] In the mid-1800s, Afro-Brazilians purposefully called cannabis both *fumo* and *tabaco* to conceal their use of the plant drug.[77]

The earliest suggestion that cannabis knowledge had departed Central Africa comes from Sierra Leone. In 1802, the Scottish author of a Susu-language word list translated *iambe* as "tobacco" and *iambe fenge* as "tobacco pipe."[78] *Fenge* corresponds to a group of Central African pipe words with an *-eng-* syllable, such as Umbundu *etenga* (Angola) and Koongo *fwanga* (Democratic Republic of the Congo [DRC]).[79] I don't know how such words might have come to Sierra Leone by 1802. Freed slaves arrived from Britain and Nova Scotia in the 1790s, when Sierra Leone for centuries had already been connected to Portuguese maritime trade networks that extended to Central Africa. In 1859, *diamba* was reported as "tobacco" in an unspecified language—probably Mandinkakan—among itinerant traders in central Senegambia,[80] and later in Maninkakan (Guinea) and Bamanankan (Mali). Like Susu, these are Manding languages, which have different, more widely shared terms for tobacco and pipe. The plant is generally *taba*, one of many West African words that can be traced ultimately to Spanish *tabaco*. Other tobacco terms are similar to Bamanankan *sira* and may derive from an Arabic term for snuff.[81] Notably, in Mandinkakan in 1891, *sira* was translated as a general term for tobacco, while *diamba* was specifically "tobacco for smoking."[82] Most pipe words in West Africa are English loanwords, such as Temne *paip* (Sierra Leone) and Susu *pèpui*, recorded later in the 1800s. Most Manding languages also include a pipe term such as *da*, which may relate to words spoken farther east in the Sahel.[83] The sole historical description of cannabis paraphernalia in Sierra Leone describes "a large wooden pipe or reed[, or] a small calabash, but common clay-pipes are also used."[84] The only descriptions of the Central African -*eng*- pipes are generic, either "water pipe" or "for smoking hemp."[85] *Iambe fenge* were likely loanwords in Susu in 1802, having arrived along now forgotten pathways.

Diamba cognates occurred in the Americas beyond Brazil. "Congoes" in Jamaica—who arrived either directly from slave ships or were transshipped from Sierra Leone, St. Helena, or somewhere else that the British were holding recaptives—used the term.[86] Central African words about smoking persisted in Jamaica into the 1970s, including the plant names *diamba* and *chianga*, which was attested as "tobacco" in the Mongo-Nkundu language (western DRC) and as "cannabis" in an unknown language in the Kwango-to-Lualaba region.[87]

Diamba is a singular noun. Commonly, however, plural nouns were used in western Central African Bantu languages. The plural gave the sense of "some herbs to smoke." Thus, *mariamba* meant "some cannabis to smoke," while *maconha* was "some tobacco to smoke."[88] Literally, *maconha* meant "plant leaves" and perhaps more generally "smokable herb." Whatever the case, *maconha* cognates in Central Africa were rarely translated as cannabis, but in diasporic communities they were normally translated as cannabis, including *maconie* and *makaia* in Sierra Leone in 1851.[89] In Brazil, *maconha* was the term selected by the author of a germinal (and negative) public health report on cannabis in 1917.[90] The word *maconha* was associated with northeastern Brazil in the 1930s, similar to *liamba*.[91] In Jamaica, cognates were *makoni*, *maka*, and *kaya*.[92] The word may have been truncated to *canyack* in Panama by 1924,[93] though I mention a more likely etymology later. In western Central African Bantu languages, the plural form seemingly could refer to the act of smoking, too, as in the Lunda phrase *Xa Mariamba*, which meant "master of *riamba* smoking." This became a title for the head of the Lunda Empire in the late 1800s.[94] In areas once under Lunda influence, "Madiamba" remains a surname today. The plural forms *madiamba*, *maruamba*, and *aliamba* persisted in Brazil in 1958.[95]

Another possible plural cognate is ambiguous. In Colombia in a community established by escaped slaves, *marimba* means drug cannabis.[96] This community's Spanish Creole bears features of Koongo and related Central African languages. *Marimba* also means cannabis more generally in Colombian Spanish and in Cuban Spanish.[97] "Marimba" is better known as the name of a musical instrument invented in western Africa and adopted around the Caribbean. Perhaps Cubans and Colombians first called cannabis *marimba* to conceal drug use. Perhaps *marimba*-meaning-cannabis arrived in Cuba via Colombian drug distribution networks after the 1960s. Like many cannabis terms, *marimba* is but recently documented. It seems likely, though, that in both countries it traces to the hundreds of thousands of Central Africans who arrived speaking languages that included cannabis words such as *mariamba*. It is unlikely that the same idiom arose in two locations or that it passed between Colombia and Cuba but not evidently elsewhere.

At last, the English word "marijuana" derives from *mariamba*. Two linguists have separately proposed this etymology,[98] which I specify here. The name "Mariguana" was first published in 1846 in a listing of Mexican medicinal plants,[99] but it was spelled *marihuana* in 1853 and most subsequent instances in Spanish.[100] The *ma-* syllable corresponds to the Bantu plural marker. The *r* is a liquid consonant that persists in many *riamba* cognates. The *g* and *h* represent similar sounds; both initiate the following vowel rather than serving as true consonants that stop air flow.[101] The *marihuana/mariguana* uncertainty follows the Atlantic-wide pattern in which the root word's pronunciation challenged people who were not native speakers of Central African Bantu languages. The *ua* diphthong corresponds to the rising vowel tone central to other *riamba* cognates. The *-na* at the end of *marihuana* is one of many variations on *-mba*, including Fang *yame* (Gabon), Hausa *rama* (Nigeria), and Jula *naman-ho* (Côte d'Ivoire).[102]

Historical writers portrayed *marihuana* as either a "Mexican" term lacking any linguistic identity or a word whose roots lay only in Mexican Indigenous languages.[103] In recent decades, a few etymologists have looked beyond Mexico for possible roots but have barely considered Africa.[104] Writers have assumed African roots could have come to Central America only from Brazil and have shown no knowledge of the diverse cannabis terminology of either Brazil or Africa. Even well-established etymologies are diluted: "The word maconha"— the only Brazilian word ever considered—"is reportedly derived from . . . a Bantu dialect."[105] Dismissiveness is unjustifiable.

An African etymology for *marihuana* is a hypothesis that is supported by historical context and can be tested through formal linguistic analysis. All other proposed etymologies are untenable. Some rest on made-up words that are absolutely undocumented, like the alleged Portuguese *maraguango*.[106] Others rise on grammatically valid phrases that are undocumented, contrary to other linguistic evidence, and unsupportable with historical facts. For instance, the Mandarin phrase *ma ren hua* (purportedly "cannabis seed flowers") has never been a name for cannabis in China,[107] where people didn't use cannabis as a psychoactive drug. Certainly, during the 1600s tens of thousands of *chinos* settled in Mexico, but most of these people were not Chinese but Filipino.[108] The few Chinese among them had been immigrants in the Philippines who were hired as servants by Spanish officials traveling to Mexico. In sum, there were effectively no Chinese immigrants in Mexico until the 1880s; no historical Mexican Spanish words demonstrably trace to Chinese. Some etymologies discover real words that are phonetically similar to *marihuana* but semantically and historically unassociated with cannabis, such as Nahuatl *mallihuan* (prisoner) and the name of the Bahamian island Mayaguana.[109] There are absurd proposals.[110] Nineteenth-century Mexicans did not adopt a version of the ancient Semitic root *mrr*, which appears in no cannabis names in the Old World. Chinese ships did not carry cannabis across the Pacific before Columbus. These far-fetched ideas have received more attention than the possibility that *marihuana* traces to Africa.[111]

(Incidentally, since a Bahamian island has been mentioned, I will note several other place names. Mount Mariamba island was a landmark for ships' pilots in Rio de Janeiro's Guanabara Bay in 1808.[112] Diamba is the name of a current town in Angola, in the center of the Kwango-to-Lualaba region, and the name of other places in western Central Africa.[113] "Diamba" and "makoni" also appear in place names in Jamaica.[114] Further, I can propose Kimbundu *mariúanu* [admiration] as a word that is phonetically similar, but semantically unrelated, to *marihuana*.[115])

Another idea is that *marihuana* somehow came from the names Maria and Juana. It is phonetically incorrect to spell *marihuana/mariguana* with a *j*, which in Spanish represents a different sound from *g* or *h*. The *j* arose in American English discourse that tagged the plant drug Juana to strengthen portrayals of its unsavory Mexicanness in the early 1900s.[116] Some Spanish speakers doubtless heard familiar names in the initially unfamiliar word. In 1853, a Mexican writer proposed that "*marihuana*" meant "rose of Maria." The woman's name seemed obvious, but he could not guess which language might include "*huana*" to mean rose or even flower.[117] The Maria moniker suggested Catholic beliefs about Mary, mother of Jesus, and thus perhaps enabled smokers to justify the plant drug.[118] Associations between Maria and the plant likely strengthened in contexts where people wanted to conceal drug use.

Semantically and morphologically, *marihuana* relates to specific words that circulated widely as a consequence of transatlantic slaving. If read as an ultimately African word, *marihuana* is part of an Atlantic-wide pattern in which traceably African loanwords name the plant. There are obviously many non-African and untraceable plant names, and other aspects of African cannabis culture—notably water pipes—didn't appear everywhere that words did. Such objections oversimplify the plant's past. Cannabis has generated innumerable nicknames everywhere it has grown; multiple non-African groups have contributed to cannabis cultures around the Atlantic; the plant, its names, and associated technologies have never been an inseparable package. "Congo" inheritances—linguistic and otherwise—have been recognized from Colombia to Mexico; *marihuana* is another. I don't know how *riamba* became words as different as Krio *giyambá* (Sierra Leone), Jula *naman-ho* (Côte d'Ivoire), Krahô *iamhô* (Brazil), Colombian Spanish *marimba*, or Mexican Spanish *marihuana*, but I do assert the unlikelihood that these and other terms are each local anomalies within a cloud of words obviously derived from *riamba*, within a bigger cloud of words that can be traced to Africa.

The word *marihuana*, despite its current global ubiquity, has a shadowy past, because *Cannabis indica* traveled with subaltern peoples whom historical writers mostly ignored. Nonetheless, the documentary record shows that *indica* came to the New World primarily from Central Africa. Its primary New World names reflect this geography.

The People Who Carried Cannabis

Angola was central to the plant's transatlantic dispersal. Luanda was the main Central African slaving port. People were farming cannabis around Luanda by 1803, the plant's earliest documented presence in the tropical Atlantic.[119] Inland, the slave trade was mostly funneled through a handful of market towns, including Bailundo, where cannabis was growing abundantly by 1832.[120] Trade followed a network of paths that connected inland market towns to seaports. Slavers generally aimed their captives toward the closest port to minimize slave deaths along the way. Slavers also considered market conditions when selecting ports, including the types of trade goods available at a port and the likelihood of quickly finding a ship that would load captives. Consequently, slaves from throughout western Central Africa were embarked all along the coast. Unfortunate captives in southern market towns might be marched far to the north, or vice versa, depending on the self-interested decisions of their captors.[121]

Specific ethnolinguistic groups periodically dominated the slave popula-tions loaded at each port, depending on which inland areas were supplying captives at a given time. However, captivity produced homogenizing influences. Enslaved people were made to conform to commercial norms. Captives mov-ing toward Luanda learned Kimbundu on the way because it was the dominant trade language and similar to other regional Bantu languages.[122] In southern Angola, Umbundu was prominent; around the mouth of the Congo, Koongo was. Slaves exchanged knowledge with one another about the institutions in which they were bound.[123] Shared knowledge included therapeutic plants.[124] Slavers recognized the broad distinctiveness of captive societies in different locations through pseudoethnic categories such as "Angola," "Congo," and "Benguela." These categories did not preexist the slave trade but encapsulated outsiders' perceptions of the social-ecological groups that commercial slaving produced.

In addition, the processes of environmental change associated with slaving—including seed transport, disease transmission, and ecological disturbances caused by slave-labor industries—produced more or less widely distributed sets of conditions. People in slavery shared environmental contexts within which relevant knowledge could circulate readily. Importantly, many of the medicinal plants that slaves valued were weedy, growing without human intervention in marginal spaces like roadsides, field edges, and cleared ground. Survivors of the Middle Passage would have recognized many plants in the Americas.[125] The oc-currence of African plant names on both sides of the ocean indicates a transfer of knowledge, not necessarily of seeds.

Slave coffles carried cannabis to the coast in 1850, because slavers thought the plant drug sustained captives on their forced marches to slave-ship ports.[126] Of the several stages of travel that brought captives across the sea, these marches produced the highest mortality.[127] Slaves valued the plant drug, too. The only known account of seed saving of any plant by a slave in Africa refers to *Can-nabis indica*. In coastal Gabon, the French-American traveler Paul Du Chaillu "once saw a few [*liamba*] seeds in the possession of a slave in a slave-factory. He was carefully preserving them, intending to plant them in the country to which he should be sold."[128] Du Chaillu encountered this slave perhaps dur-ing 1856–59 (the period of travel represented in his book), but he also lived in Gabon in the 1840s as a teenager (his father was a trader). He spent years among slave-dealing locals, and certainly visited Portuguese barracoons on the coast in 1855.[129] The Gabonese trade is poorly quantified and poorly docu-mented.[130] Most slaves were landed in African ports, particularly São Tomé.[131]

During 1799–1840, fifteen slave-ship departures are documented in the TSTD, with 2,567 slaves known to have been disembarked on São Tomé island from eleven of the voyages. This group of slaves likely introduced the plant to the island.

Oral histories of seed saving persisted across the ocean. In 1926, the Brazilian naturalist Manoel Pio Corrêa published a tradition he had collected in Brazil between 1910 and 1925.[132] He wrote, "With the heinous traffic, [cannabis] came from one side of the Atlantic to the other, the seeds brought by unfortunate captives [who] tied [them] into the edges of their wraps and loincloths, [and] who ultimately disseminated [cannabis] to all of South America and the Antilles."[133] Pio Corrêa's study of useful plants in Brazil is considered encyclopedic and reliable, having emerged from twenty years' research in South America, West Africa, Central Africa, North America, Europe, and Asia.[134] He offers a plausible mode of seed transport. Slaves entered the Middle Passage mostly unprepared and often unclothed, yet there are similar traditions in Suriname that enslaved West Africans carried concealed rice seeds.[135] Cannabis in Central Africa had lower cultural importance than rice among West African captives, but its association with slaving was strong. No other compilations of cannabis-specific Brazilian folklore repeat Pio Corrêa's story, although several folk songs include a chorus that celebrates the plant drug's past: "It's from Congo, it's from Congo! / Hey, conga / Hey, conga / Rah, rah, it's from Congo."[136]

More commonly, Brazilian folk songs reference cannabis horticulture. Lyrics describe the plant as "sweetheart of my garden," and remind people to "plant it with great care / always working on it / to see a [good] result."[137]

Brazilian cultivation of *Cannabis indica* originated with Central African seeds. When the seeds arrived is unknown.[138] The majority (69 percent) of all Central African captives were landed in Brazil—316,000 before 1750, 470,000 during 1750–1800, and 1.21 million more before 1865. After 1750, 62 percent disembarked near Rio de Janeiro or in Minas Gerais; the remainder disembarked in Brazil's northeast.[139] Two sources suggest cannabis in eighteenth-century Brazil. The weakest came from Maranhão, where the governor in 1784 offered to send samples to Lisbon of a plant "similar [to the one that] the nations of the north, and particularly the Hamburgers, use for cordage."[140] Portugal grew almost no cannabis, and few Portuguese had any experience with the plant. Portugal tried producing cannabis hemp in southernmost Brazil, with little success and, particularly, no success by 1784.[141] They also tried in the Amazon, but their eighteenth-century attempt was called "aborted" in 1866.[142] Given that the governor of Maranhão offered to "fill a boat" with the plant,[143] he likely witnessed cannabis from African seeds, if he saw cannabis at all.

The strongest eighteenth-century evidence is from 1749. A young man, accused of sodomy before the Inquisition of Lisbon in Minas Gerais, confessed that "aguardiente, with *pitar*," led to his sin. He swore never again to "drink aguardiente, nor use *pitto*."[144] This was probably short for *pito do pango*, first published in 1830. In 1749, the accused man could not have hoped to blame his behavior on tobacco, which was popular across society; was not associated with deviance; and anyway was called *petume* at that time (the word borrowed from Brazil's Indigenous Tupi language).[145] Assuming again that "*pitto*" was *pito do pango*, the plant drug's earliest Brazilian name derived from the combination of the Tupi word *pito* and the Portuguese word *bangue*. This bilingual phrase—"a pipeful of *pango*"—suggests that early knowledge of psychoactive cannabis in Brazil was shared between Indigenous pipe smokers and Portuguese travelers. The later flood of cannabis knowledge that arrived with Central African captives mostly had washed away the *pito do pango* tradition by 1900.

Accounts of Brazilian cannabis became more common after 1828. The drug plant grew widely, although details about its production and use can only be inferred. The newspaper ad from 1828 and Rio de Janeiro's law from 1830 show that there was an organized market for the plant drug. The last record showing an above-ground market came in 1847, when a man advertised *pango* alongside other medicinal plants in a Rio newspaper.[146] However, by that time *pango* was not easily available to outsiders. In 1849, French homeopaths in Rio who wanted to test the plant drug's therapeutic potential reported that it was hard to find because "hashish farming is severely prohibited."[147] Slaves likely grew it within their self-provisioning horticulture, but not openly. In 1884, another French doctor "sought it in vain from [his] regular suppliers" of medicinal plants but ultimately bought the prohibited substance from kitchen slaves in the imperial palace.[148] Cannabis controls were strictest in Rio de Janeiro, the imperial capital. Elsewhere, the cannabis economy was less hidden. Burton found that *bangue* grew everywhere in Bahia in 1869. He considered the price high in Minas Gerais, so possibly it was in short supply.[149] Minas Gerais's economy centered on mining, not farming; most slaves labored in mines, so perhaps few grew cannabis. In the 1880s, slaves in northeastern Brazil clandestinely scattered cannabis among their other garden crops and in isolated patches away from gardens.[150] A folk song suggests excuses that probably cropped up, too: "I am very ignorant / of your way / of taking to my garden / without letting me know."[151] By 1900, botanists considered cannabis "naturalized" in Brazil because it grew widely in small patches away from fields. These may have been feral populations or just concealed plots. Whatever the case, slaves certainly did not grow cannabis between rows of sugarcane, as the sociologist Gilberto

FIGURE 7.4. After slavery was abolished in Brazil in 1888, cannabis remained associated with hard laborers, such as these porters, who were ostensibly born in Africa. "Um grupo de Velhos carregadores africanos, Bahia (Brazil)," postcard, Brazil, postmarked 19[?], published by J. Mello, Bahia, Brazil. Author's collection.

Freyre claimed in 1937.[152] Workers might have been allowed to spare volunteer plants on field margins, but bosses would not have tolerated a slave's plant competing with the principal cash crop. Bosses would have been particularly intolerant of plants that were even remotely threatening. In 1843, a German botanist reported that "the Ethiopians [i.e., Afro-Brazilians] know [how] to extract from [*diamba*] powerful poisons and anodynes."[153] Brazilian slaveholders feared their captives; if *diamba* was known but vaguely as a poison, it would have survived only in hidden gardens.[154]

Oral traditions of the drug plant's Central African past also persisted among recaptives in West Africa. Sierra Leone, Liberia, and other locations received relatively small numbers of people from the same forced migration stream that populated Brazil's mines and plantations. In 1851, Robert O. Clarke, the colonial surgeon at Freetown, Sierra Leone, reported that *diamba* "ha[d] long been in use in the interior of [the] colony. . . . Its seed was brought . . . by Congoes captured by one of our cruisers. . . . It is now chiefly cultivated and prepared by these people or their descendants, but [also by] many of the other liberated African tribes."[155] The Susu word *iambe* recorded in 1802 suggests cannabis knowledge had arrived by 1802; an Englishwoman's complaint about nasty-smelling "tobacco" suggests cannabis in 1847.[156] Cannabis was known there well enough by 1869 that Burton could disparage "idle and dissolute" slaves in Brazil for "smok[ing] hemp, like the half-reclaimed savages of 'Sã Leone.'"[157] Many of the Brazilian slaves Burton critiqued were from "Congo land."

More than 90 percent of the 100,000 recaptives landed in Sierra Leone had no knowledge of cannabis, having come from ports between present-day Nigeria and Senegal, a broad region where cannabis was unknown until the late 1800s. By 1811, though, a sufficient number had arrived from western Central Africa to populate "Congo Town," near Freetown. This settlement had 350 adult inhabitants by 1820, approximately 4 percent of the colony's nonindigenous population.[158] "Congoes" subsequently remained a small minority.[159] Of the people landed in Sierra Leone during 1807–63 whose embarkation ports were recorded, the TSTD shows that 9 percent came from western Central Africa. If the same percentage of those whose origins are not documented came from the same region, this gives 7,928 people who might have been called "Congoes." However, if the plant's presence in the colony is backdated five years before the 1851 report, only 4,061 "Congoes" had arrived. Perhaps these people found the familiar plant already growing in Sierra Leone, if the 1802 dictionary recorded its presence. Otherwise, within forty years, this group of 4,100 people—many of whom died soon after landing—successfully carried seeds into and through their Middle Passage, then established a self-sustaining cannabis agriculture.

The provisioning practices of slavers may have facilitated seed transport. This was the case for some African food crops that came to the Americas.[160] Slavers sometimes allowed captives to smoke in Africa and the Middle Passage because of its presumed health and morale-boosting benefits.[161] Angolan slavers valued cannabis specifically to "support the strength and condition" of slaves.[162] The practice of rationing smoke to slaves became more common over time, peaking in the early 1800s. While most accounts of smoking on slave ships indubitably describe *Nicotiana*, some are unclear. One crew member on a slave ship observed Central African captives surreptitiously smoking below deck in the 1820s but could not identify what was smoked because they kept their pipe concealed.[163] Slave ship captains from Angola encouraged loyalty among sailors by supplying brandy and "tobacco" rations.[164] Presumably, Angolan captives were at least rarely given alcohol and made to smoke, in line with general slaving practices documented in Dutch, French, and English sources.[165] Cannabis probably boarded some ships under ambiguous names such as African tobacco, Angolan tobacco, Congo tobacco, *maconha*, and *fumo*.

Cannabis came to Liberia, too. In the 1880s, a German traveler remarked, "Congo-negroes [in Liberia] nearly all smoke hemp. This habit they have, like so many other customs, brought from their old home."[166] As in Sierra Leone, "Congoes" in Liberia farmed *diamba* and smoked it in calabash water pipes like those "made and available anywhere in Lower Guinea [i.e., Atlantic Central Africa]."[167] A later British visitor similarly reported, "I have not noticed hemp-growing or smoking anywhere in Liberia except by Americo-Liberians of Congo origin."[168] In the 1920s, *diamba* had a coastal distribution, being farmed and used from Sierra Leone to the grasslands at Liberia's center.[169]

After 1821, the U.S. Navy captured slave ships in the North Atlantic and worked with American abolitionists to resettle recaptives in Liberia. At least one group of several hundred "Congoes" arrived in the 1820s or '30s and were established in "Congo town" near Monrovia. It is hard to imagine that these people brought cannabis to Liberia. After their ship was captured near Cuba, they were enslaved for two years in Georgia before enduring another Middle Passage to Liberia.[170] I emphasize that there is no evidence or suggestion that slaves introduced cannabis to the United States. From 1858 to 1860, the U.S. Navy liberated several hundred more "Congoes" near Cuba.[171] They spent months in holding camps in Florida that were no better than barracoons in West Africa, then made the reverse Middle Passage to Liberia. Perhaps seeds miraculously survived these ordeals; people did. At most, two thousand "Congoes" arrived in Liberia between 1821 and 1860, out of seven thousand recaptives in total.[172] If these people established cannabis, the inferred frequency with which captives carried the seed (at least one instance of plant introduction per two thousand people per thirty-nine years) doubles that implied by the Sierra Leone numbers (one introduction per 4,100 people per thirty-nine years).

Sierra Leone and Liberia received slave ships captured north of the equator, which were primarily from West Africa and bound for the Antilles, Cuba, or the United States. Dozens of ships were captured in the South Atlantic, too, where demand was primarily in Brazil, supplied from western Central Africa and Mozambique. The British transferred South Atlantic recaptives to St. Helena island. At any time between 1810 and 1850, the tiny island held dozens to thousands of recaptives. "Congoes," "Mozambiques," and "Benguelas" were common in 1843, when a British surgeon observed, "There is a certain narcotic root, called by the negroes 'diamba,' . . . that many of them smoke out of an immense bamboo with a . . . reed pipe fixed to it as a mouthpiece."[173] The British physician did not know the plant drug or much about it. He reported that recaptives considered it an all-purpose remedy and acquired it from Indian sailors who visited the island's port on European ships. Weedy cannabis grew in St. Helena's main settlement in 1813,[174] but that population's origin and fate is unknown. Most likely, Europeans had tried planting *Cannabis sativa*, although

St. Helena was not settled for farming. An African introduction by 1813 is unlikely. Ships traveling between India and Europe by then had been visiting the island for three centuries; perhaps Indian seeds made it into St. Helena's soil.

St. Helena is tiny, so most recaptives were resettled elsewhere. Of 24,000 landed, at least 17,000 were shipped onward.[175] The remainder were mostly buried soon after arriving.[176] Those who left were shipped to British Caribbean colonies and Sierra Leone. Altogether, the Caribbean colonies received 52,000 recaptives. More than 11,000 went to Jamaica, including 3,900 from Sierra Leone, sent mostly as indentured laborers during 1840–67.[177] Of course, Jamaica had earlier received 89,000 slaves from western Central Africa after 1750, though it received only eight hundred following 1810.[178]

Cannabis in Jamaica heavily bore South Asian cultural influences by 1920, following the arrival of 36,000 indentured Indian workers. The number of Indians who arrived after 1850 dwarfed the number of Africans during the same period. Many Jamaicans first learned about psychoactive cannabis around the turn of the twentieth century. Most had no ancestral connections to places where the plant grew in Africa and learned about it only through contact with Indian laborers who called it *ganja*. Earlier African knowledge of cannabis was not documented, partly because European literature on psychoactive cannabis emphasized India, the Levant, and North Africa. Recaptives did bring cannabis knowledge to Jamaica, but this was not salient to colonial observers. Consider the first account of the drug plant on Jamaica, in a letter from a local magistrate in 1862:

> The Hindoo immigrants [on a plantation] were carefully cultivating the Indian Hemp,—*Cannabis Indica*[,] for the purpose of preparing the powerful narcotic known as *gunjah*,—the plant dried having in India that name. . . . [This drug produces visions for users, as described in the book *Chemistry of Common Life*. In addition, the] Congo Africans use [cannabis] in preference to tobacco;—it is known to them by the name of fuomo [i.e., *fumo*],—though the use of it is hitherto unnoticed by travellers as an African indulgence. . . . The growing of Indian hemp is the only garden cultivation I have seen among the Hindoos.—Their indifference to gardening is a strong contrast to the Chinese immigrants, and to the Africans who are careful to plant ground provisions and farinaceous fruits.[179]

This passage is the best evidence I have found for seed transport anywhere by Indian labor migrants. The book *Chemistry of Common Life*—a listing of medicinal plants published in 1855—offered several pages on Indian cannabis culture, but just one sentence relevant to "Congo Africans": "In central and tropical Africa it is almost everywhere known as a powerful medicine and a desired indulgence."[180] The magistrate overlooked this sentence and was unaware of the very few English-language works that had by his time described cannabis among "Congoes" elsewhere.

Cannabis in Jamaica has a Central African heritage, even if South Asian influences became dominant. Calabash-based water pipes were used into the 1950s. The plant names *diamba* and *makoni* are still part of the spoken language and occur in place names.[181] The plant name *kaya*—a cognate of *maconha*, as described earlier—gained global fame via the album *Kaya*, by Bob Marley and the Wailers (1973). Many Jamaicans, like reggae fans, encountered cannabis as a Rastafarian sacrament after that religion's rise in the 1930s. Rastafarianism has roots in Hindu beliefs, but the plant drug independently had significance among African Jamaicans. Into the 1970s, *diamba* had roles in the Kumina spiritual tradition, which originated in Jamaica in the 1800s when Koongo beliefs were brought from Central Africa.[182]

The British settled more recaptives in British Guiana (14,100) than Jamaica (11,400), and nearly as many as in Trinidad (9,200) and the Bahamas (7,100).[183] Between four hundred and three thousand were settled on each of the other British Caribbean islands. These colonies imported slaves as well, including 159,000 from western Central Africa after 1750, though only 4,500 after 1810.[184]

There is no historical information about cannabis in these locations except Jamaica, Guiana, and Trinidad. The colonial governments of Guiana and Trinidad were concerned about cannabis among Indian laborers by 1861, when controls were first enacted on *ganja* imports, sales, possession, and use.[185] Other than import controls, the plant drug was openly tolerated. In Guiana in 1893, Indian smokers consumed *ganja* in *chillum*-type pipes, as did people in India at the same time. *Chillum* pipes are short cones, about four inches long, without distinct bowl and stem; *chillum* is the Hindi name for the bowl of a water pipe.[186] Other immigrants in Guiana brought coconut-based water pipes from India,[187] where the pipe type was associated with poorer smokers and *ganja*. In Trinidad, South Asian influences were similarly prominent by 1920.[188] The obvious South Asian cannabis traditions around the Caribbean have discouraged research on African influences and encouraged the assumption that psychoactive cannabis arrived in the Americas only with indentured Indians. This assumption maintains a colonialist narrative about South Asian laborers that existed by 1893: "[Cannabis] owes its introduction into British Guiana and the West Indies to the coolie immigrant from India, who on quitting his native country did not leave his bad habits behind him, but brought with him the seeds of the plant to sow in a new land, where he has more wealth to indulge in a luxury."[189] Africans have no place in this narrative; colonial preoccupation with India likely obscured, then obliterated, earlier influences. African plant knowledge persists in independent Guyana, as well as in neighboring Suriname (a Dutch colony that received Indian laborers via the British). Researchers recently have found Koongo and Kimbundu names still used for many plants in these countries,[190] but none have reported information on cannabis.

Indentured Indian migrants affected the drug plant's distribution, but their influence has not been studied. During 1834–1920, nearly 464,000 people landed in the tropical Americas, including British Guiana (239,000), Trinidad (144,000), Jamaica (36,000), and Dutch Guiana (34,000), with smaller numbers on other British West Indian islands. Hard laborers in South Asia valued *ganja*.[191] All indentured migrants carried knowledge of the plant drug, and undoubtedly some of them carried seeds, but overall they may have had low motivation to carry cannabis because an international trade in *ganja* followed them from British India (see chapter 9). In the late 1800s, for instance, hundreds of kilograms of *ganja* were imported to British Guiana annually, with some transshipped from there to the British West Indies and Dutch Suriname. Some of this *ganja* bore seeds, which either started or strengthened cannabis cultivation in Caribbean colonies. Whatever the source of seeds, Indian settlers in the New World established vibrant cannabis economies. The clearest example is from Trinidad. By 1895, some immigrants had become specialized *ganja* producers, growing the drug plant in Venezuela and smuggling it back to Trinidad to avoid colonial customs authorities.[192] This is the second-best evidence I have found for seed transport by Indian laborers, but given the late date, it is more likely these entrepreneurs sowed seeds from plants already growing in the Americas rather than seeds directly from India.

Many Central Africans arrived in locations where there is scant evidence of cannabis history or no evidence of African influences in it. More than 28,000 captives came to the United States from western Central Africa after 1800, but, again, there is neither evidence nor suggestion that slaves established cannabis or knowledge of its use in the country. In Cuba, 76,000 Central Africans arrived during 1800–1867. The word *marimba* suggests their influence, but cannabis drug use was not clearly documented until 1950.[193] It is impossible to know why the plant drug caught on in some places but not others. Captives and recaptives were treated differently in different societies. They were not always able to garden, and even if a person successfully grew plants, he or she may not have been able to harvest the first crop of seeds. The plant drug is not universally appreciated, and it never became popular in some places. Cannabis was less successful than people in surviving the Middle Passage.

Conversely, there are locations with scant evidence of Central African arrivals prior to evidence of psychoactive cannabis. These cases likely represent secondary dispersals from initial points of arrival, though secondary dispersal is clearly documented only for Sierra Leone and only after 1900.

The plant probably left Sierra Leone soon after it arrived. Sierra Leonean merchant sailors had worked on European ships since in the 1600s, and after 1808 many recaptives were involuntarily enrolled in the British Navy and other armed forces.[194] Sailors became drug traffickers once colonial prohibitions started in 1926.[195] British colonial officers complained that Sierra Leonean seamen brought cannabis to ports from Gambia to Ghana. In 1938, one sailor was arrested with *diamba* in New York City. If the *diamba* recorded as "tobacco" in Senegambia in 1859 was cannabis, its presence would trace either to the few recaptives directly settled in British Gambia—estimated at just 310 people[196]— or to travelers from Sierra Leone.[197] About 3,500 recaptives left Sierra Leone for Senegambia between 1818 and 1838.[198] However the plant arrived, it was grown and smoked "pretty much everywhere in Senegal" by the 1950s, under the name *yamba*.[199] One botanist proposed that this name somehow came from Brazil,[200] because the plant's West African history has been forgotten.

Cannabis perhaps did leave Brazil to return to Africa. *Diamba*, smoked in calabash-based water pipes, was present for Burton's visit to Lagos in 1861.[201] This is the only record of cannabis in Nigeria before World War II. Lagos was a large and diverse port city in 1861. The plant-pipe combination most reasonably came from somewhere nearby—Central Africa or Sierra Leone—but there is no other record of cannabis between Liberia and Gabon until decades later. Fifteen hundred recaptives were sent to Lagos.[202] However, a Brazilian origin seems possible because Burton also mentioned the coastal towns Badagry and Porto Novo.[203] These towns, near the modern Benin-Nigeria border, had important commerce with Brazil. After 1835—the date of a major slave revolt in Brazil— Badagry and Porto Novo hosted increasing numbers of Afro-Brazilian immigrants who had been expelled from Brazil. There is no record that these people carried cannabis, but they planned their departures from South America and maintained transoceanic commerce in various plants after they arrived.[204] Nigeria's iteration of *diamba* did not persist and is known only through Burton's drug-focused eyes.

Finally, the arrival of psychoactive cannabis in Central America remains enigmatic. Except for Mexico, the regional historical record for the plant is thin.

Slaving withered early in the region. After 1750, 12,000 people came as slaves from western Central Africa, including 8,700 during 1800–1835.[205] In addition, 154,000 captives arrived from other New World ports during 1760–1867, though only 5,000 arrived after 1820, when the newly independent former Spanish colonies began formally abolishing slavery.[206] African inheritances are but weakly evident in Central America. Most likely, cannabis arrived via secondary dispersal, not directly from Africa.

Secondary dispersal is clearest for Panama and neighboring Colombia and Costa Rica. The Panamanian record began in 1916 because of concerns in the U.S. Army about soldiers along the canal.[207] Cannabis smoking was "not uncommon" among Panamanians in 1925, when an American botanist found cannabis "widely distributed," "cultivated clandestinely," and apparently "grow[ing] wild."[208] He observed other domesticates whose presence he attributed to slaves and reported (but did not recognize) at least one Central African plant name. His *guandú* for pigeon pea (*Cajanus cajan*) is a Koongo word used also in Brazil and first recorded in 1813 at the mouth of the Congo.[209]

Cannabis had two names in Panama in 1925: *canyack* and *mariahuana*.[210] Beginning in the 1850s, tens of thousands of laborers came to Costa Rica, Panama, and Colombia from across the Caribbean—mostly Jamaica—to work on plantations, build railroads, and dig the canal. Few if any of these people were African natives or even "Congo" descendants and thus most likely knew the plant drug as *ganja*, its primary Jamaican name. *Canyack* may trace to *ganja*; a link between the two is *canchac*, a 1970s term for cannabis in Costa Rica, where the plant drug was associated with communities descended from Jamaican immigrants.[211] Jamaican labor migrants reputedly brought cannabis to Panama, Costa Rica, and Colombia (and Cuba),[212] although there is only one record of cannabis among them. Around 1905, banana plantation workers on the Atlantic slope grew cannabis for smoking.[213] (By 1932, people were allegedly trafficking the plant drug to California in Central American fruit shipments.[214]) Perhaps an echo of African cannabis knowledge persisted in Panama in the 1920s, when "colored people" there appreciated cannabis tea as a therapeutic beverage.[215] Cannabis tea has been associated with African-descendant populations elsewhere in the Americas and has identifiable Central African roots. Jamaicans drank *ganja* tea into the 1970s.[216] In Brazil in 1915, herbalists who were "generally black Africans or old caboclos" made *maconha* tea.[217] Herbalists prescribed cannabis in infusion with other plants at the mouth of the Congo in 1850.[218] There is no evidence in the Atlantic (except the Mediterranean basin) of the *bhang* beverages of India or of other cannabis-laced drinks.

The word *marihuana* is another weak link to Africa in Central America. The word was published first in Mexico in 1846. The plant drug's prior history in Mexico is cloudy. Spanish colonists introduced *Cannabis sativa* for hemp as early as 1530, but that effort failed, as did many more over the following centuries. The singular instance of limited success was near Mexico City around 1760, when a family of farmers produced enough fiber for their efforts to enter the historical record but not enough to attract other farmers to the crop or end governmental enticements to produce hemp. The source of this plant population is uncertain. Perhaps it originated with *indica* seeds from sailors on European ships. No special breeding—just fertilizer, irrigation, and densely spaced planting—is necessary for most psychoactive strains to produce long, fibrous stems. Alternatively, the hemp farmers may have bred a successful strain from some of the *sativa* plants Spanish colonists had tried over previous centuries.[219] Whatever success the farming family had was short-lived, ending with the patriarch's death in 1760.

Two documents, from 1772 and 1777, indicate that Indigenous peoples used cannabis as a drug.[220] They included it within "the *pipiltzintzintlis*," a generic, plural category of plants.[221] The two accounts do not show that the cannabis itself had any psychoactive qualities. Preparations of pipiltzintzintli plants were often psychoactive, but given the plural, categorical name, these preparations were likely always mixtures. Cannabis was probably either a substitute or supplement for other pipiltzintzintli plants, such as *Salvia divinorum*, a powerfully mind-altering herb. Even *Cannabis sativa* would have been an intriguing supplement, because it is chemically complex and pharmacologically active, even though it is not psychoactive. To use pipiltzintzintlis, people ground the plant material and mixed it with water, then drank it before ceremonies, including divinations.[222] Pipiltzintzintlis were variously described as roots or leaves and were somehow associated with a psychoactive seed called *ololiuhqui*. Whatever the case, cannabis-as-pipiltzintzintli was never again documented; indeed, no mention of any pipiltzintzintli was recorded after the 1777 document.[223]

The new appellation *mariguana* in 1846 suggests that a novel use for cannabis arrived in the intervening decades. Whatever cannabis-as-pipiltzintzintli was, the new use effaced its legacy. The meanings associated with the pipiltzintzintlis were not transferred to *marihuana*; nor was the manner of use. When Mexican uses of *marihuana* were first described in the 1850s, it was a smoked drug that had limited medicinal indications and was mostly used by prisoners and soldiers for mental escapes.[224] The plant drug dispersed northward through Mexico during the nineteenth century, arriving at the Rio Grande by the 1890s.[225] It crossed into the United States overland after 1895 with migrant laborers, in-

cluding ranch hands and farmworkers.[226] Maybe cannabis gained its Mexican
foothold in the southern cities of Veracruz and Campeche, where most slaves
arrived in the 1700s. "Hemp" was reported near Veracruz in 1778,[227] although
European seeds had not previously succeeded there. Ports on Mexico's Atlantic
side were nodes in a loose network of sailors, stevedores, and slaves who transmitted knowledge and objects throughout the Caribbean as an extension of
South Atlantic networks.[228] Perhaps cannabis-as-*marimba* in Colombia and
Cuba traces to the same historical period and maritime connections. The plant
likely did not come to Mexico overland from the south; as late as 1946, cannabis seemed rare between Mexico and Panama.[229] Whatever the case, Mexico is
not an exception to the Atlantic-wide pattern wherein cannabis smoking seemingly appeared in the late 1700s or early 1800s, but was mentioned in print
only near mid-century. The final crescendo of transatlantic slaving from western Central Africa brought *Cannabis indica* as a smoked drug into societies
around the Atlantic, although its trajectories of biological and cultural dispersal are unknown.

Mexico is also unexceptional in how people in receiving societies transformed the plant drug. There is no evidence of African water pipes in Mexico
or of cannabis in dry pipes, or many mentions even of tobacco in dry pipes
after about 1750. Mexico was where cigarettes were invented and first became
dominant.[230] African smoking technologies and terminologies did not persist
widely in the Americas because of the rootedness of tobacco smoking in the
New World. Knowledge of calabash-based water pipes certainly survived the
Middle Passage to Brazil, Jamaica, Sierra Leone, and Liberia. The only African
pipe word documented in the Americas is *kinzu*, which named calabash water
pipes in Jamaica into the middle 1900s.[231] This term is attested as "pipe" or
"cannabis pipe" in Koongo, Vili, and Luba-Kasai, all spoken in Angola and the
DRC. Calabash-based water pipes persisted in Brazil into the middle 1900s,
too,[232] but no African names were recorded. Cognates of the Yao *kachimbo*
occur widely, but in the Americas they are borrowed from the Portuguese
cachimbo, the root of the widespread Spanish word *cachimba*.[233] African pipes
were not necessary accompaniments to the plant or knowledge of its drug use,
because any smoked herb can be smoked in any type of pipe or in a cigarette.

Cannabis was intricately part of Mexican society by the late 1800s, which
is also unexceptional. Mexico's Indigenous knowledge of psychoactive plants
is renowned for its breadth and depth, and native experts probably evaluated
newfound plants as soon as they encountered them, including *Cannabis sativa*
during its long, unsuccessful history in that country. In Brazil, cannabis was so
thoroughly part of caboclo society that twentieth-century outsiders called it

fumo do caboclo and considered it more Indigenous than African, despite common knowledge of its African past.[234] Its principal caboclo name, *dirijo*, was not African. Brazilian smokers used African water pipes, but their pipe name, *maricas*, was not African. Knowledge of smoking and smokable herbs arose along unknown pathways of migration, cultural exchange, and social change.

The overarching pattern of cannabis cultures around the Atlantic is of Central African inheritances, reflecting the plant's primary dispersal pathway into the Atlantic and the large size of the relevant human migration. However, Central African inheritances have rarely been strong anywhere, because in all receiving societies where the plant drug gained acceptance, it did so across a culturally, ethnically, and geographically diverse social group—labor underclasses in emerging capitalist societies.

PART III. DISCUSSION AND CONCLUSIONS

What Carried Cannabis?

EIGHT

Working under the Influence

Cannabis indica entered the Atlantic World and crossed the ocean primarily with enslaved people shipped from western Central Africa. African words for cannabis persist widely. The African water pipe is used worldwide. Other than these deep-seated features, psychoactive cannabis in the present-day Atlantic is not evidence of African heritage or tastes. This holds true often even within Africa, where global media, travel and tourism, and drug-control efforts have shaped practices of substance use.[1] Cannabis is a component of generalized world culture, with deep-seated African (and South Asian and European) roots.

Its generalized cultural condition began as soon as cannabis arrived in new landscapes. The plant dispersed with specific groups of people, but it did not remain associated with these people. Every receiving society can exemplify the plant drug's cross-cultural acceptance. In Sierra Leone, by 1851 it was valued by "Congoes," as well as by "Akoos, Eboes, and many of the other liberated African tribes, and likewise by the Maroons, Settlers, and Creoles."[2] These groups shared a society, but they had different histories and diverse origins. "Congo" represented an amalgam of peoples brought together through enslavement. "Maroons, Settlers, and Creoles" included descendants of freed slaves—mostly from West Africa—who had lived in Nova Scotia, Britain, and elsewhere. In Brazil, newspaper ads from the 1820s to the 1840s were directed to anyone who read Portuguese. A Belgian in 1886 who complained that his guides smoked *liamba* was talking about Zanzibaris working in Congo, not Congolese.[3] Jamaica's cannabis culture by 1925 had South Asian and Central African roots, but few users had ancestral connections to either region.

People of all cultural, linguistic, ethnic, and geographic groups found that they liked the newfound plant drug and adopted the drug plant into their individual ethnobotanies. People who encountered cannabis via contact with transatlantic travelers learned the name that came with it, whether Portuguese *bangue*, Koongo *riamba*, Hindi *ganja*, or something else; the persistence of these plant names did not depend on the persistence of transplanted human cultures. Almost everyone who encountered cannabis already knew how to smoke herbs. African pipes and pipe words weren't adopted as widely as plant words, which evolved and sometimes faded as new names emerged. Cannabis didn't succeed everywhere, and even where it did, more people used alcohol, tobacco, tea, coffee, and sugar.

People have always had diverse reasons for consuming cannabis. In the Atlantic World, during the period 1500–1925, work was the most commonly documented context of use. Smoking before, during, and after work was widespread. In this chapter, I argue that cannabis enhanced the capacity of laborers to perform physically demanding and emotionally taxing tasks in perpetuity. In this role, cannabis furthered political-economic relationships that simultaneously produced and depended upon labor underclasses—slaves, indentured servants, prisoners, sex workers, drafted soldiers, merchant sailors, and others—who were socially and culturally marginalized and occupied hazardous environments of disease, malnutrition, dangerous work, poor housing, and psychological trauma.

Many drugs have been called "labor enhancers," functioning to draw people into labor relationships and improve morale and endurance while working.[4] Angolan slaves, for instance, were rationed "tobacco" weekly in 1875.[5] Labor enhancers have been important in the global expansion of colonialism, capitalism, and the varied forms of exploitation these political-economic systems generated. Alcohol and tobacco are well known in this light in Africa, but not cannabis—even though scholars have shown that the plant drug facilitated work for hard laborers in India, Jamaica, Mexico, Costa Rica, Colombia, Trinidad, Guyana, Morocco, Algeria, Tunisia, and Egypt.[6] It still does in the Democratic Republic of the Congo.[7] This role was documented as early as 1598 in India, when a Dutchman characterized the main *bhang*-using social groups as "whores[,] soldiers[, and] slaves."[8] The principal *ganja* smokers in India throughout the 1800s were hard laborers, who used the drug interchangeably with opium and liquor, depending on price and availability.[9] In sub-Saharan Africa, cannabis was not as prominent or economically important as alcohol or tobacco, but it widely functioned to enhance labor performance and was commonly accepted in this role by overseers.

For centuries, cannabis drug use has been primarily associated with social class, not heritage. Race and class have been coproduced in the Atlantic World; racial categories have defined or strengthened social stratifications on which exploitative labor regimes depend. Cannabis histories have underemphasized class, interpreting drug use primarily through the lens of race. This emphasis has bolstered arguments that cannabis prohibition was fundamentally a racist undertaking.[10] In addition, race structured many historical accounts of drug use, and secondary histories have maintained this theme. Innocuous statements direct attention to race as much as virulent ones. "All races have their weaknesses," opined a pharmacist in British Guiana in 1893, "and in the matter of intoxicants I am afraid the Englishman has no peculiar right to fling stones at the Chinaman or Hindoo."[11] Racial statements might have minimally reflected geographic awareness—liquor in nineteenth-century Guiana traced to the land of the Englishman, *ganja* traced to that of the Hindu—but neglected most other factors of drug use. In particular, different drugs had different prices, which restricted accessibility based on income. Ideologies that assigned people to social classes based on race thereby linked different drugs with different racial groups.[12] Unequivocally, racial ideas have shaped drug use and responses to it. However, historical accounts consistently link cannabis drug use to the physical, mental, and environmental conditions of work, and not to any quasi-real bases for racial groupings, such as cultural, geographic, ethnic, or linguistic background.

Cannabis indica must be interpreted as an aspect and outcome of political economies, which are interactions of social, technical, and environmental systems. The dispersal of the plant and diffusion of its drug use were linked to highly stratified social systems, whose underclasses were made to complete onerous but simple tasks in risky environments and rarely with any prospect of release from those conditions. Cannabis was a low-input environmental resource that laborers valued because it enhanced their capacities to endure marginalization and exploitation. Cannabis competed principally with alcohol and tobacco for workers' attention, because all three can be subsistence drugs produced with minimal inputs from beyond the household. *Cannabis indica*, like tobacco, can grow most places in tropical and subtropical latitudes. Alcoholic drink can be made more widely. Tobacco needs more horticultural attention than cannabis to yield well. In most locations, cannabis was the cheapest option. People chose to grow it because of its pharmacology, which helped workers manage appetite, stimulate willingness to work, and treat generalized mental and physical malaise. Despite its utility to workers, in this subsistence role it ultimately functioned contrary to their interests. By helping laborers endure, cannabis enhanced the capacities of elites to profit from the exploitation they oversaw. A British colonial administrator in Trinidad recognized this relationship in 1893, observing that "if a man can undergo harder exertions under the influence of ganja than his might would allow, his health is surely to break down sooner or later, [and] it is rather a kind of inhumanity on the part of his employers to extort more work from him than his natural health and strength can permit."[13] This extraction of "more work" exemplifies the concept of surplus value in political-economic thought. Surplus value is one source of wealth that can be captured in capitalist societies when overseers take labor from workers without paying for it.[14]

Yet simultaneously, cannabis, like other drugs, has hindered capitalist endeavors because it has helped workers resist the demands of their overseers. Cannabis has enhanced work slowdowns, purposeful inefficiencies, absenteeism, subversive thought, and other activities that oppose the desires of elites. Social-ecological authorities ultimately came to see cannabis as a problem but recognized its ambivalent political-economic role. One suggestion that it ultimately benefited workers more than elites came in the attitudes that flourished at the dawn of the twentieth century. Colonial authorities increasingly bemoaned the plant drug's effects on labor supply and quality and pushed for cannabis prohibition on these bases. Their complaints were burdened with colonial and racial preoccupations yet exhibit the drug plant's political-economic significance.

In this chapter, I describe how people used cannabis in relation to work and the attitudes social elites developed toward these practices. I focus particularly on Central Africa and Southern Africa, regions where historical evidence for labor-drug relationships is strong. Despite this focus, I also mention examples where Africans, and people categorized as Blacks more generally, had no appreciable presence, but cannabis did, such as in Mexican prisons and armies in the late 1800s.[15] Such instances help underscore that cannabis's role as a labor enhancer depended not on the presence of people from Africa or the strength of African influence but, rather, on stratified social structures and the conditions these structures produced for labor underclasses.

Drugs among Laborers

Since the 1500s, cannabis has been entangled in labor relationships that developed within global economies. The plant traveled within commercial slavery, for instance, that linked human bodies, land resources, and capital in Europe, Africa,

Asia, and the Americas. The conditions that created value for cannabis in slavery persisted after slavery.

Societies include norms and rules that, among other things, make labor available for economic activities. These social relations are called labor regimes. Unfree labor regimes depend upon rules that create classes of individuals whom others can rightfully force to work against their will.[16] Chattel slavery, the form of unfree labor that sustained the transatlantic system, rested on a class of people who were not legally people but living property who could be treated like cattle. Laws allowed this treatment. Commercial rules and racist norms defined membership in the class; people whose bodies had a sale price were slaves, and racial labels sharply delimited whose bodies could be priced for sale. Following the decline of chattel slavery, unfree workers remained in prison labor, illegal slavery, and other settings. More widely, societies developed semi-free labor regimes on classes of people who were legally people but subject to norms and rules that sharply limited social and geographic mobility. An important example was the indentured servitude regime that brought workers from India to other British possessions around the Indian and Atlantic Oceans between 1819 and 1920. This labor regime was developed explicitly to replace emancipated slaves, who could no longer be forced to supply cheap labor.[17] Instead, indentured Indian laborers were legally bound to work on specific plantations for specific terms, and generally had no independent means of returning to India.[18] The "Asian" and "coolie" labels hindered mobility because they marked a semi-free labor class dominated by people with a shared geographic background; race and class were coproduced.

Different forms of labor can be compared in terms of the tasks workers are assigned and the incentives overseers use to encourage the worker performance they desire.[19] In economic terms, chattel slavery can efficiently supply workers for tasks that require strength and stamina but few technical skills. Breaking rocks requires no specialized skills, only muscle; from ancient Rome to nineteenth-century Brazil, chattel slavery was prominent in mining. The interest of those who supervise low-skill, manual tasks is to have workers work harder and longer. In this context, fear of violence is the most effective incentive supervisors have.[20] Threats of physical and mental abuse produce stress, which can motivate hard work but not attentive work. However, negative incentives can provoke resistance via wastefulness, sabotage, shirking, and so on.[21] Direct, constant surveillance is necessary to make threats of abuse tangible and to reduce opportunities for resistance.

Furthermore, it's important to recognize that, as a condition of work, the loss of privacy is as onerous as the muscular demands of heavy tasks.[22] Sex workers, domestic servants, and others whose work places them in direct, near-constant contact with their overseers experience mental stress, if not physical abuse, too. Their overseers expect compliance and are in positions to force compliance when they deem force necessary.

The view that chattel slavery is morally unacceptable became increasingly popular in Europe and North America after 1800. By mid-century, slavery was abolished in most countries, although the United States, Cuba, Brazil, and Angola were notable holdouts. In slaveholding societies, emancipation meant labor shortages, because heavy, manual tasks remained central to dominant industries, and freed slaves generally refused to continue working for their former masters. Societies mostly replaced slaves with semi-free workers. The British, for example, began in the 1830s to transport recaptives from Sierra Leone to Jamaica as "apprentices"—indentured laborers—because plantation bosses needed people to work sugarcane.[23] The recaptive supply soon dwindled, so Britain looked to India for laborers for the Caribbean sugar colonies. Although slavery persisted in western Central Africa into the 1900s, labor shortages and new labor arrangements developed there, too. By 1869, when Portugal abolished slavery in its colonies, Angola already had a system that obliged technically freed slaves to continue as "servants" for years after their technical manumission.[24] The conditions experienced by slaves and post-slave workers were indistinct. In Angola, the conditions of slaves being marched laden to the coast merged imperceptibly with the conditions of technically free commercial porters, who, into the twentieth century, sang a refrain about losing someone to slavery while marching: "She has crossed Ondumba ya Maria [a creek on the way to Benguela;] She has gone into slavery to be sold for São Thome."[25] Slavery was illegal in São Tomé, but the conditions that the "servants" there experienced merged imperceptibly with conditions earlier slaves had experienced.[26]

The social relations of slavery persisted in degrees after emancipation. Overseers retained the same interests. They wanted laborers to work harder and longer and didn't require attentive performance. With the legality of physical violence toward workers reduced (not eliminated), threats to workers increasingly centered on emotional and social consequences.[27] Fear of destitution and social ostracism still plagued wage slaves. Post-slave laborers had slim prospects to escape their conditions of employment. Debt, laws, and racism hindered their mobility. Racist thought allowed different prospects to different groups—Whites were favored—but all groups were represented in labor underclasses.

Risky environmental conditions did not disappear with emancipation. Workers were assigned hazardous tasks that produced injuries and fear of injury. Exhaustion and poor health aggravated occupational risks. Workers often had nutritionally deficient diets, whether given by overseers or afforded through income. Workers were exposed to illness in diverse ways, including poor sanitation, housing, and healthcare. Poor diet, exhaustion, and exposure aggravated the risks of sickness.

Obviously, conditions of hard labor varied greatly among people, places, and times. All who engaged in hard labor experienced physical and emotional stressors, which were produced by and necessary for the social stratification that enabled exploitative labor regimes. Cannabis enhanced the capacity of hard laborers to do their work. Yet it was not simply good or bad for those who used it or those whose workers used it. Cannabis had ambivalent roles for laborers and overseers alike.

THE EARLIEST ENTANGLEMENT cannabis had with labor in Africa directly aided capitalist expansion. Soon after Dutch settlers and merchants landed at the Cape of Good Hope in 1652, they began paying Khoisan laborers with drugs. Tobacco and alcohol were the earliest forms of payment. *Dagga* followed by 1713, when "everyone [Dutch settlers] planted [hemp] for the Hottentots."[28] For centuries, European settlers paid workers with drugs rather than food, goods, or cash.[29] Khoisan livestock and land changed ownership in exchange for cannabis, which thereby helped colonists expand control over what is now South Africa.

At the time of European contact, Khoisan peoples used many psychoactive plants for social, medicinal, and spiritual reasons, although precontact practices are not known. During the historical period, there is limited evidence of plant uses in spiritual contexts,[30] because Europeans were not invited to observe. European-observed instances of cannabis use seemingly centered on worldly socialization.[31] Colonial contexts of drug use differed from earlier ones. Distilled alcohol and tobacco were entirely new intoxicants, and cannabis was probably so in the Western Cape. Imported distillates had much higher alcohol content than indigenous fermentations.[32] All imported drugs were sometimes available in such quantities that consumption was limited only by capacity to trade labor, cattle, land, or something else in exchange. Europeans found exchange rates advantageous, especially as settlers replaced imported cannabis and tobacco with local produce. Alcohol remained an import, but in the form of cheaper and cheaper rotgut.[33] By 1800, substance use was destructive in many Khoisan communities, accelerating social disintegration that can be traced to dispossession by settler colonialism.

Khoisan traders were not helplessly naïve but acquired alcohol, cannabis, and tobacco to meet their needs, which included distributing substances to build and maintain patronage networks.[34] Yet these substances unequivocally contributed to sociocultural decline because many people developed addictions that colonists exploited.[35] In the 1770s, a traveler discovered he could better control his porters if he was "very sparing in my treats, giving out only enough for two or three pipes at a time."[36] He could not get his workers to work until they had exhausted their *dagga* or tobacco and wanted more. Beginning in 1818, Europeans expressed qualms about exchanging drugs for labor, and *dagga* farming was increasingly driven underground after 1850.[37] Nonetheless, *dagga* wages were seemingly paid into the twentieth century.[38]

Cannabis does not produce physiological dependence like nicotine, morphine, cocaine, or alcohol, but some users—about 10 percent in current Western societies—develop behavioral addictions, including the condition called cannabis use disorder in current medicine.[39] Symptoms now diagnostic of cannabis use disorder were described in 1913 among South African workers, who reported craving *dagga* and irritability and distractedness when deprived.[40] Cannabis is not a gateway drug and is less toxic than alcohol or tobacco, but any addiction can damage individual potential. Worldwide, drug trading aided colonial expansion because dependence damaged Indigenous capacities for resisting dispossession, which in turn produced conditions that encouraged coping through drug use. Consider, for example, that in the United States cannabis use disorder is most common among American Indians, although these populations had effectively no interactions with the plant drug until after 1900.[41]

Outside South Africa, employers uncommonly supplied the drug. Normally, workers bought cannabis or grew their own and used it to manage physical and mental challenges. A Brazilian scholar in 1937 reported that "*maconha* [is smoked] to alleviate greatly 'the sufferings of the profession' . . . , as a newspaper vendor, sometimes poorly nourished, told me, [and is] much used by newsboys, whores, crooks, [and] sailors."[42] This relationship existed around the Atlantic, and centuries before 1937.

Cannabis widely served to modulate hunger. Most notably, it was an appetite suppressant in Southern Africa. In the 1580s, a Portuguese visitor to Mozambique recorded that cannabis "comforted [users'] stomachs [and] sustained them several days, without eating another thing."[43] Three centuries later, in southern Tanzania, people valued cannabis because it "calms the sufferings of hunger."[44] At the turns of the twentieth and twenty-first centuries, South African laborers dulled their hunger with *dagga*.[45]

This function has an objective, pharmacological basis that traces to plant genetics. Cannabis farmers and smokers saved seeds from plants they liked. Past farmers and users in Southern Africa developed a genetically distinctive plant population by selecting for appetite-suppressing physiological effects.[46] Southern African plants produce elevated levels of the cannabinoid THCV, an appetite suppressant.[47] Plants with elevated THCV levels are globally rare, with just one other example reported, from Afghanistan.[48] The distinctive Southern African strains undoubtedly traveled with people, although plant genetic data are insufficient to reconstruct their trajectories. Anecdotal evidence suggests appetite-suppressing strains along westward plant dispersal pathways. In the Kwango-to-Lualaba region, smokers reportedly found that *diamba* "makes one forget hunger and all the illnesses that afflict man."[49] Decades later in Brazil, others reported that cannabis "eliminates the feeling of hunger and of thirst" and thereby makes work easier.[50] The plant name *soruma* came to Brazil probably from Mozambique; if seeds accompanied the word, they were almost certainly a THCV-rich strain.

Of course, in current societies marijuana is commonly considered an appetite stimulant. Historical reports of appetite-stimulating cannabis are uncommon. Nineteenth-century Western medicine did not indicate it for appetite management.[51] Physicians occasionally noted increased appetite consequent to use but did not state that this was why people valued it. In Brazil, smokers risked a "canine hunger" that "nothing can placate."[52] A physician in British Guiana reported that "overindulgence [can produce] great hunger and thirst," but his statement represented observations in India.[53] I have found one account in Africa of appetite stimulation, in a British administrator's mention of a woman—"the Sirdar"—who led an uprising in southern Anglo-Egyptian Sudan. The woman supposedly "stated that under its influence one always laughed, and a man who could normally consume only a small dish of [food] could . . . eat four."[54]

All other accounts associating cannabis and food say that people smoked after eating, not before. "As soon as he has satisfied his appetite," a Frenchman stereotyped in Tanzania in the 1880s, the Nyamwezi man "quickly takes up his devotion to hemp."[55] After-dinner smoking was noted in Angola, too.[56] In historical instances when cannabis was a postprandial drug, context implies it did not stimulate appetite. Such after-dinner use may have arisen as an objective effect of THCV-rich phytochemistry, or a subjective effect if social contexts produced satisfaction with food already eaten, rather than desire for additional food.

Whatever the case, the plant was valued in settings where appetite management was a documented medical problem. In São Tomé, slaves and indentured servants from Angola were brought in to work on cocoa plantations. In 1869, colonial officials discovered that these workers suffered numerous illnesses, including cachexia (severe appetite loss), and that they sought out cannabis. "When they are employed in the duty of cutting weeds and they encounter a *Liamba* plant, it is always spared for themselves."[57] I don't know why islanders valued the plant drug, because none of them published records of their experiences. Obviously, when facing food shortage or purposefully avoiding food, appetite suppression can reduce discomfort from hunger; when facing unappetizing food or lacking hunger, appetite stimulation can help a body take in calories. By 1800, European physicians recognized appetite loss as a common ailment among slaves. They attributed "negro cachexy" to "grief, despondency, poor diet, hard labor, and harsh treatment," and had no effective treatments.[58] I do not know whether or how slaves treated this condition. Europeans sometimes noted that soil eating accompanied cachexia. This behavior, called pica, can be spurred by mineral nutrient deficiencies, but it can also be suicidal. Cannabis could have either aided or treated cachexia.

Therapeutic potentials of cannabis tend to be greatest when a person suffers endocannabinoid deficiency, which malnutrition can cause.[59] Even if people did not explicitly identify appetite management as a therapeutic application, the plant drug's nutrition-related pharmacology reasonably contributed to generalized indications, as among recaptives on St. Helena who considered it a "sovereign remedy against all complaints."[60] Skeletons recovered from a recaptive graveyard on the island show that these people suffered multifaceted and extreme malnutrition.[61]

The historical record most clearly indicates why users valued the plant drug in instances when it was associated directly with labor. Most historical accounts of cannabis smoking south of the Sahara describe the activities of porters and canoe paddlers. Small boats and human backs were the only modes of hauling freight in most of the sub-Saharan region before railroads and automobiles. From the 1500s into the 1930s, many men worked as nominally free porters. Others rowed canoes laden with travelers and goods. Cannabis smoking among these workers gained prominence because most European documentarians oversaw large retinues of men whom they employed to haul their stuff. People in other occupations used, too—farmers, miners, herders, soldiers, sailors, hunters, fishermen—but documentarians observed few others with similar fastidiousness.

Cannabis was functional. It was a stimulant before, during, and after work. This use has objective but poorly understood chemical bases. Current sub-Saharan

FIGURE 8.1. Porters commonly carried a small box, such as the one at this man's waist, to hold smoking supplies. Angolan porters carried headloads but rested their burdens on the shoulder while posing for photographers. The poles extending to the right of the basket allowed a carrier to prop a load on the ground while resting and raise the burden again without assistance. In 1892, Angola's future governor Henrique de Paiva Couceira described the porter business from the viewpoint of an employer: "[Wherever there are] white settler[s] instilled with business temperament, all [Native] men are porters; they begin, from the age of nine or ten, to undertake marches with successively greater loads, in a manner that, [having] reached the age of strength, they have the physical capacity sufficient to transport, during successive days, weights from 60 to 80 pounds, and the detachment necessary to abandon their homes and families; nevertheless, never do they do it without reluctance, and the result of this reluctance [is] to have in general great delays in constituting and putting in march an entourage, the greatest delays when the destinations are the most distant": H. M. de Paiva Couceiro, *Relatorio de Viagem entre Bailundo e as terras do Mucusso* (Lisbon: Imprensa Nacional, 1892), 9. "Loanda. Um carregador," postcard, Angola, ca. 1910, published by J. H. Ferreira/Photographia Lisbonense, Luanda. Author's collection.

varieties represent the folk species sativa, which produces pseudo-stimulant subjective effects for most users.[62] Current marijuana aficionados value southern African strains for speedy highs.[63] The psychoactive cannabinoid THC increases the pulse rate and can produce hyperactive behavior. Subjective effects are strengthened in users who believe it is a stimulant.[64] Another cannabinoid, CBD, modulates the effects of THC. Aficionados believe that CBD-rich strains produce mellower, extended highs.[65] Southern African strains produce very little CBD, with some samples having none detectable.[66] Low-CBD material has been collected since the 1970s also in Kenya, Nigeria, Ghana, Brazil, Jamaica, Costa Rica, and Mexico.[67] India, Cyprus, Myanmar, and Thailand have yielded low-CBD material, as well as high-CBD cannabis.

European observers noticed that their porters' motivation to work increased after smoking. A Portuguese traveler in Angola reported in 1875 that "the blacks affirm that it wakes them up and warms their bodies, so that they are ready to start up with alacrity, take up their loads, and trot off quickly."[68] Twenty years later in Gabon, the British voyager Mary Kingsley discovered the same thing.[69] Some accounts hint at subjective effects; users recorded nothing. A Belgian ethnographer wrote stereotypically about Songye men (Democratic Republic of the Congo): "When the work to do is rather hard, he drinks palm wine and especially smokes hemp. He does not disdain tobacco, but tobacco, he says, *does not render* [him] *strong* like hemp."[70] Similarly, a South African miner in 1913 reported that it "makes me strong and happy and I can work well" and it "make[s] work a pleasure and [I] do not feel the day pass."[71] Nineteenth-century miners smoked in Brazil, and early twentieth-century miners smoked in Belgian Congo and Portuguese Angola.[72]

Similar subjective effects were identified in the 1970s when scholars studied how cannabis affected laborers in Jamaica, Colombia, Costa Rica, and Trinidad.[73] Although relatively recent, these studies more generally illuminate cannabis-labor relationships. Sugarcane workers in Jamaica were mechanically less efficient but had greater job satisfaction and greater willingness to work.[74] Many workers believed that *ganja* made workers more productive, and some overseers agreed, although researchers could not validate this belief with data on income or labor output.[75] Most overseers discouraged *ganja* use because they feared behavioral problems such as belligerence. However, most bosses underestimated the incidence of *ganja* smoking—on average, one-third to one-half of laborers used it—because smokers were circumspect. In Colombia, discreet use continued despite anti-cannabis laws primarily because workers valued it functionally, not because of any expressive or symbolic roles it had.[76] In Costa

Rica, most users believed cannabis positively affected their work performance by improving endurance, enjoyment, and attentiveness, although subjective effects varied significantly depending on settings of use.[77] On-the-job smoking can damage performance by impairing concentration, short-term memory, physical coordination, and judgment.[78] These effects increase occupational risks. One Jamaican overseer, who estimated that 75 percent of his workers smoked *ganja*, blamed intoxication for poor tractor driving.[79] *Cannabis indica* contributed to work-related injury and death among historical laborers, though less significantly than did alcohol, fatigue, malnutrition, and other factors.

Cannabis eased work-related discomfort. The plant drug can treat physical pain, although few analgesic applications were specified—to ease chest and stomach pain (Sierra Leone, 1851) or labor pains (Sotho, South Africa, 1906).[80] Of course, when indicated for one medical condition, cannabis may have served to treat pain as much as other symptoms. The cannabinoid profiles of current sub-Saharan varieties suggest that historical varieties offered mild analgesia: THC objectively influences pain sensations and treats painful conditions such as muscle spasms, but CBD—scarce in sub-Saharan varieties—accentuates these effects and, further, acts as an anti-inflammatory.[81]

More commonly, people smoked to assuage hunger and ward off the cold.[82] Many people smoked to start the day. Workers often ate poorly. An enlightened boss in Angola reported that, miraculously, "a mugful of hot coffee and a biscuit every morning before going to work" yielded "great benefit" to his mineworkers.[83] Porters were beasts of burden and were guaranteed neither care nor sympathy from their employers. In South Sudan, a British administrator noted, stereotypically, that the Zande man "supports fatigue well, and can carry a load of fifty pounds on his head twenty miles a day for a week on end with ease, provided that he gets his food. Without the latter, he gets very thin and tired, but even so, he carries on in a wonderful way, and soon picks up flesh again."[84] Henry Morton Stanley, traveling not far to the south, blamed cannabis, rather than his unyielding demands or their loads, diet, and constant exposure, for weakness and infirmity among his porters.[85] If Stanley's men were like the stereotypical Zande man, they smoked to warm themselves up.[86] In western Central Africa, morning smoking seemed most prominent during the cold season, from May to October in areas south of the equatorial forests.[87] The Portuguese traveler Henrique Dias de Carvalho hints of his porters' experiences: "In the early morning [in June 1892] I felt rather cold, which obliged me to use the fire of the boys and . . . smok[e] my little *mutopa* [water pipe] until the day brightened."[88] Dias de Carvalho had a hut; porters spent nights in the open, huddled around campfires.[89] Another traveler, in the midst of Angola's cold season, described how his "two or three hundred blacks . . . crouch[ed] in circles of ten or a dozen together round a fire, shivering and chattering their teeth[, and] smoking the 'diamba.'" He continued, "The natives have no efficient remedies or treatment for bronchitis, pleurisy, and pneumonia, from which they suffer so much and so fatally in the cold season."[90] In Angola, cannabis was sowed in March, near the end of the rainy season and just before the cold, whereas most crops were planted in October, just prior to the rains,[91] suggesting seasonal farming and consumption.

Porters experienced nonphysical discomfort too. They were often compulsory laborers, forced into service by local leaders or colonial administrators. They traveled for weeks to months at a time, leaving behind family, fields, and other opportunities.[92] Payment was poor. Higher pay for each carrier meant the caravan had to haul additional goods destined for payment, which meant hiring more carriers. Merchants further sought to minimize transport costs by loading slaves bound for sale with goods bound for sale.[93] From southern Angola to the lower Congo, commercial shipments of *riamba* traveled on the backs of slaves.[94]

In Angola, porters were crucial for commerce because no navigable rivers flowed far inland. The colonial administration first recorded problems recruiting porters in 1666 and had constant problems until truck drivers and railroad crews replaced them.[95] A colonial governor described the problems of commercial transport in 1814. Inland, slave dealers demanded heavy goods, particularly rifles, gunpowder, fabric, and liquor; coastal merchants could move goods only with porters, yet that occupation attracted little interest; merchants and colonial administrators forced vassal chieftains to supply porters, with minimal remuneration; thus, laborers hauled goods rather than farmed, and agricultural productivity was low, contributing to food shortages.[96]

Travel accounts suggest why men had little interest in becoming porters. In 1892, a Portuguese traveler who credited himself as being enlightened on labor issues—and who later became Angola's governor—demanded that local leaders supply men to him but rarely found enough to haul his things. He loaded each carrier with sixty to eighty pounds, not including personal effects, water, or food, which they purchased and prepared themselves. He kept them from their homes longer than agreed by lying about his itinerary and paid them one yard of fabric each for several months' work.[97] Less enlightened taskmasters were described in 1929 by an American traveler who wrote, without irony, "[H]ow fortunate it is that the whites are no longer quite free to beat and kick out their own inefficiencies on the natives." She observed truck drivers and their bosses in southern Belgian Congo. One boss was "the kind of man who, when he didn't understand a black, knocked him down," and the other boss was

> a handsome blond giant of a man with an ungovernable temper. [T]his otherwise very agreeable person seemed to thrive on [anger]. I remember [one time] the black driver of [the truck in front of us] did not hear our horn. As we drove mile after mile, taking his dust, the white driver became apoplectic, half insane with fury. At last he managed to bring his car alongside the truck. He bellowed at the blacks . . . to stop, [then] rushed on them. His powerful right arm and doubled fist shot back and forth into the cab until I wondered how there could be anybody left alive inside.[98]

Labor regimes across colonial Africa depended upon physical and psychological violence, because instances of violence expressed and reinforced the strong hierarchies necessary to produce workers suited for the labor-intensive, extractive industries on which colonial states relied. Porters—who represent just one hard-labor occupation—smoked while resting in the evening. Certainly they sometimes discussed their employers' brutality or the heartaches they had experienced, although we don't know their topics of conversation.

Many people find conversation therapeutic. In some measure and by several pathways, cannabis helped users care for their mental health. Charles Bourhill's medical dissertation about *dagga* in South Africa provides illuminating quotes, ostensibly from users, on why they valued cannabis in 1913. Users described in several ways that it simply made them feel good and lessened fear and worry.[99] Psychoactive cannabis can be a euphoriant; THC and CBD can both reduce anxiety and inhibitions.[100] (Of course, subjective effects vary between users. Some experience feelings of fear or paranoia instead.[101]) In the 1960s, Egyptian prostitutes valued the plant drug explicitly to reduce anxiety; in current U.S. society, female sex workers have higher rates of drug use than other women.[102] It should be obvious that many past users may have experienced trauma that led to posttraumatic stress disorder (PTSD). Cannabis has increasingly attracted interest as a therapy for PTSD.[103] The plant drug can also stimulate creative and introspective thought. Some users perhaps discovered peace within themselves; cannabis has been called an entheogen, or a substance that generates feelings of the divine.[104] In Rastafarianism, which arose in Jamaica in the 1930s on Indian and Central African foundations, *ganja* is euphemistically the "tree of life" that guides one toward tranquility, contrary to the forces of "Babylon" (colonialism and global capitalism).[105]

Around the Atlantic, though, many more smokers killed time in mundane rather than divine contemplations, having nothing better to do. Prisoners in Brazil, Mexico, and Arizona, and soldiers in Morocco, Mexico, New Mexico, Senegal, and Egypt smoked seemingly to relieve boredom.[106]

Drugs can enable resistance to authority.[107] Cannabis symbolized resistance against the old political-economic regime for Bena Riamba adherents. In Rastafarianism, *ganja* offers sacramental resistance to Babylon. Morocco's Ḥeddawa smoked *kif* while rejecting worldly values.[108] Ḥeddawa brethren relied on cannabis handouts at a time when the Moroccan state generated revenues by controlling the *kif* market. The act of smoking can enhance solidarity through bonding around common practices and experiences of drug use. People shared songs and stories while smoking in Brazil, Lesotho, South Africa, Jamaica, and Angola.[109] Few songs were directly about working, but any folklore strengthens group cohesion. By burning cannabis in distinctive pipes, people enacted social distancing that centered on smoking practices constructed as non-European. Social distancing provided physical space during smoke breaks; European observers saw unfamiliar smoking practices from afar, not surrounding them. The act of use can provide psychological distance from work mentalities beyond what cannabinoid pharmacology enables. A relatively recent example relates to laborers in Nigeria in the 1960s, for whom cannabis was a reward following unrewarding days at work; they used drugs more generally to even out emotional ups and downs.[110]

By easing workers' difficulties, cannabis helped achieve employers' goals. Again, Bourhill's dissertation provides illuminating quotes. Many of his respondents were miners. Some mines allowed *dagga* smoking above and below ground, with workers characteristically consuming three times daily to dull feelings of exertion and stress. One respondent said, "We forget all our troubles, we forget we are working, and so work very much."[111] Such effects directly benefited users and, indirectly, their employers. Several travelers explicitly recognized that cannabis assisted them in this way. "I have never perceived any adverse effects of hemp," wrote a traveler whose canoe paddlers on the Upper Congo were "remarkably strengthened" by smoke breaks.[112] Hermann von Wissmann, whose loads were hauled by Bena Riamba adherents, was "convinced that hemp has a taming effect on the negro, that the narcotising herb moderates unpredictable wildness . . . and makes the negro more open to and useful for civilization and culture."[113] He thought that reports of its harmfulness were exaggerated.

Cannabis did not cause everyone to trot with alacrity. According to a stereotype expressed in 1832, "When he awakens [the "Congo" man] regales himself with his . . . pipe. [Pipe smoking and other] habits of the negro render him easy to control, but at the same time [make it] difficult to get him to work as a carrier."[114] In Angola, some elites believed the plant drug caused "madness and consequent lethargy."[115] Laziness, ignorance, stupidity, forgetfulness—all are beneficially displayed to the boss sometimes. In recent decades, this behavior has been attributed to cannabis via the medical concept of the "amotivational syndrome," which makes the boss's problem (unmotivated workers) into a psychiatric problem within workers. The proposed medical syndrome has been repudiated.[116] Nonetheless, cannabis can reduce inhibitions and affect judgment and short-term memory. It is impossible to know historical intentions and contexts, but cannabis had an ambivalent role in many incidents that frustrated employers. Consider the experience of a Belgian voyager in Congo in 1897: "In back, under the veranda, thirty blacks, drunk on [palm wine] and the smoke of 'diamba,' sleep in a circle, heads supported by boxes and little kegs of powder, while in their middle smolders a small campfire!" He roused them and they moved the powder, but "one shudders [to think what] one ember or a simple spark from their pipe would have [done]."[117] But what really happened? Perhaps the colonial traveler didn't tell the porters what the boxes and kegs held; perhaps he presumed they didn't know how to handle gunpowder, but they did and considered themselves safe; perhaps they were intoxicated, showing poor judgment; perhaps they were intoxicated and messing with the boss.

Most travelers said nothing about cannabis among their employees, whether from tacit approval or ignorance. Some travelers blamed cannabis for their frustrations with transport, overlooking the demanding burdens they placed on porters, as well as other factors that influenced their rate of travel. On Lake Tanganyika in 1857, Richard Burton's hired canoes were slow because "the bhang-pipe is produced after every hour, and the paddles are taken in whilst [the paddlers] indulge in the usual screaming whooping cough." On land, his caravans were slow because porters would "lie or loiter about . . . chatting and smoking tobacco or bhang, with the usual whooping, screaming cough."[118] Other travelers condemned cannabis yet also recognized its benefits to them. Kingsley considered *liamba* the worst intoxicant available in Gabon, far worse than palm wine, which was far worse than cheap British gin. Nonetheless, she found that when "a whiff of lhiamba is taken by [porters] in the morning . . . , the effect seems to be good, enabling them to get over the ground easily and endure a long march without being exhausted."[119]

Despite morbidity and mortality associated with imported distillates,[120] Europeans considered cannabis more dangerous, for transparent reasons.

Spirits were socially and culturally more valued than cannabis. Kingsley presented chemical analyses to prove that trade gin was not poisonous; it was, instead, a profitable export for her country, and, further, colonialism only benefited Africans.[121] Europeans found medicinal justifications for alcohol, which became harmful only to those drinkers who bore the individual fault of intemperance. "It is almost as suicidal to travel in tropical Africa without brandy as without quinine," bellowed one traveler. "The risk from the climate to Europeans . . . is quite sufficient, without increasing it by withholding . . . brandy from our explorers, simply from fear of its abuse, or in deference to popular claptrap."[122] The drug wasn't the problem; immoderate users were. Further, drugs each had their social places. When porters siphoned liquor from their loads, this was considered theft,[123] not self-treatment with a substance that the boss should not safely be without. Cannabis, including its perceived health risks, was more appropriate to porters than to clear-headed bosses.

Concern about health risks was rooted in dislike of social behaviors associated with smoking. Intoxication was not the problem; behavior was. Kingsley benefited from her porters' drug-enhanced endurance but concluded that "a small tot of rum is better for them by far" because with cannabis they cough and "their society [becomes] more terrifying than tolerable."[124] The plant drug stimulated animated discourse that challenged staid visitors. Europeans perceived loud voices, excited gesticulations, and boisterous interactions as drug-induced mania tending toward aggression. Quiet, contemplative behavior became morose and immoral indolence.[125] Two Portuguese travelers in Angola found that it "inspires true pity" to see porters coughing, laughing, and talking under the influence.[126] Straitlaced Victorians looked dourly upon frolic among their employees.

Cannabis seems to have been mostly a generalized tonic in sub-Saharan Africa and elsewhere.[127] An indication of its broad, unspecific utility, perhaps, is that Afro-Brazilians in 1843 reportedly considered "incense from the leaves . . . the best remedy against hangovers."[128] It just seemed generally good to those who appreciated it.

A generalized tonic was appropriate to the generalized vile conditions that sometimes accompanied the plant drug. The plant drug's past can illustrate that reality-altering drugs attract people experiencing unhappy realities.[129] Consider Nimo, the "bush boy" servant of an American in Belgian Congo in 1929. Nimo was a wage slave, apparently an orphan, who "smoked hemp but alleged it made him work better."[130] During his time with the American, he had a fistfight, an infected foot, a poor diet, little privacy, a patronizing boss, and neither family nor a permanent home. Surely cannabis was somehow therapeutic

FIGURE 8.2. Moroccan sex workers had little freedom to leave the brothels in which they were employed. The women often spent much of their income on cannabis, tobacco, and alcohol. "128. Casablanca—Loisirs au quartier Réservé," postcard, Morocco, ca. 1920, published by Édition la Cigogne, Casablanca. Author's collection.

to Nimo, as it was for others deprived of privacy. Water pipes and *ḥashīsh* became stereotypical components of brothels in European Orientalist thought,[131] partly because prostitutes used cannabis openly when with European clients. In French North Africa, prostitutes had little freedom and spent half their income on *kif*, tobacco, and alcohol.[132] Cannabis may have been used secretly, too; in present-day Morocco, it is mixed with datura, henbane, and other plants to induce abortions.[133] Cannabis existed in demeaning, abusive environments with scarce therapeutic resources. An illustrative case was that of Sarah Baartman, an enslaved Khoikhoi woman exhibited in Britain and France as "Hottentot Venus" in the 1810s, who smoked *dagga* while on display.[134] In these worst cases, cannabis was an escape, a habit, a medicine, and a social condition.

Some historical users experienced unimaginable trauma. In Brazil, cannabis was associated with *banzo*, a deep, resentful depression in slaves that slaveholders considered fatal.[135] An account from 1882 says that afflicted slaves were emotionally unstable, suicidal, and afflicted by severe dermatosis. "The poor slaves," wrote the Brazilian observer, "beat their sufferings with the fumes of *pango*, which numb them in convulsive dances, in raging frenzy."[136] Some sufferers committed suicide, including via self-starvation. The ultimate act of resistance in unfree labor regimes is to steal one's own life from its legal owner.

7 - Maladie de sommeil

FIGURE 8.3. A victim of African trypanosomiasis. The voyeuristic quality of this postcard perhaps captures the experience of nineteenth-century doctors, who could do little but watch the progression of the illness. "7. Maladie de sommeil," postcard, Belgian Congo, ca. 1930, published by C. Zagourskis, Léopoldville, Belgian Congo. Author's collection.

African trypanosomiasis is a parasitic disease more commonly and quaintly called sleeping sickness.

In the 1800s, sleeping sickness became increasingly prevalent (or increasingly salient to Europeans) in western Central Africa and along transatlantic slave routes from there. The first symptoms of the illness—malaise, headache, fever, joint pain—are easily dismissed, especially in populations bearing multiple health burdens. This first stage can persist for months, allowing the pathogen to travel with its human vector. The second stage visibly presents swollen lymph glands on the neck and features loss of appetite, sleepiness, neurological disorders, abnormal body tone and mobility, meningoencephalitis, and seizures, preceding coma and death. Sleeping sickness is "notoriously difficult to treat," explained the World Health Organization in 2017.[137] Historically it was a death sentence.

The malady came to European notice in 1734, then again in 1803, and more consistently after 1840. Between 1896 and 1906, several hundred thousand people died in an epidemic in Central Africa.[138] Sleeping sickness was first conceptualized as an incurable condition called "negro lethargy."[139] It was clearly some sort of illness but was treated as a labor problem rather than a medical condition. A physician in 1904 recalled that sleeping sickness

> was believed to be strictly confined to the negro race and was looked upon as a peculiar form of nostalgia [i.e., PTSD]. At times, it caused considerable losses to the slave-traders of the West Coast, notwithstanding the careful isolation of the sick and the weeding-out of all such as presented [symptoms]. When any of the slaves showed symptoms of the disease on transport ships, they were mercilessly thrown overboard; some developed the malady . . . and died of it in the plantations of the Antilles. But the disease never spread in the [Antillean] places in which it was imported.[140]

Its cause was perplexing. Some nineteenth-century physicians thought sleeping sickness was psychological, like *banzo*; others blamed chronic dietary toxicity. Its cause—a protozoan transmitted through tsetse fly bites—was identified between 1895 and 1901.[141] It remains, however, a neglected disease that burdens African societies and is significantly overlooked in global medical science.[142]

CANNABIS ACCOMPANIED ILLNESSES. Cannabis-illness associations had material origins in the conditions laborers experienced and had material responses from overseers and elites. Causes and effects alike reflected the social-ecological stratification produced and needed within exploitative labor regimes.

The most important example is sleeping sickness, a trypanosomiasis endemic to sub-Saharan Africa.[143] Robert O. Clarke, the physician who found cannabis in Sierra Leone in 1851, published the first detailed description of medical treatment of sleeping sickness, among recaptives in Sierra Leone in 1840.[144] Clarke called the ailment "lethargus." His patients—boys and girls aged ten to fourteen—died. He didn't mention cannabis in his 1840 paper on lethargus or lethargus in his 1851 paper on *diamba*, but in 1860 he wrote, "At Sierra Leone, I have known several instances of [sleeping sickness] being induced in youth of both sexes from smoking 'diamba.'"[145] This offhand comment made it into a medical textbook in 1862 but was dismissed in the textbook's second edition (1886) on the reasoning that cannabis smoking existed "in the whole of the Orient," but the disease did not.[146] Before the second edition, though, the idea that cannabis causes lethargus had taken root in western Central Africa. In 1880, a Portuguese traveler in Angola gave the "averred fact that *liamba* smokers are those who most frequently succumb to this terrible illness. . . . [Thus,] in all of Africa the slave that acquires the habit of *liamba* smoking . . . is reputed lost."[147] (Not everyone agreed that cannabis spoiled slaves. In 1903, a plantation near Benguela planted rows of *liamba* to supply the slaves on the place.[148]) By 1875, some Angolan slaveholders were prohibiting their slaves from using.[149] Anti-cannabis views from Brazil certainly must have circulated to Angola, increasing concern among slaveholders about drug use among their captives.

At the end of the century, it was common knowledge for Europeans in western Central Africa that sleeping sickness was a form of poisoning caused by cannabis—if not palm wine, promiscuity, bad water, or manioc.[150] Few physicians accepted the poisoning theory, whether centered on *liamba* or not. Epidemiologists in São Tomé in 1900 rejected *liamba* because the disease occurred on Príncipe Island, where the plant was absent, and because its increased incidence correlated to increased arrivals of indentured laborers.[151] Nonetheless, colonial administrators were concerned about labor supply, and lethargus was salient. Several hundred thousand people died in the Central African epidemic of 1896–1906.[152] Common knowledge evolved to follow political-economic concerns, not medical evidence. Conclusive evidence implicating protozoans carried by flies came in 1901.[153] It then became common knowledge that cannabis might not *cause* sleeping sickness, but it made its users more susceptible.[154] Cannabis smoking was implicated insofar as "the black never ceases to weaken himself physically and morally," stated ethnographers in Belgian Congo in 1911.[155] Regarding the counterargument that "the zone infested by sleeping sickness is less expansive than that where hemp reigns," these ethnographers found it "proper to repeat that the documentation is still not conclusive."

Historians have interpreted sleeping sickness in nineteenth-century Africa as the culmination of decades of social-ecological exploitation and destruction.[156] Across western Central Africa, sleeping sickness accompanied exploitative labor relationships. Human migrations carry along other species, both intentionally (via crops and domesticated animals) and unintentionally (via weeds, vermin, and infections). An accompanying set of creatures is called a "portmanteau biota."[157] Three components of the portmanteau biota of "Congoes" were the pathogen *Trypanosoma brucei gambiense*, the tsetse fly *Glossina morsitans*, and *Cannabis indica*.

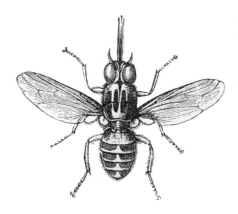

FIGURE 8.4. *Glossina morsitans*, the tsetse fly. "La mouche tsetse," engraving, in É. Charton, ed., "L'Afrique austral, premiers voyages du Dr. Livingstone (1840–1856)," *Le tour du monde* 13 (1866), 60. Author's collection.

These species had different levels of success in accompanying people. Slave caravans likely spread trypanosomes within Africa, allowing the pathogen to colonize landscapes where tsetse flies were present.[158] Sleeping sickness entered transatlantic slave trading near its end, as did cannabis. Their Atlantic distributions show parallels. In 1869, a French physician in Martinique traced sleeping sickness to "Congoes," who later carried the illness to London.[159] The disease was not contagious in the Antilles because tsetse flies did not survive the Middle Passage.[160] It was contagious in São Tomé and Príncipe because tsetse flies arrived there probably in the 1820s with cattle (and thus slaves to care for them) shipped from Gabon.[161] The pathogen and plant came to the islands during the same period, although the plant seemingly did not survive on Príncipe. *Glossina* flies occupy most of tropical Africa. People with inadequate clothing or shelter have reduced protection against bites; those unable to travel freely cannot avoid locations they consider dangerous. On São Tomé, plantation bosses rejected slaves' beliefs that tsetse flies caused sleeping sickness and forced them to work in habitats where the flies thrived.[162] On the mainland, slave coffles must have been tormented by tsetses, with bound slaves unable to swat them.

Sleeping sickness was an occupational hazard. Physicians could at one time believe it was "strictly confined to the negro race" only because people assigned to other racial categories were not enslaved in the locations where the pathogen came to European notice.[163] All people fell victim to trypanosomiasis, but those deprived of basic needs were more vulnerable. Incidence rates from São Tomé in 1900 show that 6 percent of Europeans and 18 percent of Africans became infected.[164] There is no evidence that people (including people on São Tomé from mainland Africa) acquire immunity to the malady; the trypanosome manipulates the immune system to its advantage perhaps more effectively than any other pathogen.[165] Thus, the different incidence rates represent effects of socioeconomic class on exposure and susceptibility to the disease.[166] Generalizations of habitual cannabis smokers as emaciated, listless, gaunt, weak, and without appetite may reflect observations of people self-palliating mortal infections endemic to the environments to which they were exposed.

Belief that cannabis caused so-called negro lethargy reflected the enduring attitude that illness among African workers was less a medical problem than a labor problem. Good help is hard to find, you know? This attitude preexisted modern medical science and provided the perceived truths upon which medical knowledge initially developed in African contexts. When the English physician Thomas Winterbottom described sleeping sickness in 1803, he identified swollen lymph glands in the neck as a diagnostic symptom. Slave traders considered the swollen glands "a symptom indicating a disposition to lethargy, and they either never buy such slaves, or get [rid] of them as soon as they observe any such appearances." Winterbottom also observed that "the disposition to sleep is so strong" in those who contract the illness that "even the repeated application of the whip, a remedy which has been frequently used, is hardly sufficient to keep the poor wretch awake."[167] This was the intellectual atmosphere in which the medical practice of trypanosomiasis diagnosis and treatment originated. Drs. Winterbottom and Clarke were abolitionists, yet they had no words to name the illness except one—"lethargy"—that preserved the social relations of slavery. For at least a century after Winterbottom's observations, sleeping sickness remained a blur of inexplicable illness and inexcusable laziness; it is not surprising that it remains a neglected tropical disease.

Less importantly, the attitude that illness among African workers was a labor problem led toward prohibitions of cannabis. Common knowledge of the cannabis-causes-lethargus idea explicitly motivated early administrative moves toward prohibition in Central Africa. In French Congo, the initial move (1907) rested on two points. First, "Under a climate deadly for the European, the native alone can engage in toilsome labor; . . . loss [of African labor] compromises all the colonization [effort]. Also, to not consider only our interest, it is necessary for us to defend them from epidemic and contagious illnesses." Second, "These poisons [*liamba* and alcohol] contribute powerfully to the development of contagious illnesses, such as tuberculosis and sleeping sickness," as well as rickets, madness, theft, and crime.[168] The cannabis-based etiology gave heft to ideas that workers were lazy and that cannabis abetted laziness.[169] The stereotyped Angolan "native" in 1904 sat in listless groups, passing "the *mutopa* [water pipe] of *liamba* . . . from hand to hand, with [an] indifferent and inexpressive disposition. . . . This indolence is natural, quite, so thus they act."[170] Lethargus, a fatal illness, and lethargy, an unhelpful attitude, looked alike until a person's neck showed swollen lymph glands, and then it was too late to do anything. Attitude among workers was the more pressing problem, and seemingly more soluble. Views of cannabis and of workers developed in the same moments. Generalizations about lethargy as an attribute of people and the plant drug came from interactions such as one that a Belgian had in Congo in 1888, when he "lost several hours in . . . hunt[ing] down our [guides] from the high grass on the riverside where they lounged deliciously in smoking *iamba*, with no more concern of us than of the great Turk, of whose existence they are ignorant."[171]

In sub-Saharan Africa at the turn of the twentieth century, cannabis increasingly seemed to accompany affronts to colonial authority.[172] These affronts often appeared in the behavior of workers. The Belgian traveler's guides were not the first to discover that it is sometimes pleasant to play lost and sometimes necessary to show who really leads an expedition. Afrikaner employers suspected herders who "lost" sheep ate them; these shepherds smoked *dagga* to fend off cold and hunger, relieve boredom and loneliness, and enhance their endurance, but the bosses thought simply that it made them more unreliable than they were when sober.[173] Where South African employers prohibited smoking, herders stole water pipes or made earth pipes so they could smoke while out with their animals.[174]

Colonial contexts were disrespectful, angering. It is impossible to decipher historical accounts of drug use, let alone the contexts through which the stories came into print. Cannabis seems to have widely accompanied distress, as well as enactments of social and racial order. In Natal in 1891, a magistrate asserted, "Low classes of semi-civilized Native transport wagon-drivers . . . brutally ill-treat their oxen," because *dagga* causes "acts of sudden impulsiveness, . . . and crimes of the most degraded and brutal description."[175] Perhaps the cruelty was a symptom of anger, aggressiveness, maliciousness, or illness, whether *dagga*-enhanced or not; perhaps cruelty and cannabis were symptoms of social condition, or resistance in the form of sabotage and psychological escape—or, perhaps the magistrate's sworn statement consisted of sand grains of experience embellished into nuggets of invective.

Cannabis had fraught relationships with both laborers and overseers. It helped and hindered, depending on context. By 1900, though, elites increasingly viewed cannabis as a labor problem and consequently pursued its legal prohibition.

NINE

Buying and Banning

Even if cannabis seemed increasingly like a problem to colonialists, it remained potentially valuable. In French Congo in 1885, *Cannabis indica* was considered one of several resources "that commerce will soon appreciate" in advantageous exchange for rifles, cloth, and brandy.[1] Despite damning it among his porters, Henry Morton Stanley determined cannabis was something the Congo Free State could "teach the natives to employ profitably."[2] Prohibiting the plant drug would carry economic costs. This chapter evaluates the cost-benefit relationships that preceded cannabis prohibition in Africa.

The Geneva opium convention of 1925 took cannabis into an international drug-control regime. Before the convention, many countries and colonies already had some form of legal restriction on psychoactive cannabis, ranging from import duties to full prohibition.[3] In much of Africa, cannabis was banned decades before 1925.[4] The plant drug's value and meaning varied from country to country and from colony to colony. In all cases, though, legal controls strengthened as its perceived political-economic costs outweighed its benefits.

A popular idea nowadays is that cannabis had great economic value when it was banned.[5] Cannabis histories point to the ropes and sails of European ships as evidence that prohibition destroyed vibrant economies. This idea is incorrect. Globally, cannabis hemp fiber peaked in importance around 1800. Processing cannabis into high-quality products was labor-intensive and thus either expensive or dependent on coerced workers. Fiber plants that might substitute for *Cannabis sativa* were among the first resources European naturalists sought as scientific exploration intensified in the 1700s. During the eighteenth and nineteenth centuries, European botanists discovered many plants whose fiber equaled or exceeded cannabis hemp. For those plants that produced satisfactorily at low latitudes, colonial economies helped keep labor costs down, making finished products inexpensive. Rope manufactured in places such as colonial Malaysia and the Philippines from plants such as abacá (*Musa textilis*) had swept cannabis hemp nearly out of the world market by 1900. Further, Russian hemp was cheap, abundant, and good, and had dominated global supply for centuries to the detriment of domestic industries elsewhere. New technologies helped doom hemp, too: steel cable, for instance, was more durable than plant fiber. By 1900, only a few countries—primarily Russia, France, Italy, and China—had substantial hemp industries, but all were in decline. Nonetheless, cannabis continued to tantalize people seeking economic opportunity because industrial hemp products were not valueless, and the plant could grow nearly everywhere. In South Africa, for instance, as late as 1908 settlers wishfully tried to produce cannabis fiber, unsuccessfully.[6] In few places would industrial hemp be a noticeable economic cost of prohibition.[7]

In any case, a focus on industrial hemp is misplaced because cannabis laws worldwide had exceptions for fiber and oilseed. Not until the 1970s were laws constructed to exclude *all* cannabis. Exceptions for industrial hemp were feasible because these products had economic geographies that were different from those of psychoactive products. Early laws prohibited specific psychoactive products, not cannabis generically. Names assigned to the plant drug in laws represented commercial products and the agroindustrial networks that produced them. The economic costs of prohibition lay within the networks that brought psychoactive goods to market.

To evaluate the economic logic of global prohibition, the Western commodity to consider is pharmaceutical cannabis, not rope. Cannabis traveled around the Atlantic as a subsistence plant resource whose pharmacology appealed to laborers. In those places where psychoactive cannabis was commonly used, social elites had been mostly indifferent to it. However, its political economy changed during the 1800s because social elites discovered value in the plant drug and made it a commercial commodity.

Three pathways led to commoditization. First, labor institutions that arose to supply post-slave workers did not replace the income slavers lost to abolition. European investors shifted to other activities, as did slavers in Africa and the Americas. This included a formal *liamba* export trade from Angola. (By formal, I mean trade that had published, taxed value.) Second, colonial governance impelled authorities to seek sources of revenue via taxation of established commodities and through exploitation of previously noncommercial products. Colonial governments entered previously informal cannabis trades to capture income from the plant drug. The third development was a shift in the plant drug's social meaning after 1840, when it became the "cannabis indica" of Western pharmacy. This shift produced a highly formalized pharmaceutical market centered in London that linked colonial possessions in South Asia, sub-Saharan Africa, and the Caribbean.

Prohibition had different justifications in each country and colony. However, I argue that whatever the specific justifications, anti-cannabis controls happened when the drug plant's political-economic costs exceeded its benefits. Of course, I mean only the costs and benefits perceived by social elites who had the power to enact drug prohibitions. Worldwide, a key pattern was that government shares in cannabis trading were small. Private buyers and sellers captured most of the economic benefits. Governments increasingly perceived political benefits to cannabis controls, because they could address various domestic and international concerns. Cost-benefit calculations ultimately led to strong controls on all forms of the plant drug, but initial controls targeted non-Western products and retained conditioned legality for pharmaceutical cannabis indica. To make this argument, I sketch informal market conditions, mostly in sub-Saharan Africa, then briefly examine formal markets in three African regions, as well as the global pharmaceutical trade.

Informal Cannabis Commerce

Formal cannabis markets rose from informal trades. Buying and selling of *Cannabis indica* appeared early in the plant's documentary history—thirteenth-century Egypt, eighteenth-century South Africa and Mexico, 1820s Brazil. Globally, cannabis was an economic staple only for *bhang, ganja*, and *charas* producers in South Asia.[8] Around the Atlantic, cannabis was a low-value component of economic systems but nonetheless commercially important. It helped sustain the labor regimes of colonialism and capitalism, for instance, and it was the gateway that led the Bena Riamba into its problems with rifles, ivory, slaves, and rubber.

Its informal economy is best documented in Central Africa and Southern Africa. In Angola, Europeans first noticed cannabis in informal markets in the 1850s, when regional supply networks already existed.[9] Cannabis was less valuable than tobacco because it was more easily grown, less commonly used, and not sold in export markets. Farmers sometimes smoked cannabis rather than tobacco because tobacco was worth more at market.[10] Cannabis seems to have been most valuable at the geographic edges of its availability. In southeastern Angola in 1855, *pango* was one of just three things—with beads and tobacco— that San people would exchange for copper.[11] At its simultaneous northern limit, the newfound plant drug was valued highly enough to inspire the Bena Riamba. Between these limits, cannabis was one of many valued crops.[12] Sometimes people intercropped it with staples such as manioc, or grew it along field margins.[13] It probably did best in moist locations; accounts from southern Angola to Gabon describe small riverside plots.[14] Fertile soil was beneficial but not crucial because people harvested pistillate inflorescences, and the plant prioritizes floral development when nutrients are limited. European visitors noticed cannabis in house gardens, and it persisted at abandoned settlements, alongside tomatoes and datura.[15] It seemed like an uncultivated plant to some observers. Crop theft sometimes led people to grow cannabis in secluded patches, "to remove the plantings from the eagerness of wayfarers."[16] European travelers likely underestimated the amount of cannabis grown because of secluded plantings, and when observed, secluded patches mimicked wild-growing plants. Small, dispersed plantings also suggest that farmers sowed marginal land to maximize space in prime locations for other crops. Similar planting strategies existed widely around the Atlantic.[17] In retail markets, cannabis appeared alongside foods and ethnobotanical herbs.[18] In Brazil in 1847, *pango* was advertised alongside the uncultivated medicinal plants elder (*Sambucus nigra*) and canella (trees of the genus *Nectandra*).[19] In 1875, market women in Angola sold "gourds full of . . . Indian-corn beer; live fowls and ducks, eggs, milk, Chili peppers, small white tomatoes [eggplants], bananas, and, in the season, oranges, mangoes, sour-sop, and other fruits, . . . cabbage-leaves and vegetables, firewood, tobacco, pipes and stems, wild hemp [*liamba*], mats, pumpkins, sweet potatoes, palm and ground-nut oil, and dried and salt fish."[20] Market supplies likely came from many farmers selling small amounts rather than fields of cannabis. Demand came from people on the move—day laborers, slaves, porters, and their overseers—who couldn't grow their own.

Efforts to outlaw informal economies are also well documented in Central Africa and Southern Africa. Anti-cannabis sentiment arose early in these regions and shaped horticulture before laws were enacted. In Central Africa by the 1880s, some European observers were condemning the plant drug and concluding that the drug plant grew wild.[21] "Wild" plants were, instead, probably isolated plantings. In French Congo in 1902—five years before the first official efforts to eradicate cannabis—people avoided smoking in front of European travelers and generally grew only "a few stems . . . in concealed places [that are] difficult to observe."[22] Twenty years earlier, the plant had been grown openly; twenty years later, the colonial government, in the law formally banning it, character-ized farming as "always clandestine."[23] Across Central Africa, concealed plots became more common, or more commonly noticed, as anti-cannabis sentiment grew in the 1900s.[24] Yet regional farming practices were perhaps preadapted to, rather than shaped by, cannabis-control laws. In the 1850s, sixty years before Angola's prohibition law, an Austrian botanist determined that the plant was cultivated "always in more or less hidden or solitary sites."[25] Similarly, patches in Gabon in the 1850s were removed from fields and villages,[26] six decades before prohibition. Disapproval of *dagga* wages in South Africa arose by 1818, causing growers to conceal their plots decades before prohibition began in 1904.[27]

Colonialists recognized that informally traded cannabis had economic value, because they participated in these trades. In South Africa, *dagga* wages contin-ued for two centuries. European storekeepers sold herbal cannabis in southern Zambia around 1900 and in Gabon in 1910.[28] Some travelers surely bought cannabis for their porters; slavers in Angola supplied their slaves.[29]

Nonetheless, in published discourse informal trades were worthless, and the drug plant only had *potential* value because it was evaluated only on Euro-pean terms. A British administrator in colonial South Sudan thought it should be "grown for commercial purposes, and not for the native consumption,"[30] thereby flushing all economic value from the informal market. "Commercial purposes" meant pharmaceutical cannabis indica. Colonial administrations hoped to enter the European drug market, which British India dominated. Early sub-Saharan laws banned non-Western products by name—German East Africa listed six names, in Swahili, Arabic, and Gujarati[31]—and thus the underlying commercial networks. Congo Free State's 1903 law explicitly tar-geted these networks by banning the farming, sale, transport, and possession of "hemp for smoking," thus striking valueless all activities that enabled this specific, non-European use.[32] (The law nonetheless authorized compensation payments to people who destroyed their *liamba* within two weeks of the law's enactment.) Laws included allowances for pharmaceutical horticulture and commerce, whether explicitly or implicitly via language banning only unau-thorized activities.

Most colonial governments received no direct political-economic benefits from informal markets. Few colonial states taxed cannabis before banning it. Imports were assessed tariffs, but they could not have generated meaningful revenue. Tariffs were intended to discourage imports and probably did, because inexpensive, locally grown material was widely available.[33] Perceived costs of cannabis did not need to be great to overcome minute, perceived benefits. The decision to prohibit was explicitly a political-economic one in French Congo in 1891. The following writer compares that colony with French Gabon, which at the time formally imported from Portuguese Angola:

> I accept... that we do not prohibit completely the introduction to Gabon of the poisonous plant [because] the importation of hemp... is a source of earnings for the public Treasury. But in interior regions, in the very center of the black continent, what use is it, since it is not slapped with any duty? It is simply an instrument of death, which does not even have the merit of reporting [revenues] and of being from this point of view of some usefulness.[34]

From this perspective, informal markets were economically harmful because they did not help pay for colonial governance. The regional sleeping sickness epidemic that endured from 1896 to 1906 made it politically impossible to justify an instrument of death that did not pay its way.

Sometimes the plant drug posed acute political problems. The Congo Free State collected taxes *with* cannabis, so to speak, by keeping it legal for tax-collecting employees such as the mercenary Zappo Zaps, who washed their atrocities down in 1901 with tobacco and *diamba*, mixed for smoking in a freshly fashioned skull bowl.[35] The news article that supplied this anecdote helped upend politics, ultimately overturning the Free State in 1908. Before its demise, the state banned *diamba* (in 1903).[36] This effort stimulated suppression elsewhere. In 1906, a British administrator in South Sudan cheered, "The Belgians are putting down the growing of this [plant] with a firm hand."[37] The following year, Anglo-Egyptian Sudan's "Hashish Ordinance" banned unauthorized farming, processing, sales, possession, imports, exports, and transport of herbal material and resin, as well as unauthorized use of pharmaceutical cannabis.[38] The plant drug's political costs had likely been rising in Sudan. The British in Egypt had intensified efforts against *hashish* trafficking. In Sudan, *Cannabis indica* was fully banned in 1901 in legislation meant to control commercial smuggling of all commodities; the 1907 law simply focused attention on the product *hashish*.[39] The plant drug had no perceived political-economic value to Sudan's colonial administration, but prohibition offered political benefits in intercolonial relations and in giving a display of colonial power to the natives.

Cannabis was a political symbol to Africans, not just to Europeans. The first sub-Saharan cannabis control arose in precolonial Madagascar, where Merina royalty had forbidden the plant drug by 1870.[40] Their decree was a political statement. The monarchy, based in Madagascar's central highlands, dominated

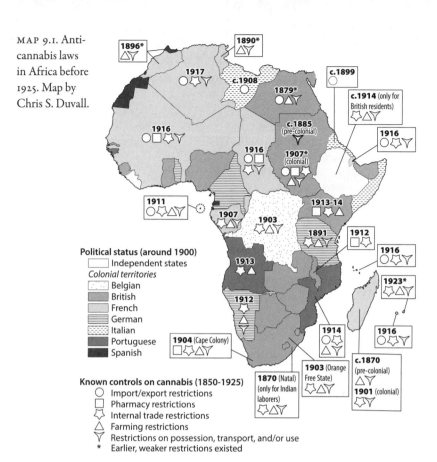

MAP 9.1. Anti-cannabis laws in Africa before 1925. Map by Chris S. Duvall.

people in the lowlands, where observers thought smoking was most common.[41] The decree was justified within the Merina monarchy's project of political-economic modernization; cannabis and alcohol were both made to represent backwardness.[42] In what today is Sudan, in the 1880s, the Mahdi—a messianic Islamic leader—banned *ḥashīsh* and punished users with brutal whippings because the plant drug represented the secularism of Anglo-Turkish rule.[43] Thirty years later, the Sirdar woman in South Sudan reportedly gave cannabis the opposite meaning to symbolize resistance to the colonial state that had outlawed the plant drug. Moralist politics propelled anti-cannabis efforts in many areas. Nineteenth-century churches in South Africa disallowed it, even though it remained legal.[44] In Belgian Congo, years after legal prohibition, churches excommunicated members who were caught smoking.[45]

In much of Africa, cannabis was banned before the 1925 opium convention.[46] In some colonies, though, cannabis was unregulated before laws based on the international convention took effect. In these cases, colonial governments were ignorant of cannabis within their borders, so that regulations were considered unnecessary before 1925, and the perceived costs of compliance were nil. Sierra Leone provides an example. Although *diamba* was present there by 1851, within decades elites were ignorant of it. In 1893, a well-educated former recaptive who came from what is now Nigeria and published a newspaper in Sierra Leone wrote that "the Congoes have a native opium called *diambah*, which they smoke immoderately like the Chinese," but he was discussing the Congo Basin and showed no awareness of cannabis in his colony.[47] In 1899, the English president of the Sierra Leone Chamber of Commerce, a twenty-year resident of the colony, testified that there was "nothing like bhang or Indian hemp" within its borders. Of course, he cared only about declared imports and exports, testifying that the colony "produces practically nothing beyond a little ginger."[48] Global lack of concern about psychoactive cannabis meant that it was absent from the Opium Convention of 1912, the first international drug-control agreement.[49] Within years, newly independent Egypt and South Africa had raised concerns. Consequently, the 1925 opium convention included cannabis resin and pistillate inflorescences "under whatever name they may be designated in commerce." The only commercial names given were "hashish, esrar, charas"—Levantine and South Asian words for resin—and "djamba," which was probably mentioned on behalf of Central African colonies.[50] Sierra Leone's law enacting the 1925 agreement used the "whatever name" formulation and betrayed no official awareness of cannabis in the colony.[51] Police on the ground probably knew of *diamba* in the 1920s,[52] but not until 1933 did Sierra Leone officially report that the "only dangerous drug known to be used illegally in this colony is a plant known locally as '*diamba*,' a species of *Cannabis sativa*."[53] At that time, Sierra Leonean sailors smuggled *diamba* to ports from Senegal to Nigeria and beyond.[54] The plant drug's identifiable past, in Sierra Leone and elsewhere, was lost in early drug-control laws.

Finally, buyers in informal markets paid for cannabis, but I have found only two past prices for informal, legal sales.[55] In Sierra Leone in 1851, dried pistillate inflorescences came in "very small packets, which are sold for one half-penny each."[56] The same source reported that a "small plant in full flower will yield . . . ten-shillings' worth of [inflorescences]"—that is, 240 half-penny packets.[57] The Sierra Leonean plants were characterized as ranging in height from six to thirteen feet, with basal diameters up to twenty feet.[58] Current marijuana growers estimate yields of one hundred to four hundred grams of inflorescences per plant for outdoor-grown plants that are physically similar to the historical ones.[59] If this range is applied to 1851, each packet of dried flowers would weigh 0.4–1.6 grams, equivalent to £1.25–£5 per kilogram.[60] The other informal price was from Richard Burton's statement that smokers in Minas Gerais, Brazil, would "readily pay as much as [one milréis] for a handful of this poison" in 1866.[61] Burton did not describe the poison—presumably inflorescences—but suggested its price was high. The internet offers guides for visually estimating the weight of harvested inflorescences. Handfuls are estimated to hold 10–25 grams. In 1869, one milréis exchanged in Brazil for 17–28 pence.[62] Taking the lower figure to avoid overvaluation, this converts to £2.8–£7.1 per kilogram.[63]

Numbers calculated this way are at best indexes of nominal value, not price or cost estimates. As indexes, they allow comparison of different markets. For instance, these index values for Sierra Leone and Brazil are higher than most values I have calculated for later, formal markets. Formal markets arose in Egypt, the Maghreb, Angola, and Mozambique, and a global trade emanated from British India and supplied pharmaceutical cannabis to widespread markets. I describe these formal markets in the sections that follow but wait until the end of the chapter to discuss value indexes for these trades.

North Africa's Markets

Cannabis commerce in North Africa was formalized for centuries, before 1300 CE in Egypt. The greatest government involvement in any historical cannabis market happened in the Maghreb, where governments sold annual monopolies for *kif, takrūri,* and tobacco.

Egypt's *hashīsh* economy was vibrant in 1800, when the government taxed imports and sales.[64] The country mostly consumed imported *hashīsh* from Turkey and re-exported some up the Nile toward Sudan.[65] Egyptian farmers grew cannabis, but in the 1800s this was principally subsistence-oriented production not destined for formal markets.[66] For centuries, coffeehouses and hash parlors retailed cannabis to a wide range of consumers and generated government revenues via permits and taxes. Although the cannabis economy benefited the state treasury, by the 1860s the political costs of allowing the plant drug had grown.[67] Religious, social, and cultural considerations led to prohibition. Egypt's leaders were concerned that *hashīsh* use violated Islamic beliefs, confirmed Orientalist stereotypes, and threatened public health. They outlawed the plant drug in 1879, but the centuries-old commercial networks easily worked through the new legal context.

The *hashīsh* economy remained vibrant well into the twentieth century, although it was transformed under prohibition.[68] Egypt's black market was the world's best documented before 1925. Drug-control laws in Turkey had ended

FIGURE 9.1. By 1900, Europeans in Egypt commonly associated *gozeḥ* water pipes and cannabis with peasant farmers, or *fellaḥin*. Although this woman was clearly made to pose with the water pipe, this representation provides more information on historical material culture than idealized Orientalist portrayals. Compare the "fumeuse de hachiche" on the postcard with Bernard's *La fumeuse de hachiche* (1900) (figure 1.3). "N. 108—Egypte—Fumeuse de Hachiche," postcard, Egypt, about 1905, published by Khardiache F., no location given. Author's collection.

N. 108 - *Egypte - Fumeuse de Hachiche*

legal sales there by 1890.[69] Greece became the main supplier and also furnished legal tobacco cigarettes.[70] Egypt's black market was profitable because consumption remained strong. Nonetheless, the British colonial government clamped down in 1903 and closed more than 1,700 cafés,[71] which drove the centuries-old institution underground. Smugglers brought concealed cannabis shipments into Egypt—such as between the walls of double-walled casks[72]—despite surveillance by the coast guard and constabulary. Smugglers landed along the coast from what is now Libya to Sudan, then carried the *hashīsh* to Egyptian cities through the desert on camels.[73] Nearly everything shipped in made it to consumers. By one estimate, during 1919–24, law enforcement seized on average just 6 percent of the imported total per year.[74] The French drug runner Henri de Monfried thought the *hashīsh* economy in the 1920s was a collusion among Egyptian officials and British and Greek businessmen, so that arrests were limited to "the occasional little fellow," not big dealers.[75] Indeed, as early as 1884 customs officers were paying themselves by selling whatever they impounded, because the state had no money to pay their salaries. Further, customs officers were impeded by European governments that did not allow the Egyptians to search warehouses owned by their citizens.[76] In the early twentieth century, coffee shops and hash parlors continued to sell *ḥashīsh* illegally, but the plant drug's social status had declined from a century before. In the 1920s, Monfried described the primary *ḥashīsh* consumers as *fellaḥin* (peasant farmers) who "rel[y] on its stimulating properties to compensate for underfeeding and to combat fatigue."[77]

Authorities in the Maghreb faced political pressures similar to those in Egypt. In the end, Morocco and Tunisia maintained legal but strictly controlled internal markets rather than producing entirely underground markets. Legal controls took the form of state-owned monopolies for both cannabis and tobacco. These monopolies generated revenue, but were intended mostly to shape colonial agriculture and limit drug consumption. Several countries in southern Europe used the same administrative strategy for tobacco,[78] but only Morocco and Tunisia monopolized cannabis.

Morocco's monopolies were morally fraught from the beginning.[79] The tobacco monopoly began in 1844, when the sultan needed to fund a war against France.[80] The monopoly overturned two centuries of religious and political disapproval of tobacco use. The revenue stream was sufficiently important by 1856 that Morocco agreed with Great Britain "to abolish all monopolies of agricultural produce . . . , except leeches, bark, tobacco, and other herbs used for smoking in pipes."[81] A *kif* monopoly was explicitly identified in 1860 by a Frenchman who suggested that it violated Islamic prohibitions on intoxicants.[82] In 1876, the tobacco and *kif* monopolies were a primary source of government income.[83] For example, in 1884 the monopolies accounted for 37 percent of revenues from an administrative region in northern Morocco.[84]

The monopolies were politically useful, too. In the 1870s, Sultan Hassan I used his authority to allow cannabis farming to build political support in the *kif*-growing Rif Mountains,[85] the home region of the Ḥeddawa brotherhood.

Hassan I thought the monopoly helped limit consumption and liked "the enormous income for the Treasury in which it results," but he had qualms about selling the intoxicant.[86] After seeking guidance from a Muslim cleric, he banned both tobacco and cannabis in 1888 (by an executive action, not legislative change). He ordered commercial stocks to be publicly burned, but allowed continued farming in the Rif.[87] His son and successor re-broadened the monopolies in 1896. As French influence subsequently grew, European diplomats agreed to maintain the Moroccan monopolies. In 1910, the tobacco monopoly was awarded to a state-owned farm; *kif* was added to its crops in 1914.[88] In 1922, under the French Protectorate, the government banned "hashish" imports and

FIGURE 9.2. Historically, Moroccans prepared *kif* by finely chopping cannabis inflorescences, then mixing them with a small quantity of chopped tobacco. "Cortador de kifi—Larache. No. 1024," postcard, Spanish Morocco, ca. 1920, photographed by García-Cortés, no publisher stated. Author's collection.

controlled access to pharmaceutical cannabis,[89] but *kif* was not mentioned. *Kif* was not fully banned until 1954.[90]

The cannabis monopoly in Ottoman Tunisia followed a different pathway. In the mid-1800s people smoked cannabis openly, but in 1875 its cultivation was banned.[91] A tobacco monopoly was established in 1884, specifying that farming was legal only with a license, and only in certain parts of the colony.[92] The state controlled sales, too. The purpose was to limit the agricultural resources expended on the crop and prevent adulteration of prepared products. In 1890, *takrūri* was added to the monopoly.[93] Restrictions on cannabis farming were less explicit because Tunisia then relied on imports from the city of Constantine, Algeria.[94] Over subsequent decades, Tunisia became self-sufficient.[95] The 1890 law set prices for two *takrūri* products—inflorescences versus mixed herbal material—but starting in 1902, a single product was offered: trimmed and chopped inflorescences in five-gram boxes.[96] This was the most common manner of preparation across the Maghreb. Tunisia's five-gram boxes remained standard for decades. In the 1910s, five thousand kilograms were sold annually.[97] The monopoly persisted into the 1950s.

Between the two monopolies, Algeria hardly worried about the plant drug. An Ottoman Algerian bey, Mohamed Chakar (ruled 1814–1818), banned *kif* prior to the French takeover (1830),[98] but it was used quite openly under the French. Some French authorities became worried that *kif* was causing insanity. In 1878, a pharmacist studied the situation and recommended that the colony regulate *kif* to reduce its use and educate people about its dangers.[99] No steps were seemingly taken in this direction, and *kif* never became a prominent concern. The administration banned psychoactive cannabis in 1917, part of France's initiative to eliminate drug use throughout its colonial empire.[100] Nonetheless, cannabis remained widespread through the mid-1900s, and the earliest record of hashish production in the Maghreb names Algeria several years after colonial prohibition began.[101] By the late 1900s, the Maghreb's cannabis growers had become Europe's principal suppliers.

Angola's *Liamba* Exports

Slavery's decline posed acute challenges in Angola, where slave trading had dominated commercial activity for centuries. Few Angolans (other than slaves) had interest in ending the trade. Political-economic globalization meant that Angola had no choice but to develop new exports if it wanted to enter foreign markets. Over the 1800s, merchants exported beeswax, ivory, rubber, tobacco, coffee, lumber, sesame seeds, peanuts, cotton, and tree gums, but the colony struggled to generate revenue and burdened the metropolitan economy.[102]

Angolan merchants saw export potential in cannabis. They sought markets by displaying *liamba* at world's fairs in London (1862), Paris (1867 and 1878), Antwerp (1885), and Liverpool (1907).[103] One entrepreneur advertised Angolan *diamba* in Brazil in 1883.[104] Cannabis was well positioned for export development because its existing commercial networks tracked slave-trading routes that extended to potential overseas markets. In 1870, *liamba* was exported from Luanda to French Gabon,[105] and a decade later the colonial government participated via taxation.

Angola's cannabis commerce linked inland growers to coastal markets. Northeastern Angola supplied Luanda and the Lower Congo region, while farmers farther south supplied Benguela, a secondary port that also exported *liamba*.[106] In 1878, a Portuguese expedition to northeastern Angola found cannabis grown as frequently as tobacco; a decade later, another expedition encountered fields of both tobacco and *liamba*.[107] *Liamba* fields were rare; commercial supplies likely came from many growers who each sold a little. One disapproving observer in 1904 generalized that northern Angolan gardens included "always, always, the inevitable . . . *liamba*."[108] Commercial shipments traveled in narrow, conical packets of inflorescences, up to two feet long and four inches in diameter at the base.[109] Smaller packets appeared in markets, tied at one-inch intervals along their whole length; each interval was the amount needed to fill an average pipe bowl.[110]

The colonial government began to tax *liamba* exports by 1880, but published records evince fraud better than trade volume. Only declared exports were documented. Smuggling of all goods was common because the colonial customs system was "absurd, petty, and vexatious" for traders.[111] Bookkeeping was terrible.[112] Traders certainly undervalued their declared exports, because in 1896 customs authorities fixed the taxable value of *liamba*.[113] During 1890–94, Angola exported a greater declared value of *liamba* than of beeswax, peanuts, sesame, or lumber, but less than that of rubber, coffee, tobacco, or ivory.[114] The volume and value of exports was last recorded in 1899, although the fixed value remained active in the Lisbon customs office in 1908.[115]

Angola principally supplied Portuguese São Tomé and French Gabon; Portugal, Britain, and Germany bought very small quantities, too. The cannabis trade to São Tomé supplied slaves on cocoa plantations. These people, mostly from Angola, carried cannabis knowledge from the mainland. In fact, the last published record of the Bena Riamba is an account of a man named Musulu, who was being shipped as a slave to São Tomé. In 1893, Musulu encountered a Belgian traveler while the two sailed from Luanda on a steamship. I quote the Belgian at length because his account illustrates points discussed in preceding chapters:

> Among those shipped from Loanda, . . . a youth . . . attracted my attention. It immediately occurred to me that he might be a Mushi-lange, and I addressed him with *Moyo!* and the other Kishi-lange words I could remember from . . . Pogge's journal. The expression of surprise and pleasure which spread over his face verified . . . my diagnosis. . . . I could fairly well understand his words, and he mine, although I was ignorant of his language and he of all but a few words of Ki-mbundu picked up on the road . . . to Loanda. . . .
>
> Musulu ([which means] river) was the young man's name; his father's, Cidibu; his mother's, Bayimbe. He was a subject of Mukenge

Kalamba.... He had come with a trading party of Bashi-lange to [Ka-sange town in north-central Angola]. Being unable to walk from a sore foot, his countrymen left him there in charge of Mbanza Kambolo ka Kitamba, a Ki-mbangala chieftain and trader.... This man-stealer sold his guest to a white trader of Malange [town] (for about $15) who resold him to the agent of a S. Thomé plantation (for about $70).... He is only one among the thousands who work as semi-slaves in the houses or plantations of refined white men, without hope of regaining their liberty or ever revisiting their homes.[116]

Musulu carried cannabis knowledge with him, though not necessarily seeds. The conditions he experienced in 1893 differed from those that transatlantic slaves had encountered in prior centuries. However, the people-cannabis relationship persisted, the only difference being that Angola kept records on exported plants as well as people. In 1893, Luanda's customs house recorded 537.25 kilograms of *liamba* exports, generating the measly equivalent of one pound sterling in taxes.[117] This minuscule declared income was a direct benefit to the colonial state of maintaining a labor-drug relationship that arose under chattel slavery.

Exports to French Gabon relied on general consumer demand, not just laborers. Gabon first published records of *liamba* imports in 1884. Unfortu-nately, colonial statistics lumped leaf tobacco and *liamba* in a single category, separate from cigars, cigarettes, and packaged tobacco.[118] Europeans valued leaf tobacco and cannabis only for trading. Tobacco leaves were a basic unit of exchange in French Gabon and Spanish Guinea.[119] Europeans disdained the leaves but smoked them when in need.[120] Gabon's colonial government entered cannabis commerce in 1884 via an import duty on the leaf-tobacco-and-*liamba* category.[121] The duty endured until at least 1903.[122]

It is impossible to extract cannabis from the combined statistical category. Leaf tobacco was more important, and the numbers primarily reflect its value. In 1890, leaf-tobacco-and-*liamba* was the colony's fifth-most-valuable import, behind cloth, clothing, rifles, and copper ingots.[123] The reported value, equiva-lent to £4,684, far exceeded Angola's declared exports of £2 of cannabis and £4 of tobacco to non-Portuguese territories.[124] The closest the two sets of records seem to come is for 1891, when Angola's declared exports to non-Portuguese ports included 910 kilograms of *liamba* and no tobacco.[125] The Gabonese per-spective was that, in the second quarter 1891, 3,129 kilograms of leaf-tobacco-and-*liamba* was imported from Portuguese territories.[126] Gabon's statistics are certainly more accurate, meaning that the intercolonial trade for 1891 might have been as high as 12,000 kilograms of *liamba*.

The *liamba* trade to São Tomé seemed substantial to historic observers, but imports were even more poorly documented than Angolan exports. Angolan records from 1884 to 1898 show that 65 percent of exports with stated destinations—more than 6,500 kilograms—went to unspecified Portuguese possessions; in the Portuguese colonies, cannabis smoking was documented only in São Tomé and Angola. Colonial authorities had identified *liamba* on São Tomé by 1869, when plantation workers smoked it.[127] These workers harvested weedy volunteer plants, so there was potential for higher-quality imports. Laborers continued to use it through the end of the century.[128] The last Angolan data come from 1899, when a Belgian diplomat reported 817 kilograms exported from Luanda to São Tomé.[129]

São Tomé's colonial government never reported any imports. It's improbable that Angola's declared exports were entirely snuck onto the islands. A hint that the administration knew about imports came when a public health study in 1901 contrasted the smaller Príncipe Island with the larger São Tomé. *Liamba* "does not exist" on Príncipe, stated the report, "nor [is it] an import article."[130] Cannabis was not outlawed on the islands until 1911, but decades earlier plantation bosses thought the plant drug damaged the health of laborers.[131] The colony's post-abolition society was supposed to provide a salubrious environment for nominally free Africans to become productive laborers. An officially drug-free economy supported São Tomé's self-portrayal as a healthy, productive setting for indentured servants.

Angola's export trade fell victim to health concerns. The colony's 1913 prohibition law stated that "'Riamba' or 'Liamba' . . . contributes to degeneration of the race, [and] debilitation of the native." Its prohibition reflected "the great advisability of . . . restricting the native customs that are absolutely harmful to them."[132] (The law also sought to increase tobacco production and allowed cannabis to be grown "for industrial ends.") The attitude that *liamba* causes illness had already shaped Angola's cannabis economy. In 1904, the inchoate black market in Cabinda (Angola's northernmost port) was linked explicitly to trypanosomiasis:

> [Since cannabis] smoke makes the smoker rapidly useless or, at least, seems to dispose him to more easily contract sleeping sickness, [the] leading natives convey support to the propaganda of the Europeans against this terrible habit. [For this reason] the plant is rarely cultivated, and . . . only very secretively and in the smallest quantities; the major part of *liamba* is trafficked from Loanda, [in] narrow packages that, in small portions and quite in secret, are distributed to the fanciers known to the importer.[133]

Similar health concerns closed Angola's external markets, although legal prohibitions came years after formal trading ended. São Tomé outlawed cannabis in 1911 to protect laborers.[134] The French Central African market technically stayed open until 1926 because earlier laws were not specific enough.[135] French colonial laws from 1916 and 1918 had weak effects because magistrates didn't know whether the French term *haschisch* in the laws was the same thing as *diamba*.[136] Colonial attitudes were clearer than laws written in Paris. In 1907, French Congo's governor ordered his administration to stamp out the (fully legal) plant drug and described *diamba* selling as "criminal profiteering" from a "public poisoning" that was "expanding each day."[137] One observer in Gabon claimed that villages had been entirely depopulated by the plant drug.[138]

For Portuguese Angola's government, formal economic benefits of *liamba* declined rapidly after 1900 as its political costs rose because of regional concerns about sleeping sickness. Official discourse after prohibition maintained that cannabis damaged labor. In 1929, the colonial public health service advised that it was "the sharp black" who informed on growers and spread the word that *liamba* was "a poison invented, in olden times, . . . to destroy enemies who [from smoking would] wast[e] away, to the point that . . . they could poorly defend their fields, huts, and families."[139] This portrayal contradicted the documented history of *liamba*, which had been a drug sanctioned by colonial elites and authorities to enhance the performance of laborers.

Mozambique's Cannabis Trades

The other formal market in Portuguese Africa was barely documented. In 1904, British consuls reported that Mozambique had begun exporting to Transvaal, a British colony that entered the Union of South Africa in 1910.[140] In that year, 129,000 kilograms crossed the border. The trade declined precipitously, to just 90 kilograms in 1910 and 52 kilograms in 1913, the last year of British records.[141] The only published Portuguese statistics show 6,000 kilograms exported in 1913 and 16,000 kilograms exported in 1914.[142] The British consuls reported exports only to Transvaal; the Mozambican source reported trade only to Zanzibar, Germany, and Britain. These were two separate trades.

The Transvaal trade disappeared probably because local producers undersold imports. In 1904, *dagga* grew in gardens "in almost every town and village in the Transvaal," and it was "carefully preserved" wherever found growing as a weed.[143] To estimate market conditions for Mozambican imports, compare the situation documented in Cape Town in 1921. *Dagga* was illegal there, but pharmacies legally sold inflorescences in the form of herbal cannabis indica from British India. (More accurately, pharmaceutical sales were technically illegal but openly tolerated.) Yet few pharmacies stocked it because there was no demand. Pharmaceutical-grade herbal cannabis was low quality from the perspective of expert *dagga* smokers. Further, cannabis grew everywhere in the Cape, and locals "knew the plant quite well and understood how to treat and prepare the leaf."[144] Mozambican *soruma* was better than pharmaceutical imports, but not so much better than cheap, local supplies to sustain the cost of importing. The market experienced an immediate and massive crash. If the British statistics are correct, imports dropped more than 99.9 percent from year one to year five.[145]

Mozambique's formal markets closed also because legality changed. The only Portuguese statistics were published in the past tense: "exportation [of *soruma*] greatly increased in 1914. Now [1915] it will be none due to the prohibition of [*soruma*] farming."[146] Prohibition came abruptly, likely spurred by São Tomé's and Angola's laws. Anti-cannabis sentiments were earlier present, and enforcement may have been swiftly apparent. Less than a year into prohibition, growers were hiding their plants in patches of tall grass. According to the law, "The plant known in the kaffir manner as *bangue* or *soruma*" caused "apathy and imbecility."[147] It was farmed widely in Mozambique, though it evidently was nowhere a major crop.[148] Portuguese colonists had tried growing opium in the 1870s,[149] but no sources suggest they dealt in cannabis.

The separate colonies that formed the Union of South Africa in 1910 managed cannabis individually before banding together. Natal banned *ganja* in 1870, the Orange Free State banned *dagga* in 1903, and Transvaal imported *soruma* from 1905 to 1913.[150] Cape Colony's 1891 pharmacy control act became the foundation of drug-control laws in the Union of South Africa.[151] Neither pharmaceutical cannabis nor *dagga* was listed in the 1891 act or its amendments.[152] However, in 1904 the Cape Colony administration announced its intent to consider "Cannabis Sativa and its preparations Dagga, Ganj, and Churrus" a poison under the terms of the 1891 law.[153] Pharmacists were immediately concerned that the administration technically outlawed pharmaceutical cannabis indica by defining *dagga* as *Cannabis*. Yet cannabis did not disappear from pharmacies; nor did *dagga* disappear from work sites. Buyers of Mozambican *soruma* in Transvaal were likely miners, whose on-the-job smoking was tolerated by mine owners.[154] Many Mozambicans migrated to the mines just after 1900,[155] so their usual supply may merely have followed for a time.

Pharmacy control was one political imperative leading toward prohibition. Another motive was labor control. Natal's law of 1870 banned *ganja* specifically among Indian laborers; the plant drug remained legal for everyone else.[156]

Other imperatives came from fear that *dagga* produced crime and immorality.[157] Some missionaries considered smoking sinful long before formal drug-control laws were enacted.[158] Fears of cannabis were heightened by the belief that *dagga* smoking was expanding and a sign of social deterioration. "In the olden days, only men of mature age were allowed to drink beer and to smoke Indian hemp. Quite small boys do both these things nowadays, and the old people are powerless to prevent them," judged an outsider.[159] Age was salient in labor-related attitudes toward *dagga*. At the end of the 1800s, Southern African authorities (i.e., older men) often characterized herders (i.e., younger men) as smokers. Chewa elders in Malawi and Afrikaner bosses alike sought to prevent their hired herders from smoking.[160] Zulu and Ronga adults tried unsuccessfully to keep pipes away from young men.[161] Settler society feared *dagga*-induced violence. When prohibition came to the Cape in 1904, a physician in support testified that "crime is rampant in the country because of the effects of *Dagga capensis* on the niggers' brains."[162] This discourse reinforced Whites' fears of Black men, who were most visible as miners, farm workers, and day laborers. Physicians and pharmacists mostly did not agree—they considered alcohol a bigger problem—but the association of crime, cannabis, and race was lodged in public discourse. Cannabis symbolized social problems to many White South Africans as the twentieth century unfolded.[163]

The political costs of *dagga* outweighed its meager direct economic benefits to the state or elites in general. Pharmaceutical sales generated some tax revenues, but racial fears were prominent in many people's daily lives. The politics of *dagga* made the Union of South Africa the driving force that caused cannabis to appear in the 1925 opium convention.[164] The country's black market in *dagga* has since been robust.

Britain's Global *Ganja*

Before 1925, Great Britain controlled the world's largest cannabis markets: the one in colonial India and the global pharmaceutical trade that depended on Indian exports. These markets were intertwined, their shared history shaped conjointly by the expertise of colonial consumers and the ignorance of Western pharmacists.

The pharmaceutical trade flourished briefly during the last decades of the nineteenth century. Western awareness of pharmaceutical cannabis dawned in 1840, after William O'Shaughnessy, a physician stationed in Calcutta (now Kolkata), published results showing its promise in treating muscle spasms associated with tetanus.[165] Physicians principally used three categories of cannabis pharmaceuticals. Extracts (and tinctures) were adopted first, following O'Shaughnessy's precedent. Doctors sometimes mixed their own, but pharmacists and then pharmaceutical companies increasingly sold premade medicines intended to treat a wide range of conditions. By 1860, pharmaceutical cigarettes of cannabis, datura, and belladonna were available for asthmatics. Smoke from these plant drugs can treat some lung complaints. Asthma cigarettes were the first form of smokable cannabis available in many locations worldwide.[166] Finally, toward the end of the century, pharmacists made corn plasters in which cannabis was merely a green colorant.

In contrast, when Britain took control of India in 1757, South Asia's cannabis economy was already millennia old. Cannabis drug production was a sophisticated industry, with specialized workers, colony-wide marketing systems, and choosy consumers with regionally varying tastes.[167] Bengal—encompassing modern India's West Bengal State and the country of Bangladesh—was known for its *ganja*, while the best *charas* (hashish) came from the mid-elevation Himalayas in northeastern India and neighboring areas across India's borders. *Bhang* (the plant) was feral across the subcontinent, but farmed *bhang* was associated especially with central India, around the city of Khandwa. *Bhang* was taxed in precolonial times, and the small Portuguese territories on the western coast—such as Goa—collected revenue on it starting in the 1500s.[168] In British India, the revenue stream grew in importance over the 1800s. Nonetheless, people in Britain and administrators in India grew concerned about the public health effects of cannabis drug use in the colony, leading the government to appoint the fact-finding Indian Hemp Drugs Commission (IHDC).[169] The IHDC report, published 1893, remains the most thorough study of cannabis in any society.[170]

The global pharmaceutical market represented an interface between colonial and international plant economies. Colonial authorities controlled cannabis prices through internal taxes and export duties. Global market prices varied depending on colonial tax policies, as well as dynamics in London's market for medicinal plants and pharmaceutical chemicals. Private trading in cannabis probably began around 1840, when O'Shaughnessy brought back enough herbal material from India for a colleague to make a batch of extract.[171] Wholesale prices were first published in 1886, when the trade journal *Chemist and Druggist* began reporting public auction results. Until 1925, cannabis appeared irregularly in these reports.

British traders were not knowledgeable about psychoactive cannabis. London trading focused on cannabis "tops," meaning inflorescences at the ends of stalks—*ganja*, by another name.[172] Lots were informally graded good, fair, ordinary, or poor, and other descriptors were common. Some seemingly related to the state of preservation: green, brown, gray, bright, and dull.[173] "Dusty" tops were probably inflorescences whose dried, resin-bearing hairs had broken off, with some adhering loosely to the plant material. Dusty tops were likely unpredictable. Inflorescences that have lost resin-bearing hairs have lost THC, although some dusty stuff may have gained hairs from other plants. "Stalky" tops had a large proportion of stems to inflorescences. "Herb" was leaves. In addition to tops, herb, and stalks, traders dealt "siftings" and "dust," loose material collected from shipping containers or during processing. Low-quality material was commonly sold in the London market. Traders who bought bales of "brown siftings" (1887), "very stalky and dusty grey [tops]" (1889), or "brown [tops], partly perished and partly with stalks" (1909) likely concocted weak medicines.[174] Seemingly poor lots received only slightly lower prices, if they were discounted at all. In August 1887, "stalk[s] with a small proportion of leaves" sold for twice as much as "very common stalky and dusty tops."[175] In 1902, siftings were sometimes one-third less valuable than tops but sometimes sold for the same price. Pharmacists measured only the weight of plant material when making extracts and sometimes chose one lot over another because they thought it would impart a desirable color to their concoctions.[176]

European buyers along the whole supply chain had no knowledge base on which to evaluate raw material. During the entire pharmaceutical market, scientists—let alone traders—didn't know how to estimate reliably the psychoactive potential of herbal material or hashish, despite numerous theories.[177] They sometimes didn't even know how to make the plain herbal drug, thinking that "the leaf" became potent through a process "similar to that used in the manufacture of tobacco, though less elaborate."[178] Pharmacists sometimes found potent herb, for sure. Daredevils in Europe, North America, and Australia wrote about what happened when they drank more than a recommended dosage of extract.[179] A few pharmacists detailed their experiences for their peers in trade journals.[180] However, many more complained about the unreliable plant drug. Pharmaceutical cannabis declined in the West because pharmacists did not know how to produce consistently potent preparations.[181] By 1894 pharmaceutical cannabis had already lost its popularity in Western medicine.[182] In 1902, British pharmacists theorized that American companies were buying tops in London, keeping the "physiologically active" ones, and re-exporting the remainder back to Britain.[183] This theory reflected poorly on British knowledge and overestimated American know-how. In 1917, American pharmacists concluded that "a standard and efficient Cannabis extract is unlikely, to say the least," because they had no way to evaluate herbal material.[184]

Sellers in India took advantage of unknowledgeable buyers. Most notably, THC deteriorates with age. Cannabis tops were harvested from February to April in India but available year-round in Europe.[185] Very rarely did seemingly fresh material appear in London, such as "new . . . , good bright quality" tops in May 1890.[186] People in Bengal considered *ganja* that was a year old impotent; if it was more than two years old, it was judged worthless. Old material that had been stored for one, two, three, or more years was nonetheless shipped to Britain. By 1894, some pharmacists recognized the problem of staleness, but it was never resolved.[187] In 1925, as cannabis trading ended, a retrospective in *Chemist and Druggist* acknowledged, "One of the reasons cannabis Indica is so unsatisfactory a drug is that the natives know that it soon deteriorates on keeping, and consequently the current year's produce is retained for home use, and only the previous year exported." And to exhibit the state of British knowledge, the trade journal's editors concluded: "It is difficult to understand why the dried and coarsely powdered upper leaves are so largely used in most subtropical countries for smoking purposes as a stimulant, as they are in Morocco under the name of 'kief'; in South Africa, as 'dagga'; in India, as 'bhang'; and in Arabia as 'hashish.'"[188] The Western pharmaceutical cannabis industry failed because it didn't learn from the world's most knowledgeable producers and consumers.

Colonial cannabis consumers were very knowledgeable, not just in India but around the world. People at the Cape in 1921 didn't buy legal (rather, tolerated) cannabis in pharmacies because illegal, local *dagga* was better. Indian laborers in Guiana, Trinidad, and elsewhere tapped the same supply as London's traders but called it *ganja* rather than tops. An anonymous "Pharmaceutical Resident" published a remarkable account of *ganja* (and opium) commerce in British Guiana in 1893.[189] Indian laborers demanded *ganja* that was "sticky with gum and strong smelling" and would "hardly look at the ordinary qualities sent out from English drug-houses."[190] The material that initially dominated the London market was "Bengal ganja" exported through Bombay (now Mumbai). However, by 1898 "Khandwa ganja"—also called "Bombay"—had become dominant.[191] In India, Khandwa was less appreciated than Bengal.[192] It was thus cheaper and preferentially selected for export by merchants who retained the better stuff for the domestic market.[193] High taxes in Bengal state further increased the price difference between Bengal and Khandwa *ganja*. A British botanist estimated that non-Bengal *ganja* sold for one-twentieth the price and recommended in 1887 that "chemists desirous of making the very best extract of Indian hemp [should] pay full price for Bengal 'Ganja' [imported] from Calcutta [not] Bombay."[194] Nonetheless, "Bombay tops" remained the standard in public wholesale auctions.

Ganja means pistillate inflorescences, but it also refers to cured and processed products made from inflorescences. The material exported to London was "flat *ganja*," dried in layers between mats.[195] Other products were more valuable in India—particularly "round *ganja*" and "*chur*"[196]—because the plant material was more manicured, trimmed of leaves and stems. In 1886, the most valuable business for European exporters operating in India was "to supply [round ganja] to the Coolie markets of the West Indies"; flat *ganja* was considered inferior.[197] In 1898, a British pharmacist in India recommended that round *ganja* should replace flat in the pharmaceutical market,[198] but flat *ganja* remained the standard. The retrospective published in 1925 in *Chemist and Druggist* noted that round *ganja* "sometimes finds its way to London, [but] it is usually re-exported to [Guiana] and Trinidad, where it is purchased by the coolies."[199] Both British and Dutch Guiana also imported directly from India, presumably round *ganja*.[200]

The international *ganja* segment developed after the pharmaceutical segment. *Ganja* buying started before 1861, when Guiana's colonial administration first tried to suppress it through import and sales restrictions.[201] Other colonies that received indentured laborers similarly enacted early controls, including the British colonies Natal (1870), Trinidad (by 1882), and Mauritius (by 1898), and Dutch Guiana (1908).[202] The Pharmaceutical Resident in Guiana in 1893 pointed out that these, "like many other laws, had any number of loopholes."[203] The main dealers in Guiana, and probably elsewhere, were commercial pharmacists who could bring controlled substances into the market. The main risk for *ganja*/tops sellers was that existing stock would be sharply discounted, or even unsaleable, if a fresher shipment arrived.[204] Pharmacists could import as much cannabis (and opium) as they wanted if they paid the import duty. They were, however, prohibited from selling more than 0.65 grams of cannabis (and 0.32 grams of opium) to one person during any twenty-four-hour period and had to record buyers' names and quantities for all sales.[205] It was plainly impossible for any pharmacist in Guiana to sell hundreds of kilograms of *ganja* (or opium) per month at less than one gram per person per day. Pharmacists falsified their records or presented records in Chinese or Hindi to befuddle law enforcement. Dealers kept limited stock on hand in the store and hid the bulk of their supply to reduce the risks of a drug bust at the pharmacy. Drug busts were rare, though. The anonymous Pharmaceutical Resident proposed that authorities went along with the pharmaceutical sales charade because they valued the revenue generated from import duties.

Colonial pharmacists had better knowledge of cannabis than their metropolitan peers, and a better business. The Pharmaceutical Resident boasted of making £400–£500 in a fortnight, though he lamented that by 1893 competition had slashed profits. I have not located retail prices for pharmaceutical tops in Guiana or elsewhere, but pharmacists marked it up, perhaps a half-pound sterling per kilogram, according to the Pharmaceutical Resident. In Trinidad, a traveler reported in 1895 that *ganja* sold for the equivalent of £1.76 per kilogram, but he was referring to locally grown plants, not pharmaceutical imports.[206] His point was that the *ganja* business was profitable. In 1885, Trinidad's colonial government attempted to stifle the drug crop by requiring an annual farming license that cost £100 per acre (or any part thereof).[207] The licensing law was ineffective.[208] Trinidadian growers could clear £500 in profit per acre even after paying the license fee. Further, some Indian immigrants grew *ganja* in Venezuela and smuggled it back to Trinidad to avoid paying official taxes and fees.[209] Imported pharmaceutical tops may have been cheaper, but local produce was probably better.

Published pharmaceutical cannabis prices were steady through the 1890s but rose starting in 1900. The rise was due to tax increases in India.[210] In addition, the British home government collected fees on imports, exports, and sales. In 1900, traders viewed export duties as an inconvenience when they wanted to clear domestic stocks to improve auction prices.[211] Thus, stale Indian stock that had languished on British shelves was passed on to other countries. Fraud likely affected prices, too. *Chemist and Druggist* alleged that sellers colluded and that speculators tried to raise prices by starting rumors of new Indian taxes.[212] By withholding stocks in the hope of better prices, speculators contributed to the staleness problem.

Although the global commerce favored Britain, colonial contexts offered entry for others. In Guiana, Chinese pharmacists were dealing *ganja* by the 1880s, cutting into the profits of British druggists.[213] Published data from 1883, 1885, and 1891 agree that approximately 5,000 kilograms came into the colony each year.[214] Guiana-based traders re-exported *ganja* to the British West Indies and Dutch Guiana, although published data are incomplete and do not agree among intercolonial trade partners. British Guiana reported shipping 2,500 kilograms to the West Indies in 1883 and 30 kilograms to Dutch Guiana in 1903.[215] The Dutch colony reported imports during 1894–1910, mostly without provenance. Some came from the Netherlands and some from Great Britain, but most came from British Guiana (several hundred kilograms reported for 1894 and 1907).[216]

African colonies were unsuccessful in the global pharmaceutical trade. Pharmacists were unsure whether "Indian hemp" not grown in India had any pharmaceutical value. European markets were nonetheless receptive to new supply sources. Angola exported 16 kilograms of *liamba* to Germany in 1890, 924 kilograms to England in 1891, and 280 kilograms to Portugal in 1892 and 1894 combined.[217] The post-1900 pharmaceutical cannabis price rise offered opportunity, but African exports barely entered Europe. Madagascar-grown cannabis was available in Germany by 1908 but never prominent.[218] Portuguese Mozambique had the most promise because its exports increased in 1913 and 1914, when the outbreak of World War I caused drug prices to spike.[219] Mozambique sold 16,000 kilograms to Germany, England, and Zanzibar in 1914, just as the colonial administration outlawed it.[220] British India continued to dominate the pharmaceutical market after the war, although other places started producing the drug—notably the United States. "Cannabis americana" was first advertised in *Chemist and Druggist* in 1917,[221] and by 1925 Britain had also imported some from northern France.[222] None of these provenances appeared in London's public auction reports and thus were sold privately or re-exported.[223]

(An aside: the American and French pharmaceutical imports were derived from East Asian *Cannabis indica* varieties bred for fiber production.[224] European and North American hemp producers shifted to this seed stock in the last half of the 1800s, because these varieties outperformed European *sativa* varieties. There is no evidence that hemp farmers acquired seeds from India or any other place where cannabis was grown specifically for psychoactive drug production. The East Asian origins of the new plant populations were forgotten, and they received names such as "Kentucky hemp" instead. In 1869, an American physician determined that extracts made from "Kentucky hemp" produced effects identical to extracts made from "Indian hemp" and recognized that domestic pharmaceutical cannabis could replace imports.[225] Decades later, when industrial hemp had foundered, the U.S. Department of Agriculture tried to help farmers by publishing instructions for producing pharmaceutical cannabis.[226] Consequently, during World War I, the United States had the capacity to replace British Indian imports unavailable due to the war. The only hint that Americans discovered how to smoke these *indica* fiber cultivars is a rumor, published 1944, that "old persons in Kentucky report seeing colored field hands break up and load their pipes with dried flowering tops of the plant and smoke them. There was never the slightest suspicion that this procedure caused abnormal behavior."[227] These field hands were not slaves; slavery had ended eighty years before. However, industrial hemp fieldwork was unpopular with free laborers worldwide.[228] In the antebellum United States, hemp was a slave occupation, and after emancipation, it was the job of semi-free workers, such as sharecroppers. If they did discover cannabis smoking, they joined many other laborers in using the plant drug. Now, back to British pharmaceuticals.)

Even British African colonies found little success in the market. Trading began in 1888 with a bale of "green dust, very seedy" from South Africa, which was offered in London but withdrawn before auction.[229] African lots did not appear again at auction for two decades, and they were not heralded then. "The market has been flooded with large quantities from Zanzibar, which do not find favour here," reported *Chemist and Druggist* in December 1907. "Such parcels can only be used for adulteration, and do not enter into competition with the Bombay product."[230] Nonetheless, when East African lots appeared at auction the following summer, a higher proportion sold than Bombay lots, although the highest price for African tops was one-tenth the lowest prices for Bombay. "African" lots—presumably from Zanzibar—appeared irregularly until 1925 but were disfavored. In November 1911, one auction included material from Bombay, Zanzibar, and, for the first time, Portuguese Goa, but only the African lot carried results from a chemical analysis meant to show its potency, information never previously published for any lot.[231] In 1923, East African cannabis reached its highest price ever, equal to the price for Bombay tops in 1906. Cannabis from Cape Town appeared at auction in 1919, Goa material appeared once more in 1914, and neither was as valuable as Bombay.

Perhaps cannabis from Zanzibar, the Cape, and Goa sold cheaply because it was poor quality. Perhaps, like contemporaneous Indians, people in those places sold what they didn't want, and by the end of the pharmaceutical market British buyers had gained knowledge of cannabis quality. Sale lots were more consistently tops in the last decade of auctions, with herb, stalks, siftings, and dust less common than before. Yet even with price increases and possible improvements in quality, pharmaceutical cannabis had little value because fewer and fewer pharmacists used it.

In the first decades of the twentieth century, Great Britain was hesitant to support international drug controls because cannabis and opium were valuable to the colonial Indian treasury. Yet political pressures mounted at home and abroad. Administrators in India and officials in the former colonies Egypt and South Africa grew concerned with the public-health effects of cannabis; in negotiations leading to the Geneva opium convention the United States gave support to Egypt and South Africa, although it lacked concern about cannabis itself.[232] In 1925, Great Britain finally agreed with other countries that pharmaceutical cannabis was a poison that should be controlled.[233] The costs of denying this had finally outweighed the benefits. India's domestic market was spared under the 1925 accord, but legal exports were mostly halted.

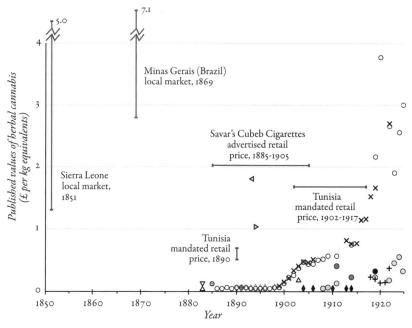

FIGURE 9.3. Value indexes for historical cannabis markets. Graphic by Chris S. Duvall.

The Economic Logic of Global Prohibition

Cannabis prohibition was a fundamentally political process in which one perspective on the plant drug was privileged in the negotiations preceding the 1925 opium convention. Yet prohibition was not purely political; it reflected economic considerations, too. The economic logic of prohibition was an unintended outcome of the collective decision to include psychoactive cannabis in Europe's colonial project. The imperative was to extract value from the drug plant as one among many exploitable resources.

Many governments levied taxes on colonial cannabis markets, but taxes within British India governed pharmaceutical cannabis prices worldwide. The inadvertently global influence of colonial Indian taxes reflected the several advantages India had in terms of cannabis production. It had the capacity to supply large quantities of the plant drug inexpensively. Value indexes before 1900 suggest this advantage.

Wholesale prices in India were lower than the reported values of exports from Angola and Mozambique, which are the most comparable data I have found, although they include the cost of exporting. (And Angola's statistics probably include significantly underreported values.) Wholesale prices in London always exceeded Indian prices, exhibiting the costs of bringing cannabis to market in Britain. Further, London prices were lower than the few import values reported elsewhere, including in Gabon and British Guiana (although these data likely represent valuation before entry into wholesale and retail markets). Prior to 1900, India and London could undersell other producers. Expectedly, the highest pre-1900 values were associated with re-export markets (especially Dutch Guiana); value-added retail products (e.g., Tunisian *takrūri*); and locations where cannabis was likely new and supplies were sparse (e.g., Sierra Leone in 1851, Dutch Guiana in 1883, and, perhaps, Minas Gerais in 1866).

After 1900, though, London prices for Indian cannabis continually rose. Value indexes in other markets did not, except for markets, such as the United States, that were closely tied to the London market. London prices rose because taxes in India rose.[234] These taxes produced colonial government revenues but were also intended to reduce *ganja* consumption by increasing prices.[235] In contrast, Tunisian colonial governments controlled the market by limiting supplies, not by reducing demand; for decades, the price of five-gram packets of *takrūri* remained steady.[236] In India, administrators repeatedly raised *ganja* taxes. They decided the market could sustain price increases because *ganja* was generally cheaper than presumed comparable quantities of *charas*, distilled alcohol, and opium.[237] The government's goal was to maximize revenue, not simply via higher taxes, but also by making colony-wide retail prices more uniform to reduce smuggling from provinces with low-cost *ganja* to those with costlier cannabis. At the same time, British attitudes toward cannabis deteriorated. Many believed that its drug use led to insanity, violence, and physical wasting, yet the widespread, widely used drug plant was impossible to eliminate. Supply-control strategies, such as the monopolies established in Tunisia and Morocco, were not feasible, leaving demand-side price control the obvious option. The complementary desires to generate revenue and reduce cannabis use pushed costs up in India, and ultimately doomed the pharmaceutical market by raising the plant drug's price above what buyers were willing to pay.

Over time, pharmacists and physicians grew distrustful of cannabis indica. "For some reason the drug [is] of uncertain strength and reliability," reported a doctor in 1912. "It has an unenviable reputation for not doing what is expected of it."[238] The quality and effects of the plant drug varied for several reasons.[239] Cannabis chemistry depends on agricultural factors, including soil fertility, crop management, plant genetics, and processing practices. Pharmaceutical markets offered a continually varying supply of plants grown in unknowable places and conditions within India, even though pharmacists wanted a chemical standard. Standardized compounding formulas were published in national pharmacopeias, but neither the plant nor commercial networks complied with the desire for uniformity.

The pharmaceutical market reflected the presumption that Western science was superior to Indigenous knowledge in assaying the quality of psychoactive cannabis. European bias against Indigenous cannabis knowledge is widely rooted. In 1803 and 1804, for example, Portuguese in Angola considered *diamba* a "terrible and disastrous" use of "*canhâmo*," meaning European cannabis varieties bred for fiber production; British in South Africa complained that "common hemp" was squandered as a "substitute for tobacco"; and Europeans in Brazil and India tried unsuccessfully to make rope from *Cannabis indica* drug cultivars.[240] During the pharmaceutical market, observers dismissed Indigenous cannabis drug uses as debauchery and failed to learn from extensive human experience. Consequently, Western pharmacists had almost no knowledge of quality control.

Historical assays were unreliable. Cannabinoid chemistry was unknown until the 1960s. Animal testing of extracts became common after 1900, but the methods, even then, were obviously subjective and unlikely to yield meaningful data:[241]

> It is necessary in selecting the test animals to pick out those that are easily susceptible to the action of cannabis, since the dogs as well as human beings vary considerably in their reactions to the drug. . . . The degree of accuracy with which the test is carried out will depend largely upon the experience and care exercised by the observer. [Further, when] standardizing cannabis [individual] dogs cannot be used indefinitely [because] they become so accustomed to the effects of the drug that they refuse to stand . . . and so do not show the typical incoordination which is the most characteristic and constant action of the drug.[242]

Decades later, assay methods remained arbitrary. In 1968, the first modern biomedical study of the plant drug's effects determined drug strength via animal testing: the researchers asked "chronic users" to smoke test material and rate it before it was administered to test subjects.[243] Had nineteenth-century pharmacists similarly built on the knowledge of chronic users—in India, South Africa, Angola, Gabon, Morocco, Egypt, Brazil, Guyana, Jamaica, Mexico, or elsewhere—they would have had a better chance of achieving consistently high-quality preparations.

Pharmaceutical cannabis was not valueless in 1925 even though it had been unreliable for decades. Yet the increasing price of pharmaceutical cannabis hindered sales after 1900, and lower-cost supplies never replaced Indian tops in the London market. New sources were severely hampered because Western society had constructed psychoactive cannabis as an Indian thing. This social construction—"Indian hemp"—produced strong brand loyalty, expressed in views that provenance was a primary indicator of a plant's pharmaceutical potential. The dog study quoted earlier was meant to test whether "one must employ the true Cannabis from India, in order to obtain physiological activity."[244] The lack of reliable assays strengthened loyalty to the imagined "Indian hemp" brand. The low values of Zanzibar, Cape, and Goa tops in London—and of domestic tops sold on the New York market—show how provenance affected cannabis prices.

Again, though, Zanzibar, Cape, and Goa tops might have been inexpensive because they were low quality. Colonial governance produced quality problems. First, by denigrating or outlawing specific Indigenous products, colonial regimes inhibited their own cannabis-production capacities. The people who successfully brought Zanzibar, Cape, and Goa tops to the London market were doubtless European businessmen intent on entering the pharmaceutical market rather than people knowledgeable about producing effective cannabis indica under some other name. Second, merchants in India, and likely elsewhere, took advantage of colonialist ignorance by selling cannabis that had little value to more knowledgeable consumers. By privileging local buyers over exporters, these merchants were resisting the socioeconomic structure imposed by colonial governance.[245] Further, colonial participants in the global market took advantage of colonial trade rules. Consumers avoided imports for better and cheaper local products; pharmacists discovered that tops were more valuable as *ganja*; and smokers found pharmaceutical *ganja* acceptable when other supplies were not available. The plant resisted governance as well, because it colonized new landscapes despite import restrictions, thus enabling people to grow their own and avoid taxed and controlled sales. Import substitution happened in the United

States during World War I because East Asian cultivars grew there readily, and because these cultivars maintained THC-dominant chemistry despite millennia of breeding for fiber and seed production. Import substitution doomed pharmaceutical *ganja* at the Cape and Mozambican *soruma* in Transvaal and perhaps made British Guiana's re-export trade to the West Indies and Dutch Guiana short-lived.

Psychoactive cannabis had a colonial economic geography. Europeans controlled market conditions and monopolized value-added segments. Colonies exported raw materials and were desired as markets for European manufactured products. Retail prices suggest the income possible from value-added markets. In 1884, herbal cannabis retailed in Britain at three times the first published wholesale price, from 1886.[246] The U.S. herbal retail price in 1913 was about eighty times the export value in Mozambique; some Mozambican material may have made it to America via Britain. Of the pharmaceutical preparations, it's possible to estimate a value index only for cigarettes. Cannabis composed a fraction of the contents of asthma cigarettes—one-sixth, in one analysis.[247] However, for illustration, if the cigarettes were entirely cannabis, retail value greatly exceeded wholesale prices. The main British brand, Savar's Cubeb Cigarettes, sold in bulk for 24 shillings for thirty-six dozen cigarettes, an equivalent of £2 per kilogram of cannabis, many times the wholesale price.[248] I don't know who smoked asthma cigarettes. They were advertised in newspapers worldwide and were marketed at least briefly to Indian laborers. A collector's card from the 1890s from Grimault's Indian Cigarettes, a French brand, is written in Bangla (the language of Bengal) and includes a picture of Shiva, a Hindi deity associated with cannabis for at least two thousand years.[249] Knowledgeable consumers certainly tried the cigarettes, but pharmaceutical tops were a better deal. Homegrown *ganja* was even better.

Colonial governance, arrogant faith in Western science, and the failure of pharmacy practice all combined to make cannabis a low-value commodity in the global pharmaceutical market by 1925, notwithstanding high wholesale prices. Participants in the negotiations preceding the International Opium Convention of 1925 perceived low economic costs and high political benefits of including cannabis in their agreement.

Nonetheless, cannabis remained more beneficial than costly to many people who were excluded from those negotiations. Many of these people had robust knowledge of cannabis as a crop and as a pharmacological agent; the exclusion of their knowledge helped doom the pharmaceutical market. In contrast, the markets that supplied high-quality psychoactive cannabis remained robust after 1925, even though they became illegal and were transformed by illegality. Decades of prohibition have shrouded the roots of today's black markets, but these markets are rooted in specific, mostly non-Western histories of people-plant interaction. Any economic value psychoactive cannabis has today has come from these long histories, not from the plant drug's brief heyday in Victorian pharmacies.

TEN

Rethinking Marijuana

Cannabis prohibitions are mostly exogenous to Africa, even if societies there had varying opinions about the plant drug and rules and norms that limited its use. Central Africans resisted cannabis prohibitions when they were first enacted.[1] Continued farming and use, there and elsewhere, constitutes continued resistance.[2] African cannabis cultures and agricultures persist as transformed through a century of prohibition.[3]

Colonial controls on cannabis in Africa were early and strict in global terms and targeted specific social and cultural groups. Its listing in the International Opium Convention of 1925 began with the request of South Africa's White minority government supported by newly postcolonial Egypt, where authorities since 1868 had suppressed cannabis to control laborers.[4] Other early laws were aimed at indentured Indian laborers in Mauritius, South Africa, Trinidad, and the British and Dutch Guianas.[5] Many colonial African laws enacted before 1925 were absolute prohibitions, outlawing essentially all forms of human interaction with the plant—with exceptions for the uses European administrators valued.[6] The 1925 agreement was mild in comparison, because, unlike prohibitory colonial laws, it established a regulatory approach to drug control. Not until 1961, with the United Nations' Single Convention on Narcotic Drugs (SCND), were international controls shifted toward legal prohibition, modeled on U.S. policies advanced under Harry Anslinger.[7] When the SCND was in discussion, India and Nepal sought to protect long-standing practices, winning *bhang, ganja,* and *charas* another twenty-five years' legality in terms of the international agreement. Africa's colonial and independent states remained neutral in the SCND negotiations, thereby disclaiming Indigenous traditions of cannabis use.[8] In the 1960s and 1970s, *Cannabis* became concerning to authorities worldwide because the plant drug symbolized political resistance.[9] Ultimately, all African states except Chad, Equatorial Guinea, Somalia, and South Sudan have signed the key United Nations conventions from 1961, 1971, and 1988 that firmly mark cannabis as an illegal crop.

Drug-policy reform is unfolding worldwide because some civil societies and governments have concluded that criminalizing drug use creates more harms than benefits. Cannabis decriminalization has been prominent in North America, Europe, and Australia, regions where many jurisdictions now allow certain instances of cultivation, sale, possession, and use. In the Global South, change has been more limited. In 2013, Uruguay took a bold step by legalizing cannabis, and Southern Africa is where many reforms have been enacted in the Global South. In late 2017, Lesotho authorized medical use, and Zimbabwe followed in May 2018; in September 2018, South Africa's constitutional court ruled that private, personal use of *dagga* is legal. No cannabis-policy reforms have been reported elsewhere in Africa, although several countries are moving toward decriminalization.

Decriminalized markets are large and growing in the Global North. In the United States, among the eight states with open recreational markets, 85 percent of all state-level retail sales taxes are expected to come from marijuana in 2017.[10] Sales have only grown in states with operating markets. The state of Nevada, including the city of Las Vegas, opened its recreational market in June 2017; total sales in the first year were $530 million, more than double what the state had anticipated.[11] Marijuana is becoming a mainstream business in the United States, with promising aspects. In 2007, seven years before the first recreational market opened in Colorado, more than 40 percent of U.S. adults had tried the plant drug, and 10 percent—about twenty-three million people—had used in the previous year.[12]

Cannabis history matters in this context. A global black market is fracturing into local, legal markets that generate legal wealth and new social meanings of drug use. In this context, African cannabis is undervalued both as an element of global cultural heritage and as an economic resource. Neglecting Africans in cannabis histories of whatever length or detail is unjustifiable. Doing so has been the norm.

In this last chapter, I argue that the neglect of Africa has real-world impacts in three ways. First, mainstream agricultural institutions have ignored the existence of cannabis in Africa, which has shifted control of *Cannabis indica*'s genetic diversity to private companies, particularly commercial sellers of marijuana seeds. The success of these businesses rests on genetically diverse seed stock, and bioprospectors identify Africa as an important storehouse of genetic diversity. African societies do not benefit from these businesses' success, despite the importance of the continent's *Cannabis* to these private enterprises. Second, medical scientists have provided a pretentious history of cannabis medicine that fails to mention Africa at all. Physicians have decided that history is relevant to understanding psychoactive cannabis today, but they only repeat rumors and factoids that are at best misleading and transparently serve to promote medical marijuana in current societies. Neglected but documented African experiences are more relevant than well-bandied falsehoods for understanding the plant drug's medical potential. Finally, cannabis histories have neglected to examine socioeconomic class in producing past drug use. By conflating race and class, history writers have enabled racially deterministic explanations of drug use. Racial determinism underpins biased drug-law enforcement, a major social problem in the United States and elsewhere. In short, the social and medical meanings of marijuana must be rethought in light of its Pan-African past.

The Value of Durban Poison

Farmers first bred *Cannabis indica* into diverse strains in South Asia. After it crossed the Indian Ocean, African farmers bred new strains by saving seeds from plants they liked. Across the Atlantic, farmers developed even more strains. These three phases of the drug plant's biological diversification have produced genetic variation that commercial bioprospectors value in their plant breeding.

Bioprospectors particularly seek out Landraces—plant populations that have distinctive characteristics, restricted geographic ranges, and lack formal improvement through selective breeding—because they carry genes that are not otherwise available to commercial growers. There is scant scholarly research on the biological diversity of *Cannabis indica* in Africa.[13] The world's de facto experts—non-scholarly marijuana aficionados—believe that the continent holds an undiscovered trove of genetic wealth. Folklore about African cannabis diversity is rich on the internet: "Africa is where the future of Sativas [the folk species] lies. It is the mothership for strains that . . . are going to be a huge factor in the future of medical cannabis that most people outside of the grow community have never even heard of."[14]

Interest in cannabis genetics has exploded with decriminalization. The marijuana seed industry is leading global bioprospecting. The number of "seed banks" doing business over the internet grew from 29 in 2002 to 354 in 2015.[15] The industry is concentrated in Amsterdam. Prominent companies are Sensi Seeds and Green House Seed Company, a highly public advocate of Africa's seed stock. Green House's Strain Hunters bioprospecting documentaries had eleven million views on YouTube by December 2017.[16] The company has sought cannabis in Malawi, Swaziland, Morocco, Jamaica, Trinidad, St. Vincent, India, and Colombia. Smaller seed companies include African Seeds, Afropips, and Seeds of Africa, which seeks to preserve "the legendary [cannabis] strains of Ancient Africa" so that "humanity . . . will not lose them forever in a world dominated by hybridised . . . varieties."[17] Marijuana seeds are only the visible aspect of bioprospecting. Pharmaceutical cannabis companies—particularly Amsterdam-based HortaPharm—have large germplasm collections but do not publicize their collections or bioprospecting.[18]

Commercial marijuana seed producers are highly capable experimental and applied scientists, even though many are not formally trained in botanical sciences. Global knowledge of *Cannabis indica*'s diversity, botany, and horticulture is exemplary citizen science, advanced by regular people interested in the topic. Research efforts with formal science-sounding names—such as the Cannabis Genomics Research Initiative, started in 2016—are privately funded and operated by marijuana aficionados, because public institutions have mostly ignored *Cannabis* during the period of prohibition. Only in the past fifteen years have formally trained, professional biologists substantially assessed cannabis's genetic diversity.[19] Their evidence and perspectives differ from those of their commercial peers, but academia trails the citizenry in understanding the extent, value, and potential of cannabis biodiversity.

Commercial bioprospectors are the world's experts because mainstream agricultural institutions ignore *Cannabis indica*. Consider Biodiversity International, part of the Consultative Group for International Agricultural Research (CGIAR), a global association of research institutes that seek to improve farming in the Global South. Biodiversity International works to "deliver scientific evidence, management practices and policy options" to conserve underutilized crops, under the vision that "agricultural biodiversity matters."[20] The organization, however, has considered only European *Cannabis sativa* strains.[21] *Cannabis sativa* is reasonably well represented in public seed banks, from which academic researchers acquire seeds for botanical studies.[22] African *indica* is absent in public collections; all provenances of *indica* are poorly represented. Academic researchers rely on the private collections of seed sellers and pharmaceutical companies, and on mostly hybrid seed stock, when studying psychoactive botany.[23] These private companies provide a globally important service—preservation of crop biodiversity—that public institutions have failed to provide.

Despite the leadership these companies have shown, the political-economic problems of private control of genetic resources must be acknowledged. Private businesses are not public services: they sell their products, and only seed companies sell germplasm. Seed companies and pharmaceutical developers use African germplasm in sophisticated breeding programs yet acknowledge no intellectual property rights for African farmers and offer no obvious benefits to them. High-value marijuana genetics come from seed stock developed and maintained by African farmers. Strains bear names like Malawi Gold, Angola Rojo (a.k.a. Liamba), and, most famous, Durban Poison. When U.S. marijuana aficionados discovered Durban Poison in the 1970s, this became the most salient knowledge of African cannabis for many Americans (see figure 2.1). Durban Poison has been continuously among the four top-selling strains since Colorado's legal recreational market opened in 2014. In the fourth quarter of 2015, it was the top seller, with $4.5 million in sales.[24] Varietal development is popular among commercial growers, which produces demand for new genetic inputs. Durban Poison was an important input in the 1970s, contributing genetics that are valued for their chemistry, which is rich in the cannabinoids THC and THCV, and low in CBD. THCV-rich varieties are rare worldwide and found principally in Southern Africa. Horticulturalists produce new strains by crossing genetic lines. For instance, by crossing Durban Poison with other strains, someone produced GSC, another of Colorado's most valuable strains.[25] Hybrid strains are the basis of the seed industry, selling for $3–$15 per seed.[26]

In the grand scheme, $4.5 million is not much, just one-tenth of 1 percent of the city budget of Durban, South Africa, in 2016–17, but it is interesting to compare numbers.[27] Across the United States, state-legalized sales reached $6.7 billion in 2016 and are expected to exceed $20 billion in five years; in 2009, the country's entire industry, both legal and illegal, was estimated at $40 billion.[28] For comparison, in 2016 the gross domestic product of Malawi was $5.5 billion; of Jamaica, $14.0 billion; and of the Democratic Republic of the Congo (DRC), $41.6 billion.[29]

Private control of germplasm takes Indigenous knowledge out of public control and enables companies to extract income from this knowledge without returning benefits to farmers who maintained seed stock from their forebears.[30] African communities should have intellectual property rights to strains that reasonably trace to their locale. South Africans, for example, should have some control over Durban Poison, whether this is a genetically traceable strain or simply an effective, informal brand name. Jamaica is the sole country to claim a strain—

Jamaican Ganja—as intellectual property.[31] Thanks to the popularity of reggae, the prominence of Rastafarianism, and the roles cannabis has in both, Jamaica has great prestige among marijuana aficionados and has smartly taken steps to protect this prestige. If intellectual property rights exist in Jamaica, they exist elsewhere. The plant came to the island with Central African and South Asian laborers whose ancestors had cultivated the crop long before. The island's Landraces probably include genetics that trace back to Victorian pharmaceutical tops, too. Guiana, Brazil, Sierra Leone, Gabon, Angola, Mozambique, Madagascar—little is known about cannabis diversity in these countries.

Debates over private versus public control of germplasm are unresolved, centering on whether property rights can or should be embedded in life forms. Regardless of the outcome of these debates, private, commercial control is the default for *Cannabis indica* because public institutions exclude the crop as an extension of drug-control policy. In Africa, colonial authorities accepted drug crops, but only those specified through their absence in drug-control laws and presence in agricultural policies—particularly tobacco, tea, and coffee. Colonial agricultural institutions actively supported these crops, which remain the bases of important industries in several countries. Cannabis has been completely excluded from African agricultural research and development, yet African societies have geographic, historical, and cultural advantages for advancing global knowledge of cannabis biodiversity. As an aspect of drug-policy reform, societies in Africa and beyond should assess how *Cannabis* genetic diversity is managed and studied.

The African cannabis crop earns less than its potential monetary value. Decriminalization reforms in North America and Europe have opened lucrative markets. However, nontariff trade barriers (i.e., drug-trafficking laws) hinder producers in the Global South from participating in these markets, despite the comparative advantages they have through strong local knowledge, lower labor costs, and low-input outdoor production. Import substitution in the Global North (via resource-intensive indoor horticulture) is simultaneously foreclosing potential export markets for Southerners and generating wealth for Northerners[32]—again, based on Southern seed stock. Countries in the Global South continue to expend resources on anti-cannabis drug-law enforcement even as Northern countries loosen controls in violation of multilateral drug-control agreements.[33]

For cannabis, drug policy and agricultural policy are inextricable. Initial cannabis-control laws in Africa directly targeted farming by proscribing crop choice according to European perspectives. Angola's 1913 law pontificated that "natives [should] substitute the cultivation of this plant with that of tobacco, making use of the opportunity to stimulate an expansion of this latter crop."[34] The colonial government was then pushing tobacco as an export. Most laws simply banned cannabis, without telling farmers what to plant instead. Farmers choose crops based on political, economic, and ecological realities. Nowadays, those who decide to grow cannabis illegally have a complicated set of calculations.[35] The crop is risky but valuable; it can produce adequately with limited inputs on marginal land, but a season's labor can be lost if police destroy a plot. Illegal cannabis attracts cash-cropping farmers who have inadequate resources— such as land rights, soil fertility, farm equipment, or labor—to earn much in legal markets.[36] The crop's hardiness and market value are embedded in the seed through the actions of generations of farmers who saved seeds from successful plants.

The drug-control strategy of alternative development centers on providing incentives for farmers to switch to legal crops.[37] Alternative development has been hardly tried in Africa, and the largest intervention, in Morocco, failed because European demand for hashish stayed strong, meaning that hashish remained a reliable source of income for both farmers and smugglers.[38] A truly alternative development strategy would be to decriminalize cannabis production in a way that allows farmers in the Global South to access lucrative markets, domestic and international.[39] Of course, open cannabis markets would favor well-capitalized farmers, probably not those who currently grow.[40] Decriminalization could face opposition from those who have profited from the conditions of prohibition, such as military commanders in the eastern DRC, whose authority enables their wives to control cannabis distribution networks.[41] Whatever the hurdles and consequences, decriminalizing cannabis in Africa could increase the legal choices farmers have when deciding what to plant in the coming season.

If European or North American cannabis markets were open to imports, and South Africa was open to exports, marijuana aficionados would surely pay a premium for fresh, THCV-rich Durban Poison, certified and sold directly from the protected geographic provenance, South Africa's Natal Province.

Queen Victoria's Marijuana Use

Queen Victoria used marijuana, according to high-end medical publications such as *The Lancet* and *New England Journal of Medicine*.[42] *Playboy* magazine has confirmed this factoid.[43]

The medical literature offers a pretentious history of cannabis in the form of introductory vignettes meant to validate current interests in the plant drug.

This history is given with an air of authoritativeness, even though it is not re-searched by the medical scientists who repeat it. The vignettes build the overarching story that marijuana use allows patients to "channel 5000 years of medical history, including the century when cannabis derivatives routinely resided in American doctors' black bags."[44] This narrative is dishonest. Falsehoods gain the appearance of truth when printed in high-end publications. The process could be called knowledge laundering.[45]

I recognize that physicians are not historians, but physicians have decided that history is relevant to understanding the plant drug. The medical literature builds its history through oft-repeated factoids that mostly originated as rumors in pro-cannabis publications of the 1960s–80s. These publications, predictably, bore the theme that cannabis has been unjustly maligned and has forgotten value. These themes remain important to physicians who see therapeutic potential in the plant drug. Anti-cannabis literature has had its own anecdotal history, with factoids tracing to colonial insane asylums and Victorian-era Orientalists. However, papers that adopt a measured view of medical marijuana tend not to bear historical vignettes anymore.[46] High-end medical authors have repeated errors from works as faulty as Jack Herer's *The Emperor Wears No Clothes*, a foundational classic for anti-prohibitionist thought whose first edition was published in 1985.[47] The book offers newspaper clippings minimally connected with conspiracy theories, gossip, and legends. Herer was a pro-marijuana po-litical activist in the United States, and the book served his efforts well. *The Emperor* is not qualified to underpin any aspect of current medical literature, including historical vignettes. High-end journals such as the *Mayo Clinic Pro-ceedings* should not launder knowledge from *The Emperor* any more than it should repeat health-advice tidbits from checkout-line magazines.[48]

For decades, most presentations of cannabis history have served to support political arguments for or against prohibition.[49] Building knowledge and test-ing assumptions have not been priorities—or, at least not commonly achieved.[50] The pretentious history of cannabis medicine exaggerates the plant drug's antiq-uity and importance, presents irrelevant past experiences as currently meaning-ful, neglects relevant past experiences, and emphasizes clinical practice over public health. Politically useful factoids have spread like contagions between doctors who use each other as sources for the history none of them have re-searched. One set of physicians who promote cannabis as a painkiller, for in-stance, cite other physicians to show that its analgesic use was "noted in ancient Chinese texts written in 2800 BC, [and in] the Athera Veda [*sic*], dating to ~2000 BC."[51] Physicians often name-drop Dioscorides, too, an ancient Greek medical luminary. The widely repeated date of 2800 BCE—sometimes specified as 2737 BCE—refers to a pharmacopeia whose current relevance has been presumed in the medical literature since 1971.[52] Since 1951, historians of science have recognized that the pharmacopeia is no older than 100 BCE and, further, that for the past millennium only hempseeds have been significant in Chinese medicine.[53] Similarly, Dioscorides's prescription of hempseed oil to treat earache does not exhibit the plant's generic therapeutic potential,[54] especially not if it is administered as smoked or edible preparations of psychoactive herbal material. Supposed references to cannabis in the Atharvaveda—which dates to approximately 1200 BCE[55]—are indecipherably cryptic. One reference says that burning a putrid rope will frighten enemies, while another says that *bhanga*, barley, and three unidentified plants "free us from distress."[56] Sanskrit scholars aren't certain what *bhanga* meant in the Atharvaveda.[57] Ancient, vaguely known uses are vaguely known because they disappeared long ago and are historically unrelated to current medical applications of cannabis.

Documented recent history is more relevant, but this record has been read incompletely and inaccurately to exaggerate the plant drug's importance. In one case, physicians recently stated that Victorian-era doctors "reported dramatic success" in treating epilepsy with cannabis, even though their nineteenth-century source actually concluded that cannabis is "sometimes, though not very frequently, useful" in this application.[58] Victorian-era physicians published many complaints and disappointments about pharmaceutical cannabis; records of success were measured, qualified, and disputed. In the years just before 1925, pharmacists mostly valued cannabis indica simply as a colorant for corn plasters. The prohibition of cannabis did not close any vibrant pharmaceutical industries.

The most embarrassing use of history to validate medical interest in cannabis is the tale that Queen Victoria used pharmaceutical cannabis for menstrual cramps.[59] Nobody knows whether she did or not. The anecdote traces to the 1971 book *Uses of Marijuana*, by the neuroscientist Solomon Snyder.[60] Many more readers came to know about Victoria and cannabis via *Playboy*, which for some time—perhaps from 1974 to 1976—ran pro-marijuana advocacy ads that repeated Snyder's tale.[61] Snyder decided that Victoria took the drug because John Russell Reynolds, a leading British physician, published a review of pharmaceutical cannabis in 1890.[62] Reynolds reported three primary applications: (1) against pain, "Indian hemp [is] by far the most useful of drugs"; (2) to calm patients with "senile insomnia, [in the] elderly person probably with brain-softening"; and (3) for muscular spasms.[63] In this last instance, the doctor listed many types of cramping and considered cannabis "of great service in cases of simple spasmodic dysmenorrhea [menstrual cramps]." He advised caution, though, because herbal material and extracts were highly variable in potency and thus unreliable. He presented the mainstream view of pharmaceutical cannabis at the height of its faddish popularity in Victorian medicine.

Coincidentally, Reynolds served on Queen Victoria's medical staff.[64] He was *not* her personal physician. His "to the Household" appointment placed him among many others who were consultants to the principal physicians who served the royal family. Reynolds likely never had any direct medical interaction with Her Highness. Further, he began his duties when Victoria was fifty-nine, so he probably wasn't consulted about menstrual cramps.[65] Reynolds wrote textbooks that reviewed many drugs, and he reported several therapeutic applications for pharmaceutical cannabis. There is no reason to presume the queen interacted with any of the drugs he wrote about, or that she suffered any of the conditions he mentioned in his paper on cannabis (including brain softening). Multiple historians of medicine have thrown out the Victoria story as nonsense, including some writing for high-end publications such as *The Lancet*.[66] Nonetheless, in 2017 medical practitioners earned CMEs—continuing medical education credits that are required to maintain licensure in the United States—for learning that "cannabis was prescribed by Queen Victoria's personal physician, Sir John Russell Reynolds, for her menstrual discomfort throughout her adult life."[67]

Stories of ancient and upper-class use transparently serve to elevate the plant drug's past status and imply that its status should rise today.[68] Yet it is simply untrue that "cannabis has been used throughout the world for thousands of years and by all types of social classes, including Queen Victoria in the 1800s," as anesthesiologists have written.[69] Most human populations had absolutely no contact with psychoactive cannabis until after 1800, however old the Atharvaveda might be. No current medical literature mentions that slavers supplied psychoactive cannabis to their captives or that enslaved people appreciated the plant drug.[70] These people's histories are much more relevant than Victoria's in understanding cannabis, even if acknowledging this past might be uncomfortable for medical marijuana advocates.

Cannabis has been entangled throughout the world for hundreds of years with disease, trauma, violence, exploitation, and poverty. The plant drug's past in public health is as pertinent as its past in clinical practice. The historic publications of Dr. Robert O. Clarke are more relevant than those of Dr. Reynolds because they exhibit the plant drug's historical epidemiology and thereby provide precedent for understanding patterns of drug use in current societies.

Clarke was a colonial surgeon in Sierra Leone during 1837–54 who treated thousands of people liberated from slave ships. His paper published in 1840 was the first treatment-oriented publication on sleeping sickness.[71] He was also the first to report *diamba* in the colony in 1851 when he associated it with "Congoes." On the basis of Clarke's observations, a subsequent colonial medical officer concluded that trypanosomiasis was not endemic to Sierra Leone but occurred only in the bodies of people coming from the Lower Congo.[72] Its incidence in Sierra Leone spiked at the height of recaptive resettlement in the 1830s and 1840s, and again in the 1890s, an extension of the Central African epidemic. The 1890s epidemic could have been worse in Sierra Leone if "the large numbers [of] Mende and T[e]mne labourers who were sent to work in . . . the Congo Free State had returned home; [many] were enlisted as soldiers when they got down to the Congo and perished in the continued warfare waged by the state among the natives. A very large number . . . also perished from disease, neglect and want."[73] These migrant laborers joined social groups in the Free State in which *diamba* was prominent. Those who came home joined social groups that included people such as Mankah, a Temne man who fell ill and died of sleeping sickness three months after returning to Freetown in 1904.[74] I don't know whether Mankah smoked cannabis. I also don't know about the recaptives rechristened Mary Coker (age fourteen), John Silver (fourteen), Thomas Caperhill (fourteen), and Sara (ten). These children, taken from slave ships, were Clarke's patients who died of trypanosomiasis in 1839.[75] Perhaps they were among the "youth of both sexes" who induced sleeping sickness by smoking *diamba*, as Clarke later reported.[76]

For two centuries around the Atlantic, cannabis has been a subsistence therapeutic resource for people on social-ecological margins, exposed to an array of health risks. The historical association between cannabis and risky environments should be understood in two ways. First, this association validates interest in certain therapeutic clinical applications, such as reducing post-traumatic stress, managing appetite, and palliating illness.[77] The people who carried *diamba* seeds to Sierra Leone (and elsewhere) emerged from slave ships as "emaciated, tottering and debilitated bod[ies in a] truly pitiable state."[78] These people experienced horrific psychological trauma: "In some . . . the countenance indicated suffering, moral and physical, of the most profound and agonizing nature. Others of them gazed vacantly . . . in the most utter helplessness. Occasionally, . . . all sense of suffering was merged in melancholic or raving madness."[79] Many died soon after landing. Some who survived to build a life in Sierra Leone occasionally spent evenings with other recaptives, drinking cheap rum and smoking *diamba*.[80] Clarke characterized these parties as "groups of merry people spend[ing] their time in conversation, [with] hearty peals of laughter, amazing vociferation, volubility, and gaiety . . . so seducing that they separate with reluctance."[81] Surely this history—of enslavement, drug use, trauma, malnutrition, injury, illness, and recovery—better validates interest in medical marijuana than rumors about Victoria's boudoir.

Second, the epidemiological history of cannabis validates interest in analyzing drug use as a product of social structure more than individual behavior.[82] Cannabis drug use has been principally a social condition for at least two centuries. For every Richard Burton and Chishimbi who chose to try cannabis because their elite social status offered them this choice, there were thousands of people with forgotten names who smoked the plant drug because it was integral to the hard-laboring occupations and risky environments they occupied. *Diamba* was not the problem when sleeping sickness flared in Central Africa; human exploitation was. *Maconha* was not a remnant of slavery in early twentieth-century Brazil but an ongoing product of inequitable social structure. Certainly, individual choice exists in instances of drug use, but in historical underclasses, the multifaceted stressors of marginality made reality-altering drugs alluring. Social-ecological conditions brought people toward cannabis, even if their drug use was justified in other terms. Morocco's Ḥeddawa brotherhood, for example, smoked *kif* ceremonially and spiritually, but they also considered it an addictive curse symbolic of poverty.[83] In 1905, the Ḥeddawa brotherhood was "open to all comers, . . . the refuge of people disgusted with existence; former bosses, businessmen, etc., who, after a series of setbacks of fortune, have retired from the world[;] even a European had been affiliated with this order."[84] "Even a European": socioeconomic class cuts across racial categories, even in colonial societies where Europeans, and Whites more generally, experienced much greater privilege than others. Morocco's Ḥeddawa was a class-based movement in a strongly stratified society, in an environment where *Cannabis indica* had grown for centuries. Around the historical Atlantic, the drug plant's biological adaptability made it a widespread, low-cost option for self-medication that appealed to people with few therapeutic resources.

This relationship, documented through 1925, has persistent echoes. Low socioeconomic status and drug use consistently correlate in current societies, although most studies have been conducted in North America, Europe, and Australia.[85] People in higher socioeconomic echelons use all manner of substances, too, but upper-class drug use is often legitimized as morally, aesthetically, and legally acceptable. Medical marijuana has gained mainstream legitimacy in the United States alongside increasing portrayals of upper-class use in popular media—even though cannabis drug use remains more common in lower socioeconomic classes.[86] The association that cannabis has had with social marginality is neither necessary nor universal. It has a history that traces to neither Chinese pharmacopeias nor Dioscorides. I have not shown that current cannabis epidemiology directly continues people-plant relationships that existed in transatlantic slavery or other contexts. My research focus stops around 1925, after which prohibition altered earlier practices and patterns of drug use. What I have provided is historical validation for the current epidemiological hypothesis that many people use drugs, whether legally or illegally, to cope with stressors produced by socioeconomic inequality and to self-treat trauma or mental illness.[87]

Queen Victoria used psychoactive cannabis, just not how medical scientists have pretended. Nineteenth-century European empires stood upon exploitative labor regimes in which workers used tobacco, alcohol, cannabis, and other substances to enhance their capacities to undertake onerous tasks, endure risky environments, and survive physical and mental trauma. Victoria's government collected taxes from Caribbean plantation bosses who worked *ganja*-smoking indentured laborers and from African colonies where workers used *chamba*, *dagga*, *bangi*, and so on. Her government collected revenues from the flawed global pharmaceutical cannabis market. Victoria's documented drug use is more relevant than anything published by anyone on her medical staff, which included 280 people during her life.[88]

The medical marijuana literature should include no anecdotes—gems such as "George Washington is reported to have used cannabis for tooth pain"—without telling who reported what.[89] If history is relevant enough to bring up, it should be researched honestly, adequately, and critically. Medical marijuana advocates must discover and contemplate how emperors like Victoria really did use psychoactive cannabis.

Race

Medical marijuana has benefited many people in current societies and has unrealized potential. However, its utility should be established through research findings, not received wisdom. The pretentious history serves to validate a political viewpoint. If psychoactive cannabis was used (almost) immemorially by (almost) everyone with (almost) no negative consequences, then it must be harmless and natural, and therefore prohibition must be bad. Cannabis drug use has been made placeless and timeless, a behavior that is natural and without history. It is true, as pharmacologists have reported, that humans have an endocannabinoid receptor system. It is not true that the existence of this system shows that marijuana is "something everyone is familiar with, whether they know it or not . . . , because the brain makes its own marijuana."[90] Instances of drug consumption are social, individual, and environmental events, not examples of natural, pan-human behavior. The idea that psychoactive cannabis is uniformly and fundamentally benign contradicts public health goals of minimizing risks in decriminalized markets.[91]

Some generalizations can be made about the plant drug's effects based on human biology. Objective effects that have been identified recently existed historically. Specific applications and objective effects recorded historically are relevant for understanding potential applications today. Based on Dioscorides, it is valid to examine whether hempseed oil can treat earaches. The internal, biological context of cannabis drug use is the only reasonably generalizable human element of the people-plant interaction, but even here there are exceptions for genetic variation among people. Subjective effects may vary as greatly as human personalities.

So, to end with a summary: instances of drug consumption have social, individual, and environmental histories. Africa's omission from cannabis history comes from an intellectual tradition that marginalizes African contributions to world culture. African knowledge is fundamental to now dominant global practices of cannabis use, particularly the act of smoking the herb and the technology of the water pipe. In the Atlantic World, African knowledge of psychoactive cannabis spread widely with slave trading. In many societies that received slaves from Central African ports between 1730 and 1900, African vocabulary and technology are historically documented. These cultural elements were not an inseparable package. Words, paraphernalia, plants, and knowledge variably survived the Middle Passage. Other things that accompanied this enslaved migration were the trypanosome that causes sleeping sickness and the tsetse fly that carries the trypanosome. Before 1925, the social groups in which cannabis smoking was most prominent were labor underclasses exposed to risky environments. The plant drug served as a tonic associated with work and socialization, a general-purpose therapeutic resource, and a pharmaceutical means of preparing for or recovering from trauma. Psychoactive cannabis use has been a social-ecological condition within exploitative labor regimes that were integral to expanding global capitalism. During the post-Columbian period, racist social structures have been coproduced with labor exploitation and caused peoples of color to experience marginality more extensively than Whites. The cannabis literature has conflated social condition with racial identity by perpetuating colonialist discourse about drugs and people. Racially deterministic accounts of drug use underpin structural racism, including biased drug-law enforcement. No form of drug use is natural to one group of people or another, but represents the outcome of social-ecological processes.

Decriminalization reduces legal risks associated with cannabis use. This is one of its greatest potential benefits, given racial bias in law enforcement.[92] In the United States, drug-law enforcement has produced race-based inequities that are comparable to historical Jim Crow laws.[93] However, cannabis decriminalization does not address the processes that produce social-ecological marginality, and it does nothing to overturn racial ideologies that enable biased law enforcement. Criminalization of cannabis doesn't solve anything either, because the plant drug is symptomatic of deeper problems; it is not the problem itself. Marijuana advocates must directly confront the underlying causes of drug use and not simply aim to facilitate one form of self-medication.

Marijuana does not cure trypanosomiasis.

Acknowledgments

Many people helped make this book, and I thank them for it. First, many colleagues and students at the University of New Mexico (UNM) helped me develop my thought through stimulating discussions. Among my colleagues, Maria Lane particularly enabled this book by giving me time to write, by willingly taking an overload of administrative work. And I thank John Carr and Tema Milstein for their flagpole. Second, I have benefited from the professional assistance of several students. I especially thank Daniel Montoya and Kyle Wilson for their development of map designs on which I have built. Jonathan K. Nelson, Maureen Meyer, and William Maxwell assisted with my research and cartography as well. Third, I have received institutional support from UNM's Department of Geography and Environmental Studies, College of Arts and Sciences, and University Libraries. I also appreciate the assistance I received from staff at Lisbon's Sociedade de Geografia; Portugal's Biblioteca Nacional and Arquivo Nacional Torre do Tombo; and the British National Archives. Fourth, I benefited from discussions at various professional meetings, including the Department of Geography's speaker series at the University of Nevada, Reno (2018); the Challenging Canada 150 conference at Nipissing University (2017); the Latin American Studies speaker series at Central New Mexico Community College (2017); the American Historical Association's annual meeting (2016); the Second International Conference of the Portuguese Center for World History at Universidade Nova de Lisboa (2015); the Second World Congress of the International Consortium of Environmental History Organizations (2014); the annual meetings of the American Association of Geographers (2012, 2013, 2015, and 2016) and its Southwest Division

(2012); the Annual Conference of Harvard University's Center for Geographic Analysis (2012); and the 50/Forward conference of the University of Wisconsin's African Studies Program (2012). Finally, I thank family in New Mexico, Wyoming, Colorado, South Australia, and elsewhere for indispensable support, especially S. G. D., L. & L. D., S. L. B., and E. J. B., and, of course, R. W. D., H. L. D., and M. J. B. Lastly, F. and S. attended much of the actual writing.

Notes

1. CANNABIS AND AFRICA

1. Data sources for the graphic on arrest rates in New York and Chicago are: Census Data.gov; M. Dumke, "Chicago Decriminalized Marijuana Possession—but Not for Everyone," *Chicago Reader*, 2014, accessed 28 August 2017, https://www.chicagoreader .com/chicago/police-bust-blacks-pot-possession-after-decriminalization/Content?oid =13004240; Substance Abuse and Mental Health Services Administration (SAMHSA), *Results from the 2010 National Survey on Drug Use and Health: Summary of National Findings* (Rockville, MD: Substance Abuse and Mental Health Services Administration, 2011); H. G. Levine, "New York City's Marijuana Arrest Crusade . . . Continues," Sociology Department, City University of New York, 2009, accessed 28 August 2017, http://marijuana-arrests.com/docs/NYC-MARIJUANA-ARREST-CRUSADE -CONTINUES-SEPT-2009.pdf.

2. By "Pan-African," I mean the peoples worldwide of recent African ancestry (roughly the past five centuries) and the intellectual movement that recognizes and seeks to strengthen solidarity among these peoples.

3. R. C. Clarke and M. D. Merlin, *Cannabis: Evolution and Ethnobotany* (Berkeley: University of California Press, 2013); E. L. Abel, *Marihuana: The First Twelve Thousand Years* (New York: Springer, 1980); M. Booth, *Cannabis: A History* (New York: St. Martin's, 2005); M. A. Lee, *Smoke Signals: A Social History of Marijuana—Medical, Recreational, and Scientific* (New York: Scribner, 2012).

4. J. Herer, *The Emperor Wears No Clothes*, 12th ed. (Van Nuys, CA: Ah Ha, 2010).

5. E. B. Russo, "The Pharmacological History of Cannabis," in *Handbook of Cannabis*, ed. R. Pertwee (Oxford: Oxford University Press, 2014), 23–43.

6. George somehow treated tooth pain with colonial European cannabis plants grown for fiber, according to P. G. Fine and M. J. Rosenfeld, "Cannabinoids for Neuropathic Pain," *Current Pain and Headache Reports* 18, no. 10 (2014): art. 451.

7. C. S. Duvall, *Cannabis* (London: Reaktion, 2015).

8. P. Sharpe and G. Smith, "Cannabis: Time for Scientific Evaluation of This Ancient Remedy?" *Anesthesia and Analgesia* 90, no. 2 (2000): 237–40.

9. See introduction chapters in J. H. Mills, *Cannabis Britannica: Empire, Trade, and Prohibition, 1800–1928* (Oxford: Oxford University Press, 2003); J. H. Mills, *Cannabis Nation: Control and Consumption in Britain, 1928–2008* (Oxford: Oxford University Press, 2012).

10. I. Campos, *Home Grown: Marijuana and the Origins of Mexico's War on Drugs* (Chapel Hill: University of North Carolina Press, 2012).

11. S. Scheerer, "North-American Bias and Non-American Roots of Cannabis Prohibition," n.d. [2011], accessed 7 August 2017, http://www.bisdro.uni-bremen.de/boellinger /cannabis/04-schee.pdf.

12. Good summaries of Anslinger's role in cannabis prohibition are D. Bewley-Taylor, T. Blickman, and M. Jelsma, *The Rise and Decline of Cannabis Prohibition* (Amsterdam: Transnational Institute, 2014); J. C. McWilliams, "Unsung Partner against Crime: Harry J. Anslinger and the Federal Bureau of Narcotics, 1930–1962," *Pennsylvania Magazine of History and Biography* 113, no. 2 (1989): 207–36; R. Carroll, "Under the Influence: Harry Anslinger's Role in Shaping America's Drug Policy," in *Federal Drug Control: The Evolution of Policy and Practice*, ed. J. Erlen, J. F. Spillane, R. Carroll, W. Mcallister, and D. B. Worthen (Binghamton, NY: Pharmaceutical Products Press, 2004), 61–100; A. Rathge, "Cannabis Cures: American Medicine, Mexican Marijuana, and the Origins of the War on Weed, 1840–1937," Ph.D. diss., Boston College, 2017. Adam Rathge's dissertation will be published as a book. I thank him for sharing a copy of his work with me.

13. H. J. Anslinger and C. R. Cooper, "Marijuana, Assassin of Youth," *American Magazine* 124 (July 1937): 19–25.

14. J. Herer, *The Emperor Wears No Clothes*, 11th ed. (Van Nuys, CA: Ah Ha, 1998), 89.

15. M. J. Routh, "Re-thinking Liberty: Cannabis Prohibition and Substantive Due Process," *Kansas Journal of Law and Public Policy* 26, no. 2 (2017): 145; M. Render and E. Nielson, "How States Can Bring African-Americans into the Marijuana Industry," 2016, accessed 9 August 2017, http://www.rollingstone.com/culture/how-to-bring-african -americans-into-marijuana-industry-w454920; W. T. Hoston, "The Racial Politics of Marijuana," in *Race and the Black Male Subculture: The Lives of Toby Waller* (New York: Palgrave Macmillan, 2016), 101.

16. Routh, *Re-thinking Liberty*, 145.

17. Rathge, "Cannabis Cures"; N. Johnson, *Grass Roots: A History of Cannabis in the American West* (Corvallis: Oregon State University Press, 2017).

18. Johnson, *Grass Roots*; D. H. Gieringer, "The Forgotten Origins of Cannabis Prohibition in California," *Contemporary Drug Problems* 26 (1999): 237–88.

19. Scheerer, "North-American Bias and Non-American Roots of Cannabis Prohibition"; Mills, *Cannabis Britannica*; Bewley-Taylor et al., *The Rise and Decline of Cannabis Prohibition*; L. Kozma, "Cannabis Prohibition in Egypt, 1880–1939: From Local Ban to League of Nations Diplomacy," *Middle Eastern Studies* 47, no. 3 (2011): 443–60; C. S. Duvall, "Drug Laws, Bioprospecting, and the Agricultural Heritage of *Cannabis* in Africa," *Space and Polity* 20, no. 1 (2016): 10–25.

20. Two qualifications. First, South Africa and Egypt were independent in 1925, but attitudes toward cannabis in those countries originated earlier, in colonial contexts. In

both countries, colonial social structures remained in place for decades after independence. Second, some other locations had strict cannabis controls before 1900—notably Greece, Turkey, and Sri Lanka. For further legal history, see chapter 9 below.

21. K. W. Hillig, "Genetic Evidence for Speciation in *Cannabis* (Cannabaceae)," *Genetic Resources and Crop Evolution* 52 (2005): 161–80; K. W. Hillig and P. G. Mahlberg, "A Chemotaxonomic Analysis of Cannabinoid Variation in *Cannabis* (Cannabaceae)," *American Journal of Botany* 91, no. 6 (2004): 966–75; J. Sawler, J. M. Stout, K. M. Gardner, D. Hudson, J. Vidmar, L. Butler, J. E. Page, and S. Myles, "The Genetic Structure of Marijuana and Hemp," *PLoS One* 10, no. 8 (2015): e0133292.

22. Sawler et al., "The Genetic Structure."

23. Jute (*Corchorus* species) from India was an early candidate and was the species George Washington grew when he instructed his gardener to grow "Indian Hemp," an incident that pro-marijuana activists have spun fancifully: Duvall, *Cannabis*, 182–85.

24. C. Fyfe, "Using Race as an Instrument of Policy: A Historical View," *Race and Class* 36, no. 2 (1994): 69–77.

25. M. Rogers, "Paul Bowles: The Rolling Stone Interview: Conversations in Morocco with the Expatriate Author and Composer," *Rolling Stone*, 23 May 1974, accessed 7 August 2017, http://www.rollingstone.com/culture/features/the-rolling-stone-interview -paul-bowles-19740523. Hashish was made in Morocco, by Moroccans, early in the twentieth century: R. Brunel, *Le monachisme errant dans l'Islam* (Paris: Maisonneuve and Larose, [1955] 2001).

26. S. J. Altoma, "Paul Bowles' Knowledge of Arabic: Personal Observations," *Journal of North African Studies* 17, no. 1 (2012): 157–72.

27. Bewley-Taylor et al., *The Rise and Decline of Cannabis Prohibition*; D. R. Bewley-Taylor, *International Drug Control: Consensus Fractured* (Cambridge: Cambridge University Press, 2012).

28. J. C. Miller, V. Brown, J. Cañizares-Esguerra, L. Dubois, and K. Ordhal Kupperman, eds., *The Princeton Companion to Atlantic History* (Princeton, NJ: Princeton University Press, 2015).

29. A. Sluyter, *Black Ranching Frontiers: African Cattle Herders of the Atlantic World, 1500–1900* (New Haven, CT: Yale University Press, 2012); R. A. Voeks, *Sacred Leaves of Candomblé: African Magic, Medicine, and Religion in Brazil* (Austin: University of Texas Press, 1997); R. A. Voeks and J. Rashford, eds., *African Ethnobotany in the Americas* (New York: Springer, 2013); L. Schiebinger, "Agnotology and Exotic Abortifacients: The Cultural Production of Ignorance in the Eighteenth-Century Atlantic World," *Proceedings of the American Philosophical Society* 149, no. 3 (2005): 316–43.

30. Duvall, *Cannabis*; Clarke and Merlin, *Cannabis*; B. M. du Toit, *Cannabis in Africa: A Survey of Its Distribution in Africa, and a Study of Cannabis Use and Users in Multiethnic South Africa* (Rotterdam: A. A. Balkema, 1980).

31. Booth, *Cannabis*, 54.

32. Clarke and Merlin, *Cannabis*, 236; Booth, *Cannabis*, 154; Lee, *Smoke Signals*, 14; M. S. Ferrara, *Sacred Bliss: A Spiritual History of Cannabis* (New York: Rowman and Littlefield, 2016), 78.

33. Abel, *Marihuana*, 143.

34. Du Toit, *Cannabis in Africa*.

35. Du Toit, *Cannabis in Africa*, 11.

36. Gambia and Senegal: E. Poisson, "Itineraire suivi par les habitants de Bakel pour se rendre à Kaouroco, d'où ils descendent la Gambia jusqu'à Sainte-Marie de Bathurst, et vocabulaire du pays de Guey," *Bulletin de la Société de Géographie* 17, 4th series (July 1859): 46–47. Liberia: J. Büttikofer, *Reisebilder aus Liberia*, vol. 2 (Leiden: E. J. Brill, 1890), 276–77; L. Lewin, *Phantastica: Die betäubenden und erregenden Genussmittel* (Berlin: Stilke, 1924), 105. Nigeria: Anonymous [Richard F. Burton], *Wanderings in West Africa from Liverpool to Fernando Po*, vol. 2 (London: Tinsley Brothers, 1863), 224–25. Sierra Leone: R. O. Clarke, "Short Notice of the African Plant Diamba, Commonly Called Congo Tobacco," *Hooker's Journal of Botany* 3 (1851): 9–11. Senegal: A. Sébire, *Les plantes utiles du Sénégal: Plantes indigènes–plantes exotiques* (Paris: J.-B. Baillière and Sons, 1899), 163; T. Chazarain, "Traitement du tétanos," *Union Médicale* 10, 3d series, no. 96 (August 13, 1870): 229–31. Guinea: H. Pobéguin, *Essai sur la flore de la Guinée Française: Produits forestiers, agricoles et industriels*, Côte Occidentale d'Afrique (Paris: Augustin Challamel Librairie Maritime et Coloniale, 1906), 110. Togo: H. L. Hammerstein, "Die Land-wirtschaft der Eingeborenen Afrikas," *Beihefte zum Tropenpflanzer* 19, no. 1 (1919): 108. Niger: F. Foureau, *Documents scientifiques de la Mission Saharienne (Mission Foureau–Lamy d'Alger au Congo par le Tchad), Premier fascicule* (Paris: Masson, 1903), 467, 519.

37. Important repositories include Google Books, Hathi Trust, Persée.fr, Gallica (of the Bibliothèque Nationale de France), and Archive.org.

38. Clarke and Merlin, *Cannabis*, 368.

39. Booth, *Cannabis*, 157.

40. Lee, *Smoke Signals*, 14. As an indication of its dismissiveness of Africa and reliance on stereotypes, the book includes in its index, "Africa, 4, 13, 14, 20/African Americans. *See* blacks": Lee, *Smoke Signals*, 495. In a five hundred-page book, ostensibly a world history, the continent garners four page mentions; a racial category is more salient than specific cultural, social, historic, geographic, linguistic, ethnic, or other more precise human descriptors.

41. Ferrara, *Sacred Bliss*, 82.

42. Clarke and Merlin, *Cannabis*, 236.

43. Abel, in 1980, offered embellishments not included in the 1927 source, which Clarke and Merlin thankfully did not repeat in 2013: Abel, *Marihuana*, 145–46; P. M. Larken, "Impressions of the Zande (Continued from Vol. IX, Part 1)," *Sudan Notes and Records* 10 (1927): 93.

44. J. M. McPartland and K. W. Hillig, "Early Iconography of *Cannabis Sativa* and *Cannabis Indica*," *Journal of Industrial Hemp* 13, no. 2 (2008): 189–203.

45. H. W. Hutchinson, "Patterns of Marihuana Use in Brazil," in *Cannabis and Culture*, ed. V. Rubin (The Hague: Mouton, 1975), 176; D. T. Courtwright, "Review of *The Cult of Pharmacology* by Richard DeGrandpre," *Addiction* 102, nos. 1006–7 (2007): 107–8.

46. D. T. Courtwright, *Forces of Habit: Drugs and the Making of the Modern World* (Cambridge, MA: Harvard University Press, 2001), 41.

47. Hutchinson, "Patterns of Marihuana Use," 176.

48. P. Rosado, "O Vício da Diamba no Estado do Pará. Uma toxicose que ressurge entre nós," in *Maconha: Coletânea de trabalhos Brasileiros*, ed. Serviço Nacional de Educação Sanitária (Rio de Janeiro: Ministério da Saúde, 1958), 91.

49. M. Pio Corrêa, *Diccionario das plantas úteis do Brasil e das exóticas cultivadas*, vol. 1 (Rio de Janeiro: Imprensa Nacional, 1926), 472. Pio Corrêa's original reads, "Com o nefando trafico, [*Cannabis*] vir de uma á outra margem do Atlantico, trazidas as sementes amarradas em boneca na ponta dos pannos ou tangas pelos desventurados captivos." Although the primary meaning of *boneca* is "doll," a secondary meaning is "[uma b]olinha de qualquer substância, amarrada num pano" (a little ball of whatever substance, tied in a cloth). This secondary meaning is connoted by the construction *em boneca*: J. P. Machado, *Dicionário da língua portuguesa*, vol. 1 (Lisbon: Sociedade de Língua Portuguesa, 1958), 1012.

50. M. Rediker, *The Slave Ship: A Human History* (New York: Viking, 2007); J. A. Carney and R. N. Rosomoff, *In the Shadow of Slavery: Africa's Botanical Legacy in the Atlantic World* (Berkeley: University of California Press, 2009).

51. G. Freyre, *Nordeste: Aspectos da influencia da canna sobre a vida e a paizagem do Nordeste do Brasil* (Rio de Janeiro: José Olympio, 1937), 15.

52. Duvall, *Cannabis*, chap. 7.

53. Carney and Rosomoff, *In the Shadow of Slavery*; J. A. Carney, *Black Rice: The African Origins of Rice Cultivation in the Americas* (Cambridge, MA: Harvard University Press, 2001); J. A. Carney and R. A. Voeks, "Landscape Legacies of the African Diaspora in Brazil," *Progress in Human Geography* 27, no. 2 (2003): 139–52; Sluyter, *Black Ranching Frontiers*; T. R. van Andel, C. I. E. A. van't Klooster, D. Quiroz, A. M. Towns, S. Ruysschaert, and M. van den Berg, "Local Plant Names Reveal That Enslaved Africans Recognized Substantial Parts of the New World Flora," *Proceedings of the National Academy of Sciences of the United States of America* 111, no. 50 (2014): E5346–53; C. S. Duvall, "A Maroon Legacy? Sketching African Contributions to Live Fencing Practices in Early Spanish America," *Singapore Journal of Tropical Geography* 30, no. 2 (2009): 232–47; A. Sluyter and C. S. Duvall, "African Rangeland Burning and Colonial Ranching Landscapes in the Neo-tropics," *Geographical Review* 106, no. 2 (2016): 294–311.

54. There is no single, overarching term accepted for generalizing about the Indigenous peoples of the Americas, comparable to "Africans" or "Europeans." Since I am writing in the United States, I will use "American Indian" as an overarching term, though I recognize it is not used in many countries and contexts. In specific countries and contexts, I will use narrower terms—most notably "Indigenous people" in the case of Brazil. My selection of "American Indian" over "Native American" in the United States follows the perspective of Russell Means, an Oglala Lakota leader: see I. Watson, "Introduction," in *Indigenous Peoples as Subjects of International Law*, ed. I. Watson (New York: Routledge, 2017).

Sources on pipe history and archaeology: E. Zangato, "Early Smoking Pipes in the North-Western Central African Republic," *Africa* (Rome) 56, no. 3 (2001): 365–95; J. E. Philips, "African Smoking and Pipes," *Journal of African History* 24, no. 3 (1983): 303–19; N. J. van der Merwe, "Antiquity of the Smoking Habit in Africa," *Transactions of the Royal Society of South Africa* 60, no. 2 (2005): 147–50; J. P. Ossah Mvondo, "L'archéologie des pipes en Afrique intertropicale," Ph.D. diss., Université de Paris I Panthéon-Sorbonne, 1988.

55. N. J. Van der Merwe, "Cannabis Smoking in 13th–14th Century Ethiopia: Chemical Evidence," in *Cannabis and Culture*, ed. V. Rubin (The Hague: Mouton, 1975), 77–80.

56. Booth, *Cannabis*, 53; W. La Barre, "History and Ethnography of Cannabis," in *Culture in Context: Selected Writings of Weston La Barre* (Durham, NC: Duke University Press, 1980), 93–107.

57. Ossah Mvondo, "L'archéologie des pipes en Afrique intertropicale," 24–32, 744–53; Zangato, "Early Smoking Pipes in the North-Western Central African Republic"; Philips, "African Smoking and Pipes"; J. P. Ossah Mvondo, "La question des pipes archéologiques en Afrique: Les nouvelles évidences," *West African Journal of Archaeology* 24 (1994): 1–19.

58. E. J. Keall, "Smokers' Pipes and the Fine Pottery Tradition of Hays," *Proceedings of the Seminar for Arabian Studies* 22 (1992): 29–46; W. Floor, "The Art of Smoking in Iran and Other Uses of Tobacco," *Iranian Studies* 35, nos. 1–3 (2002): 48.

59. E. J. Keall, "One Man's Mead Is Another Man's Persian: One Man's Coconut Is Another Man's Grenade," *Muqarnas* 10 (1993): 275–85.

60. B. Laufer, "The Introduction of Tobacco into Africa," in *Tobacco and Its Use in Africa*, Anthropology leaflet no. 29, ed. B. Laufer, W. D. Hambly, and R. Linton (Chicago: Field Museum of Natural History, 1930), 10.

61. Philips, "African Smoking and Pipes," 313.

62. Burton, *Wanderings in West Africa from Liverpool to Fernando Po*, 2:224; P. B. Du Chaillu, *Explorations and Adventures in Equatorial Africa* (New York: Harper Brothers, 1861), 420.

63. H. Nipperdey, "The Industrial Products and Food-stuffs of the Congo," *Scottish Geographical Magazine* 2, no. 8 (1886): 485–86.

64. F. R. Wulsin, *Varia Africana V: An Archaeological Reconnaissance of the Shari Basin*, ed. E. A. Hooton and N. I. Bates (Cambridge, MA: Harvard African Studies, 1932), 52–53.

65. Booth, *Cannabis*, 53. See also Courtwright, *Forces of Habit*, 40; Clarke and Merlin, *Cannabis*, 127.

66. Sluyter, *Black Ranching Frontiers*, 218.

67. Duvall, *Cannabis*, chap. 2.

68. J. dos Santos, *Ethiopia oriental e varia historia de covsas* (Evora, Portugal: Impressa no Conuento de S. Domingos, 1609), 20B; E. de Flacourt, *Histoire de la grande isle de Madagascar* (Paris: François Clouzier, 1661), 145; P. Kolbe, *Naaukeurige en Uitvoerige Beschryving van de Kaap de Goede Hoop*, vol. 1 (Amsterdam: Balthazar Lakeman, 1727), 314.

69. A. Margarido, "Les Porteurs: Forme de domination et agents de changement en Angola (XVIIe–XIXe siècles)," *Revue Française d'Histoire d'Outre-mer* 65, no. 240 (1978): 377–400.

70. Duvall, *Cannabis*, 173–75; M. Alloula, *The Colonial Harem* (Minneapolis: University of Minnesota Press, 1986), 74.

71. W. W. Reade, *The African Sketch-Book*, vol. 2 (London: Smith, Elder, 1873), 343–44.

72. D. A. Livingstone, *Missionary Travels and Researches in South Africa* (London: John Murray, 1857), 540.

73. R. F. Burton, *Scinde; or, The Unhappy Valley*, vol. 2 (London: Richard Bentley, 1851), 234–35. Despite this comment, Burton likely first used *bhang* while in the royal army in India in the 1840s.

74. R. F. Burton, *Explorations of the Highlands of Brazil*, vol. 2 (London: Tinsley Brothers, 1869), 276.

75. R. F. Burton, *Two Trips to Gorilla Land and the Cataracts of the Congo*, vol. 2 (London: Sampson Low, Marston, Low, and Searle, 1876), 296.

76. He admitted using it in Arabia, not Egypt: R. F. Burton, *Personal Narrative of a Pilgrimage to El Medinah and Meccah*, 1st ed., vol. 1 (London: Longman, Brown, Green, Longmans, and Roberts, 1856), 51.

77. See, e.g., R. F. Burton, *The Book of the Thousand Nights and a Night*, vol. 3 (London: Private Printing for the Burton Club, n.d. [1886–1888]), 93.

78. R. O. Clarke, "Short Notes of the Prevailing Diseases in the Colony of Sierra Leone," *Journal of the Royal Statistical Society* 19 (1853): 65.

79. G. Wiet, ed., *Maqrizi: El-Mawâ'iz wa'l-i'tibâr fî dhikr el-khitat wa'l-âthâr*, vol. 2 (Cairo: Institut Français d'Archéologie Orientale, 1913), 90; J. Ohrwalder, *Ten Years' Captivity in the Mahdi's Camp: 1882–1892* (Leipzig: Heinemann and Balestier, 1893), 17.

80. Duvall, *Cannabis*, 95.

81. J. F. Thackeray, N. J. Van der Merwe, and T. A. Van der Merwe, "Chemical Analysis of Residues from Seventeenth-Century Clay Pipes from Stratford-upon-Avon and Environs," *South African Journal of Science* 97 (January–February 2001): 19–21.

82. For information on Monfried, see R. P. T. Davenport-Hines, *The Pursuit of Oblivion: A Global History of Narcotics* (New York: W. W. Norton, 2004), 255. Monfried's books most relevant to cannabis are H. de Monfried and I. Treat, *Pearls, Arms, and Hashish* (New York: Coward-McCann, 1930); H. de Monfried, *La cargaison enchantée: Charas* (Paris: Bernard Grasset, 1962); H. de Monfried, *Charas* (Paris: Pavois, 1947); H. de Monfried, *La croisère du hachich* (Paris: Bernard Grasset, 1933).

83. Alloula, *The Colonial Harem*, 74.

84. W. W. Reade, *Savage Africa* (New York: Harper and Brothers, 1864), 423.

85. Paul Bowles offered a Moroccan *majūn* recipe in the *Rolling Stone* article from 1974: see Rogers, "Paul Bowles."

86. É. Dupont, *Lettres sur le Congo: Récit d'un voyage scientifique entre l'embouchure du fleuve et le confluent du Kassaï* (Paris: C. Reinwald, 1889), 644.

87. W. A. Emboden, "Ritual Use of *Cannabis Sativa* L.: A Historical-Ethnographic Survey," in *Flesh of the Gods: The Ritual Use of Hallucinogens*, ed. P. T. Furst (Prospect Heights, IL: Waveland, 1972), 226.

88. Clarke and Merlin, *Cannabis*, 127, 235.

89. H. L. Tangye, *In New South Africa: Travels in the Transvaal and Rhodesia* (London: Simpkin, Marshall, Hamilton, Kent, 1900), 313–14.

90. F. Ames, "A Clinical and Metabolic Study of Acute Intoxication with *Cannabis Sativa* and Its Role in the Model Psychoses," *British Journal of Psychiatry* 104 (1958): 975–76.

91. C. S. Duvall, "Linguistic Evidence on the Historical and Cultural Geographies of Cannabis, Tobacco, and Smoking Pipes in Africa," *Economic Botany* (forthcoming).

I discuss my linguistic data in chapter 3, which comprises words for cannabis, tobacco, and smoking pipe in several hundred African languages. I have posted my raw data openly on the internet, in the University of New Mexico's Digital Repository (https://digitalrepository.unm.edu/). To locate the data in this repository, search for the title of the forthcoming paper identified in this note.

92. Du Toit, *Cannabis in Africa*; J. B. Page, "Costa Rican Marihuana Smokers and the Amotivational Syndrome Hypothesis," Ph.D. diss., University of Florida, Gainesville, 1976; J. B. Page, "A Brief History of Mind-Altering Drug Use in Prerevolutionary Cuba," *Cuban Studies/Estudios Cubanos* 12, no. 2 (1982): 56–71; W. E. Carter, *Cannabis in Costa Rica: A Study of Chronic Marijuana Use* (Philadelphia: Institute for the Study of Human Issues, 1980); M. C. Dreher, *Working Men and Ganja: Marihuana Use in Rural Jamaica* (Philadelphia: Institute for the Study of Human Issues, 1982); A. Hamid, *The Ganja Complex: Rastafari and Marijuana* (Lanham, MD: Lexington, 2002); V. Rubin and L. Comitas, *Ganja in Jamaica: The Effects of Marijuana Use* (New York: Mouton de Gruyter, 1975); W. L. Partridge, "Exchange Relationships in a Community on the North Coast of Colombia with Special Reference to Cannabis," Ph.D. diss., University of Florida, Gainesville, 1974.

93. I describe the enslaved population movements as migrations, and enslaved people as migrants, to denote their geographic translocation. Enslaved people did not voluntarily make this movement.

94. W. F. Daniell, "On the D'amba, or Dakka, of Southern Africa," *Pharmaceutical Journal and Transactions* 9, no. 8 (1850): 363–65.

95. Such as Clarke and Merlin, *Cannabis*; Lee, *Smoke Signals*; Russo, "The Pharmacological History of Cannabis."

96. Carney, *Black Rice*; Carney and Rosomoff, *In the Shadow of Slavery*; Voeks, *Sacred Leaves of Candomblé*.

97. Duvall, *Cannabis*.

98. Du Chaillu, *Explorations and Adventures*, 420.

99. Daniell, "On the D'amba," 365.

100. C. Jeannest, *Quatre années au Congo* (Paris: G. Charpentier, 1883), 86.

101. C. d. Escayrac de Lauture, *Le désert et le Soudan* (Paris: J. Dumaine and Friedrich Klincksieck, 1853), 225.

102. T. Gautier, "Le Club des Hachichins," *Revue des Deux Mondes* 16 (February 1846): 520–35.

103. G. M'Henry, "An Account of the Liberated African Establishment at St. Helena, Chapter II," *Simmond's Colonial Magazine* 5 (1845): 437.

104. L. Parsons and M. Hill, *Endocannabinoids* (Waltham, MA: Academic Press, 2015).

105. National Academies of Sciences, Engineering and Medicine, *The Health Effects of Cannabis and Cannabinoids: The Current State of Evidence and Recommendations for Research* (Washington, DC: National Academies, 2017); R. Pertwee, ed., *Handbook of Cannabis* (Oxford: Oxford University Press, 2014); D. Castle, R. M. Murray, and D. C. D'Souza, eds., *Marijuana and Madness* (Cambridge: Cambridge University Press, 2011). See also N. D. Volkow, R. D. Baler, W. M. Compton, and S. R. B. Weiss, "Adverse Health Effects of Marijuana Use," *New England Journal of Medicine* 370, no. 23 (2014): 2219–27;

W. Hall and L. Degenhardt, "The Adverse Health Effects of Chronic Cannabis Use," *Drug Testing and Analysis* 6 (2014): 39–45; P. F. Whiting, R. F. Wolff, S. Deshpande, M. Di Nision, S. Duffy, A. V. Hernandez, C. Keurentjes, S. Lang, K. Misso, S. Ryder, S. Schmidlkofer, M. Westwood, and J. Kleijnen, "Cannabinoids for Medical Use: A Systematic Review and Meta-analysis," *Journal of the American Medical Association* 313, no. 24 (2015): 2456–73.

106. A. Dumas, *Le véloce ou Tanger, Alger et Tunis*, vol. 4 (Brussels: Ch. Muquardt, 1849), 53; E. B. Russo, A. Merzouki, J. Molero Mesa, K. A. Frey, and P. J. Bach, "Cannabis Improves Night Vision: A Case Study of Dark Adaptometry and Scotopic Sensitivity in Kif Smokers of the Rif Mountains of Northern Morocco," *Journal of Ethnopharmacology* 93 (2004): 99–104.

107. B. Hartung, S. Kauferstein, S. Ritz-Timme, and T. Daldrup, "Sudden Unexpected Death under Acute Influence of Cannabis," *Forensic Science International* 237 (2014): e11–13; J. Sachs, E. McGlade, and D. Yurgelun-Todd, "Safety and Toxicology of Cannabinoids," *Neurotherapeutics* 12, no. 4 (2015): 735–46; A. Singh, S. Saluja, S. Agrawal, M. Thind, S. Nanda, and J. Shiranj, "Cardiovascular Complications of Marijuana and Related Substances: A Review," *Cardiology and Therapy* 7, no. 1 (2018): 45–59; A. R. Turner and S. Agrawal, "Marijuana Toxicity," *StatPearls*, 2017, accessed 28 August 2017, https://www.ncbi.nlm.nih.gov/books/NBK430823.

108. T. H. M. Moore, S. Zammit, A. Lingford-Hughes, T. R. E. Barnes, P. B. Jones, M. Burke, and G. Lewis, "Cannabis Use and Risk of Psychotic or Affective Mental Health Outcomes: A Systematic Review," *The Lancet* 370, no. 9584 (2007): 319–28; P. Casadio, C. Fernandes, R. M. Murray, and M. Di Forti, "Cannabis Use in Young People: The Risk for Schizophrenia," *Neuroscience and Biobehavioral Reviews* 35 (2011): 1779–87. J. Vaucher, B. J. Keating, A. M. Lasserre, W. Gan, D. M. Lyall, J. Ward, D. J. Smith, J. P. Pell, N. Sattar, G. Paré, and M. V. Holmes, "Cannabis Use and Risk of Schizophrenia: A Mendelian Randomization Study," *Molecular Psychiatry* 23, no. 5 (2018): 1287–92.

109. See, e.g., J. Moreau, *Du hachisch et de l'aliénation mentale* (Paris: Fortin, Masson, and Co., 1845); T. Ireland, "Insanity from the Abuse of Indian Hemp," *Alienist and Neurologist* 14 (1893): 622–30; A. Maria, "Note sur la folie haschichique," *Nouvelle Iconographie de la Salpêtrière* 20 (1907): 252–57.

110. R. van Winkel and Genetic Risk and Outcome of Psychosis (GROUP) Investigators, "Family-based Analysis of Genetic Variation Underlying Psychosis-Inducing Effects of Cannabis: Sibling Analysis and Proband Follow-up," *Archives of General Psychiatry* 68, no. 2 (2011): 148–57.

111. A. T. Weil, N. T. Zinberg, and J. M. Nelsen, "Clinical and Psychological Effects of Marihuana in Man," *Science* 162, no. 859 (1968): 1234–42; N. E. Zinberg, *Drug, Set, and Setting: The Basis for Controlled Intoxicant Use* (New Haven, CT: Yale University Press, 1986).

112. Hall and Degenhardt, "The Adverse Health Effects of Chronic Cannabis Use"; Volkow et al., "Adverse Health Effects of Marijuana Use"; W. Hall and R. Pacula, *Cannabis Use and Dependence: Public Health and Public Policy* (Cambridge: Cambridge University Press, 2010).

113. C. J. G. Bourhill, "The Smoking of *Dagga* (Indian Hemp) among the Native Races of South Africa and the Resultant Evils," M.D. diss., School of Medicine, University of Edinburgh, 1913.

114. R. Brunel, *Le monachisme errant dans l'Islam* (Paris: Maisonneuve and Larose, [1955] 2001), 315–16.

115. French physicians in Morocco associated several mental illnesses with *kif*, including schizophrenia: Brunel, *Le monachisme errant dans l'Islam*, 315.

116. G. G. Nahas, "Hashish and Drug Abuse in Egypt during the 19th and 20th Centuries," *Bulletin of the New York Academy of Medicine* 61, no. 5 (1985): 430.

117. Révérend Père Colle, *Les Baluba*, vol. 1 (Brussels: Albert de Wit, 1913), 119.

118. Daniell, "On the D'amba"; A. Chevalier, "Histoire de deux plantes cultivées d'importance primordiale: Le Lin et le Chanvre," *Revue de Botanique Appliquée et d'Agriculture Coloniale* 24, nos. 269–71 (1944): 51–71; H. Ward, "Ethnographical Notes Relating to the Congo Tribes," *Journal of the Anthropological Institute of Great Britain and Ireland* 24 (1895): 295.

119. For Guiana in 1891, ten thousand pounds of *ganja* was imported, consumed primarily by the colony's 106,000 Indian laborers: Pharmaceutical Resident, "Opium-Dealing in British Guiana," *Chemist and Druggist* 42 (28 January 1893): 120–21. Mazagan, Morocco, had seven thousand to eight thousand people, who collectively consumed 2,700 kilograms of herbal cannabis: L. Raynaud, *Étude sur l'hygiène et la médecine au Maroc suivie d'une notice sur la climatologie des principales villes de l'empire* (Algiers: S. Léon, 1902), 108.

120. Bourhill, "The Smoking of *Dagga* (Indian Hemp) among the Native Races of South Africa and the Resultant Evils," 35.

121. Ireland, "Insanity from the Abuse of Indian Hemp," 629; E. L. Erickson, "The Introduction of East Indian Coolies into the British West Indies," *Journal of Modern History* 6, no. 2 (1934): 141.

122. For 3–4 shillings, .19–.25 pounds, or 85–113 grams, could be had. The 16 shilling per pound rate is from West India Royal Commission, *Report of the West India Royal Commission: Appendix C, Volume II., Containing Parts II, III, IV, and V—Proceedings, Evidence, and Documents Relating to British Guiana, Barbados, Trinidad, and Tobago* (London: Eyre and Spottiswoode, 1897), 343.

123. Y. Gaoni and R. Mechoulam, "Isolation, Structure and Partial Synthesis of an Active Constituent of Hashish," *Journal of the American Chemical Society* 86 (1964): 1646.

124. P. B. Baker, R. Bagon, and A. Gough, "Variation in the THC Content in Illicitly Imported Cannabis Products," *Bulletin on Narcotics* 33, no. 4 (1980): 47–54. More recent studies with similar findings include R. S. Londt, "An Investigation of Tetrahydrocannabinol, Cannabidiol and Cannabinol Content of Cannabis Confiscated by the South African Police Service's Forensic Laboratories from Various Regions of South Africa," Ph.D. diss., University of Cape Town, 2014; R. Maharaj, G. Singh, C. Thomas, and D. John, "Physical and Chemical Characteristics of Cannabis Found in Trinidad and Tobago," *Internet Journal of Forensic Science* 2, no. 2 (2006).

125. J. Pernambuco, "A Maconha em Pernambuco," in *Novos estudos Afro-brasileiros: Trabalhos apresentados ao 1.° Congresso Afro-brasileiro do Recife*, ed. A. Ramos, Bibliotheca

de Divulgação Scientifica, vol. 9 (Rio de Janeiro: Civilização Brasileira, 1937), 190. See also J. J. Monteiro, *Angola and the River Congo*, vol. 2 (London: Macmillan, 1875), 257.

126. E. B. Russo, "Clinical Endocannabinoid Deficiency (cecd): Can This Concept Explain Therapeutic Benefits of Cannabis in Migraine, Fibromyalgia, Irritable Bowel Syndrome and Other Treatment-Resistant Conditions?" *Neuroendocrinology Letters* 25, nos. 1–2 (2008): 31–39.

127. Important examples include Carney, *Black Rice*; Carney and Rosomoff, *In the Shadow of Slavery*; L. Head and J. Atchison, "Cultural Ecology: Emerging Human-Plant Geographies," *Progress in Human Geography* 33, no. 2 (2009): 236–45; L. Head, J. Atchison, and A. Gates, *Ingrained: A Human Bio-geography of Wheat* (Surrey, UK: Ashgate, 2012); L. Head and P. Muir, "Nativeness, Invasiveness, and Nation in Australian Plants," *Geographical Review* 94, no. 2 (2004): 199–217; S. W. Mintz, *Sweetness and Power: The Place of Sugar in Modern History* (New York: Viking, 1985); A. Crosby, *Ecological Imperialism: The Biological Expansion of Europe, 900–1900* (Cambridge: Cambridge University Press, 1986); A. W. Crosby Jr., *America, Russia, Hemp, and Napoleon: American Trade with Russia and the Baltic, 1783–1812* (Columbus: Ohio State University Press, 1965); A. W. Crosby, *The Columbian Exchange: Biological and Cultural Consequences of 1492* (Westport, CT: Greenwood, 1972).

128. Hamid, *The Ganja Complex*.

129. K. H. Offen, "Historical Political Ecology: An Introduction," *Historical Geography* 32 (2004): 19–42; P. Robbins, *Political Ecology*, 2d ed. (Malden, MA: Blackwell, 2011).

130. P. Jackson and A. H. Neely, "Triangulating Health: Toward a Practice of a Political Ecology of Health," *Progress in Human Geography* 39, no. 1 (2015): 47–64; J. Guthman, *Weighing In: Obesity, Food Justice, and the Limits of Capitalism* (Berkeley: University of California Press, 2011); M. Singer, *Drugging the Poor: Legal and Illegal Drugs and Social Inequality* (Long Grove, IL: Waveland, 2008); B. Mansfield, "Health as a Nature-Society Question," *Environment and Planning A* 40, no. 5 (2008): 1015–19.

131. L. Gezon, *Drug Effects: Khat in Biocultural and Socioeconomic Perspective* (Walnut Creek, CA: Left Coast, 2012); C. Herrick, "The Political Ecology of Alcohol as 'Disaster' in South Africa's Western Cape," *Geoforum* 43, no. 6 (2012): 1045–56. See Mintz, *Sweetness and Power*.

132. R. J. Turner and F. Marino, "Social Support and Social Structure: A Descriptive Epidemiology," *Journal of Health and Social Behavior* 35, no. 3 (1994): 193–212; M. S. Porta, S. Greenland, M. Hernán, I. dos Santos Silva, J. M. Last, and International Epidemiological Association, *A Dictionary of Epidemiology*, 6th ed. (Oxford: Oxford University Press, 2014).

133. P. Robbins, J. Hintz, and S. A. Moore, *Environment and Society: A Critical Introduction*, 2d ed. (Hoboken, NJ: Wiley-Blackwell, 2014), 98–119.

134. W. Jankowiak and D. Bradburd, *Drugs, Labor and Colonial Expansion* (Tucson: University of Arizona Press, 2003); A. A. Laudati, "Out of the Shadows: Negotiations and Networks in the Cannabis Trade in Eastern Democratic Republic of Congo," in *Drugs in Africa: Histories and Ethnographies of Use*, ed. G. Klantschnig, N. Carrier, and C. Ambler (Gordonsville, NY: Palgrave Macmillan, 2014), 161–81.

135. R. Cohen, "Resistance and Hidden Forms of Consciousness among African Workers," *Review of African Political Economy* 7, no. 19 (1980): 8–22.

136. G. Huggan and H. Tiffin, *Postcolonial Ecocriticism: Literature, Animals, Environment* (London: Routledge, 2010); D. K. Davis and E. Burke III, *Environmental Imaginaries of the Middle East and North Africa* (Athens: Ohio University Press, 2011); C. Lutz and J. L. Collins, *Reading National Geographic* (Chicago: University of Chicago Press, 1993); B. Caminero-Santangelo and G. Myers, eds., *Environment at the Margins: Literary and Environmental Studies in Africa* (Athens: Ohio University Press, 2011); M. J. Goldman, P. Nadasdy, and M. D. Turner, eds., *Knowing Nature: Conversations at the Intersection of Political Ecology and Science Studies* (Chicago: University of Chicago Press, 2011); S. Jasanoff, "Ordering Knowledge, Ordering Society," in *States of Knowledge: The Co-production of Science and Social Order*, ed. S. Jasanoff (London: Routledge, 2004), 13–45; T. Forsyth, *Critical Political Ecology: The Politics of Environmental Science* (London: Routledge, 2003).

137. J. Fairhead and M. Leach, *Misreading the African Landscape: Society and Ecology in a Forest-Savanna Mosaic* (Cambridge: Cambridge University Press, 1996); J. Fairhead and M. Leach, *Reframing Deforestation: Global Analysis and Local Realities: Studies in West Africa* (London: Routledge, 1998); M. Leach and R. Mearns, eds., *The Lie of the Land: Challenging Received Wisdom on the African Environment*, African Issues (Oxford: James Currey, 1996); K. B. Showers, *Imperial Gullies: Soil Erosion and Conservation in Lesotho* (Athens: Ohio University Press, 2005); D. K. Davis, *Resurrecting the Granary of Rome: Environmental History and French Colonial Expansion in North Africa* (Athens: Ohio University Press, 2007).

2. RACE AND PLANT EVOLUTION

1. B. Berlin, *Ethnobiological Classification: Principles of Categorization of Plants and Animals in Traditional Societies* (Princeton, NJ: Princeton University Press, 1992); R. Ellen, *The Cultural Relations of Classification* (Cambridge: Cambridge University Press, 1993).

2. L. Schiebinger, "Agnotology and Exotic Abortifacients: The Cultural Production of Ignorance in the Eighteenth-Century Atlantic World," *Proceedings of the American Philosophical Society* 149, no. 3 (2005): 316–43.

3. I am approximating the evolutionary species concept: see E. O. Wiley and R. L. Mayden, "The Evolutionary Species Concept," in *Species Concepts and Phylogenetic Theory: A Debate*, ed. Q. D. Wheeler and R. Meier (New York: Columbia University Press, 2000), 70–89.

4. J. Cracraft, "Geographic Differentiation, Cladistics, and Vicariance Biogeography: Reconstructing the Tempo and Mode of Evolution," *American Zoologist* 22 (1982): 411–24; J. Cracraft, "Speciation and Its Ontology: The Empirical Consequences of Alternative Species Concepts for Understanding Patterns and Processes of Differentiation," in *Speciation and Its Consequences*, ed. D. Otte and J. A. Endler (Sunderland, MA: Sinauer, 1989), 28–59; L. Andersson, "An Ontological Dilemma: Epistemology and Methodology of Historical Biogeography," *Journal of Biogeography* 23, no. 3 (1996): 269–77; S. Knapp, "Species Concepts and Floras: What Are Species For?" *Biological Journal of the Linnaean Society* 95, no. 1 (2008): 17–25.

5. L. H. Rieseberg, T. E. Wood, and E. J. Baack, "The Nature of Plant Species," *Nature* 440 (23 March 2006): 524–27.

6. W. A. Emboden, "The Genus *Cannabis* and the Correct Use of Taxonomic Categories," *Journal of Psychoactive Drugs* 13, no. 1 (1981): 15–21; E. Small, *The Species Problem in Cannabis: Science and Semantics*, 2 vols. (Toronto: Corpus, 1979).

7. B. S. Arbogast and G. J. Kenagy, "Comparative Phylogeography as an Integrative Approach to Historical Biogeography," *Journal of Biogeography* 28, no. 7 (2001): 819–25; M. C. Ebach and C. J. Humphries, "Ontology of Biogeography," *Journal of Biogeography* 30, no. 6 (2003): 960; D. Bickford, D. J. Lohman, N. S. Sodhi, P. K. L. Ng, R. Meier, K. Winkler, K. K. Ingram, and I. Das, "Cryptic Species as a Window on Diversity and Conservation," *Trends in Ecology and Evolution* 22, no. 3 (2007): 148–55.

8. A. Sluyter, *Black Ranching Frontiers: African Cattle Herders of the Atlantic World, 1500–1900* (New Haven, CT: Yale University Press, 2012); J. A. Carney and R. N. Rosomoff, *In the Shadow of Slavery: Africa's Botanical Legacy in the Atlantic World* (Berkeley: University of California Press, 2009); R. A. Voeks, *Sacred Leaves of Candomblé: African Magic, Medicine, and Religion in Brazil* (Austin: University of Texas Press, 1997).

9. J. A. Carney, *Black Rice: The African Origins of Rice Cultivation in the Americas* (Cambridge, MA: Harvard University Press, 2001).

10. R. C. Clarke and M. D. Merlin, *Cannabis: Evolution and Ethnobotany* (Berkeley: University of California Press, 2013), 314–17.

11. Emboden, "The Genus *Cannabis* and the Correct Use of Taxonomic Categories"; E. Small, "Evolution and Classification of *Cannabis sativa* (Marijuana, Hemp) in Relation to Human Utilization," *Botanical Review* 81 (2015): 189–294.

12. E. Small and A. Cronquist, "A Practical and Natural Taxonomy for *Cannabis*," *Taxon* 25, no. 4 (1976): 409.

13. J.-B. Lamarck, *Encyclopédie méthodique: Botanique*, vol. 1, pt. 2 (Paris: Panckouke and Plomteux, 1783), 695.

14. Clarke and Merlin, *Cannabis*; Small, "Evolution and Classification of *Cannabis sativa* (Marijuana, Hemp) in Relation to Human Utilization"; C. S. Duvall, *Cannabis* (London: Reaktion, 2015).

15. C. Acosta, *Tractado de las drogas, y medicinas de la Indias Orientales* (Burgos, Spain: Martin de Victoria, 1578), 360–61; I. Dukerley, "Note sur les différences que présente avec le chanvre ordinaire et la variété de cette espèce connue en Algérie sous les noms de *kif* et de *tekrouri*," *Bulletin de la Société Botanique de France* 3 (9 November 1866): 401–6; W. A. Emboden, "Cannabis: A Polytypic Genus," *Economic Botany* 28, no. 3 (1974): 304–10; G. Rossi and A. H. Husson, "Note sur le hachych," *Revue d'Égypte* 2 (February [1847] 1896): 525–31.

16. Small and Cronquist, "A Practical and Natural Taxonomy for *Cannabis*," 405; Small, "Evolution and Classification of *Cannabis sativa* (Marijuana, Hemp) in Relation to Human Utilization."

17. Clarke and Merlin, *Cannabis*, 317–20; K. W. Hillig and P. G. Mahlberg, "A Chemotaxonomic Analysis of Cannabinoid Variation in *Cannabis* (Cannabaceae)," *American Journal of Botany* 91, no. 6 (2004): 966–75.

18. S. L. Datwyler and G. D. Weiblen, "Genetic Variation in Hemp and Marijuana (*Cannabis Sativa* L.) According to Amplified Fragment Length Polymorphisms," *Journal of Forensic Sciences* 51, no. 2 (2006): 371–75; E. P. M. de Meijer, M. Bagatta, A. Carboni, P. Crucitti, V. M. C. Moliterni, P. Ranalli, and G. Mandolino, "The Inheritance of Chemical Phenotype in *Cannabis Sativa* L.," *Genetics* 163 (2003): 335–46; H. van Bakel, J. M. Stout, A. G. Cote, C. M. Tallon, A. G. Sharpe, T. R. Hughes, and J. E. Page, "The Draft Genome and Transcriptome of *Cannabis Sativa*," *Genome Biology* 12, no. 10 (2011): R102; S. Gilmore, R. Peakall, and J. Robertson, "Organelle DNA Haplotypes Reflect Crop-Use Characteristics and Geographic Origins of *Cannabis Sativa*," *Forensic Science International* 172 (2007): 179–90; J. Sawler, J. M. Stout, K. M. Gardner, D. Hudson, J. Vidmar, L. Butler, J. E. Page, and S. Myles, "The Genetic Structure of Marijuana and Hemp," *PLoS One* 10, no. 8 (2015): e0133292.

19. K. W. Hillig, "Genetic Evidence for Speciation in *Cannabis* (Cannabaceae)," *Genetic Resources and Crop Evolution* 52 (2005): 161–80.

20. Hillig and Mahlberg, "A Chemotaxonomic Analysis of Cannabinoid Variation in *Cannabis* (Cannabaceae)," 973.

21. Sawler et al., "The Genetic Structure of Marijuana and Hemp."

22. Hillig, "Genetic Evidence for Speciation in *Cannabis* (Cannabaceae)," 177–78; De Meijer et al., "The Inheritance of Chemical Phenotype in *Cannabis Sativa* L."; K. W. Hillig, "A Combined Analysis of Agronomic Traits and Allozyme Allele Frequencies for 69 *Cannabis* Accessions," *Journal of Industrial Hemp* 10, no. 1 (2005): 17–30.

23. Hillig, "Genetic Evidence for Speciation in *Cannabis* (Cannabaceae)." The East Asian plant population has distinctive chemical characteristics, including high levels of the cannabinoid cannabigerol monomethylether (CBGM).

24. Hillig and Mahlberg, "A Chemotaxonomic Analysis of Cannabinoid Variation in *Cannabis* (Cannabaceae)"; Clarke and Merlin, *Cannabis*; R. E. Schultes and A. Hofmann, *The Botany and Chemistry of Hallucinogens*, 2d ed. (Springfield, IL: Charles C. Thomas, 1980).

25. Duvall, *Cannabis*, 49–57, 81–82.

26. Hillig and Mahlberg, "A Chemotaxonomic Analysis of Cannabinoid Variation in *Cannabis* (Cannabaceae)," 972.

27. Duvall, *Cannabis*, 109–11.

28. Hillig and Mahlberg, "A Chemotaxonomic Analysis of Cannabinoid Variation in *Cannabis* (Cannabaceae)."

29. M. S. Chauhan and M. F. Quamar, "Pollen Records of Vegetation and Inferred Climate Change in Southwestern Madhya Pradesh during the Last circa 3800 Years," *Journal of the Geological Society of India* 80, no. 4 (2012): 470–80.

30. A. de Candolle, *Géographie botanique raisonnée*, vol. 2 (Paris: Masson, 1855), 833; V. Hehn, *Kulturpflanzen und Hausthiere in ihrem übergang aus Asien nach Griechenland und Italien sowie das übrige Europa* (Berlin: Gebrüder Borntraeger, 1870), 157.

31. E. P. M. de Meijer, "The Chemical Phenotypes (Chemotypes) of *Cannabis*," in *Handbook of Cannabis*, ed. R. Pertwee (Oxford: Oxford University Press, 2014), 90.

32. De Meijer, "The Chemical Phenotypes (Chemotypes) of *Cannabis*"; Small, "Evolution and Classification of *Cannabis sativa* (Marijuana, Hemp) in Relation to Human Utilization."

33. Hillig, "Genetic Evidence for Speciation in *Cannabis* (Cannabaceae)"; Sawler et al., "The Genetic Structure of Marijuana and Hemp."

34. Schiebinger, "Agnotology and Exotic Abortifacients"; P. Robbins, "Tracking Invasive Land Covers in India, or Why Our Landscapes Have Never Been Modern," *Annals of the Association of American Geographers* 91, no. 4 (2001): 637–59; P. Robbins, "Comparing Invasive Networks: Cultural and Political Biographies of Invasive Species," *Geographical Review* 94, no. 2 (2004): 139–56.

35. Emboden, "The Genus *Cannabis* and the Correct Use of Taxonomic Categories."

36. Small, "Evolution and Classification of *Cannabis sativa* (Marijuana, Hemp) in Relation to Human Utilization."

37. Clarke and Merlin, *Cannabis*, 51.

38. Clarke and Merlin, *Cannabis*, 311–12.

39. Duvall, *Cannabis*, 146–77.

40. Clarke and Merlin, *Cannabis*, 111.

41. S. Jasanoff, "Ordering Knowledge, Ordering Society," in *States of Knowledge: The Co-production of Science and Social Order*, ed. S. Jasanoff (London: Routledge, 2004), 13–45.

42. Small and Cronquist, "A Practical and Natural Taxonomy for *Cannabis*"; Small, "Evolution and Classification of *Cannabis sativa* (Marijuana, Hemp) in Relation to Human Utilization."

43. I. Campos, *Home Grown: Marijuana and the Origins of Mexico's War on Drugs* (Chapel Hill: University of North Carolina Press, 2012), 64.

44. De Meijer et al., "The Inheritance of Chemical Phenotype in *Cannabis Sativa* L."; Hillig and Mahlberg, "A Chemotaxonomic Analysis of Cannabinoid Variation in *Cannabis* (Cannabaceae)"; E. Small, H. D. Beckstead, and A. Chan, "The Evolution of Cannabinoid Phenotypes in *Cannabis*," *Economic Botany* 29, no. 3 (1975): 219–32; E. P. M. de Meijer, K. M. Hammond, and A. Sutton, "The Inheritance of Chemical Phenotype in *Cannabis Sativa* L. (IV): Cannabinoid-Free Plants," *Euphytica* 168 (2009): 95–112.

45. Clarke and Merlin, *Cannabis*, 22, 39, 51–52, 317, 325, 353, 360–61.

46. Hillig and Mahlberg, "A Chemotaxonomic Analysis of Cannabinoid Variation in *Cannabis* (Cannabaceae)"; De Meijer et al., "The Inheritance of Chemical Phenotype in *Cannabis Sativa* L."; D. Pacifico, F. Miselli, M. Micheler, A. Carboni, P. Ranalli, and G. Mandolino, "Genetics and Marker-Assisted Selection of the Chemotype in *Cannabis Sativa* L.," *Molecular Breeding* 17 (2006): 257–68.

47. G. Zanni and J. M. Opitz, "Annals of Morphology. Atavisms: Phylogenetic Lazarus?" *American Journal of Medical Genetics, Part A* 161A, no. 11 (2013): 2822–35.

48. M. Conan and W. J. Kress, "A Historical View of Relationships between Humans and Plants," in *Botanical Progress, Horticultural Innovations, and Cultural Changes*, ed. M. Conan (Washington, DC: Dumbarton Oaks, 2007), 6.

49. Zanni and Opitz, "Annals of Morphology."

50. R. Thapar, "The Theory of Aryan Race and India: History and Politics," *Social Scientist* 24, nos. 1–3 (1996): 3–29; B. N. Mukherjee, "The Unsolved Aryan Problem," *Indologica Taurinensia* 23–24 (1997–1998): 71–80.

51. Thapar, "The Theory of Aryan Race and India," 5.

52. J. G. Shaffer, "The Indo-Aryan Invasions: Cultural Myth and Archaeological Reality," in *The People of South Asia*, ed. J. R. Lukacs (New York: Plenum, 1984): 77–90; M. Danino, "A Brief Note on Aryan Invasion Theory," *Pragati* 3, no. 108 (2009): 5–20; E. F. Bryant and L. L. Patton, eds., *The Indo-Aryan Controversy: Evidence and Inference in Indian History* (New York: Routledge, 2005).

53. A. de Candolle, *Origin of Cultivated Plants* (London: Kegan Paul, Trench, 1885), 148; F. M. Müller, *Vedic Hymns, Part I: Hymns to the Maruts, Rudra, Vâyu, and Vâta*, vol. 1 (Oxford: Clarendon, 1869), 233; C. T. Buckland, "Ganjah," *National Review* 2, no. 11 (1884): 620.

54. E. L. Abel, *Marihuana: The First Twelve Thousand Years* (New York: Springer, 1980), 16–17.

55. Clarke and Merlin, *Cannabis*, 91, 98–99.

56. Small and Cronquist, "A Practical and Natural Taxonomy for *Cannabis*," 406, 416.

57. The cases of other plants cited as evidence for an Aryan invasion also do not bear scrutiny: see B. B. Lal, "Aryan Invasion of India: Perpetuation of a Myth," in Bryant and Patton, *The Indo-Aryan Controversy*, 50–74.

58. R. B. Strassler, ed., *The Landmark Herodotus: The Histories* (New York: Pantheon, 2007), 311–20.

59. S. I. Rudenko, *Frozen Tombs of Siberia: The Pazyryk Burials of Iron-Age Horsemen* (Berkeley: University of California Press, [1953] 1970), 285.

60. Duvall, *Cannabis*, 50–52; B. Derham, "Archaeological and Ethnographic Toxins in Museum Collections," in *Impact of the Environment on Human Migration in Eurasia*, ed. E. M. Scott, A. Y. Alexseev, and G. Zaitseva (Dordrecht, the Netherlands: Kluwer Academic, 2003): 185–97; R. C. Clarke, *Hashish!* 2d ed. (Los Angeles: Red Eye, 2010), 24.

61. M. Madells, "Investigating Agriculture and Environment in South Asia: Present and Future Contributions of Opal Phytoliths," in *Indus Ethnobiology: New Perspectives from the Field*, ed. S. A. Weber and W. R. Belcher (Lanham, MD: Lexington, 2003), 199–250.

62. Duvall, *Cannabis*, 42.

63. Duvall, *Cannabis*, 40–41.

64. Duvall, *Cannabis*, 34–36.

65. Duvall, *Cannabis*, 50.

66. Bryant and Patton, *The Indo-Aryan Controversy*.

67. Carney and Rosomoff, *In the Shadow of Slavery*; J. M. Diamond, *Guns, Germs, and Steel: The Fates of Human Societies* (New York: W. W. Norton, 1997); A. Crosby, *Ecological Imperialism: The Biological Expansion of Europe, 900–1900* (Cambridge: Cambridge University Press, 1986); A. W. Crosby, *The Columbian Exchange: Biological and Cultural Consequences of 1492* (Westport, CT: Greenwood, 1972).

68. Carney and Rosomoff, *In the Shadow of Slavery*.

69. Carney, *Black Rice*; Carney and Rosomoff, *In the Shadow of Slavery*; Voeks, *Sacred Leaves of Candomblé*; J. A. Carney and R. A. Voeks, "Landscape Legacies of the African Diaspora in Brazil," *Progress in Human Geography* 27, no. 2 (2003): 139–52.

70. M. Booth, *Cannabis: A History* (New York: St. Martin's, 2005), 156.

71. Among Levantine immigrants in California: see "Local Hashish-Eaters," *San Francisco Call*, 24 June 1895, 7.

72. J. C. Munch, "Marihuana and Crime," UNODC *Bulletin on Narcotics* 18, no. 2 (1965): 22.

73. J. C. Adiala, *O Problema da Maconha no Brasil: Ensaio sobre Racismo e Drogas* (Rio de Janeiro: Instituto Universitario de Pesquisas do Rio de Janeiro, 1986).

74. Clarke and Merlin, *Cannabis*, 82, 129; R. J. Schafer, *The Economic Societies in the Spanish World, 1763–1821* (Syracuse, NY: Syracuse University Press, 1958), 322.

75. D. P. West, *Final Status Report* (Honolulu: Hawai'i Industrial Hemp Research Project, 2003); P. Ranalli, ed., *Advances in Hemp Research* (New York: Food Products, 1999); R. C. Clarke, *Marijuana Botany* (Berkeley, CA: Ronin, 1981).

76. A. Humboldt, *Ensayo político sobre la Isla de Cuba*, trans. J. L. Bustamante (Paris: Jules Renouard, 1827), 218; *Diccionario Marítimo Español* (Madrid: Real, 1831), 350.

77. A. Haney and F. A. Bazzazz, "Some Ecological Implications of the Distribution of Hemp (*Cannabis Sativa* L.) in the United States of America," in *The Botany and Chemistry of Cannabis*, ed. C. R. B. Joyce and S. H. Curry (London: J. and A. Churchill, 1970): 39–48.

78. J. T. Schneider, *Dictionary of African Borrowings in Brazilian Portuguese* (Hamburg: Helmut Buske, 1991), 87, 172.

79. Adiala, *O Problema da Maconha no Brasil*.

80. D. Northrup, *Indentured Labor in the Age of Imperialism, 1834–1922* (Cambridge: Cambridge University Press, 1995); K. Saunders, ed., *Indentured Labour in the British Empire, 1834–1920* (London: Croom Helm, 1984).

81. K. Bilby, "The Holy Herb: Notes on the Background of Cannabis in Jamaica," *Caribbean Quarterly* (1985): 82–95.

82. Clarke and Merlin, *Cannabis*, 29, 123.

83. Northrup, *Indentured Labor in the Age of Imperialism*; Saunders, *Indentured Labour in the British Empire*.

84. Schafer, *The Economic Societies in the Spanish World*, 29, 290, 322–23; E. Pérez-Arbaláez, *Plantas útiles de Colombia*, 3d ed. (Bogotá, Colombia: Camacho Roldan, 1956), 513–14; C. de Souza Moraes, *Feitoria do Linho Cânhamo* (Porto Alegre, Brazil: Parlenda, 1994); R. M. Serrera Contreras, *Cultivo y manufactura de lino y canamo en Nueva España (1777–1800)* (Seville, Spain: Escuela de Estudios Hispano-Americanos de Sevilla, 1974).

85. M. Pollan, *The Botany of Desire: A Plant's Eye View of the World* (New York: Random House, 2001).

86. Clarke and Merlin, *Cannabis*, 26.

87. Duvall, *Cannabis*, 28–29.

88. Schultes and Hofmann, *The Botany and Chemistry of Hallucinogens*; Hillig, "Genetic Evidence for Speciation in *Cannabis* (Cannabaceae)."

89. Clarke, *Marijuana Botany*, 124; Small, "Evolution and Classification of *Cannabis sativa* (Marijuana, Hemp) in Relation to Human Utilization," 208–9.

90. Small, "Evolution and Classification of *Cannabis sativa* (Marijuana, Hemp) in Relation to Human Utilization," 244.

91. J. Lydon, A. H. Teramura, and C. B. Coffman, "UV-B Radiation Effects on Photosynthesis, Growth and Cannabinoid Production of Two *Cannabis Sativa* Chemotypes,"

Photochemistry and Photobiology 46, no. 2 (1987): 201–6; D. W. Pate, "Possible Role of Ultraviolet Radiation in Evolution of *Cannabis* Chemotypes," *Economic Botany* 37, no. 4 (1983): 396–405; D. W. Pate, "Chemical Ecology of *Cannabis*," *Journal of the International Hemp Association* 2 (1994): 29, 32–37; P. G. Mahlberg and J. K. Hemphill, "Effect of Light Quality on Cannabinoid Content of Cannabis Sativa L. (Cannabaceae)," *Botanical Gazette* 144, no. 1 (1983): 43–48; D. J. Potter and P. Duncombe, "The Effect of Electrical Lighting Power and Irradiance on Indoor-Grown Cannabis Potency and Yield," *Journal of Forensic Sciences* 57, no. 3 (2012): 618–22.

92. Lydon et al., "UV-B Radiation Effects on Photosynthesis, Growth and Cannabinoid Production of Two *Cannabis Sativa* Chemotypes"; Hillig and Mahlberg, "A Chemotaxonomic Analysis of Cannabinoid Variation in *Cannabis* (Cannabaceae)."

93. Pate, "Possible Role of Ultraviolet Radiation in Evolution of *Cannabis* Chemotypes"; Pate, "Chemical Ecology of *Cannabis*."

94. P. K. Zeitler, N. M. Johnson, C. W. Naeser, and R. A. K. Tahirkheli, "Fission-Track Evidence for Quaternary Uplift of the Nanga Parbat Region, Pakistan," *Nature* 298 (1982): 255–57; A. Dambricourt-Malassé, "Relations between Climatic Changes and Prehistoric Human Migrations during Holocene between Gissar Range, Pamir, Hindu Kush and Kashmir: The Archaeological and Ecological Data," *Quaternary International* 229, nos. 1–2 (2011): 123–31.

95. M. Beckmann, T. Václavík, A. M. Manceur, L. Šprtová, H. von Wehrden, E. Welk, and A. F. Cord, "gIUV: A Global UV-B Radiation Data Set for Macroecological Studies," *Methods in Ecology and Evolution* 5, no. 4 (2014): 372–83.

96. O. E. Agkhanyantz and I. K. Lopatin, "Main Characteristics of the Ecosystems of the Pamirs, USSR," *Arctic and Alpine Research* 10, no. 2 (1978): 397–407.

97. Haney and Bazzazz, "Some Ecological Implications of the Distribution of Hemp (*Cannabis Sativa* L.) in the United States of America."

98. B. J. Borougerdi, "Cord of Empire, Exotic Intoxicant: Hemp and Culture in the Atlantic World, 1600–1900," Ph.D. diss., University of Texas, Arlington, 2014. Borougerdi's dissertation has been published by Lexington Books, with the title *Commodifying Cannabis: A Cultural History of a Complex Plant in the Atlantic World*. I thank him for sharing a copy of his work with me.

99. Pate, "Possible Role of Ultraviolet Radiation in Evolution of *Cannabis* Chemotypes," 397.

100. Duvall, *Cannabis*, 89–108.

3. ROOTS OF AFRICAN CANNABIS CULTURES

1. M. D. Merlin, "Archaeological Evidence for the Tradition of Psychoactive Plant Use in the Old World," *Economic Botany* 57, no. 3 (2003): 295–323.

2. C. S. Duvall, "Linguistic Evidence on the Historical and Cultural Geographies of Cannabis, Tobacco, and Smoking Pipes in Africa," *Economic Botany* (forthcoming). My raw data are openly available on the internet, in the University of New Mexico's Digital Repository (https://digitalrepository.unm.edu/).

3. I have adopted the spelling of my sources for words published just once, or have selected a common spelling in instances where multiple sources reported one word.

4. C. S. Duvall, "Cannabis and Tobacco in Precolonial and Colonial Africa," in *Oxford Research Encyclopedia of African History*, ed. T. Spear (New York: Oxford University Press, 2017), accessed 24 April 2018, http://africanhistory.oxfordre.com/view/10.1093/acrefore/9780190277734.001.0001/acrefore-9780190277734-e-44.

5. J. Vansina, "Histoire du manioc en Afrique centrale avant 1850," *Paideuma* 43 (1997): 255–79; J. Vansina, "Communications between Angola and East Central Africa before circa 1700," in *Angola on the Move: Transport Routes, Communications and History*, ed. B. Heintze and O. von Achim (Frankfurt: Otto Lembeck, 2008), 130–43; R. Blench, "Trees on the March: The Dispersal of Economic Trees in the Prehistory of West Central Africa," 2001, accessed 24 April 2018, http://www.rogerblench.info/Ethnoscience/Plants/Trees/SAFA%202000%20paper.pdf; C. Ehret and M. Posnansky, *The Archaeological and Linguistic Reconstruction of African History* (Berkeley: University of California Press, 1982).

6. F. A. Flückiger, "Pharmaceutische Reiseeindrucke," pt. 1, *Pharmaceutische Central-halle für Deutschland* 8, no. 49 (1867): 436–42.

7. B. M. du Toit, *Cannabis in Africa: A Survey of Its Distribution in Africa, and a Study of Cannabis Use and Users in Multi-ethnic South Africa* (Rotterdam: A. A. Balkema, 1980).

8. C. Paterson, "Prohibition and Resistance: A Socio-political Exploration of the Changing Dynamics of the Southern African Cannabis Trade, circa 1850–the Present," M.A. thesis, Rhodes University, Grahamstown, South Africa, 2009.

9. I list my language references for the African plant and pipe words in Duvall, "Linguistic Evidence on the Historical and Cultural Geographies of Cannabis, Tobacco, and Smoking Pipes in Africa." I provide references for non-African words in this book.

10. K. W. Hillig and P. G. Mahlberg, "A Chemotaxonomic Analysis of Cannabinoid Variation in *Cannabis* (Cannabaceae)," *American Journal of Botany* 91, no. 6 (2004): 966–75; R. E. Schultes and A. Hofmann, *The Botany and Chemistry of Hallucinogens*, 2d ed. (Springfield, IL: Charles C. Thomas, 1980).

11. United Nations Office on Drugs and Crime, *World Drug Report 2006*, vol. 1 (Vienna: United Nations, 2006), 172, 187–91; J. Cervantes, *Marijuana Horticulture: The Indoor/Outdoor Medical Grower's Bible* (Sacramento, CA: Van Patten, 2006), 10–11; S. T. Oner, *Cannabis Indica: The Essential Guide to the World's Finest Marijuana Strains* (San Francisco: Green Candy, 2011); S. T. Oner, *Cannabis Sativa: The Essential Guide to the World's Finest Marijuana Strains* (San Francisco: Green Candy, 2012).

12. M. Starks, *Marijuana Chemistry*, 2d ed. (Berkeley, CA: Ronin, 1990); Hillig and Mahlberg, "A Chemotaxonomic Analysis of Cannabinoid Variation in *Cannabis* (Cannabaceae)." In current marijuana commerce, the sativa and indica labels are unreliable markers of genetic similarity between plant strains: J. Sawler, J. M. Stout, K. M. Gardner, D. Hudson, J. Vidmar, L. Butler, J. E. Page, and S. Myles, "The Genetic Structure of Marijuana and Hemp," *PLoS One* 10, no. 8 (2015): e0133292.

13. Indian Hemp Drugs Commission, *Report of the Indian Hemp Drugs Commission, 1893–1894* (Simla, India: Government Central Printing Office, 1894).

14. F. Rosenthal, *The Herb: Hashish versus Medieval Muslim Society* (Leiden: E. J. Brill, 1971).

15. Burton believed that Homer's antidepressant substance *nepenthe* (*Odyssey*, book 4, v. 219–21, eighth century BCE) came from an Old Arabic word similar to Coptic *nibanj* (Egypt), which named an edible anesthetic that included cannabis, datura, and henbane. In Southeast Asia, a few *bhang* cognates have been published, such as Burmese *bhén* (Myanmar), and Bahasa Malay *bang* (Indonesia). However, these may be Portuguese loanwords, not Hindi; Portuguese *bangue* was a trade item in Indonesia by 1708. See G. Watt, *The Commercial Products of India* (London: John Murray, 1908), 249; R. F. Burton, *The Book of the Thousand Nights and a Night*, vol. 1 (London: Private Printing for the Burton Club, n.d. [1886–1888]), 70; P. J. Veth, "Varia," *Tijdschrift voor Nederlandsch Indië* 4, no. 2 (1870): 84–86; B. J. Leonardo de Argensola, *The Discovery and Conquest of the Molucco and Philippine Islands* (London: J. Knapton, 1708), 143.

16. A. Stanziani, *Sailors, Slaves, and Immigrants: Bondage in the Indian Ocean World, 1750–1914* (New York: Palgrave Macmillan, 2014), 23.

17. C. Ward and U. Baram, "Global Markets, Local Practice: Ottoman-Period Clay Pipes and Smoking Paraphernalia from the Red Sea Shipwreck at Sadana Island, Egypt," *International Journal of Historical Archaeology* 10, no. 2 (2006): 135–58.

18. H. A. Yassa, A.-W. A. Dawood, M. M. Shehata, R. H. Abdel-Hady, and K. M. Abdel-Aal, "Risk Factors for Bango Abuse in Upper Egypt," *Environmental Toxicology and Pharmacology* 28, no. 3 (2009): 397–402; Republic of Yemen, *Law on the Control of Illicit Trafficking in the Abuse of Narcotics and Psychotropic Substances, No. 3 of 1993*, Article 57, 1993, accessed 28 August 2017, http://www.unodc.org/enl/showDocument.do ?documentUid=2447&country=YEM; E. M. M. Ali, E. Fadul, A. Khalid, A. A. Elgamel, D. A. Hassan, S. H. Abdelrehman, and S. M. E. Khojali, "In Vitro Anti-Oxidant Activity, Phytochemical Screening and Amino Acids Profile of *Cannabis Sativa*," *Journal of Ethnobiology and Ethnopharmacology* 2, no. 1 (2013): 5–8; A. F. Broun and R. E. Massey, *Flora of the Sudan* (London: T. Murphy, 1929), 217.

19. G. Watt, *A Dictionary of the Economic Products of India: Cabbage to Cyperus*, vol. 2 (Calcutta: Department of Revenue and Agriculture, Government of India, 1889), 104.

20. R. C. Clarke, *Hashish!*, 2d ed. (Los Angeles: Red Eye, 2010).

21. C. S. Duvall, *Cannabis* (London: Reaktion, 2015).

22. Hillig and Mahlberg, "A Chemotaxonomic Analysis of Cannabinoid Variation in *Cannabis* (Cannabaceae)."

23. R. C. Clarke, *Marijuana Botany* (Berkeley, CA: Ronin, 1981).

24. G. J. Meulenbeld, "The Search for Clues to the Chronology of Sanskrit Medical Texts, as Illustrated by the History of *Bhanga* (Cannabis Sativa Linn.)," *Studien zur Indologie und Iranistik* 15 (1989): 59–70; D. Wujastyk, "Cannabis in Traditional Indian Herbal Medicine," in *Ayurveda at the Crossroads of Care and Cure*, ed. A. Salema (Lisbon: Universidade Nova de Lisboa, 2002): 45–73; G. A. Grierson, "The Hemp Plant in Sanskrit and Hindi Literature," *Indian Antiquary* 23 (September 1894): 260–62; E. Russo, "Cannabis in India: Ancient Lore and Modern Medicine," in *Cannabinoids as Therapeutics*, ed. R. Mechoulam (Geneva: Birkhäuser, 2005): 1–22.

25. T. Bowrey, *A Geographical Account of Countries round the Bay of Bengal, 1669 to 1679* (Cambridge: Hakluyt Society, [1701] 1905), 79.

26. The Sinhala word is now written *gaṁjā* and the Malayalam word *kañcāv*. Current vocabularies in Southeast Asia include Thai *kạn chā*, Vietnamese *cần sa*, and Khmer *kanhchhea* (Cambodia); on the other side of the Bay of Bengal, on the southern Indian peninsula, there is Telugu *gañjāyi* in addition to the Sinhala and Malayalam words: W. Derham, ed., *Philosophical Experiments and Observations of the Late Eminent Dr. Robert Hooke* (London: W. Derham, 1726), 210; R. J. Wilkinson, *A Malay–English Dictionary* (Hong Kong: Kelly and Walsh, 1901), 577; G. E. Rumpf, *Herbarium amboinense*, vol. 5 (Amsterdam: François Changuion, Hermanus Uytwerf, 1747), 209; H. D. Gaub, *Sermones academici de regimine mentis quod medicorum est*, vol. 1 (Brittenburg, Germany: Balduinum Vander), 114.

27. W. V. Erickson, P. K. Jarvie, and F. L. Miller, "Water Pipe or Bong," US Patent 4,216,785, issued 12 August 1980.

28. Despite internet rumors, Mount Bong, Liberia, has nothing to do with the smoking device. For the Khmer word, see J. P. Lee and S. Kirkpatrick, "Social Meanings of Marijuana Use for Southeast Asian Youth," *Journal of Ethicity and Substance Abuse* 4, nos. 3–4 (2005): 135–52.

29. Postcard photos from around the turn of the twentieth century depict opium pipes made of bamboo, but these appear to be dry pipes.

30. T. Herbert, *A Relation of Some Yeares Travaile, Begunne Anno 1626* (London: William Standby and Jacob Bloome, 1634), 24; F. Le Vaillant, *Voyage de M. Le Vaillant dans l'interieur de l'Afrique*, vol. 2 (Paris: Leroy, 1790), 71–72.

31. R. Drury, *Madagascar: Or, Robert Drury's Journal, during Fifteen Years Captivity on That Island* (London: Meadows. Marshall, Worrall, and Drury, 1729), 276.

32. Duvall, "Linguistic Evidence on the Historical and Cultural Geographies of Cannabis, Tobacco, and Smoking Pipes in Africa."

33. R. Carnac Temple, ed., *The Travels of Peter Mundy in Europe and Asia, 1608–1667*, vol. 3, pt. 2 (London: Hakluyt Society, 1919), 384; W. White, *Journal of a Voyage Performed in the Lion Extra Indiaman* (London: John Stockdale, 1800), 34; A. Sparrman, *A Voyage to the Cape of Good Hope*, 2d ed., vol. 1 (London: G. G. J. and J. Robinson, 1785), 230.

34. The most basic water container is the mouth. Historical users in South Africa sometimes inhaled through water: see C. J. G. Bourhill, "The Smoking of *Dagga* (Indian Hemp) among the Native Races of South Africa and the Resultant Evils," M.D. diss., School of Medicine, University of Edinburgh, 1913, 16.

35. W. Cremer, *Pfeifen, Hanf und Tabak in Schwarzafrika: Eine historische Darstellung* (Idstein, Germany: Baum, 2004); E. Zangato, "Early Smoking Pipes in the North-Western Central African Republic," *Africa* 56, no. 3 (2001): 365–95; N. J. van der Merwe, "Antiquity of the Smoking Habit in Africa," *Transactions of the Royal Society of South Africa* 60, no. 2 (2005): 147–50; J. E. Philips, "African Smoking and Pipes," *Journal of African History* 24, no. 3 (1983): 303–19. In addition, fourteenth-century pipes have been reported from Sierra Leone, but Hill rejects this date for technical reasons: M. H. Hill, "Archaeological Smoking Pipes from Central Sierra Leone," *West African Journal of Archaeology* 6 (1976): 116.

36. Zangato, "Early Smoking Pipes in the North-Western Central African Republic";
J. P. Ossah Mvondo, "L'archéologie des pipes en Afrique intertropicale," Ph.D. diss.,
Department of Art and Archaeology, Université de Paris I Panthéon Sorbonne, 1988;
J. P. Ossah Mvondo, "La question des pipes archéologiques en Afrique: Les nouvelles
évidences," *West African Journal of Archaeology* 24 (1994): 1–19. In 2015, I erroneously in-
dicated that these pipes came from the middle Niger Delta in Mali rather than the lower
Niger Delta in Nigeria: Duvall, *Cannabis*, 108.

37. Van der Merwe, "Antiquity of the Smoking Habit in Africa."

38. Ossah Mvondo, "L'archéologie des pipes en Afrique intertropicale."

39. Ossah Mvondo, "L'archéologie des pipes en Afrique intertropicale"; van der
Merwe, "Antiquity of the Smoking Habit in Africa"; Zangato, "Early Smoking Pipes in
the North-Western Central African Republic"; Philips, "African Smoking and Pipes."

40. M. Shaw, "Native Pipes and Smoking in South Africa," *Annals of the South African
Museum* 24 (1938): 281.

41. N. J. Van der Merwe, "Cannabis Smoking in 13th–14th Century Ethiopia: Chemical Evidence," in *Cannabis and Culture*, ed. V. Rubin (The Hague: Mouton, 1975), 77–80.

42. In southern Chad, in a study that predated both absolute dating and diagnostic
knowledge of cannabis chemistry, Wulsin found residue in a pipe stratigraphically assigned to the 500s BCE. The residue was spectrographically more similar to that from
herbal cannabis than hashish or tobacco: F. R. Wulsin, *Varia Africana V: An Archaeological Reconnaissance of the Shari Basin*, ed. E. A. Hooton and N. I. Bates (Cambridge, MA:
Harvard African Studies, 1932), 55–56.

43. Duvall, "Linguistic Evidence on the Historical and Cultural Geographies of
Cannabis, Tobacco, and Smoking Pipes in Africa."

44. G. W. Stow, *The Native Races of South Africa* (London: Swan Sonnenschein,
1905), 52; C. G. Sampson, "'Zeer grote liefhebbers van tobak': Nicotine and Cannabis
Dependency of the Seacow River Bushmen," *Digging Stick* 10, no. 1 (1993): 2–6; D.
Kidd, *The Essential Kafir* (London: Adam and Charles Black, 1904), 346; D. Gordon,
"From Rituals of Rapture to Dependence: The Political Economy of Khoikhoi Narcotic
Consumption, c. 1487–1870," *South African Historical Journal* 35 (November 1996): 86;
J. W. Jennings and C. Addison, *With the Abyssinians in Somaliland* (London: Hodder
and Stoughton, 1905), 234.

45. Le Vaillant, *Voyage de M. Le Vaillant dans l'interieur de l'Afrique*, 72; H. A. Fos-
brooke, "A Stone Age Tribe in Tanganyika," *South African Archaeological Bulletin* 11,
no. 41 (1956): 3–8.

46. Drury, *Madagascar*, 276.

47. Carnac Temple, *The Travels of Peter Mundy in Europe and Asia*, 384; R. Linton, *The
Tanala: A Hill Tribe of Madagascar* (Chicago: Field Museum of Natural History, 1933), 76.

48. Le Vaillant, *Voyage de M. Le Vaillant dans l'interieur de l'Afrique*, 71.

49. G. M'Henry, "An Account of the Liberated African Establishment at St. Helena.
Chapter II," *Simmond's Colonial Magazine* 5 (1845): 437.

50. E. W. Lane, *An Account of the Manners and Customs of the Modern Egyptians*, vol. 1
(London: Charles Knight, 1837), 187; L. Leclerc, *Kachef er-roumoûz (Révélation des énigmes) d'Abd er-Rezzaq ed-Djezaïry* (Paris: Baillière et Fils, and Leroux, 1874), 365; L. Krapf

and J. Rebman, *A Nika-English Dictionary* (London: Society for Promoting Christian Knowledge), 17; C. G. Büttner, *Wörterbuch der Suaheli-Sprache* (Stuttgart and Berlin: Spemann, 1890), 42; Anonymous, "La littérature populaire des Israélites tunisiens," *Revue Tunisienne* 12, no. 49 (1905): 121–35.

51. J.-B. Douville, *Voyage au Congo et dans l'interieur de l'Afrique equinoxiale, fait dans les années 1828, 1829, et 1830*, vol. 1 (Paris: Chez Jules Renouard, 1832), 127.

52. Bourhill, "The Smoking of *Dagga* (Indian Hemp) among the Native Races of South Africa and the Resultant Evils"; G. F., "Le Chemin de Fer du Congo Français," *Globe Trotter* 5, no. 233 (1906): 38–39.

53. Lane, *An Account of the Manners and Customs of the Modern Egyptians*, 1:187.

54. British travelers in North Africa often wrote "hookah," from the Arabic *ḥuqqa* (jar), for glass-based water pipes. This word was earliest recorded in the mid-1700s, in South Asia: H. Yule and A. C. Burnell, *Hobson-Jobson: A Glossary of Colloquial Anglo-Indian Words and Phrases* (London: John Murray, 1903), 428. It was not recorded historically in North African languages.

55. Although Lane writes that the container is made from a coconut, his illustration shows a ceramic container. His other descriptions, and other sources, show ceramic containers: see Lane, *An Account of the Manners and Customs of the Modern Egyptians*, 1:184–87.

56. Lane, *An Account of the Manners and Customs of the Modern Egyptians*, 1:188.

57. H. A'lam, "Coconut," in *Encyclopedia Iranica*, ed. E. Yarshater, vol. 5, fasc. 8 (London: Routledge and Kegan Paul, 1992), 882–83.

58. W. R. Wilde, *Narrative of a Voyage to Madeira, Teneriffe, and along the Shores of the Mediterranean*, vol. 1 (Dublin: William Curry Jr., 1840), 325; E. W. Lane, *An Account of the Manners and Customs of the Modern Egyptians*, vol. 2 (London: Charles Knight, 1836), 39.

59. Lane, *An Account of the Manners and Customs of the Modern Egyptians*, 1:184.

60. E. J. Keall, "Smokers' Pipes and the Fine Pottery Tradition of Hays," *Proceedings of the Seminar for Arabian Studies* 22 (1992): 29–46; E. J. Keall, "One Man's Mead Is Another Man's Persian: One Man's Coconut Is Another Man's Grenade," *Muqarnas* 10 (1993): 275–85. Persian sources attribute the invention of the water pipe to an early sixteenth-century leader, but the relevant historical accounts describe elaborated devices (similar to the shisha and narguilé that I described in the prior paragraph of the main text): S. Razpush, "Ḡalyān," in *Encyclopedia Iranica*, ed. E. Yarshater, vol. 10, fasc. 3 (London: Routledge and Kegan Paul, 2000), 261–65.

61. A'lam states that Persians began manufacturing coconut-based water pipes in the "seventeenth century": A'lam, "Coconut." The earliest description of coconut-based water pipes I've found from the Levant is from Syria in around 1790: A. Russell, *The Natural History of Aleppo*, 2d ed., vol. 1 (London: G. G. and J. Robinson, 1794), 125. There are descriptions of glass and ceramic pipes from early in 1600s in southwestern Asia, e.g., Persia around 1630 (Herbert, *A Relation of Some Yeares Travaile*, 150), and southwestern India in 1616 (E. Terry, *A Voyage to East-India*, reprint ed. [London: Wilkie, Cater, Hayes, and Easton, (1665) 1777], 96). For other descriptions of early water pipes: Keall, "One Man's Mead Is Another Man's Persian"; Razpush, "Ḡalyān"; W. Floor, "The Art of Smoking in Iran and Other Uses of Tobacco," *Iranian Studies* 35, nos. 1–3 (2002): 47–85.

62. J. Fryer, *A New Account of East India and Persia in Eight Letters, Being Nine Years Travels, Begun 1672 and Finished 1681* (London: Richard Chiswell, 1698), 8. Additionally, in 1645, escaped slaves in Brazil made coconut-based pipes, but it's not recorded if these were water pipes. The escaped slaves might have brought knowledge of such pipes from Africa, but by that date essentially all captives had come from Atlantic Africa, and none from the Indian Ocean. These people likely learned to smoke from sailors: A. Carvalho, "Diario da viagem do capitão João Blaer aos Palmares em 1645," *Revista do Insituto Archeológico e Geográphico Pernambucano* 10, no. 56 (1902): 87–96, 93.

63. B. F. Gunn, L. Baudouin, and K. M. Olsen, "Independent Origins of Cultivated Coconut (*Cocos Nucifera* L.) in the Old World Tropics," *PLoS One* 6, no. 6 (2011): e21143.

64. A'lam, "Coconut."

65. L. Perera, L. Baudouin, R. Bourdeix, A. Bait Fadhil, F. C. C. Hountondji, and A. Al-Shanfari, "Coconut Palms on the Edge of the Desert: Genetic Diversity of *Cocos Nucifera* L. in Oman," *Cord* 27, no. 1 (2011): 1–11.

66. C. Allibert, "Austronesian Migration and the Establishment of the Malagasy Civilization: Contrasted Readings in Linguistics, Archaeology, Genetics and Cultural Anthropology," *Diogenes* 218 (2008): 9.

67. M. Schuiling and H. C. Harries, "The Coconut Palm in East Africa: 1. East African Tall," *Principes* 38, no. 1 (1994): 4–11.

68. *Kiko* is also documented as "smoking pipe" in Bondei and Shambala, both spoken in Tanzania. A cognate of the Kigiryama *bororo* is the Zande *mbololo* (South Sudan), translated as "water pipe"; only bamboo- and horn-based water pipes are recorded among the Zande: see C. R. Lagae and V. H. Vanden Plas, *La langue des Azande, Volume II: Dictionnaire Français-Zande* (Ghent, Belgium: Éditions Dominicaines "Veritas," 1922). Many sources document the Swahili term for "coconut." For the Kigiryama word for "coconut," see W. E. Taylor, *Giryama Vocabulary and Collections* (London: Society for Promoting Christian Knowledge, 1891), 109.

69. Allibert, "Austronesian Migration and the Establishment of the Malagasy Civilization," 15.

70. Wilde, *Narrative of a Voyage to Madeira, Teneriffe, and along the Shores of the Mediterranean*, 325; Lane, *An Account of the Manners and Customs of the Modern Egyptians*, 1:187; Lane, *An Account of the Manners and Customs of the Modern Egyptians*, 2:39; Russell, *The Natural History of Aleppo*, 125; L. Leclerc, *Kachef er-roumoûz (Révélation des énigmes)*, 365; J.-H. Grose, *A Voyage to the East-Indies, with Observations on Various Parts There* (London: Hooper and Morley), 235.

71. T. Shaw, "Early Smoking Pipes: In Africa, Europe, and America," *Journal of the Royal Anthropological Institute of Great Britain and Ireland* 90, no. 2 (1960): 272–305.

72. White, *Journal of a Voyage Performed in the Lion Extra Indiaman*, 34–35.

73. Keall, "Smokers' Pipes and the Fine Pottery Tradition of Hays"; Keall, "One Man's Mead Is Another Man's Persian."

74. Relevant sources use the term *qalyān*, which refers to the water pipe's bubbling sound: Razpush, "Ḡalyān." Floor proposes that people smoked "indigenous tobacco" before American tobacco arrived and dismisses the possibility of pre-tobacco cannabis smoking: Floor, "The Art of Smoking in Iran and Other Uses of Tobacco."

75. J. Green, "Southeast Asian Ceramic Smoking Pipes," *International Journal of Nautical Archaeology* 15, no. 2 (1986): 167–69.

76. Also, Burton concluded that cannabis use by the "S. African Bushman" was "the earliest form of smoking" but was unsure whether they used pipes anciently or something comparable to the fabled, smoke-filled tents of Herodotus's Scythians: see Burton, *The Book of the Thousand Nights and a Night*, 70.

77. If pipes were used, they were completely unlike the pipes Portuguese smokers used subsequently: Philips, "African Smoking and Pipes"; Shaw, "Early Smoking Pipes."

78. J. P. Machado, *Dicionário da língua portuguesa*, vol. 1 (Lisbon: Sociedade de Língua Portuguesa, 1958); J. T. Schneider, *Dictionary of African Borrowings in Brazilian Portuguese* (Hamburg: Helmut Buske, 1991).

79. E. Axelson, *Portuguese in South-East Africa, 1488–1600* (Johannesburg: C. Struik, 1973).

80. P. E. H. Hair, "Portuguese Contacts with the Bantu Languages of the Transkei, Natal and Southern Mozambique, 1497–1650," *African Studies* 39, no. 1 (1980): 3–46.

81. Duvall, *Cannabis*, 132.

82. Examples of the two types were on display in 2015 in the museum at the Castelo de São Jorge historic site in Lisbon and in 2016 at the African Burial Mounds National Monument in New York City.

83. Duvall, *Cannabis*, 133–34.

84. The Zinacantán Tzotzil and Q'eqchi' words likely came from Portuguese via Spanish. Sources for American languages include H. G. Lenz, *Tupi e Guarani: A língua dos bandeirantes—séculos XVII e XVIII* (Timburi, Brazil: Cia do Ebook, 2007); C. H. Brown, "Loanwords in Zinacantán Tzotzil, a Mayan Language of Mexico," in *Loanwords in the World's Languages: A Comparative Handbook*, ed. M. Haspelmath and U. Tadmor (The Hague: De Gruyter Mouton, 2009), 848–72; S. Wichmann and K. Hull, "Loanwords in Q'eqchi', a Mayan Language of Guatemala," in Haspelmath and Tadmor, *Loanwords in the World's Languages*, 873–96.

85. R. E. Dennett, *Notes on the Folklore of the Fjort (French Congo)* (London: David Nutt, 1898), 154.

86. E. Holub, *Von der Capstadt ins Land der Maschakulumbe: Reisen im südlichen Afrika in den Jahren 1883–1887*, vol. 2 (Vienna: Alfred Hölder, 1890), 81.

87. Kidd, *The Essential Kafir*, 346.

88. O. Lenz, *Timbuktu: Reise durch Marokko, die Sahara und den Sudan*, vol. 1 (Leipzig: F. A. Brockhaus, 1892), 207; H. Johnston, *The Uganda Protectorate* (London: Hutchinson, 1902), 189; H. Ward, "Ethnographical Notes Relating to the Congo Tribes," *Journal of the Anthropological Institute of Great Britain and Ireland* 24 (1895): 295; H. Johnston, *George Grenfell and the Congo: A History and Description of the Congo Independent State and Adjoining Districts of Congoland*, vol. 2 (London: Hutchinson, 1908), 609; M. Barbedor, "Note sur la faune et la flore du Gabon," *Bulletin de la Société de Géographie* 18, 5th series (July–December 1869): 11; C. van Overbergh, *Les Bangala* (Brussels: Albert de Wit, 1907), 113.

89. Mattos e Silva, *Contribução para o estudo da Região de Cabinda* (Lisbon: Typographia Universal, 1904), 264; C. Jeannest, *Quatre années au Congo* (Paris: G. Charpentier,

1883), 106; R. F. Burton, *Two Trips to Gorilla Land and the Cataracts of the Congo*, vol. 2 (London: Sampson Low, Marston, Low, and Searle, 1876), 295; W. P. Hiern, *Catalogue of the African Plants Collected by Dr. Friedrich Welwitsch in 1853–1861: Dicotyledons, Part I* (London: Trustees of the British Museum [Natural History], 1896), 80; A.-J. Wauters, *Le Congo au point de vue économique* (Brussels: Institut National de Geographie, 1885), 43.

90. H. H. Methuen, *Life in the Wilderness; or, Wanderings in South Africa*, 2d ed. (London: Richard Bentley, 1848), 46. Earth pipes were reported in Central Asia in 1922, and Indian soldiers fighting in Europe in World War I made earth pipes in the trenches and expedient water pipes from bottles: Duvall, *Cannabis*, 97; H. Balfour, "Earth Smoking-Pipes from South Africa and Central Asia," *Man* 22 (1922): 65–69.

91. Kidd, *The Essential Kafir*, 346; Bourhill, "The Smoking of *Dagga* (Indian Hemp) among the Native Races of South Africa and the Resultant Evils," 35; C. van Overbergh, *Les Basonge (État Ind. du Congo)* (Brussels: Albert de Wit, 1908), 140.

92. Bourhill, "The Smoking of *Dagga* (Indian Hemp) among the Native Races of South Africa and the Resultant Evils," 16–18; F. Ames, "A Clinical and Metabolic Study of Acute Intoxication with *Cannabis Sativa* and Its Role in the Model Psychoses," *British Journal of Psychiatry* 104 (1958): 972–99; J. Rebman, *Dictionary of the Kiniassa Language* (St. Chrischona, Switzerland: Church Missionary Society, 1877), 134; O. R. O'Neil, *Adventures in Swaziland: The Story of a South African Boer* (New York: Century, 1921), 308.

93. Erickson et al., "Water Pipe or Bong"; "Biggest Seizure of 'Pot' Is Made," *Lebanon [PA] Daily News*, 5 January 1973, 1, 13.

94. J.-B. Douville, *Voyage au Congo et dans l'interieur de l'Afrique equinoxiale, fait dans les années 1828, 1829, et 1830*, vol. 2 (Paris: Chez Jules Renouard, 1832), 127. See also H. A. Dias de Carvalho, *Expedição portugueza ao Muatiânvua: Ethnographia e historia tradicional dos povos da Lunda* (Lisbon: Imprensa Nacional, 1890), 293–94. The sound made on releasing a carb hole while smoking can be heard in several popular songs, such as "Shake Your Rump" (at 2:01 within the song) by the Beastie Boys on the album *Paul's Boutique* (1989).

95. Dias de Carvalho, *Expedição portugueza ao Muatiânvua*, 294.

96. Révérend Père Colle, *Les Baluba*, vol. 1 (Brussels: Albert de Wit, 1913), 119.

97. Burton, *Two Trips to Gorilla Land and the Cataracts of the Congo*, 295.

4. CANNABIS COLONIZES THE CONTINENT

1. D. A. Burney, G. A. Brook, and J. B. Cowart, "A Holocene Pollen Record for the Kalahari Desert of Botswana from a U-Series Dated Speleothem," *The Holocene* 4, no. 3 (1994): 225–32.

2. C. S. Duvall, *Cannabis* (London: Reaktion, 2015), chap. 2.

3. J. dos Santos, *Ethiopia oriental e varia historia de covsas* (Evora, Portugal: Impressa no Conuento de S. Domingos, 1609), 20B.

4. N. J. van der Merwe, "Antiquity of the Smoking Habit in Africa," *Transactions of the Royal Society of South Africa* 60, no. 2 (2005): 147–50.

5. D. A. Burney, "Pre-settlement Vegetation Changes at Lake Tritrivakely, Madagascar," *Paleoecology of Africa* 18 (1987): 374.

6. M. P. Cox, M. G. Nelson, M. K. Tumonggor, F.-X. Ricaut, and H. Sudoyo, "A Small Cohort of Island Southeast Asian Women Founded Madagascar," *Proceedings of the Royal Society B* 279 (2012): 2761–68.

7. Révérend Pères Abinal and Malzac, *Dictionnaire Malgache-Français* (Antananarivo, Madagascar: Mission Catholique Mahamasina, 1888), 272, 589; E. de Flacourt, *Histoire de la grande isle de Madagascar* (Paris: François Clouzier, 1661), 145–46; R. Drury, *Madagascar; or, Robert Drury's Journal, during Fifteen Years Captivity on That Island* (London: Meadows, Marshall, Worrall, and Drury, 1729), 276; J. Guiol, "Topographie médicale de Nossi-Bé (Extraits—Suite et fin)," *Archives de Médecine Navale* 38 (1882): 341; R. Baron, "Jottings on Some of the Plants of Imerina," *Antananarivo Annual and Madagascar Magazine* 3 (1878): 109. The sailor Robert Drury (1729) recorded *"Jermaughler."* This spelling reflects that he, probably illiterate, dictated his book in a Cockney accent: J. Richardson, "Drury's 'Vocabulary of the Madagascar Language,' with Notes," *Antananarivo Annual and Madagascar Magazine* 1 (1875): 98–106. Finally, in Ferrand's commentary on Flacourt, he gives "Ahitr'aṇdriana" (*r'aṇdriana* plant) as a modern word in the central highlands, which suggests that what Europeans heard as *rongony* may have been pronounced somewhat differently. Ferrand also provides cognates of "Ahitr'aṇdriana" for the southeast, without citing or describing the source of these words, and writes "*ahets*" as "*ahi*" in modern pronunciation: G. Ferrand, *Étienne de Flacourt: Dictionnaire de la langue de Madagascar, d'après l'édition de 1658 et l'histoire de la grande Isle de Madagascar de 1661* (Paris: Ernest Leroux, 1905), 75.

8. M. Serva, F. Petroni, D. Volchenkov, and S. Wichmann, "Malagasy Dialects and the Peopling of Madagascar," *Journal of the Royal Society Interface* 9, no. 66 (2012): 54–67.

9. G. E. Rumpf, *Herbarium amboinense*, vol. 5 (Amsterdam: François Changuion, Hermanus Uytwerf, 1747), 209–10.

10. P. J. Veth, "Varia," *Tijdschrift voor Nederlandsch Indië* 4, no. 2 (1870): 84–86.

11. C. S. Duvall, "Cannabis and Tobacco in Precolonial and Colonial Africa," in *Oxford Research Encyclopedia of African History*, ed. T. Spear (New York: Oxford University Press, 2017), accessed 24 April 2018, http://africanhistory.oxfordre.com/view/10.1093/acrefore/9780190277734.001.0001/acrefore-9780190277734-e-44. I do not know the meaning of *boule*, and thus of *ahetsboule* (lit., *boule* plant), in Malagasy. Jeffreys proposed that *ahetsmanga* means "plant of Arabia," taking the Swahili word *Manga* (i.e., the Muscat region) as the root: M. D. W. Jeffreys, "Arab-Introduced Exotics in East Africa," *African Studies* 33, no. 1 (1974): 56. However, southeastern Madagascar is far removed from shipping networks across the Arabian Sea, and northern and western Malagasy terms bear no resemblance to Hindi, Arabic, or Swahili.

12. C. Allibert, "Austronesian Migration and the Establishment of the Malagasy Civilization: Contrasted Readings in Linguistics, Archaeology, Genetics and Cultural Anthropology," *Diogenes* 218 (2008): 9.

13. Studies of cannabis phylogeography are needed, based on genetic-clock analyses of Landraces in multiple locations.

14. For slave geographies and histories involving Madagascar, see W. Wilson-Fall, *Memories of Madagascar and Slavery in the Black Atlantic* (Athens: Ohio University Press, 2015); G. Campbell, "Madagascar and the Slave Trade, 1810–1895," *Journal of*

African History 22, no. 2 (1981): 203–27; A. Stanziani, *Sailors, Slaves, and Immigrants: Bondage in the Indian Ocean World, 1750–1914* (New York: Palgrave Macmillan, 2014).

15. J. Benoist, "Réunion: Cannabis in a Pluricultural and Polyethnic Society," in *Cannabis and Culture*, ed. V. Rubin (The Hague: Mouton, 1975): 227–28.

16. A. Engler, *Die Pflanzenwelt Ost-Afrikas und der Nachbargebiete, Theil A* (Berlin: Geographische Verlagshandlung Dietrich Reimer, 1895), 468.

17. Govêrno Geral da Colonia de Moçambique, "Portaria provincial proibindo na colonia de Moçambique a importação, cultura, venda e consumo da planta conhecida cafrealmente por *bangue* ou *suruma*," in *Colecçao da Legislação Colonial da República Portuguesa, 1914 (Janeiro a Dezembro)* (Coimbra, Portugal: Imprensa da Universidade, 1914), 386.

18. P. Bruschi, M. Morganti, M. Mancini, and M. A. Signorini, "Traditional Healers and Laypeople: A Qualitative and Quantitative Approach to Local Knowledge on Medicinal Plants in Muda (Mozambique)," *Journal of Ethnopharmacology* 138, no. 2 (2011): 543–63.

19. S. M. Rucina, V. M. Muiruri, L. Downton, and R. Marchant, "Late-Holocene Savanna Dynamics in the Amboseli Basin, Kenya," *Holocene* 20, no. 5 (2010): 667–77.

20. J. E. Philips, "African Smoking and Pipes," *Journal of African History* 24, no. 3 (1983): 303–19.

21. N. J. Van der Merwe, "Cannabis Smoking in 13th–14th Century Ethiopia: Chemical Evidence," in Rubin, *Cannabis and Culture*, 77–80.

22. P. Shipton, *Bitter Money: Cultural Economy and Some African Meanings of Forbidden Commodities* (Washington, DC: American Anthropological Association, 1989), 35.

23. Abinal and Malzac, *Dictionnaire Malgache-Français*, 41, 272, 397, 506, 554, 589, 678; A. T. Bryant, *A Zulu-English Dictionary* (Pinetown, South Africa: Mariannhill Mission Press, 1905), 205, 271, 441, 548, 554, 595, 645; D. C. Scott, *A Cyclopaedic Dictionary of the Mang'anja Language Spoken in British Central Africa* (Edinburgh: Foreign Mission Committee of the Church of Scotland, 1892), 42, 103, 344, 371, 700, 706; E. Dahl, *Nyamwesi-Wörterbuch* (Hamburg: L. Friederichsen, 1915), 64, 480.

24. R. F. Burton, *Zanzibar: City, Island, and Coast*, vol. 1 (London: Tinsley Brothers, 1872), 381.

25. C. H. Stigand, *The Land of Zinj* (London: Frank Cass, [1913] 1966), 77–78. This source deserves an asterisk. It is ostensibly based on Swahili documents but does not cite them. The Swahili literature has not been studied for cannabis history.

26. See M. Haspelmath, "Lexical Borrowing: Concepts and Issues," in *Loanwords in the World's Languages: A Comparative Handbook*, ed. M. Haspelmath and U. Tadmor (The Hague: De Gruyter Mouton), 45.

27. La Barre mysteriously decided that *bangi* derives from "Bengal": W. La Barre, "History and Ethnography of Cannabis," in *Culture in Context: Selected Writings of Weston La Barre* (Durham, NC: Duke University Press, 1980), 98.

28. Dos Santos, *Ethiopia oriental e varia historia de covsas*, 20B.

29. R. Knox, *An Historical Relation of the Island Ceylon in the East-Indies* (London: Robert Chiswell, 1681), 154.

30. For more, see chapter 5 in this volume. Key sources are: G. Casati, *Ten Years in Equatoria* (London: Frederick Warne, 1898), 429; A. C. Madan, *Swahili-English Dictionary*

(Oxford: Clarendon, 1903), 22; F. Rosenthal, *The Herb: Hashish versus Medieval Muslim Society* (Leiden: E. J. Brill, 1971).

31. Burton, *Zanzibar*, 381.

32. A piece of nonevidence must be identified specifically. Nerlich and colleagues report that a mummy (attributed to 950 BCE) carried traces of cannabinoids (implying psychoactive drug use), as well as nicotine and cocaine (from tobacco and coca, New World plants that crossed the Atlantic after 1492). This report clearly shows poor research practice—the mummy's provenance and storage conditions were unknown—and the findings must be dismissed as sample contamination: A. G. Nerlich, F. Parsche, I. Wiest, P. Schramel, and U. Löhrs, "Extensive Pulmonary Haemorrhage in an Egyptian Mummy," *Virchows Archive* 427, no. 4 (1995): 423–29.

33. A. Emery-Barbier, "L'homme et l'environnement en Egypte durant la période pré-dynastique," in *Man's Role in Shaping the Eastern Mediterranean Landscape*, ed. S. Bottema, G. Entjes-Nieborg, and W. Van Zeist (Rotterdam: A. A. Balkema, 1990), 319–26; S. A. G. Leroy, "Palynological Evidence of *Azolla Nilotica* Dec. in Recent Holocene of the Eastern Nile Delta and Palaeo Environment," *Vegetation History and Archaeobotany* 1 (1992): 43–52; A. Leroi-Gourhan, "Les pollens et l'embaument," in *La momie de Ramsès II*, ed. L. Balout and C. Roubet (Paris: Recherche sur les Civilisations, 1985), 162–65.

34. This evidence deserves an asterisk. A rough wad of fibers was seemingly used to close a gap in a coffin, similar to oakum in European shipbuilding. There were no finished, processed fibers, as would have been used in textile or rope production. The age of the fiber wad is not certain; it may have been introduced to the tomb millennia after Akhenaten's death, in the Egyptian Roman period: G. T. Martin, *The Royal Tomb at El-'Amarna: The Rock Tombs at El-'Amarna, Part VII, II. The Reliefs, Inscriptions, and Architecture* (London: Egypt Exploration Society, 1989), 50, 62, plate 87.

35. W. R. Dawson, "Studies in the Egyptian Medical Texts: III (Continued)," *Journal of Egyptian Archaeology* 20, nos. 1–2 (1934): 44.

36. A. J. Veldmeijer, "Cordage Production," in *UCLA Encyclopedia of Egyptology* 1, no. 1, ed. W. Wendrich (Los Angeles: UCLA Department of Near Eastern Languages and Cultures, 2009), accessed 28 August 2017, http://escholarship.org/uc/item/1w90v76c.

37. D. P. Ryan, "The Misidentification of Ancient Egyptian Plant Fibers," *Varia Aegyptiaca* 1 (1985): 143–49.

38. Cf. E. B. Russo, "History of Cannabis and Its Preparations in Saga, Science, and Sobriquet," *Chemistry and Biodiversity* 4 (2007): 1620–26.

39. C. Scholtz, *Lexicon Aegyptiaco-Latinum* (Oxford: Typeographeo Clarendoniano, 1775), 17.

40. G. J. Dimmendaal, "Language Ecology and Linguistic Diversity on the African Continent," *Language and Linguistics Compass* 2, no. 5 (2008): 847.

41. C. S. Duvall, "Linguistic Evidence on the Historical and Cultural Geographies of Cannabis, Tobacco, and Smoking Pipes in Africa," *Economic Botany* (forthcoming).

42. S. D. Muller, L. Rhazi, B. Andrieux, M. Bottollier-Curtet, S. Fauquette, E.-R. Saber, N. Rifai, and A. Daoud-Bouattour, "Vegetation History of the Western Rif Mountains (Northwestern Morocco): Origin, Late-Holocene Dynamics and Human Impact," *Vegetation History and Archaeobotany* 24, no. 4 (2015): 487–501.

43. Duvall, *Cannabis*, 53.

44. L. Arata, "Nepenthes and Cannabis in Ancient Greece," *Janus Head* 7, no. 1 (2004): 34–49; T. F. Brunner, "Evidence of Marijuana Use in Ancient Greece and Rome? The Literary Evidence," *Bulletin of the History of Medicine* 47, no. 4 (1973): 344–55.

45. I. Lozano Cámara, "Terminología científica árabe del cáñamo," in *Ciencias naturaleza en al-Andalus: Textos y estudios IV*, ed. C. Álvarez de Morales (Granada, Spain: Consejo Superior de Investigaciones Científicas, 1996), 147–64; I. Lozano Cámara, "El uso terapéutico del *Cannabis sativa* L. en la medicina Árabe," *Asclepio* 49, no. 2 (1997): 199–208.

46. Several Levantine languages include *qinnab* cognates, and the Arabic term perhaps came from another tongue. A Greek derivation, however, better matches known geographies of cannabis dispersal and historical traditions of use. The cases made for a non-Greek, Levantine derivation are: S. Benet, "Early Diffusion and Folk Uses of Hemp," in Rubin, *Cannabis and Culture*, 39–49; R. Mechoulam, W. A. Devane, A. Breuer, and J. Zahalka, "A Random Walk through a Cannabis Field," *Pharmacology Biochemistry and Behavior* 40, no. 3 (1991): 461–64.

47. Lozano Cámara, "El uso terapéutico del *Cannabis sativa* L. en la medicina Árabe."

48. Lozano Cámara, "Terminología científica árabe del cáñamo."

49. C. du Gast, *Le Maroc agricole: Rapport adressé au Ministre de l'agriculture* (Paris: Imprimerie Nationale, 1908), 80.

50. J.-L. de Lanessan, *La Tunisie* (Paris: Félix Alcan, 1887), 52; I. Dukerley, "Note sur les différences que présente avec le chanvre ordinaire et la variété de cette espèce connue en Algérie sous les noms de *kif* et de *tekrouri*," *Bulletin de la Société Botanique de France* 3 (9 November 1866): 401–6.

51. A. Mouliéras, *Le Maroc inconnu: Deuxième partie, Exploration des Djebala (Maroc Septentrional)* (Paris: Augustin Challamel, 1899), 491. For historical European processing, see R. C. Clarke, and M. D. Merlin, *Cannabis: Evolution and Ethnobotany* (Berkeley: University of California Press, 2013).

52. Clarke and Merlin, *Cannabis*, 330.

53. Russo, "History of Cannabis and Its Preparations in Saga, Science, and Sobriquet."

54. C. Galen, *De alimentorum facultatibus, libri tres* (Lyon, France: Gulielmum Rouillium, 1547), 84–85.

55. R. C. Clarke, *Hashish!*, 2d ed. (Los Angeles: Red Eye, 2010), 24–35.

56. G. Gnoli, "Bang in Ancient Iran," in *Encyclopedia Iranica*, ed. E. Yarshater (London: Routledge and Kegan Paul, 1989), 689–90.

57. This word has been transcribed in many ways in European languages, including *haschisch, hachiche, h'echicha, hchich, habtchy, abchy, assis, axis*, and *achicha*. I use modern standard Arabic *ḥashīsh* to refer to specific historical contexts, and modern English "hashish" to refer generally to collected cannabis resin.

58. Rosenthal, *The Herb*. See also P. Alpino, *De medicina Aegyptiorum libri quatuor* (Venice: Franciscum de Franciscis Senensem, 1591), 121B.

59. Bureau of Foreign Commerce, U.S. Department of State, "Italian East Africa, Erythrean Colony: Tariff of Duties and Accessory Taxes Applicable in the Custom-House at Massowah, 1898–99," in *Tariffs of Foreign Countries, Volume 16, Part 3—Asia, Africa,*

Australasia, and Polynesia, ed. Bureau of Foreign Commerce, U.S. Department of State (Washington, DC: U.S. Government Printing Office), 447. Cognates of *ḥashīsh* have been recorded recently in Oromo and Amharic (Ethiopia) and Somali (Somalia). These loanwords likely trace to twentieth-century popular culture, drug smuggling, and anti-drug laws.

60. D. Lemordant, "Cannabis et Datura en Ethiopie," *Journal d'Agriculture Tropicale et de Botanique Appliquée* 27, no. 2 (1980): 133–52; C. Bosc-Tiessé, "La tête qui fume de l'église de Nārgā," *Afriques* 1 (2010), http://afriques.revues.org/414.

61. Van der Merwe, "Cannabis Smoking in 13th–14th Century Ethiopia."

62. Bosc-Tiessé, "La tête qui fume de l'église de Nārgā." In the late 1840s, smoking was rare in the Abyssinian highlands and common in the non-Christian lowlands: M. Parkyns, *Life in Abyssinia: Being Notes Collected during Three Years' Residence and Travels in That Country*, vol. 1 (London: Murray, 1853), 12.

63. F. H. Apel, *Drei Monate in Abyssinien und Gefangenschaft unter König Theodorus II* (Zurich: Carl Meyer, 1866), 10.

64. H. de Monfried and I. Treat, *Pearls, Arms, and Hashish* (New York: Coward-McCann, 1930), 308.

65. A. Sebaut, *Dictionnaire de la législation tunisienne*, new ed. (Dijon, France: Imprimerie Sirodot, 1896), 149–67, *chīra* on 150.

66. "La littérature populaire des Israélites tunisiens," *Revue Tunisienne* 12 no. 49 (1905): 121–35; A. Russell, *The Natural History of Aleppo*, 2d ed., vol. 1 (London: G. G. and J. Robinson, 1794), 125.

67. The 1735 documentation is weak because the original Arabic (or Berber) name is unknown. The nineteenth-century Frenchman who summarized the original Arabic-language source wrote of "hashish" smoking: L. Godard, *Description et histoire du Maroc* (Paris: Charles Tanera, 1860), 540. Regarding religious use, see text box 2 on page 96.

68. "Local Hashish-Eaters," *San Francisco Call*, 24 June 1895, 7.

69. Dukerley, "Note sur les différences que présente avec le chanvre ordinaire et la variété de cette espèce connue en Algérie sous les noms de *kif* et de *tekrouri*."

70. The words *Takrūr* and *takrūri* have been spelled in multiple ways, the main point of variation being the first vowel (e.g., *takrūri* versus *tekrūri*). I transliterate the vowel mark *fatḥah* as English *a*: see U. Al-Naqar, "Takrūr: The History of a Name," *Journal of African History* 10, no. 3 (1969): 365–74; A. E. Robinson, "The Tekruri Sheikhs of Gallabat (Southeastern Sudan)," *Journal of the Royal African Society* 26, no. 101 (1926): 47–53; G. Ellero, "I Tacruri in Eritrea," *Rassegna di Studi Etiopici* 6, no. 2 (1947): 189–99.

71. "La littérature populaire des Israélites tunisiens."

72. L. Leclerc, *Kachef er-roumoûz (Révélation des énigmes) d'Abd er-Rezzaq ed-Djezaïry* (Paris: Baillière et Fils, and Leroux, 1874), 365–66; J. R. Morell, *Algeria: The Topography and History, Political, Social, and Natural, of French Africa* (London: Nathaniel Cooke, 1854), 108.

73. W. G. Browne, *Travels in Africa, Egypt, and Syria, from the Year 1792 to 1798* (London: Cadell Junior, Davies, Longman, and Rees, 1799), 274.

74. F. Foureau, *Documents scientifiques de la Mission Saharienne (Mission Foureau–Lamy d'Alger au Congo par le Tchad), Premier fascicule* (Paris: Masson, 1903), 467, 519.

Foureau also recorded that the plant was grown in Saharan oases in northern Niger but did not visit these sites: Foureau, *Documents scientifiques de la Mission Saharienne*, 467. In addition, there is an account of water-pipe smoking in northern Nigeria from 1889; this mode of smoking was associated with *takrūri* in Tunisia and Algeria. However, the 1889 account was in a fictional portrayal of a slave's experiences, though ostensibly an accurate portrayal of conditions in the area: H. Johnston, *The History of a Slave* (London: Kegan Paul, Trench, 1889), 90.

75. Robinson, "The Tekruri Sheikhs of Gallabat"; A. Paul, *A History of the Beja Tribes of the Sudan* (Cambridge: Cambridge University Press, [1954] 2012); N. McHugh, *Holymen of the Blue Nile: The Making of an Arab-Islamic Community in the Nilotic Sudan, 1500–1850* (Evanston, IL: Northwestern University Press, 1994).

76. The word *shahdānej* referred to hemp fiber: Leclerc, *Kachef er-roumoûz*, 365.

77. For the reasons stated here, I have changed my perspective regarding the direction of the desert crossing. Earlier, I proposed a south-to-north crossing: Duvall, "Cannabis and Tobacco in Precolonial and Colonial Africa."

78. Arabic loanwords for edible cannabis concoctions, such as *majuni*, are reported in one Swahili dictionary: Madan, *Swahili-English Dictionary*, 204.

79. A. Chevalier, "Histoire de deux plantes cultivées d'importance primordiale: Le Lin et le Chanvre," *Revue de Botanique Appliquée et d'Agriculture Coloniale* 24, nos. 269–71 (1944): 67.

80. E. Zangato, "Early Smoking Pipes in the North-Western Central African Republic," *Africa* (Rome) 56, no. 3 (2001): 365–95; J.-P. Lebeuf, "Pipes et plantes à fumer chez les Kotoko," *Notes africaines* 93, no. 1 (1962): 16–17.

81. Chevalier, "Histoire de deux plantes cultivées d'importance primordiale," 67.

82. P. M. Larken, "Impressions of the Zande (Continued from Volume IX, Part 1)," *Sudan Notes and Records* 10 (1927): 93–94; P. de Schlippe, *Shifting Cultivation in Africa: The Zande System of Agriculture* (London: Routledge and Kegan Paul, 1956), 75–76, 107; J. P. Browne, "The Lado Enclave and Its Commercial Possibilities," *Scottish Geographical Magazine* 22, no. 10 (1906): 528, 533.

83. H. L. Hammerstein, "Die Landwirtschaft der Eingeborenen Afrikas," *Beihefte zum Tropenpflanzer* 19, no. 1 (1919): 108.

84. H. Johnston, *George Grenfell and the Congo: A History and Description of the Congo Independent State and Adjoining Districts of Congoland*, vol. 1 (London: Hutchinson, 1908), 78.

85. R. F. Burton, *The Lake Regions of Central Africa: A Picture of Exploration* (New York: Harper Brothers, 1860), 81.

86. G. da Orta, *Colloquies on the Simples and Drugs of India* (London: Henry Sotheran, [1563] 1913), 56.

87. Knox, *An Historical Relation of the Island Ceylon in the East-Indies*, 154; Drury, *Madagascar*, 276; T. Bowrey, *A Geographical Account of Countries round the Bay of Bengal, 1669 to 1679* (Cambridge: Hakluyt Society, [1701] 1905), 79.

88. G. M'Henry, "An Account of the Liberated African Establishment at St. Helena, Chapter II," *Simmond's Colonial Magazine* 5 (1845): 437.

89. Duvall, *Cannabis*, 97.

90. P. B. Beaumont and J. C. Vogel, "Environment, Settlement and State Formation in Pre-colonial Nigeria," in *Frontiers: Southern African Archaeology Today*, ed. M. Hall, G. Avery, D. M. Avery, M. L. Wilson, and A. J. B. Humphreys (Oxford: British Archaeological Reports, 1984), 80–95.

91. H. A. Junod, *The Life of a South African Tribe, I. The Social Life* (Neuchatel, Switzerland: Attinger Frères, 1912), 21.

92. P. J. Mitchell, "Prehistoric Exchange and Interaction in Southeastern Southern Africa: Marine Shells and Ostrich Eggshell," *African Archaeological Review* 13, no. 1 (1996): 59; P. J. Mitchell and A. Hudson, "Psychoactive Plants and Southern African Hunter-Gatherers: A Review of the Evidence," *South African Humanities* 16 (2004): 46.

93. *Dagga* also has a meaning in South Africa that has nothing to do with cannabis. Consider how the equipment manufacturer Turner Morris describes one of its products: "The MM270 mortar mixer range is used to mix plaster, which is known as dagga in [South] Africa"; see the Turner Morris online catalogue at http://www.turnermorris.co .za/product/mortardagga-mixer-270l-s-tmm270dlom-diesel-operated-lombardini-powered -engine. The origins of this usage are unknown. It has also not been recognized in the cannabis literature, including in my 2015 book, *Cannabis*, which I must correct. The photograph on page 96 of that book, entitled "Making Dagga," certainly shows men producing adobe, not "cannabis masses for storage" as I wrote in the photo caption. I identified it as cannabis based on Bourhill's description of processing *dagga* (i.e., cannabis) for smoking: C. J. G. Bourhill, "The Smoking of *Dagga* (Indian Hemp) among the Native Races of South Africa and the Resultant Evils," M.D. diss., School of Medicine, University of Edinburgh (1913), 14. I summarize Bourhill's description in chapter 5 of the present volume.

94. H. C. V. Leibbrandt, ed., *Riebeeck's Journal, etc., January, 1656–December, 1658* (Cape Town: W. A. Richards and Sons, 1897), 129.

95. H. H. Methuen, *Life in the Wilderness; or, Wanderings in South Africa*, 2d ed. (London: Richard Bentley, 1848), 46; E. Holub, *Von der Capstadt ins Land der Maschakulumbe: Reisen im südlichen Afrika in den Jahren 1883–1887*, vol. 2 (Vienna: Alfred Hölder, 1890), 81, 424.

96. D. Gordon, "From Rituals of Rapture to Dependence: The Political Economy of Khoikhoi Narcotic Consumption, circa 1487–1870," *South African Historical Journal* 35 (November 1996): 66.

97. O. Dapper, *Description d'Afrique, contenant les noms, la situation and les confins de toutes ses parties, leurs rivieres, leurs villes and leurs habitations, leurs plantes and leurs animaux; les moeurs, les coûtumes, la langue, les richesses, la religion and le gouvernement de ses peuples* (Amsterdam: Wolfgang, Waesberge, Boom and van Someren, 1686), 386. See also Leibbrandt, *Riebeeck's Journal*, 129.

98. P. Kolbe, *Naaukeurige en Uitvoerige Beschryving van de Kaap de Goede Hoop*, vol. 1 (Amsterdam: Balthazar Lakeman, 1727), 314.

99. A. Sparrman, *A Voyage to the Cape of Good Hope*, 2d ed., vol. 1 (London: G. G. J. and J. Robinson, 1785), 145, 230–31, 265.

100. Gordon, "From Rituals of Rapture to Dependence," 65.

101. C. P. Thunberg, *Travels in Europe, Africa, and Asia, Made between the Years 1770 and 1779*, 2d ed., vol. 2 (London: F. and C. Rivington, 1795), 191–92.

102. Gordon, "From Rituals of Rapture to Dependence," 68.

103. Bourhill, "The Smoking of *Dagga*," 13–14; Godard, *Description et histoire du Maroc*, 178; R. O. Clarke, "Short Notice of the African Plant Diamba, Commonly Called Congo Tobacco," *Hooker's Journal of Botany* 3 (1851): 9–11; W. F. Daniell, "On the D'amba, or Dakka, of Southern Africa," *Pharmaceutical Journal and Transactions* 9, no. 8 (1850): 363–65; C. M. Doke, *The Lambas of Northen Rhodesia: A Study of Their Customs and Beliefs* (London: George G. Harrap, 1931), 110; M. H. Kingsley, *Travels in West Africa: Congo Français, Corisco and Cameroons* (London: Macmillan, 1897), 667–68.

104. F. M. Barroso da Silva, "Descripção de algumas drogas e medicamentos da India, feita em 1799 pelos Facultativos de Goa," *Archivo de Pharmacia e Sciencias Accessorias da India Portugueza* 1, no. 12 ([1799] 1864): 185–91.

105. K. W. Hillig, "Genetic Evidence for Speciation in *Cannabis* (Cannabaceae)," *Genetic Resources and Crop Evolution* 52 (2005): 161–80; K. W. Hillig and P. G. Mahlberg, "A Chemotaxonomic Analysis of Cannabinoid Variation in *Cannabis* (Cannabaceae)," *American Journal of Botany* 91, no. 6 (2004): 966–75.

106. C. S. Duvall, "Drug Laws, Bioprospecting, and the Agricultural Heritage of *Cannabis* in Africa," *Space and Polity* 20, no. 1 (2016): 10–25.

107. J. Mackenzie, "Bechuanaland, with Some Remarks on Mashonaland and Matebeleland," *Scottish Geographical Magazine* 3, no. 6 (1887): 298; F. Elton, "Journal of an Exploration of the Limpopo River," *Journal of the Royal Geographical Society of London* 42 (1872): 1–49.

108. G. Thompson, *Travels and Adventures in Southern Africa* (London: Henry Colburn, 1827), 54.

109. Duvall, "Drug Laws, Bioprospecting, and the Agricultural Heritage of *Cannabis* in Africa."

110. Mitchell, "Prehistoric Exchange and Interaction in Southeastern Southern Africa"; B. J. Brochado, "Terras do Humbe, Camba, Mulondo, Quanhama, e Outras, Contendo uma Idéa da Sua População, Seus Costumes, Vestuarios, etc.," *Annaes do Conselho Ultramarino, Parte Não Official* series 1 (November 1867 [1855]): 187–97; C. Paterson, C. "Prohibition and resistance: A socio-political exploration of the changing dynamics of the Southern African cannabis trade, c. 1850–the present," M.A. thesis, Department of History, Rhodes University, Grahamstown, South Africa (2009).

111. Gordon, "From Rituals of Rapture to Dependence," 67.

112. Gordon, "From Rituals of Rapture to Dependence," 67.

113. Leibbrandt, *Riebeeck's Journal*, 48, 61; Kolbe, *Naaukeurige en Uitvoerige Beschryving van de Kaap de Goede Hoop*, 314; Thompson, *Travels and Adventures in Southern Africa*, 54; Sparrman, *A Voyage to the Cape of Good Hope*, 265; A. Sparrman, *A Voyage to the Cape of Good Hope*, 2d ed., vol. 2 (London: G. G. J. and J. Robinson, 1785), 73, 126, 258; F. Le Vaillant, *Voyage de M. Le Vaillant dans l'interieur de l'Afrique*, vol. 2 (Paris: Leroy, 1790), 72; C. I. Latrobe, *Journal of a Visit to South Africa in 1815 and 1816* (New York: Negro Universities Press, [1818] 1969), 325.

114. C. G. Sampson, "'Zeer grote liefhebbers van tobak': Nicotine and Cannabis Dependency of the Seacow River Bushmen," *Digging Stick* 10, no. 1 (1993): 2–6.

115. Elton, "Journal of an Exploration of the Limpopo River"; J. Tyler, *Forty Years among the Zulus* (Boston: Congregational Sunday-School and Publishing Society, 1891), 122; J. M. Wood, "Native Hemp," *Natal Agricultural Journal* 10, no. 11 (1907): 1365–67.

116. G. A. Farini, *Through the Kalahari Desert* (London: Sampson Low, Marston, Searle, and Rivington, 1886), 125.

117. H. Schinz, *Deutsch-Südwest-Afrika* (Oldenburg: Schulzesche Hol-Buchhandlung und Hof-Buchdruckerei, 1891), 161; "Reviews and Literary Notes," *Chemist and Druggist* 41 (30 January 1892): 174–75; Mr. Dinter, "Vegetation of German South-West Africa," *Gardeners' Chronicle*, no. 687 (24 February 1900): 113–15.

118. Leibbrandt, *Riebeeck's Journal*, 61. Dutch settlers surely planted European hemp-seeds, given that their other crops (including wheat, barley, and peas) were European.

119. Wood, "Native Hemp."

120. F. Eyles, "Vegetable Fibres for Rhodesia," *Rhodesian Agricultural Journal* 5, no. 4 (1907): 297.

121. Published spellings of these plant names vary. Makonde is spoken in northern Mozambique; the other languages are spoken in the lower Zambezi basin.

122. Comte de Ficalho, *Plantas úteis da África portuguesa*, 2d ed. (Lisbon: Agéncia Geral das Colónias, [1884] 1947), 264; H. Johnston, *George Grenfell and the Congo: A History and Description of the Congo Independent State and Adjoining Districts of Congo-land*, vol. 2 (London: Hutchinson, 1908), 608.

123. Linguists call these sounds voiceless alveolar affricate (like *ch* in English "charm"), alveolar lateral approximant (*l* in "line"), alveolar approximant (*r* in "ride"), and palatal approximant (*y* in "you").

124. J. Ladhams, "In Search of West African Pidgin Portuguese," *Revista Internacional de Linguistica Iberoamericana* 4, no. 1 (2006): 96.

125. H. A. Dias de Carvalho, *Expedição portugueza ao Muatiânvua: Ethnographia e historia tradicional dos povos da Lunda* (Lisbon: Imprensa Nacional, 1890), 584; H. A. Dias de Carvalho, *Expedição portugueza ao Muatiânvua: Descripção da viagem á Mussumba do Muatiânvua, Vol. IV: Do Liembe ao Calanhe e Regresso a Lisboa* (Lisbon: Typographia do Jornal, 1894), 775.

126. J. Vansina, "Communications between Angola and East Central Africa before c. 1700," in *Angola on the Move: Transport Routes, Communications and History*, ed. B. Heintze and O. von Achim (Frankfurt: Otto Lembeck, 2008), 130–43; J. Vansina, *How Societies Are Born: Governance in West Central Africa before 1600* (Charlottesville: University of Virginia Press, 2004).

127. Vansina, "Communications between Angola and East Central Africa before c. 1700"; Vansina, *How Societies are Born*; J. Vansina, "Long-Distance Trade-Routes in Central Africa," *Journal of African History* 3, no. 3 (1962): 375–90; B. M. Fagan, "Early Trade and Raw Materials in South Central Africa," *Journal of African History* 10, no. 1 (1969): 1–13.

128. Vansina, "Long-Distance Trade-Routes in Central Africa," 382.

129. J. C. Miller, *Way of Death: Merchant Capitalism and the Angolan Slave Trade, 1730–1839* (Madison: University of Wisconsin Press, 1988); D. B. Domingues da Silva,

The Atlantic Slave Trade from West Central Africa, 1780–1867 (Cambridge: Cambridge University Press, 2017).

130. Vansina, "Communications between Angola and East Central Africa before c. 1700," 138; Vansina, "Long-Distance Trade-Routes in Central Africa," 382.

131. Vansina, "Communications between Angola and East Central Africa before c. 1700"; J. Vansina, *Kingdoms of the Savanna* (Madison: University of Wisconsin Press, 1966).

132. I. Cunnison, "Kazembe and the Portuguese, 1798–1832," *Journal of African History* 2, no. 1 (1961): 61–76.

133. Miller, *Way of Death*, 143–61.

134. Holub, *Von der Capstadt ins Land der Maschakulumbe*, 81; Mackenzie, "Bechuanaland, with Some Remarks on Mashonaland and Matebeleland," 298; Monsieur van Wincxtenhoven, *Exposition Universelle d'Anvers de 1894: Les colonies et l'État Indépendant du Congo, Rapport* (Brussels: Commissariat Général du Gouvernement, 1895), 12; D. Macdonald, *Africana; or, The Heart of Heathen Africa, Volume 1: Native Customs and Beliefs* (London: Simpkin Marshall, 1882), 30.

135. D. B. Domingues da Silva and B. Bukas-Yakabuul, "From beyond the Kwango: Tracing the Linguistic Origins of Slaves Leaving Angola, 1811–1848," *Almanack* 12 (2016): 34–43.

136. A. de Saldanha da Gama, *Memoria sobre as colonias de Portugal: Situadas na costa occidental d'Afrique* (Paris: Typographia de Casimir, 1839), 73.

137. Duvall, *Cannabis*, 65–67.

138. Daniell, "On the D'amba," 363.

139. F. Welwitsch, *Synopse explicativa das amostras de madeiras e drogas medicinaes e de otros objectivos normente ethnographicos colligidos na provincia de Angola* (Lisbon: Imprensa Nacional, 1862), 45; J. J. Monteiro, *Angola and the River Congo*, vol. 2 (London: Macmillan, 1875), 257.

140. Clarke, "Short Notice of the African Plant Diamba"; Ficalho, *Plantas úteis da África portuguesa*, 264; J. Büttikofer, *Reisebilder aus Liberia*, vol. 2 (Leiden: E. J. Brill, 1890), 276; M'Henry, "An Account of the Liberated African Establishment at St. Helena," 437; F. A. Flückiger, "Pharmaceutische Reiseeindrucke [Part I]," *Pharmaceutische Centralhalle für Deutschland* 8, no. 49 (1867): 436–42.

141. P. B. Du Chaillu, *Explorations and Adventures in Equatorial Africa* (New York: Harper Brothers, 1861), 420.

142. H. Baum, *Kunene—Sambesi-Expedition* (Berlin: Kolonial-Wirtschaftlichen Komitees, 1903), 7; A. F. F. da Silva Porto, *Viagens e Apontamentos de um Portuense em África* (Lisbon: Divisão de Publicações e Biblioteca, Agência Geral das Colónias, [ca. 1885] 1942), 231.

143. C. Smith, "The Journal of Professor Smith," in *Narrative of an Expedition to Explore the River Zaire, Usually Called the Congo, in South Africa, in 1816, under the Direction of Captain J. K. Tuckey, R.N.*, ed. Lords Commissioners of the Admiralty (London: Frank Cass, [1818] 1967), 304.

144. The brief, anonymous notice cites *Union Médicale*—a contemporaneous journal—but I have been unable to trace this source: "Deïamba, nouveau narcotique," *Journal de Pharmacie et de Chimie* 14 (1848): 201.

145. Daniell, "On the D'amba."

146. Generalized accounts associated the plant specifically with rivers, although this may have represented observation bias, because travelers principally followed rivers: see, e.g. F. Goffart, *Traité méthodique de géographie du Congo* (Antwerp: Clément Thibaut, 1897), 87.

147. M. Decazes, "L'ouest africain: Relation de voyage," *Société Normande de Géographie Bulletin de l'Année* 10 (1888): 59.

148. H. Nipperdey, "The Industrial Products and Food-stuffs of the Congo," *Scottish Geographical Magazine* 2, no. 8 (1886): 487.

149. Chevalier, "Histoire de deux plantes cultivées d'importance primordiale," 67–68; Monsieur Ponel, "Note sur les M'Bochis," *Bulletin de la Société de Géographie* 7, 7th series (1886): 377; J. Dybowski, "La Mission Jean Dybowski vers le Tchad," in *Le Tour du Monde: Nouveau Journal des Voyages*, ed. É. Charton (Paris: Librairie Hachette, 1893), 126; Contre-amiral du Quilio, "Voyage dans l'Ogoway," *Revue Maritime et Coloniale* 41 (April 1874): 16; G. di Brazza Savorgnan, "E. Tre anni e mezzo nella regione dell'Ogóue e del Congo [part 5]," *Bollettino della Società Geographica Italiana* 21, series 2, no. 12 (1887): 364; C. van Overbergh, *Les Basonge (État Ind. du Congo)* (Brussels: Albert de Wit, 1908), 139.

150. Nipperdey, "The Industrial Products and Food-stuffs of the Congo," 487; H. Ward, "Ethnographical Notes Relating to the Congo Tribes," *Journal of the Anthropological Institute of Great Britain and Ireland* 24 (1895): 295.

151. Ponel, "Note sur les M'Bochis," 377; C. Coquilhat, *Sur le Haut-Congo* (Paris: J. Lebègue, 1888), 348.

152. E. Viaene and F. Bernard, "L'art de guérir chez les peuplades congolaises," *Bulletin de la Société Royale Belge de Géographie* 35 (1911): 40.

153. J. de Mattos e Silva, *Contribução para o estudo da Região de Cabinda* (Lisbon: Typographia Universal, 1904), 263.

154. Du Chaillu, *Explorations and Adventures in Equatorial Africa*, 420. See also P. B. Du Chaillu, *Journey to Ashango-Land, and Further Penetration into Equatorial Africa* (New York: Harper Brothers, 1871), 326, 335.

155. Du Chaillu, *Explorations and adventures in Equatorial Africa*, 419; Quilio, "Voyage dans l'Ogoway," 16; E. Jardin, "Aperçu sur la flore du Gabon avec quelques observations sur les plantes les plus importantes," *Bulletin de la Société Linnéenne de Normandie* 4, 4th series (10 November 1890): 179; Monsieur Lartigue, "Contributions à la géographie médicale: La lagune de Fernand-Vaz et le delta de l'Ogo-Wé," *Archives de Médecine Navale* 14 (1870): 175; E. Trivier, "Le Gabon, le Komo, l'Ogowé," *Bulletin de la Société de Géographie de Rochefort* 7 (1885): 262–308; C. Ivens, "Consulat général de Belgique à Sainte-Croix de Ténériffe," in *Recueil consulaire contenant les rapports commerciaux des agents belges à l'étranger publié en execution de l'Arrêté royal du 13 novembre 1855, Tome 100: 1898* (Brussels: P. Weissenbruch, 1898), 12.

156. C. Seguin, "Les hallucinations d'un fumeur de chanvre au Gabon," *Journal des Voyages* 704 (29 May 1910): 427.

157. Viaene and Bernard, "L'art de guérir chez les peuplades congolaises," 39; J.-B. Douville, *Voyage au Congo et dans l'interieur de l'Afrique equinoxiale, fait dans les années 1828, 1829, et 1830*, vol. 1 (Paris: Chez Jules Renouard, 1832), 127.

158. Delgado-Matas and colleagues describe the cropping system but do not mention cannabis. Nonetheless, the drug plant's role is clearly documented in nineteenth-century sources. See C. Delgado-Matas, B. Mola-Yudego, D. Gritten, D. Kiala-Kalusinga, and T. Pukkala, "Land Use Evolution and Management under Recurrent Conflict Conditions: Umbundu Agroforestry System in the Angolan Highlands," *Land Use Policy* 42 (2015): 460–70.

159. Monteiro, *Angola and the River Congo*, 258; Welwitsch, *Synopse explicativa das amostras de madeiras e drogas medicinaes e de otros objectivos normente ethnographicos colligidos na provincia de Angola*, 45; Baum, *Kunene*, 7; H. A. Dias de Carvalho, *Expedição portugueza ao Muatiânvua: Descripção da viagem á Mussumba do Muatiânvua, Vol. 2: Do Cuango ao Chicapa* (Lisbon: Imprensa Nacional, 1892), 56; H. Capello and R. Ivens, *De Benguela as Terras de Iácca*, vol. 2 (Lisbon: Imprensa Nacional, 1881), 259.

160. A. Sisenando Marques, *Expedição portugueza ao Muata-Ianvo: Os climas e as producções das Terras de Malange á Lunda* (Lisbon: Imprensa Nacional, 1889), 103.

161. J. W. Lapsley, *Life and Letters of Samuel Norvell Lapsley, Missionary to the Congo Valley, West Africa, 1866–1892* (Richmond, VA: Whittet and Shepperson, 1893), 212.

5. A CONVENIENT CROP

1. C. S. Duvall, *Cannabis* (London: Reaktion, 2015), chap. 2.

2. C. Galen, *De alimentorum facultatibus, libri tres* (Lyon: Gulielmum Rouillium, 1547), 84–85.

3. F. Rosenthal, *The Herb: Hashish versus Medieval Muslim Society* (Leiden: E. J. Brill, 1971).

4. R. J. Bouquet, "Cannabis," UNODC *Bulletin on Narcotics* 4, no. 2 (1950): 14–30; H. Yule and A. C. Burnell, *Hobson-Jobson: A Glossary of Colloquial Anglo-Indian Words and Phrases* (London: John Murray, 1903). For Moroccan recipes: L. Raynaud, *Étude sur l'hygiène et la médecine au Maroc suivie d'une notice sur la climatologie des principales villes de l'empire* (Algiers: S. Léon, 1902), 107; M. Rogers, "Paul Bowles: Conversations in Morocco with the Expatriate Author and Composer," *Rolling Stone*, 23 May 1974, accessed 7 August 2017, http://www.rollingstone.com/culture/features/the-rolling-stone -interview-paul-bowles-19740523. For global recipes, see H. Bey and A. Zug, eds., *Orgies of the Hemp Eaters: Cuisine, Slang, Literature and Ritual of Cannabis Culture* (Brooklyn: Autonomedia, 2004).

5. Only tobacco smoking was evident: E. J. Keall, "One Man's Mead Is Another Man's Persian: One Man's Coconut Is Another Man's Grenade," *Muqarnas* 10 (1993): 275–85. Prospero Alpini, a Venetian botanist resident in Cairo during the 1580s, recorded only oral consumption of cannabis: P. Alpino, *De medicina Aegyptiorum: Libri quatuor* (Venice: Franciscum de Franciscis Senensem, 1591), 121B.

6. L. Godard, *Description et histoire du Maroc* (Paris: Charles Tanera, 1860), 540; P. Paquignon, "Le monopole du tabac au Maroc," *Revue du Monde Musulman* 5, no. 3 (1911): 499–500. Paquignon claimed to identify a sixteenth-century allusion to cannabis smoking in an Arabic history (*Nozhet al Hâdi*, in French translation), but I have not located the passage he paraphrases.

7. G. Wiet, ed., *Maqrizi: El-Mawâ'iz wa'l-i'itibâr fi dhikr el-khitat wa'l-âthâr*, vol. 2 (Cairo: Institut Français d'Archéologie Orientale, 1913), 90.

8. W. H. Salmon, *An Account of the Ottoman Conquest of Egypt in the Year A.H. 922 (A.D. 1516)* (London: Royal Asiatic Society, 1921), 94–95.

9. Alpino, *De medicina Aegyptiorum*, 121B.

10. G. G. Nahas, "Hashish and Drug Abuse in Egypt during the 19th and 20th Centuries," *Bulletin of the New York Academy of Medicine* 61, no. 5 (1985): 428–44; E. Daumas and A. de Chancel, *Le grand désert, ou itinéraire d'une caravane du Sahara au pays des nègres (Royaume de Haoussa)* (Paris: Napoléon Chaix, 1848), 399–400; L. Kozma, "Cannabis Prohibition in Egypt, 1880–1939: From Local Ban to League of Nations Diplomacy," *Middle Eastern Studies* 47, no. 3 (2011): 443–60.

11. J. P. Brown, *The Dervishes; or, Oriental Spiritualism* (London: Trübner, 1868), 309.

12. J. S. Trimingham, *The Sufi Orders in Islam* (Oxford: Clarendon, 1971), 199.

13. Rosenthal, *The Herb*.

14. R. Brunel, *Le monachisme errant dans l'Islam* (Paris: Maisonneuve and Larose, [1955] 2001).

15. Regarding cannabis in the Rif: T. H. Mikuriya, "Kif Cultivation in the Rif Mountains," *Economic Botany* 21, no. 3 (1967): 231–34; R. Joseph, "The Economic Significance of *Cannabis Sativa* in the Moroccan Rif," *Economic Botany* 27, no. 2 (1973): 235–40; A. Merzouki and J. Molero Mesa, "Concerning Kif, a *Cannabis Sativa* L. Preparation Smoked in the Rif Mountains of Northern Morocco," *Journal of Ethnopharmacology* 81 (2002): 403–6; P.-A. Chouvy, "Production de cannabis et de haschich au Maroc: Contexte et enjeux," *L'Espace Politique* 4, no. 1 (2008): art. 59; K. Afsahi and K. Mouna, "Cannabis dans le Rif central (Maroc): Construction d'un espace de déviance," Espaces-Temps.net, 30 September 2014, accessed 28 August 2017, https://www.espacestemps.net /en/articles/cannabis-dans-le-rif-central-maroc-2.

16. The 1921 date relates to a source that documents hashish production near Constantine, Algeria: L. Livet, "Les fumeurs de Kif," *Bulletin de la Société Clinique de Médecine Mentale* 9 (17 January 1921): 40–45. It's reasonable to infer that the practice was more widespread in the Atlas Mountains. Indeed, some earlier accounts of the Ḥeddawa suggest that people made dry-sifted hashish in Morocco, although the descriptions could simply describe hand-crushed, dried inflorescences: Raynaud, *Étude sur l'hygiène et la médecine au Maroc suivie d'une notice sur la climatologie des principales villes de l'empire*, 107.

17. P. Bowles, "Kif: Prologue and Compendium of Terms," in *The Book of Grass: An Anthology on Indian Hemp*, ed. G. Andrews and S. Vinkenoog (New York: Grove, 1967), 108–14.

18. Chouvy, "Production de cannabis et de haschich au Maroc."

19. Key works on the Ḥeddawa include Brunel, *Le monachisme errant dans l'Islam*; Afsahi and Mouna, "Cannabis dans le Rif central"; A. Mouliéras, *Le Maroc inconnu, deuxième partie: Exploration des Djebala (Maroc Septentrional)* (Paris: Augustin Challamel, 1899); R. Touceda Fontenia, *Los heddaua de Beni Arós y su extraño rito* (Tétouan, Morocco: Marroquí, 1955).

20. Brunel, *Le monachisme errant dans l'Islam*.

21. Afsahi and Mouna, "Cannabis dans le Rif central."

22. Grupo Senderismo en el Rif, "La zaouia de Sidi Heddi en Beni Aros (July 15, 2011)," Randonnées dans le Rif (blog), accessed 29 August 2017, http://tetuangorgues.blogspot .com/2011/07/la-zaouia-de-sidi-heddi-en-beni-aross.html.

23. Brunel, *Le monachisme errant dans l'Islam*.

24. M. G. Marchand, "Conte en dialecte marocain," *Journal Asiatique* 6, 10th series (November–December 1905): 458, 463.

25. Marquis de Segonzac, *Voyages au Maroc (1899–1901)* (Paris: Armand Colin, 1903), 291.

26. Raynaud, *Étude sur l'hygiène et la médecine au Maroc suivie d'une notice sur la climatologie des principales villes de l'empire*, 108–10; M. Morelet, "Les Maures de Constantine en 1840," *Mémoires de l'Académie des Sciences, Arts et Belles-Lettres de Dijon* 3, 3d series (1876): 275; J. H. Dunant, *Notice sur la régence de Tunis* (Geneva: Jules-Germaine Fick, 1858), 206.

27. A. Dumas, *Le véloce, ou, Tanger, Alger et Tunis*, vol. 4 (Brussels: Muquardt, 1849), 53.

28. Raynaud, *Étude sur l'hygiène et la médecine au Maroc suivie d'une notice sur la climatologie des principales villes de l'empire*, 108–9. Photos of adherents published in 1955 show men in worn clothes, without spears, and not particularly unclean looking. The photos were published in Touceda Fontenia, *Los heddaua de Beni Arós y su extraño rito*. Many of the photos have been posted online at Grupo Senderismo en el Rif, "La zaouia de Sidi Heddi en Beni Aros."

29. R. Leydi, *Chants, rythmes et influences du Maroc* [compact disc] (Ivry-sur-Seine, France: Disques Dom, [1972] 2000). The chant can be found on the internet by searching "Heddaoua chante."

30. Marchand, "Conte en dialecte marocain," 462.

31. Brunel, *Le monachisme errant dans l'Islam*, 238, 291.

32. Brunel and Touceda Fontenia provide detailed analyses of Ḥeddawa theology and devotional practices.

33. Recipes for both edible and smoked preparations are at Brunel, *Le monachisme errant dans l'Islam*, 303–5.

34. Afsahi and Mouna, "Cannabis dans le Rif central."

35. Brunel, *Le monachisme errant dans l'Islam*, 291.

36. On the donations, see Brunel, *Le monachisme errant dans l'Islam*, 291. On the sales price, see: C. de Foucauld, *Reconnaissance au Maroc, 1883–1884* (Paris: Challamel, 1888), 35.

37. Afsahi and Mouna, "Cannabis dans le Rif central."

38. Foucauld, *Reconnaissance au Maroc*, 35, 255. Some marabouts also drank liquor (though this is clearly prohibited in Islam) to aid their meditation.

39. Afsahi and Mouna, "Cannabis dans le Rif central"; Chouvy, "Production de cannabis et de haschich au Maroc."

40. Afsahi and Mouna, "Cannabis dans le Rif central."

41. Afsahi and Mouna, "Cannabis dans le Rif central."

42. Brunel, *Le Monachisme errant dans l'Islam*, 304.

43. P.-A. Chouvy and K. Afsahi, "Hashish Revival in Morocco," *International Journal of Drug Policy* 25, no. 3 (2014): 416–23.

44. Primary documents are in French, Spanish, and German; secondary sources are in French and Spanish. There are also documents in Arabic, but I have not researched this literature. I do acknowledge that there are scattered one-sentence mentions in English books about Sufism, all based on Brunel's *Le monachisme errant dans l'Islam*. The English literature on cannabis completely omits the Ḥeddawa: see, e.g., M. S. Ferrara, *Sacred Bliss: A Spiritual History of Cannabis* (New York: Rowman and Littlefield, 2016). Finally,

an anthology of poetry by Beat writers, including Bowles, William S. Burroughs, and the Moroccan writer Mohammed Mrabet, was published in 1967 as "An Heddaoua Publication," with no further explanation: see I. Cohen and R. Richkin, eds., *The Great Society* (N.p.: Heddaoua, 1967).

45. See, e.g., Docteur Décugis, "Relation d'un voyage dans l'intérieur du Maroc," *Bulletin de la Société de Géographie* 16 (September 1878): 267.

46. E. W. Lane, *An Account of the Manners and Customs of the Modern Egyptians*, vol. 2 (London: Charles Knight, 1836), 37.

47. N. Hanna, "Culture in Ottoman Egypt," in *The Cambridge History of Egypt*, ed. C. F. Petry (Cambridge: Cambridge University Press, 1998), 107.

48. Monsieur Rouyer, "Notice sur les médicaments usuels des Égyptiens," in *Description de l'Égypte*, ed. Commission des Sciences et des Artes d'Égypte (Paris: Impériale, 1809), 220.

49. Lane, *An Account of the Manners and Customs of the Modern Egyptians*, 40.

50. W. R. Wilde, *Narrative of a Voyage to Madeira, Teneriffe, and along the Shores of the Mediterranean*, vol. 1 (Dublin: William Curry Jr., 1840), 325; E. W. Lane, *An Account of the Manners and Customs of the Modern Egyptians*, vol. 1 (London: Charles Knight, 1837), 183–88.

51. Rouyer, "Notice sur les médicaments usuels des Égyptiens," 220.

52. Lane, *An Account of the Manners and Customs of the Modern Egyptians*, 1:188.

53. Lane, *An Account of the Manners and Customs of the Modern Egyptians*, 1:187.

54. Brown, *The Dervishes*, 311.

55. Rouyer, "Notice sur les médicaments usuels des Égyptiens," 220.

56. J. L. Burckhardt, *Travels in Arabia*, vol. 1 (London: Henry Colburn, 1829), 48.

57. K. Baedeker, ed., *Egypt: Handbook for Travellers, Part First: Lower Egypt, with the Fayûm and the Peninsula of Sinai* (Leipzig: Karl Baedeker and Dulau, 1878), xxii.

58. Lane, *An Account of the Manners and Customs of the Modern Egyptians*, 2:39.

59. Monsieur Larue du Barry, "Note sur l'usage du chanvre en Algérie," *Journal de Chimie Médicale, de Pharmacie et de Toxicologie* 21 (January 1845): 31; J. Navarrete, *Desde Vad-Ras à Sevilla: Acuarelas de la campaña de África* (Madrid: Víctor Saiz, 1880), 221.

60. Rouyer, "Notice sur les médicaments usuels des Égyptiens," 220.

61. Baedeker, *Egypt*, 428–46; Brown, *The Dervishes*, 311.

62. G. Beauclerk, *A Journey to Morocco in 1826* (London: Poole and Edwards and William Harrison Ainsworth, 1828), 275; L. Washington, "Geographical Notice of the Empire of Morocco," *Geographical Journal* 1, no. 1 (1832): 146. In Morocco in 1902, the proportion was one part tobacco to six parts *kif*: Raynaud, *Étude sur l'hygiène et la médecine au Maroc suivie d'une notice sur la climatologie des principales villes de l'empire*, 109.

63. Sebaut, *Dictionnaire de la législation tunisienne*, new ed. (Dijon, France: Imprimerie Sirodot, 1896), 149–67, *chīra* on page 150.

64. Livet, "Les fumeurs de Kif."

65. Navarrete, *Desde Vad-Ras à Sevilla*, 221; Foucauld, *Reconnaissance au Maroc*, 34; M. Seghir ben Youssef, "Soixante ans d'histoire de la Tunisie (1705–1765) (suite)," *Revue Tunisienne* 3, no. 11 (1896): 41; C. Féraud, *Kitab el Adouani, ou le Sahara de Constantine et de Tunis* (Constantine, Algeria: Arnolet, 1868), 197; M. de Chénier, *Recherches histo-*

riques sur les Maures, et histoire de l'empire de Maroc, vol. 3 (Paris: Chénier, Bailly, and Royer, 1787), 76, 439.

66. The lounging and smoking are described on pages 435 and 437; the quote, from page 436, compares the man's drug use to that of Ḥeddawa: Marchand, "Conte en dialecte marocain."

67. Révérends Pères Abinal and Malzac, *Dictionnaire Malgache-Français* (Antananarivo, Madagascar: Mission Catholique Mahamasina, 1888), 41, 272, 397, 506, 554, 589, 678; R. Baron, "Jottings on Some of the Plants of Imerina," *Antananarivo Annual and Madagascar Magazine* 3 (1878): 109; J. Sibree, *The Great African Island* (London: Trübner, 1880), 95.

68. F. M. Barroso da Silva, "Descripção de algumas drogas e medicamentos da India, feita em 1799 pelos Facultativos de Goa," *Archivo de Pharmacia e Sciencias Accessorias da India Portugueza* 1, no. 12 ([1799] 1864): 185–91.

69. V. Giraud, *Les lacs d'Afrique équatoriale: Voyage d'exploration éxécuté de 1883 à 1885* (Paris: Hachette, 1890), 73.

70. Duvall, *Cannabis*, chaps. 3, 5.

71. Giraud, *Les lacs d'Afrique équatoriale*, 73.

72. The word was *katrinia*, unrelated to known Arabic or Hindi terms: Abinal and Malzac, *Dictionnaire Malgache-Français*, 292.

73. The other words were *boza* and *palu*, both unrelated to known foreign terms: A. C. Madan, *Swahili-English Dictionary* (Oxford: Clarendon, 1903), 30, 204, 301.

74. G. Casati, *Ten Years in Equatoria* (London: Frederick Warne, 1898), 429; Madan, *Swahili-English Dictionary*, 22; C. de Martrin-Donos, *Les Belges dans l'Afrique Centrale: Voyages, aventures et découvertes d'après les documents et journaux des explorateurs, Le Congo et ses affluents*, vol. 2 (Brussels: P. Maes, 1886), 166; Ministério das Colónias, Portugal, "Portaria provincial proibindo, na provincia de Angola, o fornecimento a indigenas da *riamba*, ou *liamba*, por ter efeitos perniciosos semelhantes aos do ópio," in *Colecção da Legislação Colonial da República Portuguesa, 1913 (Janeiro a Dezembro)*, vol. 4 (Lisbon: Imprensa Nacional, 1918), 262.

75. "Deïamba, nouveau narcotique," *Journal de Pharmacie et de Chimie* 14 (1848): 201; J. Dybowski, "La mission Jean Dybowski vers le Tchad," in *Le tour du monde: Nouveau journal des voyages*, ed. É. Charton (Paris: Hachette, 1893), 126; C. van Overbergh, *Les Basonge (État Ind. du Congo)* (Brussels: Albert de Wit, 1908), 139; A. de Saldanha da Gama, *Memoria sobre as colonias de Portugal: Situadas na costa occidental d'Afrique* (Paris: Casimir, 1839), 73; W. F. Daniell, "On the D'amba, or Dakka, of Southern Africa," *Pharmaceutical Journal and Transactions* 9, no. 8 (1850): 364; C. M. Doke, *The Lambas of Northen Rhodesia: A Study of Their Customs and Beliefs* (London: George G. Harrap, 1931), 110.

76. Van Overbergh, *Les Basonge*, 140.

77. C. Jeannest, *Quatre années au Congo* (Paris: G. Charpentier, 1883), 106.

78. Daniell, "On the D'amba, or Dakka, of Southern Africa," 364; J. R. Jackson, "On the Products of the Hemp Plant (*Cannabis Sativa*)," *The Technologist* 2 (1862): 176–78; J. de Mattos e Silva, *Contribução para o estudo da Região de Cabinda* (Lisbon: Universal, 1904), 263; F. A. Flückiger, "Pharmaceutische Reiseeindrucke [Part I]," *Pharmaceutische Centralhalle für Deutschland* 8, no. 49 (1867): 440. Daniell, Jackson, and Flückiger

describe open, legal markets; Mattos e Silva describes a clandestine market under European scrutiny, though technically still legal. In Chichewa (Malawi), such packets were called *mfani* or *mpaka*: D. C. Scott, *A Cyclopaedic Dictionary of the Mang'anja Language Spoken in British Central Africa* (Edinburgh: Foreign Mission Committee of the Church of Scotland, 1892), 344, 371.

79. E. Dahl, *Nyamwesi-Wörterbuch* (Hamburg: L. Friederichsen, 1915), 114, 583; J. M. Watt, "Dagga in South Africa," *Bulletin on Narcotics* 13 (1961): 9–14.

80. C. J. G. Bourhill, "The Smoking of *Dagga* (Indian Hemp) among the Native Races of South Africa and the Resultant Evils," M.D. diss., School of Medicine, University of Edinburgh, 1913, 14.

81. C. S. Duvall, "Drug Laws, Bioprospecting, and the Agricultural Heritage of *Cannabis* in Africa," *Space and Polity* 20, no. 1 (2016): 10–25.

82. D. Gordon, "From Rituals of Rapture to Dependence: The Political Economy of Khoikhoi Narcotic Consumption, circa 1487–1870," *South African Historical Journal* 35 (November 1996): 62–88; C. Paterson, "Prohibition and Resistance: A Socio-political Exploration of the Changing dynamics of the Southern African Cannabis Trade, circa 1850–the Present," M.A. thesis, Department of History, Rhodes University, Grahamstown, South Africa, 2009.

83. A. Werner, *The Natives of British Central Africa*, vol. 3 (London: Archibald Constable, 1906), 178–79.

84. This term was translated as *sarro de cachimbo* (lit., fun of the pipe) in J. D. Cordeiro da Matta, *Ensaio de Diccionario Kimbúndu-Portuguez* (Lisbon: Antonio Maria Pereira, 1893), 149.

85. H. A. Dias de Carvalho, *Expedição portugueza ao Muatiânvua: Ethnographia e historia tradicional dos povos da Lunda* (Lisbon: Imprensa Nacional, 1890), 367; Martrin-Donos, *Les Belges dans l'Afrique Centrale*, 311; A. Chapaux, *Le Congo historique, diplomatique, physique, politique, économique, humanitaire et colonial* (Brussels: Charles Rozez, 1894), 46; C. S. L. Bateman, *The First Ascent of the Kasaï: Being Some Records of Service under the Lone Star* (New York: Dodd, Mead, 1889), 113–81.

86. Dias de Carvalho, *Expedição portugueza ao Muatiânvua*, 367.

87. R. F. Burton, "The Lake Regions of Central Africa, with Notices of the Lunar Mountains and the Sources of the White Nile," *Journal of the Royal Geographical Society* 29 (1859): 298. See also A. Burdo, *Les Belges dans l'Afrique Centrale: De Zanzibar au Lac Tanganyika* (Brussels: P. Maes, 1890), 312.

88. D. Kidd, *The Essential Kafir* (London: Adam and Charles Black, 1904), 346; H. A. Junod, *The Life of a South African Tribe, I: The Social Life* (Neuchatel, Switzerland: Attinger Frères, 1912), 312–16; J. Tyler, *Forty Years among the Zulus* (Boston: Congregational Sunday-School and Publishing Society, 1891), 123; L. H. Samuelson, *Some Zulu Customs and Folk-lore* (London: Church Printing, 1905), 81. Samuelson also described games in which players drew mazes to challenge their opponents or battled one another with "armies" of "soldiers"—bubble marks on the ground. In Zulu, the maze game may have been called "*u-Sogerre*"; the language had several other words that linked saliva and cannabis smoking: A. T. Bryant, *A Zulu-English Dictionary* (Pinetown, South Africa: Mariannhill Mission Press, 1905), 281, 551, 595, 601, 667.

89. T. Maggs, "Neglected Rock Art: The Rock Engravings of Agriculturist Communities in South Africa," *South African Archaeological Bulletin* 50, no. 162 (1995): 140.

90. Government of the Colony of Natal, *Departmental Reports: 1893–94* (Pietermaritzburg: William Watson, 1895), B14.

91. M. Decazes, "L'ouest africain: Relation de voyage," *Société Normande de Géographie, Bulletin de l'Année* 10 (1888): 59.

92. D. A. Livingstone, *Missionary Travels and Researches in South Africa* (London: John Murray, 1857), 356; H. Chatelain, "Angolan Customs," *Journal of American Folk-Lore* 9, no. 23 (1896): 13.

93. Martrin-Donos, *Les Belges dans l'Afrique Centrale*, 180, 223; C. Gouldsbury and H. Sheane, *The Great Plateau of Northern Rhodesia* (London: Edward Arnold, 1911), 27; H. M. da Paiva Couceiro, *Relatorio de viagem entre Bailundo e as terras do Mucusso* (Lisbon: Imprensa Nacional, 1892), 154; H. Capello and R. Ivens, *De Benguela as terras de Iácca. Descripção de uma viagem na Africa central e occidental*, vol. 1 (Lisbon: Imprensa Nacional, 1881), 188. See also J. Fabian, *Out of Our Minds: Reason and Madness in the Exploration of Central Africa* (Berkeley: University of California Press, 2000).

94. Dias de Carvalho, *Expedição portugueza ao Muatiânvua*, 584.

95. J. C. Curto, *Enslaving Spirits: The Portuguese-Brazilian Alcohol Trade at Luanda and Its Hinterland, circa 1550–1830* (Leiden: E. J. Brill, 2004).

96. Burdo, *Les Belges dans l'Afrique Centrale*, 312.

97. Giraud, *Les lacs d'Afrique équatoriale*, 337.

98. J. J. Monteiro, *Angola and the River Congo*, vol. 2 (London: Macmillan, 1875), 257.

99. R. F. Burton, *The Lake Regions of Central Africa: A Picture of Exploration* (New York: Harper Brothers, 1860), 81. The sound of coughing caused by cannabis appears at the beginning of the song "Sweet Leaf," by Black Sabbath, on *Master of Reality*, LP, 1971.

100. A.-J. Wauters, *Le Congo au point de vue économique* (Brussels: Institut National de Geographie, 1885), 44.

101. Dahl, *Nyamwesi-Wörterbuch*, 64, 480; W. P. Johnson, *Nyasa, the Great Water* (London: Oxford University Press, 1922), 99.

102. G. W. Stow, *The Native Races of South Africa* (London: Swan Sonnenschein, 1905), 53.

103. A. Sparrman, *A Voyage to the Cape of Good Hope*, 2d ed., vol. 1 (London: G. G. J. and J. Robinson, 1785), 230.

104. Perhaps he did not inhale and thus did not experience the sensation that leads to the cannabis cough. At the time, the common smoking practice among Europeans was to hold smoke in the mouth rather than filling the lungs. The quote is from R. F. Burton, *Two Trips to Gorilla Land and the Cataracts of the Congo*, vol. 2 (London: Sampson Low, Marston, Low, and Searle, 1876), 296.

105. R. F. Burton, *Personal Narrative of a Pilgrimage to El Medinah and Meccah*, 2d ed., vol. 1 (London: Longman, Brown, Green, Longmans, and Roberts, 1857), 44.

106. D. Hobson, "A Hunting Trip to Mozambique in 1868," *Geographical Journal* 149, no. 2 (1983): 208.

107. "Deïamba, nouveau narcotique"; A. Chevalier, "Histoire de deux plantes cultivées d'importance primordiale: Le Lin et le Chanvre," *Revue de Botanique Appliquée et d'Agriculture Coloniale* 24, nos. 269–71 (1944): 66.

108. J. C. Miller, *Way of Death: Merchant Capitalism and the Angolan Slave Trade, 1730–1839* (Madison: University of Wisconsin Press, 1988), 248.

109. H. A. Dias de Carvalho, *Expedição portugueza ao Muatiânvua: Descripção da viagem á Mussumba do Muatiânvua, Vol. 4: Do Liembe ao Calanhe e regresso a Lisboa* (Lisbon: Typographia do Jornal, 1894), 162–63, 430.

110. O. R. O'Neil, *Adventures in Swaziland: The Story of a South African Boer* (New York: Century, 1921), 309; J. Macdonald, "Bantu Customs and Legends," *Folklore* 3, no. 3 (1892): 352.

111. Government of the Colony of Natal, *Departmental Reports*, B13.

112. J. F. Siler, W. L. Sheep, G. W. Cook, W. A. Smith, L. B. Bates, and G. F. Clark, "Mariajuana Smoking in Panama," *Military Surgeon* 73 (1933): 273; Bourhill, "The Smoking of *Dagga* (Indian Hemp) among the Native Races of South Africa and the Resultant Evils," 57.

113. B. M. du Toit, "Historical and Cultural Factors Influencing Cannabis Use among Indians in South Africa," *Journal of Psychoactive Drugs* 9, no. 3 (1977): 235–46.

114. Indian Immigrants (Wragg) Commission, "Report," in *Documents of Indentured Labour, Natal, 1851–1917*, ed. Y. S. Meer (Durban, South Africa: Institute of Black Research, [1887] 1980), 258.

115. Duvall, "Drug Laws, Bioprospecting, and the Agricultural Heritage of *Cannabis* in Africa."

116. See, among others, I. Nabukenya, C. Rubaire-Akiiki, D. Olila, K. Ikwap, and J. Höglund, "Ethnopharmacological Practices by Livestock Farmers in Uganda: Survey Experiences from Mpigi and Gulu Districts," *Journal of Ethnobiology and Ethnomedicine* 10 (2014): art. 9; P. Tugume, E. K. Kakudidi, M. Buyinza, J. Namaalwa, M. Kamatenesi, P. Mucunguzi, and J. Kalema, "Ethnobotanical Survey of Medicinal Plant Species Used by Communities around Mabira Central Forest Reserve, Uganda," *Journal of Ethnobiology and Ethnomedicine* 12 (2016): art. 5.

117. B. M. du Toit, *Cannabis in Africa: A Survey of Its Distribution in Africa, and a Study of Cannabis Use and Users in Multi-ethnic South Africa* (Rotterdam: A. A. Balkema, 1980), 58; F. Ames, "A Clinical and Metabolic Study of Acute Intoxication with *Cannabis Sativa* and Its Role in the Model Psychoses," *British Journal of Psychiatry* 104 (1958): 976; Bryant, *A Zulu-English Dictionary*, 3, 275, 646.

118. E. P. Phillips, "A Contribution to the Flora of the Leribe Plateau and Environs: With a Discussion on the Relationships of the Floras of Basutoland, the Kalahari, and the South-eastern Regions," *Annals of the South African Museum* 16, no. 1 (1917): 260.

119. This statement deserves an asterisk. Hewat's anecdote is not clearly attributed to the Sotho, who are mentioned several pages earlier. Watt and Breyer-Brandwijk, apparently borrowing from Hewat, attribute it to Sotho, and others have followed: M. L. Hewat, *Bantu Folk Lore (Medical and General)* (New York: Negro Universities Press, [1906] 1970), 98; J. Watt and M. Breyer-Brandwijk, *The Medical and Poisonous Plants of South Africa* (Edinburgh: E. and S. Livingstone, 1932), 35–36.

120. A. T. Bryant, "Zulu Medicine and Medicine-Men," *South African Humanities* 2, no. 1 (1909): 102; R. O. Clarke, "Short Notice of the African Plant Diamba, Commonly Called Congo Tobacco," *Hooker's Journal of Botany* 3 (1851): 11. Western

physicians prescribed cannabis cigarettes to treat asthma from about the 1860s to the 1940s.

121. Du Toit, *Cannabis in Africa*, 58; Ames, "A Clinical and Metabolic Study of Acute Intoxication with *Cannabis Sativa* and Its Role in the Model Psychoses," 976; Bryant, *A Zulu-English Dictionary*, 3, 275, 646.

122. B.-E. van Wyk, "A Review of Khoi-San and Cape Dutch Medical Ethnobotany," *Journal of Ethnopharmacology* 119 (2008): 331–41.

123. J. W. D. Moodie, *Ten Years in South Africa: Including a Particular Description of the Wild Sports of that Country*, vol. 2 (London: Richard Bentley, 1835), 169.

124. G., "Fowl Cholera, or 'Black Comb Sickness'" (letter to the editor), *Agricultural Journal of the Cape of Good Hope* 22, no. 3 (1903): 354.

125. Du Toit, *Cannabis in Africa*, 58–59; van Wyk, "A Review of Khoi-San and Cape Dutch Medical Ethnobotany," 335.

126. Such a generality might represent the observer's generalization rather than the users' view: G. M'Henry, "An Account of the Liberated African Establishment at St. Helena, Chapter II," *Simmond's Colonial Magazine* 5 (1845): 437.

127. Bourhill, "The Smoking of *Dagga* (Indian Hemp) among the Native Races of South Africa and the Resultant Evils," 38.

128. Bourhill, "The Smoking of *Dagga* (Indian Hemp) among the Native Races of South Africa and the Resultant Evils," 27.

129. Gordon, "From Rituals of Rapture to Dependence"; M. Winkelman and M. Dobkin de Rios, "Psychoactive Properties of !Kung Bushman Medicine Plants," *Journal of Psychoactive Drugs* 21, no. 1 (1989): 51–59.

130. Macdonald, "Bantu Customs and Legends," 351.

131. P. Jolly, "Late Baroa in Lesotho," *Digging Stick* 20, no. 3 (2003): 5–7, 10.

132. P. J. Mitchell and A. Hudson, "Psychoactive Plants and Southern African Hunter-Gatherers: A Review of the Evidence," *South African Humanities* 16 (2004): 39–57.

133. D. Macdonald, *Africana; or, The Heart of Heathen Africa, Volume I: Native Customs and Beliefs* (London: Simpkin Marshall, 1882), vii–viii, 62, 104.

134. Gouldsbury and Sheane, *The Great Plateau of Northern Rhodesia*, 75, 87.

135. Gouldsbury and Sheane, *The Great Plateau of Northern Rhodesia*, 188; J. M. G. Lotens, *L'état indépendant du Congo: Notice descriptive* (Alost, Belgium: SAR Monseigneur le Comte de Flandre, 1899), 48; E. W. Smith, *A Handbook of the Ila Language* (London: Oxford University Press, 1907), 321.

136. H. Waller, *The Last Journals of David Livingstone, in Central Africa* (New York: Harper Brothers, 1875), 279.

137. Livingstone, *Missionary Travels and Researches in South Africa*, 198, 330.

138. J. W. Jennings and C. Addison, *With the Abyssinians in Somaliland* (London: Hodder and Stoughton, 1905), 197.

139. T. L. Kane, *Amharic-English Dictionary: H–N*, vol. 1 (Wiesbaden, Germany: Otto Harassowicz, 1990), 1039.

140. A. Naty, "The Thief-Searching (Leba Shay) Institution in Aariland, Southwest Ethiopia, 1890s–1930s," *Ethnology* 33, no. 3 (1994): 261–72.

141. I am explicitly avoiding the term *shaman*, which initially denoted Central Asian spiritual/medicinal practitioners and has since been applied to people with diverse roles in cultures on all continents. Although *nganga* is less familiar in English-language publications, it is the accurate term; *shaman* is often used sloppily, to imply spirituality that is not properly evidenced. Finally, I note that Smith's unclear 1818 account of "leimba" associates it with "the fetishman," which suggests the subsequently documented association between cannabis and *nganga*: C. Smith, "The Journal of Professor Smith," in *Narrative of an Expedition to Explore the River Zaire, Usually Called the Congo, in South Africa, in 1816, under the Direction of Captain J. K. Tuckey, R.N.*, ed. Lords Commissioners of the Admiralty (London: Frank Cass, [1818] 1967): 304.

142. Daniell does not specify which *Abrus* part was used. Its seeds are highly toxic: Daniell, "On the D'amba, or Dakka, of Southern Africa," 365.

143. F. Hagenbucher-Sacripanti, *Santé et rédemption par les génies au Congo* (Paris: Publisud, 1989), 180.

144. J. M. Janzen, "De l'ancienneté de l'usage des psychotropes en Afrique centrale," *Psychotropes* 1 (1983): 105–7.

145. Chapaux, *Le Congo historique, diplomatique, physique, politique, économique, humanitaire et colonial*, 573–74.

146. I have found no information on a THC dosage sufficient to produce unconsciousness. However, in 2001 doses of 2–22 μg/L THC in whole blood were present in six people whose deaths were attributed to cardiovascular complications caused by cannabis overdoses: L. Bachs and H. Mørland, "Acute Cardiovascular Fatalities Following Cannabis Use," *Forensic Science International* 124, no. 2 (2001): 200–203, doi: http://dx.doi.org/10.1016/S0379-0738(01)00609-0.

147. H. Trilles, *Le totémisme chez les Fân*, Bibliotheque Anthropos, vol. 1, no. 4 (Munich: Aschendorffsche, 1912), 232. Abel inaccurately summarizes this source and provides a nearly untraceable citation (his "Tulles"): E. L. Abel, *Marihuana: The First Twelve Thousand Years* (New York: Springer, 1980), 143, 281.

148. More accurately, in at least four movements. In 1921, the Congolese prophet Kimbangu banned cannabis within his Christian movement: S. Asch, *L'eglise du prophète Kimbangu: De ses origines à son rôle actuel au Zaïre, 1921–1981* (Paris: Karthala, 1983). I exclude this example from the main text because many European-led churches banned cannabis, as did many Muslim leaders.

149. J. M. Janzen, *Lemba, 1650–1930: A Drum of Affliction in Africa and the New World* (New York: Garland, 1982), 3.

150. A "Lemba" label affixed to a pipe might have simply represented the belief of a collector that a pipe owner was a Lemba adherent. For descriptions of the pipes, see Janzen, "De l'ancienneté de l'usage des psychotropes en Afrique centrale."

151. Janzen, *Lemba*, 222.

152. P. M. Larken, "Impressions of the Zande [Continued from Volume 9, Part 1]," *Sudan Notes and Records* 10 (1927): 93. Abel inaccurately summarizes this source and provides a nearly untraceable citation: Abel, *Marihuana*, 146.

153. S. Raafat, "The Sirdaria," *Cairo Times*, 15 February 2001, accessed 26 April 2018, http://www.egy.com/zamalek/01-02-15.php.

6. SOCIETY OVERTURNED: THE BENA RIAMBA

1. *Bena Riamba* is the most common formulation. *Bena Liamba* or *Bena Diamba* would be accurate, too.

2. J. Conrad, *Heart of Darkness and The Secret Sharer* (New York: Signet, [1899] 1983); A. Hochschild, *King Leopold's Ghost: A Story of Greed, Terror, and Heroism in Colonial Africa* (Boston: Mariner Houghton Mifflin, 1998).

3. P. Kleinfeld, "Mass Graves, Missing Bodies, and Mysticism: Inside Congo's Spiraling Kasai Conflict," IRIN News, 12 September 2017, accessed 27 August 2018, https://www.irinnews.org/feature/2017/09/12/mass-graves-missing-bodies-and-mysticism-inside-congo-s-spiralling-kasai-conflict; United Nations High Commissioner for Human Rights, "La situation au Kasaï", report A/HRC/38/31 (advance edited version), 3 July 2018, accessed 27 August 2018, https://www.ohchr.org/Documents/HRBodies/HRCouncil/DRC/A_HRC_38_31_FR.docx.

4. For more on Pogge and Wissmann, see J. Fabian, *Out of Our Minds: Reason and Madness in the Exploration of Central Africa* (Berkeley: University of California Press, 2000).

5. Another overlooked source is Bateman, a British employee of the Congo Free State who published his account of the Kasai Valley in 1889. Bateman supported Wissmann's view on regional politics and generally supported Wissmann's view of the Bena Riamba but ultimately and contradictorily condemned "such organizations of evil as the Lubuku brotherhood": C. S. L. Bateman, *The First Ascent of the Kasaï: Being Some Records of Service under the Lone Star* (New York: Dodd, Mead, 1889), x. *Lubuku* is the proper term of the Bena Riamba, as I describe later. Dias de Carvalho's first book, closely preceding an eight-volume travelogue, was a rebuttal of Bateman's political views about Portuguese in Central Africa. The Bena Riamba supplied Dias de Carvalho's title; *O Lubuco* was the Portuguese form of *lubuku*: H. A. Dias de Carvalho, *O Lubuco: Algumas observações sobre o livro do Sr. Latrobe Bateman* (Lisbon: Imprensa Nacional, 1889).

6. A. De Clerq, "Indications pratiques pour faire des observations en matière religieuse chez les peuples incultes," *Anthropos* 8, no. 1 (1913): 15–16.

7. The Bena Riamba episode has garnered much attention in cannabis histories; I am thus compelled to offer more detail on the relevant chronology, characters, and sources. The sources that I identify by surname in this note are cited at the end of the note. First, Dias de Carvalho provides the clearest historical account of the movement's origins. He seemingly relied on oral histories from Africans and Luso-Africans who traded with Bena Riamba adherents. Libata's 1987 history is the best secondary source; he relied on published primary sources I cite and on published and unpublished Belgian sources I have not located. Libata gives a date range (1861–68) for the movement's beginning; Dias de Carvalho is more precise. Second, the names of characters in the Bena Riamba story are uncertain. I mostly follow Libata but use English orthography based on Chatelain and Summers. Wissmann, Pogge, Bateman, and Dias de Carvalho attribute different names to characters in the Bena Riamba story. Zetterström and Fabian mostly follow Wissmann; neither cites Dias de Carvalho. Vansina cites Dias de Carvalho but mostly uses Wissmann's nomenclature.

The character I call Chishimbi corresponds to Dias de Carvalho's "Kishimbi" and Libata's "Kashonga Tshishimbi." Wissmann and colleagues barely mention this character, and they call him "Kassongo." Wissmann focuses instead on the successor of "Kassongo," "Kalamba-Mukenge," an ally whom Wissmann promotes as the rightful political authority of the Lulua Valley. Third, regarding Kalamba Mukenge, whom I call Mukenge, Dias de Carvalho defines *Mukenge* as a superlative title, "chief of chiefs," etymologically related to *mukulenge*, which I define later. His nomenclature is supported by Chatelain and Summers's and Morrison's word lists, although Chatelain and Summers relied on Dias de Carvalho regarding the Bena Riamba. Pogge and Wissmann use *Mukenge* inconsistently as either a title or an individual's name. Kabongo defines *Mukenge* as "great chief" in Cokwe (Kabongo, p. 290). Libata states that "Mukenge Tunsele" was the first Lulua Valley potentate to take "the dynastic title Kalamba (name of the Cokwe Land Chief)" (Libata, pp. 100–1). He lists several others who later took the title. My selection of "Mukenge" as a name, not a title, follows Libata, although I do not assert that this is correct. "Mukenge" instead may be the title and "Kalamba" the name. Fourth, the character I call Mukwajanga was, in Dias de Carvalho's account, "Kilunga" but also known as "Mucanjanga." To Wissmann and colleagues, "Mukanjanga" was a "notorious [Cokwe] chief" (Wissmann et al., p. 94). Wissmann did not attribute to him the name "Kilunga" but wrote that "Kalunga" meant "great mind," and was the name by which the Cokwe called their homelands (Wissmann et al., p. 313). Dias de Carvalho writes that "Kalunga" was "the ocean," from which Europeans came (Dias de Carvalho, p. 12). Zetterström also gives this translation and does not reference Dias de Carvalho. See also Fabian, *Out of Our Minds,* 156–66, for comments on names and sources. Sources identified in this note: Dias de Carvalho, *O Lubuco*; K. Zetterström, "Bena Riamba: Brothers of Hemp," *Studia Ethnographica Upsaliensia* 26, no. 2 (1966): 151–66; H. Chatelain and W. R. Summers, "Bantu Notes and Vocabularies, No. 1: The Language of the Bashi-Lange and Ba-Luba," *Journal of the American Geographical Society of New York* 25, no. 4 (1893): 512–41; J. Vansina, *Kingdoms of the Savanna* (Madison: University of Wisconsin Press, 1966); W. M. Morrison, *Grammar and Dictionary of the Buluba-Lulua Language as Spoken in the Upper Kasai and Congo Basin* (New York: American Tract Society, 1906); E. Kabongo, "La conclusion du mariage chez les Lulua face au message Chrétien," *Africa* 28, no. 2 (1973): 289–300; M.-B. Libata, "Regroupement des Baluba et ses consequences géo-politiques dans la péripherie de Luluabourg (1891–1960)," *Annales Aequatoria* 8 (1987): 99–130; H. von Wissmann, L. Wolf, C. von François, and H. Mueller, *Im Innern Afrikas: Die Erforschung des Kassai während der Jahre 1883, 1884, und 1885,* 3d ed. (Leipzig: Brockhaus, 1891).

8. Vansina, *Kingdoms of the Savanna*, 219–21.

9. Dias de Carvalho, *O Lubuco,* 10. Cokwe men carried calabash-based water pipes into the 1930s: W. D. Hambly, *The Ovimbundu of Angola* (Chicago: Field Museum of Natural History, 1934), 165.

10. Libata, "Regroupement des Baluba et ses consequences géo-politiques dans la péripherie de Luluabourg," 100.

11. Libata recognizes that Chishimbi was remembered as "Mwamba Mputu" in some sources: Libata, "Regroupement des Baluba et ses consequences géo-politiques dans la péripherie de Luluabourg," 100. This name perhaps means "Portuguese Mwamba": Fabian, *Out of Our Minds,* 295. Mwamba was a locally common given name. *Mputo,* meaning "Portu-

guese," was used in many regional languages: J. C. Miller, *Way of Death: Merchant Capitalism and the Angolan Slave Trade, 1730–1839* (Madison: University of Wisconsin Press, 1989), 4–6. Wissmann writes "Moamba Mputt": Wissmann et al., *Im Innern Afrikas*, 312. Dias de Carvalho writes "Muene Puto Kasongo": Dias de Carvalho, *O Lubuco*, 20. Wissmann presents "Katende" as a contemporary rival of Mukenge, and not the same person as "Moamba Mputt," whereas Vansina discusses "Mwamba Mputo or Katende" as a contemporary rival to Mukenge, and head of his own *lubuku*: Vansina, *Kingdoms of the Savanna*, 220–21.

12. Dias de Carvalho, *O Lubuco*, 12.

13. Libata, "Regroupement des Baluba et ses consequences géo-politiques dans la péripherie de Luluabourg," 101.

14. Dias de Carvalho, *O Lubuco*, 15; Zetterström, "Bena Riamba," 151.

15. Dias de Carvalho, *O Lubuco*, 15.

16. P. Pogge, *Im Reiche des Muata Jamwo* (Berlin: Dietrich Reimer, 1880), 49–51. The trader was Saturnino de Sousa Machado, who is discussed in several histories of Angola.

17. Dias de Carvalho, *O Lubuco*, 16.

18. Dias de Carvalho, *O Lubuco*, 16.

19. See Vansina, *Kingdoms of the Savanna*, 220.

20. Dias de Carvalho, *O Lubuco*, 17; Libata, "Regroupement des Baluba et ses consequences géo-politiques dans la péripherie de Luluabourg," 101.

21. Irresoluble is whether the movement was of the *bena* (people; plural of *muena*) or *bana* (children; plural of *muana*): see Morrison, *Grammar and Dictionary of the Buluba-Lulua Language as Spoken in the Upper Kasai and Congo Basin*, 162, 238. European observers did not have the aural comprehension or language fluency to distinguish the terms and did not report translations of whatever term they heard. Pogge translates *bena* as "sons," but he relied on translators: Pogge, *Im Reiche des Muata Jamwo*, 257. Johnston, a secondary source, is adamant that *bena* means "brothers," not "sons": H. Johnston, *George Grenfell and the Congo: A History and Description of the Congo Independent State and Adjoining Districts of Congoland*, vol. 2 (London: Hutchinson, 1908), 608, 684. Kabongo and Libata both suggest *bena* is a participle denoting group membership: Kabongo, "La conclusion du mariage chez les Lulua face au message Chrétien," 290; Libata, "Regroupement des Baluba et ses consequences géo-politiques dans la péripherie de Luluabourg," 101. Fabian translates *bena* as "children of" but provides no linguistic source to support this; he disagrees with the gendered "sons of": Fabian, *Out of Our Minds*, 295. Chatelain and Summers do not define *bena* but write "Bena Riamba" while defining "mu-ana" as "child": Chatelain and Summers, "Bantu Notes and Vocabularies," 537. I take *bena* to mean "people of," as it was used historically in phrases such as *bena kuabo* (people of their village) and *bena Kasai* (people of the Kasai valley): Morrison, *Grammar and Dictionary of the Buluba-Lulua Language as Spoken in the Upper Kasai and Congo Basin*, 46, 229, 238, 373. Vansina and Libata both use "Bena" in this sense to name many political/ethnic groups in the region; Vansina uses *lubuku* rather than any formulation of "Bena Riamba" to name the movement. The "people of" translation offers a neutral connotation; "children of" imparts a sensational tone.

22. P. Pogge, "Im Bericht über die Reise von Mukenge nach Nyangwe und zurück; und über die Begründung der Station in Mukenge," *Mittheilungen der Afrikanischen Gesellschaft in Deutschland* 4, no. 1 (1883–84): 66.

23. I have been unable to locate the creek on modern maps: J.-L. Vellut, ed., *Émeri Cambier: Correspondance du Congo (1888–1899), un apprentissage missionnaire* (Brussels: Brepols, 2001), 403. Alternatively, Vervaecke suggests the name comes from a Cokwe town, "Tshilunga," which I have also been unable to locate: J. Vervaecke, "Les Bena-Lulua," *Revue congolaise* 1, no. 1 (1910): 69–86, 71.

24. H. von Wissmann, *Meine zweite Durchquerung Äquatorial-Afrikas vom Longo zum Zambesi* (Frankfurt: Trowitzsch and Son, 1890), 242–46.

25. The term "Luba Empire" was applied by outsiders, not by people who might have considered themselves subjects of the Balopwe kings who ruled the polity. Those who followed the Balopwe represented a political grouping of some Luba-speaking peoples, led by hereditary kings whose ancestor overthrew an earlier, violent leader: see Vansina, *Kingdoms of the Savanna*, 221; Libata, "Regroupement des Baluba et ses consequences géo-politiques dans la périphérie de Luluabourg"; T. Q. Reefe, *The Rainbow and the Kings: A History of the Luba Empire to 1891* (Berkeley: University of California Press, 1981).

26. *Mukelenge* is a singular noun; *bakelenge* is the plural: Morrison, *Grammar and Dictionary of the Buluba-Lulua Language as Spoken in the Upper Kasai and Congo Basin*, 375.

27. Wissmann called this group "Tschipulumba" and described them either as "people who refused to accept the hemp cult and did not want to abandon their old wild martial customs" or as "thieves": Wissmann, *Meine zweite Durchquerung Äquatorial-Afrikas vom Longo zum Zambesi*, 56, 107. The people in question were hostile toward Wissmann (and Pogge) because the Germans were allied with the Bena Riamba. Yet Wissmann recognized that fault for the poor relations "lay not only on the side of the Tschipulumba, but often our Baschilange were led to violence by their feelings of superiority and their hatred against them [the Tschipulumba]": Wissmann, *Meine zweite Durchquerung Äquatorial-Afrikas vom Longo zum Zambesi*, 110. See also Morrison, *Grammar and Dictionary of the Buluba-Lulua Language as Spoken in the Upper Kasai and Congo Basin*, 366; H. A. Dias de Carvalho, *Expedição portugueza ao Muatiânvua: Descripção da viagem á Mussumba do Muatiânvua, Volume 3: Do Chicapa ao Luembe.* (Lisbon: Typographia do Jornal, 1892), 647; H. von Wissmann, *Unter deutscher Flagge quer durch Afrika von West nach Ost* (Berlin: Walther and Apolant, 1889), 93–94.

28. Dias de Carvalho writes "Quinguengé"; the historian Libata writes "Tschinkenke."

29. Wissmann, *Unter deutscher Flagge quer durch Afrika von West nach Ost*, 97, 321; Wissmann, *Meine zweite Durchquerung Äquatorial-Afrikas vom Longo zum Zambesi*, 249.

30. Wissmann, *Meine zweite Durchquerung Äquatorial-Afrikas vom Longo zum Zambesi*, 68.

31. Vansina interprets the situation as a rivalry rather than succession fight, although he identifies the characters involved differently from other sources: Vansina, *Kingdoms of the Savanna*, 222.

32. Dias de Carvalho, *O Lubuco*, 18.

33. Bateman, *The First Ascent of the Kasaï*, 114.

34. Zetterström, "Bena Riamba," 159; Fabian, *Out of Our Minds*, 175.

35. Thus, she was Chishimbi's sister, too, if Chishimbi and Mukenge were siblings. This is the relationship Wissmann and colleagues presented, although Wissmann called Chishimbi "Kassongo." Alternatively, Dias de Carvalho suggests Sangula Meta was Chingenge's wife. See Dias de Carvalho, *O Lubuco*, 18; Wissmann et al., *Im Innern Afrikas*, 173.

36. Wissmann, *Unter deutscher Flagge quer durch Afrika von West nach Ost*, 321.

37. Bateman, *The First Ascent of the Kasaï*, 112.

38. For first-degree murder, people were burned at the stake: Wissmann, *Unter deutscher Flagge quer durch Afrika von West nach Ost*, 154; P. Pogge, "Mittheilungen aus Dr. Paul Pogge's Tagebüchern, bearbeitet von Dr. A. von Danckelman," *Mittheilungen der Afrikanischen Gesellschaft in Deutschland* 4, no. 4 (1883–84): 228–64, 258.

39. Vansina, *Kingdoms of the Savanna*, 221–23.

40. H. Chatelain, "Lettre de Loulouabourg, du Dr. Summers, transmise de Malangé par M. H. Châtelain," *L'Afrique Explorée et Civilisée* 8, no. 8 (1893): 245–47.

41. Vansina, *Kingdoms of the Savanna*, 221.

42. This population estimate is far too high, certainly for the number of people who were truly Bena Riamba adherents. The "several million" number seemingly originated as an exaggeration of Wissmann's estimate of 1.4 million people in the "land of the Bashilange": Wissmann, *Meine zweite Durchquerung Äquatorial-Afrikas vom Longo zum Zambesi*, 250. In contrast, consider these various estimates. Summers (in his letter to Chatelain published in 1893, and from which the quote in the text is taken) describes the relevant area as densely settled, with Mukenge's town having eight thousand inhabitants: Chatelain, "Lettre de Loulouabourg," 246. Elsewhere, Chatelain (in a work published years after Summers's death, although Chatelain listed him as coauthor) states that Mukenge's town had five thousand people: Chatelain and Summers, "Bantu Notes and Vocabularies," 525. Pogge did not estimate population size but described the areas controlled by Mukenge and Chingenge as "small districts" of twenty to thirty square miles: Pogge, "Im Bericht über die Reise von Mukenge nach Nyangwe und zurück," 72. Libata reports census data from 1938, showing 38,000 people in the area around Luluabourg (now Kananga): Libata, "Regroupement des Baluba et ses consequences géo-politiques dans la périphérie de Luluabourg," 128–29. It seems far-fetched that even 38,000 were ever directly under the control of Mukenge and/or Chingenge, though there have been no historical demographies of the area.

43. Morrison, *Grammar and Dictionary of the Buluba-Lulua Language as Spoken in the Upper Kasai and Congo Basin*, 226, 242.

44. Vellut, *Émeri Cambier*, 335.

45. Vellut, *Émeri Cambier*, 335. See also Zetterström, "Bena Riamba."

46. Bateman, *The First Ascent of the Kasaï*, 115–16.

47. Fabian characterizes Wissmann's action as betrayal of his erstwhile allies: Fabian, *Out of Our Minds*, 179.

48. B. Heintze, "Long-Distance Caravans and Communication beyond the Kwango (circa 1850–1890)," in *Angola on the Move: Transport Routes, Communications and History*, ed. B. Heintze and A. von Oppen (Frankfurt: Otto Lembeck, 2008), 148.

49. On the chili oil incident, see Vellut, *Émeri Cambier*, 335. Libata dates Mukenge's refusal to 1891: Libata, "Regroupement des Baluba et ses consequences géo-politiques dans la péripherie de Luluabourg."

50. Chatelain and Summers, "Bantu Notes and Vocabularies," 525.

51. Libata, "Regroupement des Baluba et ses consequences géo-politiques dans la péripherie de Luluabourg"; Fabian, *Out of Our Minds*, 178–79; Vansina, *Kingdoms of the Savanna*, 222; T. Turner, "'Batetela,' 'Baluba,' 'Basonge': Ethnogenesis in Zaire," *Cahiers d'Études Africaines* 33, no. 132 (1993): 587–612.

52. G. Nzongola-Ntalaja, *The Congo, from Leopold to Kabila: A People's History* (London: Zed, 2002), 103.

53. Bateman, *The First Ascent of the Kasaï*, 114–15.

54. Wissmann et al., *Im Innern Afrikas*, 152–53.

55. Zetterström, "Bena Riamba," 160–61.

56. Wissmann, *Unter deutscher Flagge quer durch Afrika von West nach Ost*, 321.

57. P. Pogge, "Bericht über die Station Mukenge bis October 1883," *Mittheilungen der Afrikanischen Gesellschaft in Deutschland* 4, no. 3 (1883–84): 182.

58. Fabian, *Out of Our Minds*, 176.

59. Pogge, "Mittheilungen aus Dr. Paul Pogge's Tagebüchern," 247.

60. Many people clearly did not kill their animals. Pogge, Wissmann, and other travelers frequently traded for goats and chickens. Further, the Bena Riamba–imposed punishment for theft included repayment with either a goat or a quantity of salt: see Zetterström, "Bena Riamba," 159–60; Pogge, "Mittheilungen aus Dr. Paul Pogge's Tagebüchern," 257; Wissmann, *Unter deutscher Flagge quer durch Afrika von West nach Ost*, 321–22.

61. Wissmann et al., *Im Innern Afrikas*, 152–53; Chatelain, "Lettre de Loulouabourg."

62. Pogge, "Im Bericht über die Reise von Mukenge nach Nyangwe und zurück," 69–70.

63. Zetterström, "Bena Riamba," 164.

64. Heintze, "Long-Distance Caravans and Communication beyond the Kwango," 148.

65. Fabian, *Out of Our Minds*, 295.

66. Bateman, *The First Ascent of the Kasaï*, 115–16.

67. Zetterström, "Bena Riamba," 153.

68. Zetterström, "Bena Riamba," 162–63.

69. Wissmann, *Meine zweite Durchquerung Äquatorial-Afrikas vom Longo zum Zambesi*, 249; Bateman, *The First Ascent of the Kasaï*, 115.

70. Pogge, "Im Bericht über die Reise von Mukenge nach Nyangwe und zurück," 72.

71. Pogge, "Im Bericht über die Reise von Mukenge nach Nyangwe und zurück," 72.

72. Wissmann, *Unter deutscher Flagge quer durch Afrika von West nach Ost*, 136–37.

73. Chatelain and Summers, "Bantu Notes and Vocabularies," 527–28.

74. De Clerq, "Indications pratiques pour faire des observations en matière religieuse chez les peuples incultes," 16; Vellut, *Émeri Cambier*, 382–90; A. Verbeken, *La révolte des Batetela en 1895: Textes inédits* (Gembloux, Belgium: J. Duculot, 1957), 23, 44. Death

from cannabis smoking would entail a massive dose or cardiovascular susceptibility in the smoker: L. Bachs and H. Mørland, "Acute Cardiovascular Fatalities Following Cannabis Use," *Forensic Science International* 124, no. 2 (2001): 200–203.

75. Révérend Père Colle, *Les Baluba,* vol. 1 (Brussels: Albert de Wit, 1913), 119.

76. "Massacre in Congo State," *New York Times,* 5 January 1900, 1.

77. D. C. Rankin, "Atrocities in the Kongo Free State," *The Independent* 52, no. 2670 (1 February 1900): 304–6.

78. Ł. Kamieński, *Shooting Up: A Short History of Drugs and War* (New York: Oxford University Press, 2016). This book provides a good global overview, although it is poorly founded regarding African cases.

79. J. H. de Faria Leal, "Memorias d'Africa, Capitulo 4: Como se foi ocupando a antiga circunscrição de S. Salvador do Congo [Continuação]," *Boletim da Sociedade de Geographia de Lisboa* 33, no. 1 (1915): 18.

80. I have been unable to trace Du Toit's statements about Zulu and Swazi warriors in his cited sources: B. M. du Toit, *Cannabis in Africa: A Survey of Its Distribution in Africa, and a Study of Cannabis Use and Users in Multi-ethnic South Africa* (Rotterdam: A. A. Balkema, 1980), 23. Other untraceable anecdotes can be found in S. S. Dornan, "Some Notes on Rhodesian Native Poisons," *South African Journal of Science* 13 (1916): 357; A. Shorter, *Chiefship in Western Tanzania* (Oxford: Oxford University Press, 1972), 277; W. Blohm, *Die Nyamwezi: Land und Wirtschaft* (Hamburg: Friederichsen, De Gruyter, 1931), 136.

81. S. S. Dornan, "Witchcraft," *South African Quarterly* (December–June 1924–25): 11. This paper embellishes Dornan, "Some Notes on Rhodesian Native Poisons."

82. C. W. Hobley, *Eastern Uganda: An Ethnological Survey* (London: Anthropological Institute of Great Britain and Ireland, 1902), 30.

83. D. A. Livingstone, *Missionary Travels and Researches in South Africa* (London: John Murray, 1857), 504. Livingstone's word choice, "frenzy," continues to echo, without citation, into this century: J. F. Sobiecki, "A Preliminary Inventory of Plants Used for Psychoactive Purposes in Southern African Healing Traditions," *Transactions of the Royal Society of South Africa* 57, nos. 1–2 (2002): 1–24.

84. H. M. Stanley, *Through the Dark Continent,* vol. 1 (London: Sampson Low, Marston, Searle, and Rivington, 1878), 506; J. Becker, *La vie en Afrique ou Trois ans dans l'Afrique centrale,* vol. 2 (Paris: J. Lebègue, 1887), 508.

85. C. S. Duvall, "Drug Laws, Bioprospecting, and the Agricultural Heritage of *Cannabis* in Africa," *Space and Polity* 20, no. 1 (2016): 10–25.

86. A. Chevalier, "Histoire de deux plantes cultivées d'importance primordiale: Le Lin et le Chanvre," *Revue de Botanique Appliquée et d'Agriculture Coloniale* 24, nos. 269–71 (1944): 68.

87. B. M. du Toit, "Linguistic Subterfuge: Its Use by Drug Users in South Africa," *Anthropological Linguistics* 22, no. 1 (1980): 22–28.

7. CANNABIS CROSSES THE ATLANTIC

1. J. C. Adiala, *O problema da maconha no Brasil: Ensaio sobre racismo e drogas* (Rio de Janeiro: Instituto Universitario de Pesquisas do Rio de Janeiro, 1986).

2. E. E. Telles, *Race in Another America: The Significance of Skin Color in Brazil* (Princeton, NJ: Princeton University Press, 2004), 166–69.

3. Compare with plants analyzed in J. A. Carney, *Black Rice: The African Origins of Rice Cultivation in the Americas* (Cambridge, MA: Harvard University Press, 2001); J. A. Carney and R. N. Rosomoff, *In the Shadow of Slavery: Africa's Botanical Legacy in the Atlantic World* (Berkeley: University of California Press, 2009); J. J. Parsons, "Spread of African Pasture Grasses to the American Tropics," *Journal of Range Management* 25, no. 1 (1972): 12–17; R. A. Voeks, *Sacred Leaves of Candomblé: African Magic, Medicine, and Religion in Brazil* (Austin: University of Texas Press, 1997), 307–26; R. A. Voeks and J. Rashford, eds., *African Ethnobotany in the Americas* (New York: Springer, 2013).

4. Most notably, D. T. Courtwright, *Forces of Habit: Drugs and the Making of the Modern World* (Cambridge, MA: Harvard University Press, 2001), 41.

5. F. A. Flückiger, "Pharmaceutische Reiseeindrucke [Part I]," *Pharmaceutische Central-halle für Deutschland* 8, no. 49 (1867): 436–42.

6. C. S. Duvall, *Cannabis* (London: Reaktion, 2015), 66–67.

7. E. L. Abel, "Marijuana on Trial: The Panama Canal Zone Report," *International Journal of the Addictions* 17, no. 4 (1982): 667–78.

8. W. P. Chamberlain and D. P. Curry, *Report of the Health Department of the Panama Canal for the Calendar Year 1925* (Canal Zone: Panama Canal Press, 1926), 32.

9. J. F. Siler, W. L. Sheep, G. W. Cook, W. A. Smith, L. B. Bates, and G. F. Clark, "Mariajuana Smoking in Panama," *Military Surgeon* 73 (1933): 273.

10. D. Domingues da Silva, D. Eltis, P. Misevich, and O. Ojo, "The Diaspora of Africans Liberated from Slave Ships in the Nineteenth Century," *Journal of African History* 55, no. 3 (2014): 347–69.

11. M. Ferreira Ribeiro, *Relatorio ácerca do Serviço de Saude Publica na Provincia de S. Thomé e Principe no Anno de 1869* (Lisbon: Imprensa Nacional, 1871), 104.

12. Domingues da Silva et al., "The Diaspora of Africans Liberated from Slave Ships in the Nineteenth Century."

13. R. J. Turner and F. Marino, "Social Support and Social Structure: A Descriptive Epidemiology," *Journal of Health and Social Behavior* 35, no. 3 (1994): 193–212.

14. The role of Levantine immigrants is documented just once, in California: "Local Hashish-Eaters," *San Francisco Call*, 24 June 1895, 7.

15. The Trans-Atlantic Slave Trade Database is at http://www.slavevoyages.org.

16. C. A. Palmer, *Human Cargoes: The British Slave Trade to Spanish America, 1700–1739*, Blacks in the New World (Urbana: University of Illinois Press, 1981).

17. A. Borucki, D. Eltis, and D. Wheat, "Atlantic History and the Slave Trade to Spanish America," *American Historical Review* 120, no. 2 (2015): 433–61.

18. Domingues da Silva et al., "The Diaspora of Africans Liberated from Slave Ships in the Nineteenth Century."

19. From 1819 to 1834, laborers were transported only across the Indian Ocean, predominantly to Mauritius. Transports to the Caribbean began in 1834, although very few arrived before 1840: D. Northrup, *Indentured Labor in the Age of Imperialism, 1834–1922* (Cambridge: Cambridge University Press, 1995); K. Saunders, ed., *Indentured Labour in the British Empire, 1834–1920* (London: Croom Helm, 1984).

20. Northrup, *Indentured Labor in the Age of Imperialism*. British Guiana included the counties Demerara and Berbice, which were often listed separately in trade and population statistics. I have merged all counties in compiling statistics.

21. A. Hamid, *The Ganja Complex: Rastafari and Marijuana* (Lanham, MD: Lexington, 2002); A. Mansingh and L. Mansingh, "Hindu Influences on Rastafarianism," · *Caribbean Quarterly* (1985): 96–115.

22. K. Bilby, "The Holy Herb: Notes on the Background of Cannabis in Jamaica," *Caribbean Quarterly* (1985): 82–95.

23. H. W. Hutchinson, "Patterns of Marihuana Use in Brazil," in *Cannabis and Culture*, ed. V. Rubin (The Hague: Mouton, 1975), 173–83; M. Y. Monteiro, "Folclore da maconha," *Revista Brasileria de Folclore* 6, no. 16 (1966): 285–300; L. Mott, "A maconha na história do Brasil," in *Diamba sarabamba*, ed. A. Henman and O. Pessoa Jr. (São Paulo: Ground, 1986), 117–35; "O Dicionário da Maconha," *O Estado de São Paulo*, 1958, n.p., Centro Nacional de Folclore e Cultura Popular, Rio de Janeiro, accessed 30 April 2018, http://docvirt.com/docreader.net/DocReader.aspx?bib=Tematico&PagFis=30147&Pesq=; "Aspectos folk-lóricos da Maconha," *Diário de Sergipe*, 26 August 1948, 4, Centro Nacional de Folclore e Cultura Popular, Rio de Janeiro, accessed 30 April 2018, http://docvirt.com/docreader.net/DocReader.aspx?bib=tematico&pagfis=30149.

24. R. F. Burton, *Explorations of the Highlands of Brazil*, vol. 1 (London: Tinsley Brothers, 1869), 276.

25. Monteiro, "Folclore da maconha," 291. Mott proposes that this is a Tupi word: Mott, "A maconha na história do Brasil."

26. Monteiro, "Folclore da maconha."

27. This term has been spelled in various ways (e.g., *suruma*). I write *soruma* solely for consistency. See chapter 4 for information on African instances of this term. The earliest Brazilian source is J. L. Taylor, *A Portuguese-English Dictionary* (Stanford, CA: Stanford University Press, 1958).

28. For information on this trade, see A. F. Isaacman, E. Alpers, and B. Zimba, *Slave Routes and Oral Tradition in Southeastern Africa* (Maputo, Mozambique: Filsom Entertainment, 2005); and the Trans-Atlantic Slave Trade Database, http://www.slavevoyages.org (search embarkations in southeastern Africa, and disembarkations from southeastern Africa).

29. A. de Serpa Pinto, *How I Crossed Africa*, vol. 2 (London: Sampson Low, Marston, Searle, and Rivington, 1881), 33; C. de Figueiredo, *Novo diccionário da língua portuguesa comprehendendo: Além do vocabulário*, vol. 2 (Lisbon: Tavares Cardoso and Irmão, 1899), 771.

30. Câmara Municipal do Rio de Janeiro, "Posturas da Camara Municipal do Rio de Janeiro a que se refere o Aviso acima," in *Collecção das Decisões do Governo do Imperio do Brazil de 1832* (Rio de Janeiro: Typographia Nacional, 1830), 53–74.

31. B. M. du Toit, "Linguistic Subterfuge: Its Use by Drug Users in South Africa," *Anthropological Linguistics* 22, no. 1 (1980): 22–28; R. Tomei, *Forbidden Fruits: The Secret Names of Plants in Caribbean Culture* (Rome: Morlacchi, 2008).

32. C. de Figueiredo, *Novo diccionário da língua portuguesa comprehendendo: Além do vocabulário*, vol. 1 (Lisbon: Tavares Cardoso and Irmão, 1899), 331.

33. J. Luccock, "A Grammar and Vocabulary of the Tupi Language, Rio de Janeiro, 1818 [Continued]," *Revista do Instituto Histórico e Geográfico Brasileiro* 44, no. 1 (1881): 15. See also J. B. von Spix and C. F. P. von Martius, *Travels in Brazil, in the Years 1817–1820*, vol. 2 (London: Longman, Hurst, Rees, Orme, Brown, and Green, 1824), 100.

34. P. A. Correa Garção, *Obras poeticas de Pedro Antonio Correa Garção* (Lisbon: Impressão Regia, [1812] 1825), 93. Regarding slave commerce between southern Angola and Rio de Janeiro, see M. Pinho Candido, *An African Slaving Port and the Atlantic World: Benguela and Its Hinterland* (Cambridge: Cambridge University Press, 2015).

35. Burton, *Explorations of the Highlands of Brazil*, 1:275.

36. This folk song was originally published as having been recorded in Rio Grande do Sul. Variations were subsequently published from multiple locations, including Pernambuco, Alagoas, and Bahia: S. Roméro, *Cantos populares do Brazil* (Rio de Janeiro: Livraria Classica de Alves, 1897), 344.

37. A. Deodato, *Cannaviaes: Contos e novellas* (Rio de Janeiro: Annuario do Brasil, 1922), 59–60.

38. Dictionaries into the 1900s maintained this meaning. In the 1773 dictionary, see the last page headed "MAR-MAR-MAR": A. Vieyra Transtagano, *A Dictionary of the Portuguese and English Languages, in Two Parts, Portuguese and English: and English and Portuguese* (London: J. Nourse, 1773).

39. Monteiro, "Folclore da maconha"; J. R. da Costa Doria, "Os fumadores de maconha: Effeitos males do vicio," in *Proceedings of the Second Pan American Scientific Congress*, ed. G. L. Swiggett (Washington, DC: US Government Printing Office, 1917), 151–61; R. Cordeiro de Farias, "Use of Maconha (*Cannabis sativa* L.) in Brazil," *Bulletin on Narcotics* 7, no. 2 (1955): 5–19. Cordeiro de Farias proposes that *maricas* is "an adapted form of the Persian 'narghile'": Cordeiro de Farias, "Use of Maconha," 5. His idea perpetuates the notion that African water pipes are knockoffs of Levantine technology.

40. Deodato, *Cannaviaes*, 59–60; Glaziou, as cited in A. Chevalier, "Histoire de deux plantes cultivées d'importance primordiale: Le Lin et le Chanvre," *Revue de Botanique Appliquée et d'Agriculture Coloniale* 24, nos. 269–71 (1944): 68.

41. G. Pfaus, "Drogues et ethnologie au Brésil: Débats publics et productions intellectuelles," mémoire de DEA, Department of Sociology and Anthropology, Université Lumière Lyon II, n.d. [2002?], 15.

42. A. R. de Pinho, "Social and Medical Aspects of the Use of *Cannabis* in Brazil," in Rubin, *Cannabis and Culture*, 294.

43. The sociologist Edward Telles argues that language and stories about drug use have been coproduced with racial ideas: Telles, *Race in Another America*, 166–69.

44. It is not clear whether this indicates imports; *pango d'Angola* could mean "*pango* (brought) from Angola" (thus indicating an import) or "*pango* known from Angola" (suggesting local production). See "Vendas: 5 Quem quizar comprar . . . ," *Jornal do Commercio*, 11 November 1828, 3.

45. Câmara Municipal do Rio de Janeiro, "Posturas da Camara Municipal do Rio de Janeiro a que se refere o Aviso acima."

46. "Noticias Particulares: 25 Lourenço Lopes Pecegueiro . . . ," *Jornal do Commercio*, 17 July 1832, 3.

47. V. de Beaurepaire-Rohan, *Diccionario de vocabulos brazileiros* (Rio de Janeiro: Imprense Nacional, 1889), 116.

48. Tribunal do Santo Ofício do Inquisição de Lisboa, "[Confissão de] Antonio do Carmo: aprez. de sodom. Valentim Pra. sodom," in *Caderno 20° do Nefando, fl. 89*, 1749, Arquivo Nacional da Torre do Tombo, Lisbon.

49. C. A. Taunay, *Manual do agricultor brazileiro*, 2d ed. (Rio de Janeiro: J. Villeneuve, 1839), 250.

50. D. Granada, *Vocabulario rioplatense razonada* (Montevideo: Imprenta Rural, 1890), 306. Granada wrote that *pango* is smoked in a *pito* or *cachimbo*. This is the most recent record that *pito* was in use in Brazil; the term has appeared in subsequent lists of Brazilian cannabis terms because it appeared in Rio's 1830 law. Notably, in current Colombian Spanish, the phrase "to take *pito*" means "to be extremely high," on any drug. The ultimately Tupi word *pito* has no known cognates in Colombian Indigenous languages. The Colombian phrase suggests an undocumented arrival of drug-loaded pipes from Brazil. See J. Aguirre, J. Molina, and B. Romero, "Análisis léxico-semántico del argot de las reclusas de la cárcel 'El Buen Pastor' de Bogotá," *Lenguaje* 41, no. 1 (2013): 35–57.

51. J. Pernambuco, "A maconha em Pernambuco," in *Novos estudos Afro-brasileiros: Trabalhos apresentados ao 1.° Congresso Afro-brasileiro do Recífe*, ed. A. Ramos, Bibliotheca de Divulgação Scientífica, vol. 9 (Rio de Janeiro: Civilização Brasileira, 1937), 187.

52. A. Batista Pereira and J. Putzke, *Dicionário brasileiro de botânica* (Curitiba, Brazil: CRV, 2010), 74, 132, 233.

53. Beaurepaire-Rohan, *Diccionario de vocabulos brazileiros*, 104; A. J. de Macedo Soares, "Estudos lexicographicos do dialecto Brazileiro IV: Sobre algumas palavras africanas introduzidas no Portuguez que se fala no Brazil," *Revista Brazileira* 1, no. 4 (1880): 267.

54. M. E. Viaro, M. J. Ferreira, and Z. O. Guimarães Filho, "Derivação ou terminação: Limites para a semântica, lexicologia e morfologia históricas," in *Morfologia histórica*, ed. M. E. Viaro (São Paulo: Cortez, 2013), 75. A nineteenth-century Portuguese scholar believed that *bangue* was an Arabic loanword that survived from the Islamic Iberian period, but he showed no knowledge of its use in India, Africa, or Brazil: J. de Sousa, *Vestigios da lingoa arabica em Portugal* (Lisbon: Academia Real das Sciencias, 1830), 93.

55. W. Derham, ed., *Philosophical Experiments and Observations of the Late Eminent Dr. Robert Hooke* (London: W. Derham, 1726), 210.

56. H. Monteagudo, ed., *Martín Sarmiento: Sobre a lingua galega, Antoloxía* (Madrid: Editorial Galaxia, 2002), 377.

57. F. de Paula Mas y Artigas and L. Gonzaga Bachs y Mas, *Diccionario español-latino* (Barcelona: Herederos de la viuda Pla, 1854), 110; P. Labernia, *Diccionario de la lengua castellana*, vol. 1 (Barcelona: Esteven Pujal, 1861), 262.

58. W. H. Sanders and W. E. Fay, *Vocabulary of the Umbundu Language* (Boston: Beacon, 1885); Padres Missionarios, *Diccionario Portuguez-Olunyaneka* (Huilla, Angola: Typographia da Missão, 1896).

59. Pinho Candido, *An African Slaving Port and the Atlantic World*; J. C. Miller, *Way of Death: Merchant Capitalism and the Angolan Slave Trade, 1730–1839* (Madison: University of Wisconsin Press, 1988); D. B. Domingues da Silva, *The Atlantic Slave Trade from West Central Africa, 1780–1867* (Cambridge: Cambridge University Press, 2017).

60. "Deïamba, nouveau narcotique," *Journal de Pharmacie et de Chimie* 14 (1848): 201.

61. G. M'Henry, "An Account of the Liberated African Establishment at St. Helena, Chapter II," *Simmond's Colonial Magazine* 5 (1845): 437.

62. K. Demuth, "Bantu Noun Class Systems: Loan Word and Acquisition Evidence of Semantic Productivity," in *Classification Systems*, ed. G. Senft (Cambridge: Cambridge University Press, 2000), 270–92.

63. The *ri-* is dropped in *maconha*, as in some other 5/6 nouns in western Central African Bantu languages. *Maconha* has been spelled many ways; I use the dominant Brazilian spelling. The *nh* combination in Portuguese approximates *ñ* in Spanish and *ny* or *ni* in English (as in "canyon" or "onion").

64. Beaurepaire-Rohan, *Diccionario de vocabulos brazileiros*, 104. One published etymology acknowledges a Bantu language other than Kimbundu. The etymology, though, merely shows the influence, and distortion, of the Bena Riamba tale: "[*riamba* is] the African Baluba word for hemp, and among the Bantu there is a secret society with a riamba-smoking cult." Taylor, *A Portuguese-English Dictionary*, 226.

65. C. de Almeida, "Generos coloniaes" (advertisement), in *Novo almanach de lembranças Luso Brazileiro para o anno de 1884*, ed. A. X. Rodrigues Cordeiro (Lisbon: Lallement Frères, 1883), 189.

66. Pernambuco, "A maconha em Pernambuco," 187.

67. L. Goncalves, *O Amazonas: Esboço historico, chorographico e estatistico até o anno de 1903* (New York: Hugo J. Hanf, 1904), 30; V. Chermont de Miranda, *Glossario paraense; ou, Collecão de vocabulos peculiares à Amazonia e especialmente á Ilha de Marajó* (Pará, Brazil: Livraria Maranhense, 1906), 35; R. de Luna Antonio, N. Scalco, T. Andrade Medeiros, J. Soares Neto, and E. Rodrigues, "Smoke of Ethnobotanical Plants Used in Healing Ceremonies in Brazilian Culture," in *Ethnomedicinal Plants* (Boca Raton, FL: CRC, 2011), 166–91.

68. J. F. Johnston, *The Chemistry of Common Life*, 4th ed., vol. 2 (New York: D. Appleton, 1855), 95.

69. In Portugal, *liamba* is current slang for psychoactive cannabis, but I have found no documentation of its use prior to the 1970s, when people returning from postcolonial Angola brought the term with them.

70. Ferreira Ribeiro, *Relatorio ácerca do Serviço de Saude Publica na Provincia de S. Thomé e Principe no Anno de 1869*, 104.

71. De Luna Antonio et al., "Smoke of Ethnobotanical Plants Used in Healing Ceremonies in Brazilian Culture," 296; Ministério das Colónias, Portugal, *Colecção Oficial de Legislação Portuguesa: Ano de 1911, Primeiro semestre* (Lisbon: Imprensa Nacional, 1915), 694.

72. R. O. Clarke, "Short Notice of the African Plant Diamba, Commonly Called Congo Tobacco," *Hooker's Journal of Botany* 3 (1851): 10; J. Büttikofer, *Reisebilder aus Liberia*, vol. 2 (Leiden: E. J. Brill, 1890), 276.

73. One French traveler suspected that some of his peers in Central Africa had mistranslated cannabis terms as "tobacco": É. Dupont, *Lettres sur le Congo: Récit d'un voyage scientifique entre l'embouchure du fleuve et le confluent du Kassaï* (Paris: C. Reinwald, 1889), 645.

74. Anonymous, *A Residence at Sierra Leone* (London: John Murray, 1849), 262.

75. R. Hill, "[Letter: Indian Report, from Richard Hill, Stipendiary Magistrate, Spanish Hill, Jamaica]; enclosed in No. 106, Edward Eyre to Duke of Newcastle, 25 June 1862, CO (Colonial Office) 137/368," National Archives, London.

76. Costa Doria, "Os fumadores de maconha," 151.

77. G. Freyre, *O escravo nos anuncios de jornais brasileiros do seculo XIX*, 2d ed. (São Paulo: Nacional, 1979), 79–80.

78. Anonymous, *A Grammar and Vocabulary of the Susoo Language* (Edinburgh: J. Ritchie, 1802), 84.

79. C. S. Duvall, "Linguistic Evidence on the Historical and Cultural Geographies of Cannabis, Tobacco, and Smoking Pipes in Africa," *Economic Botany* (forthcoming).

80. E. Poisson, "Itineraire suivi par les habitants de Bakel pour se rendre à Kaouroco, d'où ils descendent la Gambia jusqu'à Sainte-Marie de Bathurst, et vocabulaire du pays de Guey," *Bulletin de la Société de Géographie* 17, 4th series (July 1859): 48.

81. The etymology of tobacco terms such as Bamanankan *sira* and Yoruba *āsara* needs further research. Wiener proposes that they trace to Arabic and suggests that there are cognate Arabic terms that mean "snuff": L. Wiener, *Africa and the Discovery of America*, vol. 1 (Philadelphia: Innes and Sons, 1920), 110–11. However, it is challenging to accept this proposed etymology. Wiener provides many dubious etymologies—he makes remarkable leaps of meaning between morphologically similar terms—in support of his overall argument that African navigators discovered the Americas and introduced tobacco to the New World. I have found just one instance of a morphologically similar Arabic term, "snuff (*nashwār*)" in Aitchison (p. 219), who lists Arabic terms he encountered in Persia and Afghanistan: J. E. T. Aitchinson, "Notes to Assist in a Further Knowledge of the Products of Western Afghanistan and of North-eastern Persia," *Transactions of the Botanical Society (Edinburgh)* 18, no. 54 (1891): 1–228. In contrast, *chīra* is attested historically as "hashish" in Tunisia and Algeria and is morphologically similar to words like *sira* and *āsara*. I will suggest that these *sira*-type terms hint at a trans-Saharan transfer of knowledge about tobacco and/or cannabis. See also C. S. Duvall, "Cannabis and Tobacco in Precolonial and Colonial Africa," in *Oxford Research Encyclopedia of African History*, ed. T. Spear (New York: Oxford University Press, 2017), accessed 24 April 2018, http://africanhistory.oxfordre.com/view/10.1093/acrefore/9780190277734.001.0001/acrefore-9780190277734-e-44.

82. M. É. Péroz, *Dictionaire Français-Mandingue* (Paris: Moderne–J. D. Maillard, 1891), 86.

83. Duvall, "Linguistic Evidence on the Historical and Cultural Geographies of Cannabis, Tobacco, and Smoking Pipes in Africa."

84. Clarke, "Short Notice of the African Plant Diamba," 10.

85. A. Raponda-Walker and R. Sillans, *Les plantes utiles du Gabon* (Paris: Paul Lechevalier, 1961), 489; W. D. Hambly, *The Ovimbundu of Angola* (Chicago: Field Museum of Natural History, 1934), 236.

86. Bilby, "The Holy Herb"; M. Schuler, *"Alas, alas, Kongo": A Social History of Indentured African Immigration into Jamaica, 1841–1865* (Baltimore: Johns Hopkins University Press, 1980).

87. The Jamaican *chianga* was translated as "cannabis": Bilby, "The Holy Herb," 85, 87. The unknown language was spoken in the Aruhimi and Lomami River valleys (DRC): Dupont, *Lettres sur le Congo*, 665; J. B. Eddie, *A Vocabulary of Kilolo as Spoken by the Bankundu, a Section of the Balolo Tribe, at Ikengo (Equator), Upper Congo* (London: East London Institute, n.d.), 75.

88. J. Pereira do Nascimento, *Grammatica do Umbundu ou lingua de Benguella* (Lisbon: Imprensa Nacional, 1894), 29; J. Pereira do Nascimento, *Kimbundu Grammar: Grammatica elementar do Kimbundu ou lingua de Angola* (Geneva: Charles Schuchardt, 1888–89), 122.

89. Clarke, "Short Notice of the African Plant Diamba."

90. Costa Doria, "Os fumadores de maconha."

91. Pernambuco, "A maconha em Pernambuco," 187.

92. Bilby, "The Holy Herb," 87. Tomei proposes that *kaya* derives from Hindi *kali* (plant bud) or Kali (wife of Shiva): Tomei, *Forbidden Fruits*, 50. I disagree. First, neither word is documented as a cannabis term in India or among Hindi speakers. Second, the numerous *kaya* cognates in Central Africa and elsewhere show that the term, shared among several Bantu languages, was used to name smoked herbs, including cannabis.

93. P. C. Standley, *Contributions from the United States National Herbarium, Volume 28: Flora of the Panama Canal Zone* (Washington, DC: US Government Printing Office, 1928), 164.

94. H. A. Dias de Carvalho, *Expedição portugueza ao Muatiânvua: Ethnographia e historia tradicional dos povos da Lunda* (Lisbon: Imprensa Nacional, 1890), 584.

95. "O Dicionário da Maconha."

96. N. del Castillo Mathieu, "El léxico negro-africano de San Basilio de Palenque," *Thesaurus* 39, nos. 1–3 (1984): 143.

97. D. Fasla Fernández, "El Español hablado en Cuba: Préstamos vigentes, lexicogénesis y variación lingüística," *Cuadernos de Investigacion Filologica* 33–34 (2007–2008): 88.

98. Castillo Mathieu, "El léxico negro-africano de San Basilio de Palenque," 143; Y. Pessoa de Castro, "Towards a Comparative Approach to Bantuisms in Iberoamerica," in *AfricAmericas: Itineraries, Dialogues, and Sounds*, ed. I. Phaf-Rheinberger and T. de Oliveira Pinto (Madrid: Iberoamericana, 2008), 86.

99. Academia Farmacéutica, *Farmacopea Mexicana* (Mexico City: Manuel N. de la Vega, 1846), 63.

100. Anonymous [Leonardo Oliva], *Lecciones de farmacologicia*, vol. 1 (Mexico City: Tipografia de Rodriguez, 1853), 200.

101. The *h* is silent, serving in this instance as a glottal stop; the *g* is what linguists call an approximant, meaning it falls between a consonant and a vowel in terms of pronunciation.

102. The Hausa term is an unrelated homonym of the cannabis nickname *rama* (branch) in Mexican Spanish.

103. F. A. Ober, *Travels in Mexico*, rev. ed. (Boston: Estes and Lauriat, 1887), 670.

104. I. Campos, *Home Grown: Marijuana and the Origins of Mexico's War on Drugs* (Chapel Hill: University of North Carolina Press, 2012), 74–77; A. Piper, "The Mysterious Origins of the Word 'Marihuana,'" *Sino-Platonic Papers* 153 (2005): 1–17.

105. Piper, "The Mysterious Origins of the Word 'Marihuana,'" 11.

106. Siler et al., "Mariajuana Smoking in Panama," 70.

107. Piper, "The Mysterious Origins of the Word 'Marihuana,'" 4. I have been unable to trace Piper's claim that *ren hua* is attested in another Chinese plant name. The untenable Chinese etymology perhaps began with the anthropologist Weston La Barre, who decided inexplicably that people in Mexico learned to smoke cannabis from "emigrant [*sic*] oriental laborers": W. La Barre, "History and Ethnography of Cannabis," in *Culture in Context: Selected Writings of Weston La Barre* (Durham, NC: Duke University Press, 1980), 94, 99.

108. H. H. Dubs and R. S. Smith, "Chinese in Mexico City in 1635," *Far Eastern Quarterly* 1, no. 4 (1942): 387–89; E. R. Slack Jr., "The Chinos in New Spain: A Corrective Lens for a Distorted Image," *Journal of World History* 20, no. 1 (2009): 35–67.

109. Haugen points out the Nahuatl etymology is untenable: J. D. Haugen, "Borrowed Borrowings: Nahuatl Loan Words in English," *Lexis Journal in English Lexicology* 3 (2009): art. 638, 94. See also Campos, *Home Grown*, 77.

110. Piper, "The Mysterious Origins of the Word 'Marihuana,'" 5–13.

111. Piper gives two pages each to the Semitic root and to pre-Columbian Chinese connections and less than one page to the possibility of African connections.

112. J. Pike, "Hydrography, Pilotage, etc., South America, Brazil," *Naval Chronicle for 1813*, 30 (July–December 1808): 211–13.

113. The town is at 8°54′S, 24°2′E. For a listing of *diamba* place names, see Office of Geography, US Department of the Interior, *Gazetteer No. 80: Republic of the Congo (Léopoldville)* (Washington, DC: US Board on Geographic Names, 1964), 78, 81.

114. Bilby, "The Holy Herb"; K. Bilby, and K. B. Fu-Kiau, "Kumina: A Kongo-based Tradition in the New World," *Les Cahiers du CEDAF Série 4: Linguistique* 8 (1983): 1–114.

115. J. D. Cordeiro da Matta, *Ensaio de diccionario Kimbúndu-Portuguez* (Lisbon: Antonio Maria Pereira, 1893), 91.

116. Haugen, "Borrowed Borrowings," 94; Real Academia Española, *Diccionario panhispánico de dudas* (Madrid: Real Academia Española, 2016).

117. [Oliva], *Lecciones de Farmacologicia*, 201.

118. Campos, *Home Grown*, 61.

119. A. de Saldanha da Gama, *Memoria sobre as colonias de Portugal: Situadas na costa occidental d'Afrique* (Paris: Typographia de Casimir, 1839), 73.

120. J.-B. Douville, *Voyage au Congo et dans l'interieur de l'Afrique equinoxiale, fait dans les années 1828, 1829, et 1830*, vol. 1 (Paris: Jules Renouard, 1832), 127.

121. Miller, *Way of Death*; Domingues da Silva, *The Atlantic Slave Trade from West Central Africa*.

122. R. Ferreira, "Slavery and the Social and Cultural Landscapes of Luanda," in *Early Modern Americas: The Black Urban Atlantic in the Age of the Slave Trade*, ed. J. Cañizares-Esguerra, M. D. Childs, and J. Sidbury (Philadelphia: University of Pennsylvania Press, 2013), 195.

123. Miller, *Way of Death*.

124. Carney and Rosomoff, *In the Shadow of Slavery*; Voeks, *Sacred Leaves of Candomblé*; Voeks and Rashford, *African Ethnobotany in the Americas*; L. Schiebinger, "Agnotology and Exotic Abortifacients: The Cultural Production of Ignorance in the Eighteenth-

Century Atlantic World," *Proceedings of the American Philosophical Society* 149, no. 3 (2005): 316–43.

125. Voeks, *Sacred Leaves of Candomblé.*

126. W. F. Daniell, "On the D'amba, or Dakka, of Southern Africa," *Pharmaceutical Journal and Transactions* 9, no. 8 (1850): 363–65.

127. Miller, *Way of Death.*

128. P. B. Du Chaillu, *Explorations and Adventures in Equatorial Africa* (New York: Harper Brothers, 1861), 420.

129. K. D. Patterson, "Paul B. Du Chaillu and the Exploration of Gabon, 1855–1865," *International Journal of African Historical Studies* 7, no. 4 (1974): 647–67.

130. H. Bucher, "The Atlantic Slave Trade and the Gabon Estuary: The Mpongwe to 1860," in *Africans in Bondage: Studies in Slavery and the Slave Trade*, ed. P. D. Curtin and P. E. Lovejoy (Madison: University of Wisconsin Press, 1986), 137–54.

131. K. D. Patterson, "Early Knowledge of the Ogowe River and the American Exploration of 1854," *International Journal of African Historical Studies* 5, no. 1 (1972): 75–90.

132. *Cannabis* is not in his 1909 list of useful Brazilian plants: M. Pio Corrêa, *Flora do Brazil: Algumas plantas úteis, suas applicações e distribução geographica* (Rio de Janeiro: Typographia da Estatistica, 1909).

133. M. Pio Corrêa, *Diccionario das plantas úteis do Brasil e das exóticas cultivadas*, vol. 1 (Rio de Janeiro: Imprensa Nacional, 1926), 472. Regarding my translation of Pio Corrêa, see note 49 in chapter 1 above.

134. Pio Corrêa, *Diccionario das plantas úteis do Brasil e das exóticas cultivadas*, vii–ix; W. B. Mors, "Leonam de Azeredo Penna and Pio Corrêa's Dictionary of Useful Plants of Brazil," *Economic Botany* 35, no. 1 (1981): 1–3.

135. M. Rediker, *The Slave Ship: A Human History* (New York: Viking, 2007), 265–66; J. S. Handler, "The Middle Passage and the Material Culture of Captive Africans," *Slavery and Abolition* 30, no. 1 (2009): 1–26; J. Carney, "Rice and Memory in the Age of Enslavement: Atlantic Passages to Suriname," *Slavery and Abolition* 26, no. 3 (2005): 325–47.

136. A. Duarte, "O tema da maconha no folclore," Historia de Alagoas, 2015, accessed 15 August 2017, http://www.historiadealagoas.com.br.

137. Monteiro, "Folclore da maconha," 291–94.

138. The Brazilian historian Edison Carneiro suggested cannabis was grown in 1645 at Quilombo dos Palmares, a famed community of escaped slaves in seventeenth-century Alagoas. This is too early. The 1645 date is from a Dutch account of the quilombo, which told that its residents made pipes from coconut husks. Carneiro assumed a water pipe and thus assumed cannabis rather than tobacco or something else, but the historical source only stated "pipe" and made no mention of herbs: see E. Carneiro, *O Quilombo dos Palmares* (Rio de Janeiro: Civilização Brasileira, 1966), 18; A. Carvalho, "Diario da viagem do capitão João Blaer aos Palmares em 1645," *Revista do Insituto Archeológico e Geográphico Pernambucano* 10, no. 56 (1902): 93.

139. S. Liet, *La philosophie absolue par le Docteur Mure* (Rio de Janeiro: L'Institute Homéopathique de Brésil, 1884).

140. C. A. Marques, *Dicionário histórico-geografico da Provincia do Maranhão* (Rio de Janeiro: Fon-Fon e Seleta, [1870] 1970), 517.

141. Duvall, *Cannabis*, chap. 3.

142. *History of Brazil* (Rio de Janeiro: E. and H. Laemmert, 1857), 266.

143. Marques, *Dicionário histórico-geografico da Provincia do Maranhão*, 517.

144. Tribunal do Santo Ofício do Inquisição de Lisboa, "[Confissão de] Antonio do Carmo." Two hundred years later, the inferred drug combination survived in a folk song that also suggested homosexuality: "Because there is no law / Everywhere I sing/ My face is shameless / I gave up on baby *cachaça* [*aguardente*] / Now [I] just take *maconha* / Hey *Marica* [effeminate man, or water pipe], *Marica* tell a friend": "Aspectos folk-lóricos da Maconha."

145. Mott, "A maconha na história do Brasil."

146. "Manoel Francisco Pedroso . . . ," *Jornal do Commercio*, 21 February 1847, 3.

147. Anonymous [Benoît Mure], *Doctrine de l'École de Rio de Janeiro et Pathogénésie Brésilienne* (Rio de Janeiro: L'Institute Homéopathique de Brésil, 1849).

148. Liet, *La philosophie absolue par le Docteur Mure*, 33.

149. Burton, *Explorations of the Highlands of Brazil*, 1:276; R. F. Burton, *Explorations of the Highlands of Brazil*, vol. 2 (London: Tinsley Brothers, 1869), 295.

150. Glaziou, as cited in Chevalier, "Histoire de deux plantes cultivées d'importance primordiale," 68; Conde de Ficalho, *Plantas úteis da África portuguesa*, 2d ed. (Lisbon: Agência Geral das Colónias, [1884] 1947), 265. Similar horticultural practices existed among caboclos in the 1960s and Indigenous peoples in the Brazilian Amazon in the 1970s: Monteiro, "Folclore da maconha"; A. Henman, "War on Drugs Is War on People," *The Ecologist* 10, nos. 8–9 (1980): 282–89.

151. Monteiro, "Folclore da maconha," 295.

152. G. Freyre, *Nordeste: Aspectos da influencia da canna sobre a vida e a paizagem do Nordeste do Brasil* (Rio de Janeiro: José Olympio, 1937), 15.

153. C. F. P. von Martius, *Systema materiae medicae vegetabilis brasiliensis* (Vienna: Friedrich Beck, 1843), 121.

154. One story that suggests slaveholders considered it a poison deserves mention, but cannot be accepted without corroborating evidence. Supposedly, in 1830 Carlota Joaquina, queen consort of Portugal, asked for Brazilian *diamba* from her Iberian deathbed. She sought it as an ingredient in an arsenic-based concoction used in assassinations—and, evidently, suicides. The only source of this story is a scandal-mongering, sensationalized book published in 1934 that is ostensibly based on historical sources, which are not cited: F. de A. Cintra, *Os escandalos de Carlota Joaquina* (Rio de Janeiro: Civilização Brasileira, 1934), 272. See also: Mott, "A maconha na história do Brasil," 127.

155. Clarke, "Short Notice of the African Plant Diamba," 10.

156. *A Residence at Sierra Leone*, 262.

157. Burton, *Explorations of the Highlands of Brazil*, 1:237–38. Burton did not mention cannabis in his disparaging description of Freetown in 1861: Anonymous [Richard F. Burton], *Wanderings in West Africa from Liverpool to Fernando Po*, vol. 2 (London: Tinsley Brothers, 1863).

158. E. Bickersteth, "Religious Intelligence: Church Missionary Society, Substance of the Report of the Rev. E. Bickersteth's Visit to the Settlements of the Society on the Western Coast of Africa," *Christian Observer*, 11 November 1816, 757; "Religious and Missionary Intelligence: State of Religion in Africa, an extract from 'The Report of the Weslyan Methodist Missionary Society of 1819,'" *Methodist Magazine*, vol. 4, April 1821, 148.

159. In registers of orphaned recaptives from 1821 to 1824, 1.5 percent came from western Central Africa: A. Jones, "Recaptive Nations: Evidence Concerning the Demographic Impact of the Atlantic Slave Trade in the Early Nineteenth Century," *Slavery and Abolition* 11, no. 1 (1990): 42–57. In an 1848 census of adult recaptives, 3.3 percent came from western Central Africa: P. D. Curtin, *The African Slave Trade: A Census* (Madison: University of Wisconsin Press, 1969), 244–50.

160. Carney and Rosomoff, *In the Shadow of Slavery*.

161. Rediker, *The Slave Ship*; Handler, "The Middle Passage and the Material Culture of Captive Africans."

162. Daniell, "On the D'amba, or Dakka, of Southern Africa."

163. W. Butterworth, *Three Years Adventures of a Minor in England, Africa, the West Indies, South-Carolina and Georgia*, 2d ed. (Leeds, UK: Edward Baines, 1831), 126–27.

164. Rediker, *The Slave Ship*, 195.

165. Handler, "The Middle Passage and the Material Culture of Captive Africans."

166. Büttikofer, *Reisebilder aus Liberia*, 276.

167. Büttikofer, *Reisebilder aus Liberia*, 277.

168. H. Johnston, *Liberia*, vol. 2 (New York: Dodd, Mead, 1906), 994.

169. R. C. F. Maugham, *The Republic of Liberia: Being a General Description of the Negro Republic* (London: George Allen and Unwin, 1920), 172; L. Lewin, *Phantastica: Die betäubenden und erregenden Genussmittel* (Berlin: Stilke, 1924), 105.

170. D. F. Bacon, *Wanderings on the Seas and Shores of Africa* (New York: Joseph W. Harrison, 1843), 127.

171. S. M. Fett, "Middle Passages and Forced Migrations: Liberated Africans in Nineteenth-Century U.S. Camps and Ships," *Slavery and Abolition* 31, no. 1 (2010): 75–98.

172. See population estimates in Fett, "Middle Passages and Forced Migrations"; Domingues da Silva et al., "The Diaspora of Africans Liberated from Slave Ships in the Nineteenth Century."

173. M'Henry, "An Account of the Liberated African Establishment at St. Helena," 437.

174. A. Beatson, *Tracts Relative to the Island of St. Helena* (London: W. Bulmer, 1816), 302.

175. Domingues da Silva et al., "The Diaspora of Africans Liberated from Slave Ships in the Nineteenth Century."

176. A. Pearson, B. Jeffs, A. Witkin, and H. MacQuarrie, *Infernal Traffic: Excavation of a Liberated African Graveyard in Rupert's Valley, St. Helena* (Bootham, UK: Council for British Archaeology, 2011).

177. Schuler, *"Alas, alas, Kongo"*; Domingues da Silva et al., "The Diaspora of Africans Liberated from Slave Ships in the Nineteenth Century."

178. Disembarkations in Jamaica from: Trans-Atlantic Slave Trade Database, http://www.slavevoyages.org.

179. Hill, "[Letter . . .]," 19.

180. Johnston, *The Chemistry of Common Life*, 91.

181. Bilby and Fu-Kiau, "Kumina."

182. Schuler, *"Alas, alas, Kongo"*; Bilby and Fu-Kiau, "Kumina," 2.

183. Domingues da Silva et al., "The Diaspora of Africans Liberated from Slave Ships in the Nineteenth Century."

184. Disembarkations on British Caribbean islands, from: Trans-Atlantic Slave Trade Database, http://www.slavevoyages.org.

185. Indian Hemp Drugs Commission, *Report of the Indian Hemp Drugs Commission, 1893–1894*, vol. 1 (Simla, India: Government Central Printing Office, 1894), 154–55; A Pharmaceutical Resident, "Opium-Dealing in British Guiana," *Chemist and Druggist* 42 (28 January 1893): 120–21.

186. H. Yule and A. C. Burnell, *Hobson-Jobson: A Glossary of Colloquial Anglo-Indian Words and Phrases* (London: John Murray, 1903).

187. H. Kirke, *Twenty-five Years in British Guiana* (London: S. Low, Marston, 1898), 337.

188. Hamid, *The Ganja Complex*.

189. T. Ireland, "Insanity from the Abuse of Indian Hemp," *Alienist and Neurologist* 14 (1893): 622–30.

190. M. Schuler, "Liberated Central Africans in Nineteenth-Century Guyana," in *Central Africans and Cultural Transformations in the American Diaspora*, ed. L. M. Heywood (Cambridge: Cambridge University Press, 2001), 319–52; J. A. Carney and R. N. Rosomoff, "African Crops in the Environmental History of New World Plantation Societies," in *Environmental History in the Making, Volume II: Acting*, ed. C. Joanaz de Melo, E. Vaz, and L. M. Costa Pinto (New York: Springer International, 2017), 173–88; T. R. van Andel, C. I. E. A. van 't Klooster, D. Quiroz, A. M. Towns, S. Ruysschaert, and M. van den Berg, "Local Plant Names Reveal That Enslaved Africans Recognized Substantial Parts of the New World Flora," *Proceedings of the National Academy of Sciences* 111, no. 50 (2014): E5346–53.

191. Indian Hemp Drugs Commission, *Report of the Indian Hemp Drugs Commission*.

192. This is the first record of cannabis in Venezuela: A. Sinclair, *In Tropical Lands: Recent Travels to the Sources of the Amazon, the West Indian Islands, and Ceylon* (Aberdeen, UK: D. Wyllie and Son, 1895), 130; West India Royal Commission, *Report of the West India Royal Commission, Appendix C, Volume 2, Containing Parts II, III, IV, and V: Proceedings, Evidence, and Documents relating to British Guiana, Barbados, Trinidad, and Tobago* (London: Eyre and Spottiswoode, 1897), 343.

193. J. B. Page, "A Brief History of Mind-Altering Drug Use in Prerevolutionary Cuba," *Cuban Studies/Estudios Cubanos* 12, no. 2 (1982): 56–71.

194. R. Anderson, "The Diaspora of Sierra Leone's Liberated Africans: Enlistment, Forced Migration, and 'Liberation' at Freetown, 1808–1863," *African Economic History* 41, no. 1 (2013): 101–38.

195. E. Akyeampong, "Diaspora and Drug Trafficking in West Africa: A Case Study of Ghana," *African Affairs* 104, no. 416 (2005): 429–47.

196. This number is 9 percent of the total known to have been landed in British Gambia (3,445 people). This was the percentage of Central Africans among the total landed in Sierra Leone: Domingues da Silva et al., "The Diaspora of Africans Liberated from Slave Ships in the Nineteenth Century."

197. Perhaps *Cannabis indica* came to Senegal from elsewhere, too. French doctors had tried to grow pharmaceutical cannabis by the 1890s, but it is undocumented whether they brought in seeds from an unknown location or experimented with local plants: A. Sébire, *Les plantes utiles du Sénégal: plantes indigènes—plantes exotiques* (Paris: J.-B. Baillière and Sons, 1899), 163.

198. Anderson, "The Diaspora of Sierra Leone's Liberated Africans."

199. H. Collomb, M. Diop, and H. Ayats, "Intoxication par le chanvre indien au Sénégal," *Cahiers d'Études Africaines* 3, no. 9 (1962): 139.

200. J. Kerharo, *La pharmacopée sénégalaise traditionelle* (Paris: Vigot Frères, 1974), 312.

201. Burton actually called *diamba* "the local European name": [Burton], *Wanderings in West Africa from Liverpool to Fernando Po*, 224.

202. Domingues da Silva et al., "The Diaspora of Africans Liberated from Slave Ships in the Nineteenth Century."

203. [Burton], *Wanderings in West Africa from Liverpool to Fernando Po*, 222.

204. Voeks, *Sacred Leaves of Candomblé*.

205. Disembarkations from West Central Africa in Spanish Central America, from: Trans-Atlantic Slave Trade Database, http://www.slavevoyages.org.

206. Borucki et al., "Atlantic History and the Slave Trade to Spanish America."

207. Abel, "Marijuana on Trial"; Siler et al., "Mariajuana Smoking in Panama."

208. Siler et al., "Mariajuana Smoking in Panama"; Standley, *Contributions from the United States National Herbarium*, 164; Chamberlain and Curry, *Report of the Health Department of the Panama Canal for the Calendar Year 1925*, 32.

209. Standley, *Contributions from the United States National Herbarium*, 215; J. T. Schneider, *Dictionary of African Borrowings in Brazilian Portuguese* (Hamburg: Helmut Buske, 1991), 12, 157.

210. Standley, *Contributions from the United States National Herbarium*, 164; Chamberlain and Curry, *Report of the Health Department of the Panama Canal for the Calendar Year 1925*, 32.

211. J. B. Page, "Costa Rican Marihuana Smokers and the Amotivational Syndrome Hypothesis," Ph.D. diss., Department of Anthropology, University of Florida, Gainesville, 1976.

212. Page, "A Brief History of Mind-Altering Drug Use in Prerevolutionary Cuba"; W. L. Partridge, "Exchange Relationships in a Community on the North Coast of Colombia with Special Reference to Cannabis," Ph.D. diss., Department of Anthropology, University of Florida, Gainesville, 1974; W. E. Carter and P. L. Doughty, "Social and Cultural Aspects of Cannabis Use in Costa Rica," *Annals of the New York Academy of Sciences* 282, no. 1 (1976): 2–16.

213. This evidence, first reported by Carter and Doughty, deserves an asterisk. It is secondhand. In 1971, the Costa Rican scholar Otón Jiménez published a story that was

passed to him, as early as 1920, that the Swiss botanist Adolphe Tonduz observed cannabis plantings and use among laborers at an unstated date. Jiménez generically wrote "coolies," employed by the United Fruit Company (UFC). Carter and Doughty assumed that these "coolies" were Chinese, but they were almost certainly Jamaicans, who strongly dominated among UFC laborers. Carter and Doughty's interpretation of Jimenez bears errors: (1) Jimenez identified plantation workers, who were almost entirely from Jamaica, not railroad construction crews, who had more diverse origins; (2) the observation came not in the 1880s but circa 1904–10, when the Swiss botanist Henri Pittier, who ordered Tonduz to conduct a plant survey, directed agricultural research for the UFC; and (3) there is no history of cannabis smoking in China, in contrast to Jamaica. I state "1905" in the text to simplify the sentence and insert "banana" because this was the primary crop. See Carter and Doughty, "Social and Cultural Aspects of Cannabis Use in Costa Rica," 14; O. Jiménez, "Tonduzia," *Revista de Agricultura (San José)* 43, nos. 5–8 (1971): 55–67.

214. State Narcotic Committee, "The Trend of Drug Addiction in California," in *Appendix to the Journals of the Senate and Assembly of the Forty-Ninth Session of the Legislature of the State of California, Vol. 5*, ed. Legislature of the State of California (Sacramento: California State Printing Office, 1932): doc. 9, 17.

215. Siler et al., "Mariajuana Smoking in Panama."

216. V. Rubin and L. Comitas, *Ganja in Jamaica: The Effects of Marijuana Use* (New York: Mouton de Gruyter, 1975).

217. Costa Doria, "Os fumadores de maconha," 154.

218. Daniell, "On the D'amba, or Dakka, of Southern Africa," 365.

219. Campos, *Home Grown*, 78.

220. For an analysis of these two sources, see Campos, *Home Grown*, 252–54. I have not seen the archival document from 1777 that Campos references. He presents it as showing that Indigenous laborers had "begun cultivating their own medicinal cannabis" (53). He does not indicate whether the document described their usage of the plant. The "medicinal" descriptor seems anachronistic; such terminology does not appear in contemporaneous sources, including those he quotes. Pipiltzintzintlis were not considered medicinal by Spanish-writing documentarians but were associated with (evil) Indigenous religions. The document from 1772 is from the Mexican scholar José Antonio de Alzate, who specified that *pipiltzintzintlis* was a plural term used for multiple substances with varying effects. He bought some in a market, grew the seeds it contained, and discovered they sprouted into cannabis. He argued that the pipiltzintzintlis should be treated legally and socially like herbal medicine, comparable to *cáñamo* (hemp) in Europe. Alzate did not describe use of cannabis-the-pipiltzintzintli but suggests the seeds were consumed orally: J. A de Alzate, "Memoria sobre el uso que hacen los Indios de los pipiltzintzintlis," in *Memorias y ensayos*, ed. R. Moreno (Mexico City: Universidad Nacional Autónoma de México, 1985), 55, 61–62. Aguirre Beltrán also summarizes primary sources as describing oral consumption. I assume the archival usage from 1777 was similar. See: G. Aguirre Beltrán, *Medicina y magia: El proceso de aculturatión en la estructura colonial* (Mexico City: Instituto Nacional Indigenista, 1963), 138.

221. Alzate, "Memoria sobre el uso que hacen los Indios de los pipiltezintzintlis," 55;
J. L. Diaz, "Ethnopharmacology of Sacred Psychoactive Plants Used by the Indians of
Mexico," *Annual Review of Pharmacology and Toxicology* 17, no. 1 (1977): 650.

222. Aguirre Beltrán, *Medicina y magia*, 138; Alzate, "Memoria sobre el uso que hacen
los Indios de los pipiltezintzintlis." I don't know whether this vague recipe would make
Salvia divinorum pharmacologically active. It would not do the same for water-insoluble
compounds such as THC and other cannabinoids.

223. Campos, *Home Grown*.

224. A. Ochoa, "Las investigaciones de Crescencio García sobre medicina popular:
'Fragmento para la materia médica mexicana (1859),'" *Relaciones, Zamora, El Colegio de
Michoacán* 4 ([1859] 1980): 76–99.

225. J. G. Bourke, "The American Congo," *Scribner's Magazine*, vol. 15, no. 5, 1894,
590–610. The river along the U.S.-Mexico border is called the Río Bravo in Mexico.

226. N. Johnson, *Grass Roots: A History of Cannabis in the American West* (Corvallis:
Oregon State University Press, 2017).

227. Campos, *Home Grown*, 55.

228. W. Johnson, *The Chattel Principle: Internal Slave Trades in the Americas,
1808–1888* (New Haven, CT: Yale University Press, 2004), 205.

229. P. C. Standley and J. A. Steyermark, *Flora of Guatemala, Part 4, Fieldiana: Botany*,
vol. 24 (Chicago: Chicago Natural History Museum, 1946), 17.

230. Campos, *Home Grown*, 51.

231. Bilby, "The Holy Herb," 85.

232. Monteiro, "Folclore da maconha."

233. Notably, the Spanish *cachimba* referred specifically to cannabis pipes in Costa Rica
in the 1970s: W. E. Carter, *Cannabis in Costa Rica: A Study of Chronic Marijuana Use*
(Philadelphia: Institute for the Study of Human Issues, 1980), 214.

234. Pernambuco, "A maconha em Pernambuco," 188–89. For descriptions of Indigenous knowledge of cannabis in Amazonian Brazil in the 1970s, see Henman, "War on
Drugs Is War on People."

8. WORKING UNDER THE INFLUENCE

1. G. Klantschnig, N. Carrier, and C. Ambler, eds., *Drugs in Africa: Histories and Ethnographies of Use* (Gordonsville, NY: Palgrave Macmillan, 2014).

2. R. O. Clarke, "Short Notice of the African Plant Diamba, Commonly Called
Congo Tobacco," *Hooker's Journal of Botany* 3 (1851): 9–11.

3. C. de Martrin-Donos, *Les Belges dans l'Afrique Centrale: Voyages, aventures et découvertes d'après les documents et journaux des explorateurs, Le Congo et ses affluents*, vol. 2
(Brussels: P. Maes, 1886), 453.

4. W. Jankowiak and D. Bradburd, *Drugs, Labor and Colonial Expansion* (Tucson:
University of Arizona Press, 2003).

5. J. J. Monteiro, *Angola and the River Congo*, vol. 2 (London: Macmillan, 1875), 26.

6. M. C. Dreher, *Working Men and Ganja: Marihuana Use in Rural Jamaica* (Philadelphia: Institute for the Study of Human Issues, 1982); I. C. Chopra and R. N. Chopra,
"The Use of the Cannabis Drugs in India," *UNODC Bulletin on Narcotics* 11, no. 1 (1957):

4–29; R. N. Chopra and G. S. Chopra, "Present Position of Hemp Drug Addiction in India," *British Journal of Inebriety* 38, no. 2 (1940): 71–74; R. P. Walton, *Marihuana: America's New Drug Problem* (Philadelphia: J. B. Lippincott, 1938), 117; W. E. Carter, *Cannabis in Costa Rica: A Study of Chronic Marijuana Use* (Philadelphia: Institute for the Study of Human Issues, 1980); A. Hamid, *The Ganja Complex: Rastafari and Marijuana* (Lanham, MD: Lexington, 2002); G. G. Nahas, "Hashish and Drug Abuse in Egypt during the 19th and 20th Centuries," *Bulletin of the New York Academy of Medicine* 61, no. 5 (1985): 428–44; J. B. Page, "Costa Rican Marihuana Smokers and the Amotivational Syndrome Hypothesis," Ph.D. diss., Department of Anthropology, University of Florida, Gainesville, 1976; Indian Hemp Drugs Commission, *Report of the Indian Hemp Drugs Commission, 1893–1894* (Simla, India: Government Central Printing Office, 1894), 405–6.

7. A. A. Laudati, "Out of the Shadows: Negotiations and Networks in the Cannabis Trade in Eastern Democratic Republic of Congo," in Klantschnig et al., *Drugs in Africa*, 164.

8. J. H. Van Linschoten, *The Voyage of John Huyghen van Linschoten to the East Indies: From the Old English Translation of 1598*, vol. 2 (London: Hakluyt Society, [1598] 1885), 125.

9. S. Chandra and A. Swoboda, "Are Spatial Variables Important? The Case for Multiple Drugs in British Bengal," in *Geography and Drug Addiction*, ed. Y. F. Thomas, D. Richardson, and I. Cheung (New York: Springer, 2008), 221–42.

10. C. S. Duvall, *Cannabis* (London: Reaktion, 2015), chap. 7.

11. A Pharmaceutical Resident, "Opium-Dealing in British Guiana," *Chemist and Druggist* 42 (28 January 1893): 120–21.

12. D. T. Courtwright, *Forces of Habit: Drugs and the Making of the Modern World* (Cambridge, MA: Harvard University Press, 2001).

13. Indian Hemp Drugs Commission, *Report of the Indian Hemp Drugs Commission*, 406.

14. For a summary of political-economic theory, see P. Robbins, J. Hintz, and S. A. Moore, *Environment and Society: A Critical Introduction*, 2d ed. (Hoboken, NJ: Wiley-Blackwell, 2014), 101–2.

15. I. Campos, *Home Grown: Marijuana and the Origins of Mexico's War on Drugs* (Chapel Hill: University of North Carolina Press, 2012).

16. P. Kolchin, *Unfree Labor: American Slavery and Russian Serfdom* (Cambridge, MA: Harvard University Press, 1987); T. Brass, *Labour Regime Change in the Twenty-First Century: Unfreedom, Capitalism, and Primitive Accumulation* (Leiden: E. J. Brill, 2011).

17. E. L. Erickson, "The Introduction of East Indian Coolies into the British West Indies," *Journal of Modern History* 6, no. 2 (1934): 127–46.

18. Indian Immigrants (Wragg) Commission, "Report," in *Documents of Indentured Labour, Natal 1851–1917*, ed. Y. S. Meer (Durban: Institute of Black Research, [1887] 1980): 246–633.

19. S. Fenoaltea, "Slavery and Supervision in Comparative Perspective: A Model," *Journal of Economic History* 44, no. 3 (1984): 635–68.

20. Fenoaltea, "Slavery and Supervision in Comparative Perspective"; Kolchin, *Unfree Labor*.

21. J. C. Scott, "Everyday Forms of Resistance," in *Everyday Forms of Peasant Resistance*, ed. F. D. Colburn (Armonk, NY: M. E. Sharpe, 1989), 3–33; R. Cohen, "Resistance and

Hidden Forms of Consciousness amongst African Workers," *Review of African Political Economy* 7, no. 19 (1980): 8–22.

22. Fenoaltea, "Slavery and Supervision in Comparative Perspective."

23. M. Schuler, *"Alas, alas, Kongo": A Social History of Indentured African Immigration into Jamaica, 1841–1865* (Baltimore: Johns Hopkins University Press, 1980); M. Schuler, "The Recruitment of African Indentured Labourers for European Colonies in the Nineteenth Century," in *Colonialism and Migration: Indentured Labour before and after Slavery*, ed. P. C. Emmer (Dordrecht: Springer Netherlands, 1986), 125–61.

24. W. A. Cadbury, *Labour in Portuguese West Africa*, 2d repr. ed. (New York: Negro Universities Press, [1910] 1969); L. J. Satre, *Chocolate on Trial: Slavery, Politics, and the Ethics of Business* (Athens: Ohio University Press, 2005); C. Higgs, *Chocolate Islands: Cocoa, Slavery, and Colonial Africa* (Athens: Ohio University Press, 2012); J. Vos, "Work in Times of Slavery, Colonialism, and Civil War: Labor Relations in Angola from 1800 to 2000," *History in Africa* 41 (2014): 363–85.

25. H. W. Nevinson, *A Modern Slavery* (London: Harper Brothers, 1906), 171.

26. Higgs, *Chocolate Islands*.

27. Fenoaltea, "Slavery and Supervision in Comparative Perspective."

28. P. Kolbe, *Naaukeurige en Uitvoerige Beschryving van de Kaap de Goede Hoop*, vol. 1 (Amsterdam: Balthazar Lakeman, 1727), 314.

29. D. Gordon, "From Rituals of Rapture to Dependence: The Political Economy of Khoikhoi Narcotic Consumption, circa 1487–1870," *South African Historical Journal* 35 (November 1996): 62–88; C. Paterson, "Prohibition and Resistance: A Socio-political Exploration of the Changing Dynamics of the Southern African Cannabis Trade, circa 1850–the Present," M.A. thesis, Department of History, Rhodes University, Grahamstown, South Africa, 2009.

30. J. Macdonald, "Bantu Customs and Legends," *Folklore* 3, no. 3 (1892): 351.

31. Gordon, "From Rituals of Rapture to Dependence"; C. G. Sampson, "'Zeer grote liefhebbers van tobak': Nicotine and Cannabis Dependency of the Seacow River Bushmen," *Digging Stick* 10, no. 1 (1993): 2–6.

32. The increasing strength of imported alcohol is described for Angola: J. C. Curto, *Enslaving Spirits: The Portuguese-Brazilian Alcohol Trade at Luanda and Its Hinterland circa 1550–1830* (Leiden: E. J. Brill, 2004).

33. Gordon, "From Rituals of Rapture to Dependence," 84–85.

34. Gordon, "From Rituals of Rapture to Dependence," 76.

35. W. F. Daniell, "On the D'amba, or Dakka, of Southern Africa," *Pharmaceutical Journal and Transactions* 9, no. 8 (1850): 365.

36. A. Sparrman, *A Voyage to the Cape of Good Hope*, 2d ed., vol. 2 (London: G. G. J. and J. Robinson, 1785), 73.

37. Sampson, "'Zeer grote liefhebbers van tobak,'" 6; C. I. Latrobe, *Journal of a Visit to South Africa in 1815 and 1816* (New York: Negro Universities Press, [1818] 1969), 325.

38. Paterson reports this based on an interview with a farm owner in 2006, who was presumably not the farm owner early in the twentieth century: Paterson, "Prohibition and Resistance," 50. What is more certain is that mine owners, and potentially other employers, found no harm in on-the-job *dagga* use at least in 1908, and probably into the

early 1920s: see M. Chanock, *Making of South African Legal Culture, 1902–1936: Fear, Favour, and Prejudice* (Cambridge: Cambridge University Press, 2001), 92.

39. Evidence on rates of cannabis use disorder are mostly from current U.S. society. Reported rates vary from around 9 percent to 30 percent: see F. S. Stinson, W. J. Ruan, R. Pickering, and B. F. Grant, "Cannabis Use Disorders in the USA: Prevalence, Correlates and Co-morbidity," *Psychological Medicine* 36, no. 10 (2006): 1447–60; C. Coffey, J. B. Carlin, L. Degenhardt, M. Lynskey, L. Sanci, and G. C. Patton, "Cannabis Dependence in Young Adults: An Australian Population Study," *Addiction* 97, no. 2 (2002): 187–94; W. M. Compton, B. F. Grant, J. D. Colliver, M. D. Glantz, and F. S. Stinson, "Prevalence of Marijuana Use Disorders in the United States: 1991–1992 and 2001–2002," *Journal of the American Medical Association* 291, no. 17 (2004): 2114–21; R. F. Farmer, D. B. Kosty, J. R. Seeley, S. C. Duncan, M. T. Lynskey, P. Rohde, D. N. Klein, and P. M. Lewinsohn, "Natural Course of Cannabis Use Disorders," *Psychological Medicine* 45, no. 1 (2014): 63–72; D. S. Hasin, T. D. Saha, B. T. Kerridge, R. B. Goldstein, S. P. Chou, H. Zhang, J. Jung, R. P. Pickering, W. J. Ruan, S. M. Smith, B. Huang, and B. F. Grant, "Prevalence of Marijuana Use Disorders in the United States between 2001–2002 and 2012–2013," *Journal of the American Medical Association Psychiatry* 72, no. 12 (2015): 1235–42; D. S. Hasin, B. T. Kerridge, T. D. Saha, B. Huang, R. Pickering, S. M. Smith, J. Jung, H. Zhang, and B. F. Grant, "Prevalence and Correlates of DSM-5 Cannabis Use Disorder, 2012–2013: Findings from the National Epidemiologic Survey on Alcohol and Related Conditions–III," *American Journal of Psychiatry* 173, no. 6 (2016): 588–99.

40. C. J. G. Bourhill, "The Smoking of *Dagga* (Indian Hemp) among the Native Races of South Africa and the Resultant Evils," M.D. diss., School of Medicine, University of Edinburgh, 1913, 35.

41. Stinson et al., "Cannabis Use Disorders in the USA."

42. J. Pernambuco, "A maconha em Pernambuco," in *Novos estudos Afro-brasileiros: Trabalhos apresentados ao 1.° Congresso Afro-brasileiro do Recife*, ed. A. Ramos (Rio de Janeiro: Civilização Brasileira, 1937), 190.

43. J. dos Santos, *Ethiopia oriental e varia historia de covsas* (Evora, Portugal: Impressa no Conuento de S. Domingos, 1609), 20B.

44. V. Giraud, *Les lacs d'Afrique équatoriale: Voyage d'exploration éxécuté de 1883 à 1885* (Paris: Hachette, 1890), 73.

45. Bourhill, "The Smoking of *Dagga*," 38; K. Peltzer and S. Ramlagan, "Cannabis Use Trends in South Africa," *South African Journal of Psychiatry* 13, no. 4 (2007): 126–31; Government of the Colony of Natal, *Departmental Reports: 1893–94* (Pietermaritzburg: William Watson, 1895), B14.

46. C. S. Duvall, "Drug Laws, Bioprospecting, and the Agricultural Heritage of *Cannabis* in Africa," *Space and Polity* 20, no. 1 (2016): 10–25.

47. C. M. Williams, B. J. Whalley, and C. McCabe, "Cannabinoids and Appetite (Dys) regulation," in *Cannabinoids in Neurologic and Mental Disease*, ed. L. Fattore (London: Academic Press, 2015), 322; M. Backes, *Cannabis Pharmacy: The Practical Guide to Medical Marijuana* (New York: Black Dog and Leventhal, 2014), 146–47; E. P. M. de Meijer, "The Chemical Phenotypes (Chemotypes) of *Cannabis*," in *Handbook of Cannabis*, ed. R. Pertwee (Oxford: Oxford University Press, 2014), 101; K. W.

Hillig and P. G. Mahlberg, "A Chemotaxonomic Analysis of Cannabinoid Variation in *Cannabis* (Cannabaceae)," *American Journal of Botany* 91, no. 6 (2004): 973.

48. Hillig and Mahlberg, "A Chemotaxonomic Analysis of Cannabinoid Variation in *Cannabis* (Cannabaceae)."

49. This is reportedly what Mukwajanga said to Chishimbi when Mukwajanga introduced Chishimbi to *riamba*, giving rise to the Bena Riamba movement: H. A. Dias de Carvalho, *O Lubuco: Algumas observações sobre o livro do Sr. Latrobe Bateman* (Lisbon: Imprensa Nacional, 1889), 12.

50. M. Y. Monteiro, "Folclore da maconha," *Revista Brasileria de Folclore* 6, no. 16 (1966): 293.

51. See J. R. Reynolds, "Therapeutical Uses and Toxic Effects of Cannabis Indica," *The Lancet* 68 (22 March 1890): 637–38; J. F. Johnston, *The Chemistry of Common Life*, 4th ed., vol. 2 (New York: D. Appleton, 1855).

52. J. R. da Costa Doria, "Os fumadores de maconha: Effeitos males do vicio," in *Proceedings of the Second Pan American Scientific Congress*, ed. G. L. Swiggett (Washington, DC: U.S. Government Printing Office, 1917), 155–56. See also Pernambuco, "A maconha em Pernambuco," 190.

53. T. Ireland, "Insanity from the Abuse of Indian Hemp," *Alienist and Neurologist* 14 (1893): 622–30.

54. P. M. Larken, "Impressions of the Zande [Continued from Vol. 9, Part 1]," *Sudan Notes and Records* 10 (1927): 94. In addition, a faint suggestion of appetite stimulation is from Burton in Tanzania, who grumbled that his porters ate more than he had budgeted, and "between their dozen meals they puff clouds of pungent tobacco, [and] jungle-bhang." Perhaps they ate so much because they smoked so much, but Burton always griped about porters: R. F. Burton, *The Lake Regions of Central Africa: A Picture of Exploration* (New York: Harper Brothers, 1860), 246.

55. A. Burdo, *Les Belges dans l'Afrique Centrale: De Zanzibar au Lac Tanganyika* (Brussels: P. Maes, 1890), 312.

56. A. Castilho, ed., *Exposition Universelle d'Anvers: Exposition Coloniale du Portugal, Catalogue Officiel* (Anvers, Belgium: Kockx, 1885), 809; Monsieur Bernardin, "Notes sur divers produits," *Bulletin of the Société de Géographie Commerciale de Bordeaux*, 9th year, 2d series (15 February 1886): 116.

57. A. F. Moller, "Exploração botanica nas possessões Portuguezas," *Jornal de Horticultura Pratica* 17 (1886): 41. For health, diet, and environment of these workers, see M. Ferreira Ribeiro, *Relatorio ácerca do Serviço de Saude Publica na Provincia de S. Thomé e Principe no Anno de 1869* (Lisbon: Imprensa Nacional, 1871).

58. R. Thomas, *The Modern Practice of Physic*, vol. 2 (London: Murray and Highley, 1802), 100.

59. E. B. Russo, "Clinical Endocannabinoid Deficiency (CECD): Can This Concept Explain Therapeutic Benefits of Cannabis in Migraine, Fibromyalgia, Irritable Bowel Syndrome and Other Treatment-Resistant Conditions?" *Neuroendocrinology Letters* 25, nos. 1–2 (2008): 31–39.

60. G. M'Henry, "An Account of the Liberated African Establishment at St. Helena, Chapter II," *Simmond's Colonial Magazine* 5 (1845): 437.

61. A. Pearson, B. Jeffs, A. Witkin, and H. MacQuarrie, *Infernal Traffic: Excavation of a Liberated African Graveyard in Rupert's Valley, St. Helena* (Bootham, UK: Council for British Archaeology, 2011).

62. S. T. Oner, *Cannabis Sativa: The Essential Guide to the World's Finest Marijuana Strains* (San Francisco: Green Candy, 2012); United Nations Office on Drugs and Crime, *World Drug Report 2006* (Vienna: United Nations, 2006), 188. Cannabis is not classified as a pharmacological stimulant, a category consisting of amphetamine-type compounds and various alkaloids. There is no identified pharmacological difference that relates to the sativa versus indica folk species that marijuana aficionados recognize. Nonetheless, these folk species seem to have had broadly different historical distributions, and different genetic characters, although sativa versus indica labels on commercially available marijuana do not reliably relate to either provenance or genetics: see Hillig and Mahlberg, "A Chemotaxonomic Analysis of Cannabinoid Variation in *Cannabis* (Cannabaceae)"; J. Sawler, J. M. Stout, K. M. Gardner, D. Hudson, J. Vidmar, L. Butler, J. E. Page, and S. Myles, "The Genetic Structure of Marijuana and Hemp," *PLoS One* 10, no. 8 (2015): e0133292.

63. In Malawi in 2008, the bioprospector Franco Loja reported being "energized by the local weed, sometimes to the point of needing less food than normal": Strain Hunters, "Africa Expedition—Malawi, " Green House Seed Company, 2010, accessed 16 August 2017, http://forums.strainhunters.com/index.html/expeditions/africa-expedition-malawi-r5.

64. J. M. Kirk, P. Doty, and H. De Wit, "Effects of Expectancies on Subjective Responses to Oral Δ9-Tetrahydrocannabinol," *Pharmacology Biochemistry and Behavior* 59, no. 2 (1998): 287–93; J. McDonald, L. Schleifer, J. B. Richards, and H. de Wit, "Effects of THC on Behavioral Measures of Impulsivity in Humans", *Neuropsychopharmacology* 28, no. 7 (2003): 1356.

65. United Nations Office on Drugs and Crime, *World Drug Report 2006*, 89, 178.

66. R. S. Londt, "An Investigation of Tetrahydrocannabinol, Cannabidiol and Cannabinol Content of Cannabis Confiscated by the South African Police Service's Forensic Laboratories from Various Regions of South Africa," Ph.D. diss., Faculty of Health Sciences, University of Cape Town, 2014.

67. United Nations Office on Drugs and Crime, *World Drug Report 2006*, 204.

68. Monteiro, *Angola and the River Congo*, 2:257.

69. M. H. Kingsley, *Travels in West Africa: Congo Français, Corisco and Cameroons* (London: Macmillan, 1897), 668.

70. C. van Overbergh, *Les Basonge (État Ind. du Congo)* (Brussels: Albert de Wit, 1908), 139, emphasis in original.

71. Bourhill, "The Smoking of *Dagga*," 38.

72. J. Higginson, *A Working Class in the Making: Belgian Colonial Labor Policy, Private Enterprise, and the African Mineworker, 1907–1951* (Madison: University of Wisconsin Press, 1990); J. Redinha, *Relatorio annual 1945* (Dundo, Angola: Companhia de Diamantes de Angola, 1946); R. F. Burton, *Explorations of the Highlands of Brazil*, vol. 2 (London: Tinsley Brothers, 1869), 276.

73. For Trinidad, see Hamid, *The Ganja Complex*.

74. Dreher, *Working Men and Ganja*; L. Comitas, "Cannabis and Work in Jamaica: A Refutation of the Amotivational Syndrome," *Annals of the New York Academy of Science* 282 (1976): 24–32.

75. M. Dreher, "Marihuana and Work: Cannabis Smoking on a Jamaican Sugar Estate," *Human Organization* 42, no. 1 (1983): 1–8.

76. W. L. Partridge, "Exchange Relationships in a Community on the North Coast of Colombia with Special Reference to Cannabis," Ph.D. diss., Department of Anthropology, University of Florida, Gainesville, 1974, 255.

77. Page, "Costa Rican Marihuana Smokers and the Amotivational Syndrome Hypothesis," 65–68, 159–60.

78. N. D. Volkow, R. D. Baler, W. M. Compton, and S. R. B. Weiss, "Adverse Health Effects of Marijuana Use," *New England Journal of Medicine* 370, no. 23 (2014): 2219–27.

79. Dreher, "Marihuana and Work," 3.

80. Clarke, "Short Notice of the African Plant Diamba," 10; M. L. Hewat, *Bantu Folk Lore (Medical and General)*, repr. ed. (New York: Negro Universities Press, [1906] 1970), 98.

81. S. Burstein, "Cannabidiol (CBD) and Its Analogs: A Review of Their Effects on Inflammation," *Bioorganic and Medicinal Chemistry* 23, no. 7 (2015): 1377–85.

82. C. Jeannest, *Quatre années au Congo* (Paris: G. Charpentier, 1883), 106.

83. Monteiro, *Angola and the River Congo*, 245.

84. P. M. Larken, "An Account of the Zande," *Sudan Notes and Records* 9, no. 1 (1926): 13.

85. H. M. Stanley, *Through the Dark Continent*, vol. 1 (London: Sampson Low, Marston, Searle, and Rivington, 1878), 68.

86. Larken, "Impressions of the Zande," 93–94.

87. Monteiro, *Angola and the River Congo*, 256–58.

88. De Carvalho implied his *mutopa* held tobacco; earlier, he had sworn off cannabis: H. A. Dias de Carvalho, *Expedição portugueza ao Muatiânvua: Descripção da viagem á Mussumba do Muatiânvua, Volume 4: Do Liembe ao Calanhe e regresso a Lisboa* (Lisbon: Typographia do Jornal, 1894), 162–63, 430.

89. Monteiro, *Angola and the River Congo*, 256–58; H. Capello and R. Ivens, *De Benguela as terras de Iácca*, vol. 2 (Lisbon: Imprensa Nacional, 1881), 26–27.

90. Monteiro, *Angola and the River Congo*, 256.

91. Daniell indicates planting in March and says this was just prior to the rains, which is contrary to precipitation patterns in northern Angola. I am accepting his date, not his description of seasonality: Daniell, "On the D'amba, or Dakka, of Southern Africa," 364. See also H. Baum, *Kunene—Sambesi-Expedition* (Berlin: Kolonial-Wirtschaftlichen Komitees, 1903), 7; J. J. d'Almeida, "Na Provincia de Angola: Administração colonial debaixo do ponto de vista agricola," pt. 1, *Revista Agronómica* 2, no. 5 (1904): 142.

92. A. Margarido, "Les porteurs: Forme de domination et agents de changement en Angola (XVIIe–XIXe siècles)," *Revue Française d'Histoire d'Outre-mer* 65, no. 240 (1978): 377–400.

93. Monteiro, *Angola and the River Congo*, 181–82.

94. A. F. F. da Silva Porto, *Viagens e apontamentos de um portuense em África* (Lisbon: Divisão de Publicações e Biblioteca, Agência Geral das Colónias, [ca. 1885] 1942), 231; Daniell, "On the D'amba, or Dakka, of Southern Africa," 365.

95. Margarido, "Les porteurs." Of course, the new transport technologies did not end labor problems; they only doomed the specific occupation of commercial, pedestrian porter.

96. A. de Saldanha da Gama, *Memoria sobre as colonias de Portugal: Situadas na costa occidental d'Afrique* (Paris: Typographia de Casimir, 1839), 74–79.

97. H. M. de Paiva Couceiro, *Relatorio de viagem entre Bailundo e as terras do Mucusso* (Lisbon: Imprensa Nacional, 1892), 9–10.

98. G. Flandrau, *Then I Saw the Congo* (New York: Harcourt, Brace, 1929), 104–5.

99. Bourhill, "The Smoking of *Dagga*," 33–38.

100. Such drugs are termed anxiolytic: S. Tambaro and M. Bortolato, "Cannabinoid-Related Agents in the Treatment of Anxiety Disorders: Current Knowledge and Future Perspectives," *Recent Patents on CNS Drug Discovery* 7, no. 1 (2012): 25–40.

101. An account suggesting paranoia: Bourhill, "The Smoking of *Dagga*," 33–34.

102. S. Ali, *Le haschisch en Égypte* (Paris: Payot, 1971), 95; J. D. Griffith, S. Mitchell, C. L. Hart, L. T. Adams, and L. L. Gu, "Pornography Actresses: An Assessment of the Damaged Goods Hypothesis," *Journal of Sex Research* 50, no. 7 (2012): 621–32; T. Bennett, K. Holloway, and D. Farrington, "The Statistical Association between Drug Misuse and Crime: A Meta-analysis," *Aggression and Violent Behavior* 13, no. 2 (2008): 107–18.

103. R. K. Das, S. K. Kamboj, M. Ramadas, K. Yogan, V. Gupta, E. Redman, H. V. Curran, and C. J. Morgan, "Cannabidiol Enhances Consolidation of Explicit Fear Extinction in Humans," *Psychopharmacology* 226, no. 4 (2013): 781–92; V. Trezza and P. Campolongo, "The Endocannabinoid System as a Possible Target to Treat Both the Cognitive and Emotional Features of Post-traumatic Stress Disorder (PTSD)," *Frontiers in Behavioral Neuroscience* 9, no. 7 (2013): 100–110. However, CBD—low in sub-Saharan cannabis—appears to have an important role in this pharmacology.

104. M. S. Ferrara, *Sacred Bliss: A Spiritual History of Cannabis* (New York: Rowman and Littlefield, 2016).

105. E. B. Edmonds, *Rastafari: A Very Short Introduction* (Oxford: Oxford University Press, 2012), 38–39, 48.

106. Campos, *Home Grown*; Pernambuco, "A maconha em Pernambuco," 190; A. Chevalier, "Histoire de deux plantes cultivées d'importance primordiale: Le lin et le chanvre," *Revue de Botanique Appliquée et d'Agriculture Coloniale* 24, nos. 269–71 (1944): 68; J. Navarrete, *Desde Vad-Ras à Sevilla: Acuarelas de la Campaña de África* (Madrid: Víctor Saiz, 1880), 221; J. F. Siler, W. L. Sheep, G. W. Cook, W. A. Smith, L. B. Bates, and G. F. Clark, "Mariajuana Smoking in Panama," *Military Surgeon* 73 (1933): 269–80; "Military Police Start War against Mariahuana Users," *Evening Herald* (Albuquerque, NM), 6 September 1917, 3.

107. Cohen, "Resistance and Hidden Forms of Consciousness amongst African Workers."

108. R. Brunel, *Le monachisme errant dans l'Islam* (Paris: Maisonneuve et Larose, [1955] 2001).

109. Bourhill, "The Smoking of *Dagga*"; Monteiro, "Folclore da maconha"; K. Bilby, "The Holy Herb: Notes on the Background of Cannabis in Jamaica," *Caribbean Quarterly* (1985): 82–95; H. Chatelain and W. R. Summers, "Bantu Notes and Vocabularies, No. 1: The Language of the Bashi-Lange and Ba-Luba," *Journal of the American Geographical Society of New York* 25, no. 4 (1893): 512–41; B. M. du Toit, "Linguistic

Subterfuge: Its Use by Drug Users in South Africa," *Anthropological Linguistics* 22, no. 1 (1980): 22–28; R. Bucher, "La marihuana en el folklore y la cultura popular brasileña," *Revista Takiwasi* 2, no. 3 (1995): 119–28; E. Dias, "A influência da maconha no folclore maranhense," *Revista Maranhense de Cultura* 1 (1974): 1; "O Dicionário da Maconha," *O Estado de São Paulo*, 1958, n.p., Centro Nacional de Folclore e Cultura Popular, Rio de Janeiro, accessed 30 April 2018, http://docvirt.com/docreader.net/DocReader.aspx ?bib=Tematico&PagFis=30147&Pesq=; "Aspectos folk-lóricos da Maconha," *Diário de Sergipe*, 26 August 1948, 4, Centro Nacional de Folclore e Cultura Popular, Rio de Janeiro, accessed 30 April 2018, http://docvirt.com/docreader.net/DocReader.aspx?bib =tematico&pagfis=30149.

110. Cohen, "Resistance and Hidden Forms of Consciousness amongst African Workers," 9, 19.

111. Bourhill, "The Smoking of *Dagga*," 35.

112. O. Lenz, *Timbuktu: Reise durch Marokko, die Sahara und den Sudan*, vol. 1 (Leipzig: F. A. Brockhaus, 1892), 207.

113. H. von Wissmann, *Unter deutscher Flagge quer durch Afrika von West nach Ost* (Berlin: Walther und Apolant, 1889), 254.

114. In this instance, I am quoting a well-phrased English-language encapsulation of Douville's book: "[Review of] *Voyage au Congo, et dans l'Interieur de l'Afrique Equinoxiale*, . . . By J. B. Douville, . . . Paris, 1832," *Nautical Journal* 1, no. 4 (1832): 202. The book is J.-B. Douville, *Voyage au Congo et dans l'interieur de l'Afrique equinoxiale, fait dans les années 1828, 1829, et 1830*, vol. 1 (Paris: Chez Jules Renouard, 1832), 132.

115. H. Capello and R. Ivens, *De Benguela as terras de Iácca: Descripção de uma viagem na Africa central e occidental*, vol. 1 (Lisbon: Imprensa Nacional, 1881), 359.

116. Dreher, *Working Men and Ganja*; Comitas, "Cannabis and Work in Jamaica"; Page, "Costa Rican Marihuana Smokers and the Amotivational Syndrome Hypothesis"; R. Hirst, L. Sodos, S. Gade, and L. Rathke, "Motivation in Chronic Cannabis Use," in *Handbook of Cannabis and Related Pathologies: Biology, Pharmacology, Diagnosis, and Treatment*, ed. V. R. Preedy (London: Academic, 2016), 288–97. The amotivational syndrome hypothesis remains attractive to some medical researchers, who have reported evidence in its support: A. Lac and J. W. Luk, "Testing the Amotivational Syndrome: Marijuana Use Longitudinally Predicts Lower Self-Efficacy Even after Controlling for Demographics, Personality, and Alcohol and Cigarette Use," *Prevention Science* 19, no. 2 (2017): 117–26, https://doi.org/10.1007/S11121-017-0811-3; W. Lawn, T. P. Freeman, R. A. Pope, A. Joye, L. Harvey, C. Hindocha, C. Mokrysz, A. Moss, M. B. Wall, and M. A. Bloomfield, "Acute and Chronic Effects of Cannabinoids on Effort-Related Decision-Making and Reward Learning: An Evaluation of the Cannabis 'Amotivational' Hypotheses," *Psychopharmacology* 233, nos. 19–20 (2016): 3537–52.

117. C. Söllner, *Un voyage au Congo*, 2d ed. (Namur, Belgium: Auguste Godenne, 1897), 89.

118. Burton, *The Lake Regions of Central Africa*, 243, 343.

119. Kingsley, *Travels in West Africa*, 668.

120. See Curto, *Enslaving Spirits*.

121. Kingsley, *Travels in West Africa*, 668.

122. Monteiro, *Angola and the River Congo*, 245.

123. Margarido, "Les porteurs"; D. A. Livingstone, *Missionary Travels and Researches in South Africa* (London: John Murray, 1857), 356.

124. Kingsley, *Travels in West Africa*, 668.

125. For examples, see Capello and Ivens, *De Benguela as terras de Iácca*, 2:26; Martrin-Donos, *Les Belges dans l'Afrique Centrale*, 268; P. B. Du Chaillu, *Explorations and Adventures in Equatorial Africa* (New York: Harper Brothers, 1861), 420; J. de Mattos e Silva, *Contribução para o estudo da Região de Cabinda* (Lisbon: Typographia Universal, 1904), 263; A. de Serpa Pinto, *How I Crossed Africa*, vol. 2 (London: Sampson Low, Marston, Searle, and Rivington, 1881), 32–33.

126. Capello and Ivens, *De Benguela as terras de Iácca*, 2:27.

127. Bourhill, "The Smoking of *Dagga*"; F. C. Wellman, "Some Medicinal Plants of Angola, with Observations on Their Use by Natives of the Province," *American Medicine* 11, no. 3 (1906): 94–99; M'Henry, "An Account of the Liberated African Establishment at St. Helena," 437.

128. C. F. P. von Martius, *Systema materiae medicae vegetabilis brasiliensis* (Vienna: Friedrich Beck, 1843), 121.

129. Courtwright, *Forces of Habit*.

130. Flandrau, *Then I Saw the Congo*, 140.

131. M. Alloula, *The Colonial Harem* (Minneapolis: University of Minnesota Press, 1986).

132. D. Maghraoui, "Knowledge, Gender, and Spatial Configuration in Colonial Casablanca," in *Revisiting the Colonial Past in Morocco*, ed. D. Maghraoui (New York: Routledge, 2013), 64–86. Colonial French troops smoked and drank with women whom they paid for sexual services: see C. Taraud, "Jouer avec la marginalité: Le cas des filles soumises 'indigènes' du quartier réservé de Casablanca dans les années 1920–1950," *Clio: Histoire, Femmes et Sociétés* 17 (2003), https://doi.org/10.4000/clio.582; C. Taraud, "Urbanisme, hygiénisme et prostitution à Casablanca dans les années 1920," *French Colonial History* 7 (2006): 97–108; A.-P. Comor, "Les plaisirs des légionnaires au temps des colonies : L'alcool et les femmes," *Guerres Mondiales et Conflits Contemporains* 2, no. 222 (2006): 33–42.

133. A. Merzouki, F. Ed-derfoufi, and J. Molero Mesa, "Hemp (*Cannabis Sativa* L.) and Abortion," *Journal of Ethnobiology* 73 (2000): 501–3.

134. Her use in Europe deserves an asterisk. This is stated in recent cultural studies that do not cite primary sources. See, e.g., Z. S. Strother, "Display of the Body Hottentot," in *Africans on Stage: Studies in Ethnological Show Business*, ed. B. Lindfors (Bloomington: Indiana University Press, 1999), 20. Drawings of Baartman show her smoking a dry pipe, but no source of cannabis supply in Europe is documented for the time that she was there.

135. L. Mott, "A maconha na história do Brasil," in *Diamba sarabamba*, ed. A. Henman and O. Pessoa Jr. (São Paulo: Ground, 1986), 117–35; A. M. G. R. Oda, "Escravidão e nostalgia no Brasil: O banzo," *Revista Latinoamericana de Psicopatologia Fundamental* 11 (2008): 735–61.

136. [A. J.] Mello Moraes Filho, *Revista da Exposição Anthropologica Brazileira* (Rio de Janeiro: Pinheiro, 1882), 30.

137. "Human African Trypanosomiasis," World Health Organization, 2017, accessed 17 September 2018, http://www.who.int/trypanosomiasis_african/disease /diagnosis/en/.

138. M. Lyons, *The Colonial Disease: A Social History of Sleeping Sickness in Northern Zaire, 1900–1940* (Cambridge: Cambridge University Press, 1992); L. Sambon, "The Elucidation of Sleeping Sickness," *Journal of Tropical Medicine* 7 (15 February 1904): 61–63.

139. D. Steverding, "The History of African Trypanosomiasis," *Parasites and Vectors* 1 (2008): 3, https://doi.org./10-1186/1756-3305-1-3.

140. Sambon, "The Elucidation of Sleeping Sickness," 61.

141. Steverding, "The History of African Trypanosomiasis."

142. "Neglected Tropical Diseases," World Health Organization, 2017, accessed 17 September 2018, http://www.who.int/neglected_diseases/diseases/en/.

143. This association is not mentioned in previous histories of cannabis or of sleeping sickness.

144. Sierra Leoneans called it "sleepy dropsy": R. O. Clarke, "Observations on the Disease Lethargus: With Cases and Pathology," *London Medical Gazette* 26 (1839–40): 973. Robert O. Clarke is not to be confused with Robert Connell Clarke, the leading field biologist of cannabis today.

145. He was stationed in Gold Coast Colony (modern Ghana) in 1860: R. O. Clarke, "Gold Coast, Enclosure No. 1, Medical Report for the Year 1858," in *The Reports Made for the Year 1858 to the Secretary of State Having the Department of the Colonies: The Past and Present State of Her Majesty's Colonial Possessions, Part II* (London: George Edward Eyre and William Spottiswoode, 1860): 29.

146. The textbook's first edition is A. Hirsch, *Handbuch der historisch-geographischen Pathologie*, vol. 2 (Erlangen, Germany: Ferdinand Enke, 1862–64), 661. In the second edition, palm wine was similarly rejected as a cause: A. Hirsch, *Handbuch der historisch-geographischen Pathologie*, 2d ed., vol. 3 (Stuttgart: Ferdinand Enke, 1886), 418.

147. Baum, *Kunene*, 106; A. de Sarmento, *Os sertões d'África (Apontamentos de Viagem)* (Lisbon: Francisco Arthur da Silva, 1880), 106.

148. Baum, *Kunene*, 106. Of course, sleeping sickness was more prominent farther north, mostly from Luanda to Cameroon, including inland and on the Gulf of Guinea islands.

149. Monteiro, *Angola and the River Congo*, 257.

150. Gleim characterizes the knowledge as "often rehearsed" among "the laity," meaning nonphysicians on the western Central African coast: Dr. Gleim, "Berichte über die Schlafkrankheit der Neger im Kongogebiete," *Archiv für Schiffs- und Tropen-Hygiene* 4, no. 6 (1900): 361–62.

151. Ministerio da Marinha e Ultramar, *Doença do Somno: Relatorios enviados ao ministerio da marinha pela missão scientifica nomeada por portaria de 21 de fevereiro de 1901* (Lisbon: Libanio da Silva, 1901), 5–6.

152. Lyons, *The Colonial Disease*; Sambon, "The Elucidation of Sleeping Sickness."

153. Steverding, "The History of African Trypanosomiasis."

154. Mattos e Silva, *Contribuição para o estudo da Região de Cabinda*, 263.

155. E. Viaene and F. Bernard, "L'art de guérir chez les peuplades congolaises," *Bulletin de la Société Royale Belge de Géographie* 35 (1911): 44. A complementary narrative was, "As excessive hemp-smoking produces impotence, it is one among the many checks to the increase of population in uncontrolled negro Africa": H. Johnston, *George Grenfell and the Congo: A History and Description of the Congo Independent State and Adjoining Districts of Congoland*, vol. 2 (London: Hutchinson, 1908), 609.

156. Lyons, *The Colonial Disease*; J. Ford, *The Role of the Trypanosomiases in African Ecology: A Study of the Tsetse Fly Problem* (Oxford: Clarendon, 1971).

157. A. Crosby, *Ecological Imperialism: The Biological Expansion of Europe, 900–1900* (Cambridge: Cambridge University Press, 1986).

158. F. L. Lambrecht, "Aspects of the Evolution and Ecology of Tsetse Flies and Trypanosomiasis in the Prehistoric African Environment," in *Papers in African Prehistory*, ed. J. D. Fage and R. A. Oliver (Cambridge: Cambridge University Press, 1970), 93.

159. Sambon, "The Elucidation of Sleeping Sickness," 61; Steverding, "The History of African Trypanosomiasis."

160. R. Matas, "Morbid Somnolence," *New Orleans Medical and Surgical Journal* 11 (1883–84): 510–525, 523.

161. Higgs, *Chocolate Islands*, 58–64.

162. Higgs, *Chocolate Islands*, 58.

163. Sambon, "The Elucidation of Sleeping Sickness," 61.

164. The mortality rate was given simultaneously as an *incidence* rate: "12 deaths per 178 Europeans . . . ; 821 deaths for 4,569 individuals of the black race." Confirmation that the statistics are simultaneously incidence and death rates is that, on one farm, "all the individuals in which the illness was verified, died": see Ministerio da Marinha e Ultramar, *Doença do Somno*, 8–9.

165. F. La Greca and S. Magez, "Vaccination against Trypanosomiasis: Can It Be Done or Is the Trypanosome Truly the Ultimate Immune Destroyer and Escape Artist?" *Human Vaccines* 7, no. 11 (2011): 1225–33.

166. Admittedly, some of the laborers in the São Tomé sample may have arrived carrying the infection from the mainland.

167. T. Winterbottom, *An Account of the Native Africans in the Neighbourhood of Sierra Leone*, vol. 2 (London: C. Whittingham, 1803), 30. The diagnostic symptom, swollen lymph glands, is still called Winterbottom's sign.

168. Commissariat General du Gouvernement, "Circulaire au sujet des mesures à prendre contre l'usage et la diffusion du chanvre," *Bulletin Officiel Administratif des Possessions du Congo Français et Dépendances et du Moyen-Congo* (March 1907): 161–62.

169. Monteiro, *Angola and the River Congo*, 256; Capello and Ivens, *De Benguela as terras de Iácca*, 1:188, 359.

170. d'Almeida, "Na Provincia de Angola," 145.

171. These guides were from Zanzibar: Martrin-Donos, *Les Belges dans l'Afrique Centrale*, 453.

172. O. Likaka, *Naming Colonialism: History and Collective Memory in the Congo, 1870–1960* (Madison: University of Wisconsin Press, 2009), 46.

173. Government of the Colony of Natal, *Departmental Reports*, B14; Government of the Colony of Natal, *Supplement to the Blue Book for the Colony of Natal: Departmental Reports, 1890–91* (Pietermaritzburg: P. Davis and Sons, 1892), B95.

174. J. Rebman, *Dictionary of the Kiniassa Language* (St. Chrischona, Switzerland: Church Missionary Society, 1877), 134; H. A. Junod, *The Life of a South African Tribe, 1: The Social Life* (Neuchatel, Switzerland: Attinger Frères, 1912), 314; J. Tyler, *Forty Years among the Zulus* (Boston: Congregational Sunday-School and Publishing Society, 1891), 123.

175. Government of the Colony of Natal, *Supplement to the Blue Book for the Colony of Natal*, B95.

9. BUYING AND BANNING

1. A. Bordier, *La colonization scientifique et les colonies françaises* (Paris: C. Reinwald, 1884), 326.

2. H. M. Stanley, *The Congo and the Founding of Its Free State: A Story of Work and Exploration*, vol. 2 (New York: Harper Brothers, 1885), 345.

3. D. Bewley-Taylor, T. Blickman, and M. Jelsma, *The Rise and Decline of Cannabis Prohibition* (Amsterdam: Transnational Institute, 2014); A. Rathge, "Cannabis Cures: American Medicine, Mexican Marijuana, and the Origins of the War on Weed, 1840–1937," Ph.D. diss., Department of History, Boston College, 2017. Africa has been neglected in recent studies of international cannabis-control laws: see, e.g., D. R. Bewley-Taylor, *International Drug Control: Consensus Fractured* (Cambridge: Cambridge University Press, 2012), 152–218.

4. C. S. Duvall, "Drug Laws, Bioprospecting, and the Agricultural Heritage of *Cannabis* in Africa," *Space and Polity* 20, no. 1 (2016): 10–25.

5. C. S. Duvall, *Cannabis* (London: Reaktion, 2015), chap. 5; C. S. Duvall, "Book Review: *Cannabis: Evolution and Ethnobotany*, by Robert C. Clarke and Mark D. Merlin," *Geographical Review* 104, no. 4 (2014): 523–26.

6. J. M. Wood, "Native Hemp," *Natal Agricultural Journal* 10, no. 11 (1907): 1365–67.

7. In the United States in 1927, for example, ten years before the country effectively prohibited the plant, less than half of 1 percent of cordage came from cannabis, and most of that was packaging twine, the cheapest, lowest-quality line available: H. T. Lewis, "Distribution of Hard Fiber Cordage," Bulletin 82, *Publications of the Graduate School of Business Administration, Harvard University* 17, no. 1 (1930): 9.

8. Indian Hemp Drugs Commission, *Report of the Indian Hemp Drugs Commission, 1893–1894* (Simla, India: Government Central Printing Office, 1894).

9. W. F. Daniell, "On the D'amba, or Dakka, of Southern Africa," *Pharmaceutical Journal and Transactions* 9, no. 8 (1850): 363–65; D. A. Livingstone, *Missionary Travels and Researches in South Africa* (London: John Murray, 1857), 356; F. Welwitsch, *Synopse explicativa das amostras de madeiras e drogas medicinaes e de otros objectivos normente ethnographicos colligidos na provincia de Angola* (Lisbon: Imprensa Nacional, 1862), 45.

10. H. M. de Paiva Couceiro, *Relatorio de viagem entre Bailundo e as terras do Mucusso* (Lisbon: Imprensa Nacional, 1892), 44.

11. B. J. Brochado, "Terras do Humbe, Camba, Mulondo, Quanhama, e outras, contendo uma idéa da sua população, seus costumes, vestuarios, etc.," *Annaes do Conselho Ultramarino, Parte Não Official*, series 1 (November [1855] 1867): 195.

12. Welwitsch, *Synopse explicativa das amostras de madeiras e drogas medicinaes e de otros objectivos normente ethnographicos colligidos na provincia de Angola*, 45.

13. Daniell, "On the D'amba, or Dakka, of Southern Africa," 363.

14. Daniell, "On the D'amba, or Dakka, of Southern Africa," 363; H. Baum, *Kunene— Sambesi-Expedition* (Berlin: Kolonial-Wirtschaftlichen Komitees, 1903), 7; "Deïamba, nouveau narcotique," *Journal de Pharmacie et de Chimie* 14 (1848): 201; Monsieur Ponel, "Note sur les M'Bochis," *Bulletin de la Société de Géographie* 7, 7th series (1886): 377; C. Coquilhat, *Sur le Haut-Congo* (Paris: J. Lebègue, 1888), 348; P. B. Du Chaillu, *Journey to Ashango-Land: And Further Penetration into Equatorial Africa* (New York: Harper Brothers, 1871), 35, 326.

15. Daniell, "On the D'amba, or Dakka, of Southern Africa," 363; "Deïamba, nouveau narcotique"; A. Sisenando Marques, *Expedição portugueza ao Muata-Ianvo: Os climas e as producções das terras de Malange á Lunda* (Lisbon: Imprensa Nacional, 1889), 172; J.-B. Douville, *Voyage au Congo et dans l'interieur de l'Afrique equinoxiale, fait dans les années 1828, 1829, et 1830*, vol. 1 (Paris: Jules Renouard, 1832), 127; A. Werner, *The Natives of British Central Africa*, vol. 3 (London: Archibald Constable, 1906), 179.

16. Welwitsch, *Synopse explicativa das amostras de madeiras e drogas medicinaes e de otros objectivos normente ethnographicos colligidos na provincia de Angola*, 45.

17. For accounts of cannabis horticulture beyond Central and Southern Africa, see P. C. Standley, *Contributions from the United States National Herbarium, Volume 28: Flora of the Panama Canal Zone* (Washington, DC: U.S. Government Printing Office, 1928), 164, 215; R. F. Burton, *The Lake Regions of Central Africa: A Picture of Exploration* (New York: Harper Brothers, 1860), 81; Conde de Ficalho, *Plantas úteis da África portuguesa*, 2d ed. (Lisbon: Agência Geral das Colónias, [1884] 1947), 265; A. J. de Macedo Soares, "Estudos lexicographicos do dialecto Braziliero, 4: Sobre algumas palavras africanas introduzidas no Portuguez que se fala no Brazil," *Revista Brazileira* 1, no. 4 (1880): 267; I. Dukerley, "Note sur les différences que présente avec le chanvre ordinaire et la variété de cette espèce connue en Algérie sous les noms de *kif* et de *tekrouri*," *Bulletin de la Société Botanique de France* 3 (9 November 1866): 401–6; J. A. de Alzate, "Memoria sobre el uso que hacen los Indios de los pipiltezintzintlis," in *Memorias y ensayos*, ed. R. Moreno (Mexico City: Universidad Nacional Autónoma de México, 1985), 57.

18. For Mexican markets, see I. Campos, *Home Grown: Marijuana and the Origins of Mexico's War on Drugs* (Chapel Hill: University of North Carolina Press, 2012).

19. "Manoel Francisco Pedroso . . . ," *Jornal do Commercio*, 21 February 1847, 3.

20. J. J. Monteiro, *Angola and the River Congo*, vol. 2 (London: Macmillan, 1875), 28. On the influence of market women in historic Angolan society, see S. Pantoja, "Women's Work in the Fairs and Markets of Luanda," in *Women in the Portuguese Colonial Empire: The Theatre of Shadows*, ed. C. Sarmento (Newcastle upon Tyne, UK: Cambridge Scholars, 2008), 81–94.

21. É. Dupont, *Lettres sur le Congo: Récit d'un voyage scientifique entre l'embouchure du fleuve et le confluent du Kassaï* (Paris: C. Reinwald, 1889), 643.

22. A. Chevalier, "Histoire de deux plantes cultivées d'importance primordiale: Le lin et le chanvre," *Revue de Botanique Appliquée et d'Agriculture Coloniale* 24, nos. 269–71 (1944): 67.

23. Ponel, "Note sur les M'Bochis," 377; Présidence de la République, France, "Interdiction de la culture du chanvre et repression de son emploi comme stupéfiant en Afrique équatoriale française: Rapport et Décret de 29 août 1926," *Journal Officiel de la République Française* 58, no. 207 (1926): 10017.

24. J. de Mattos e Silva, *Contribução para o estudo da Região de Cabinda* (Lisbon: Universal, 1904), 263; J. Redinha, *Relatorio annual 1945* (Dundo, Angola: Companhia de Diamantes de Angola, 1946), 27; E. Viaene and F. Bernard, "L'art de guérir chez les peuplades congolaises," *Bulletin de la Société Royale Belge de Géographie* 35 (1911): 41; J. Gossweiler, *Flora exótica de Angola: Nomes vulgares e origem das plantas cultivadas ou subespontâneas* (Luanda: Imprensa Nacional, 1950), 35.

25. Welwitsch, *Synopse explicativa das amostras de madeiras e drogas medicinaes e de otros objectivos normente ethnographicos colligidos na provincia de Angola*, 45.

26. People in Gabon grew cannabis in sunny, hilltop patches: P. B. Du Chaillu, *Explorations and Adventures in Equatorial Africa* (New York: Harper Brothers, 1861), 420.

27. C. G. Sampson, "'Zeer grote liefhebbers van tobak': Nicotine and Cannabis Dependency of the Seacow River Bushmen," *Digging Stick* 10, no. 1 (1993): 6; C. I. Latrobe, *Journal of a Visit to South Africa in 1815 and 1816* (New York: Negro Universities Press, [1818] 1969), 325.

28. C. Seguin, "Les hallucinations d'un fumeur de chanvre au Gabon," *Journal des Voyages* 704 (29 May 1910): 427; D. J. Harvey, "Stability of Cannabinoids in Dried Samples of Cannabis Dating from around 1896–1905," *Journal of Ethnopharmacology* 28 (1990): 120.

29. A German associate of Wissmann and Pogge bought *riamba* for his Bena Riamba porters when returning to the Atlantic coast in 1883: J. Fabian, *Out of Our Minds: Reason and Madness in the Exploration of Central Africa* (Berkeley: University of California Press, 2000), 162.

30. J. P. Browne, "The Lado Enclave and Its Commercial Possibilities," *Scottish Geographical Magazine* 22, no. 10 (1906): 533.

31. Kaiserlichen Gouverneurs in Deutsch-Ostafrika, "Verordnung des kaiserlichen Gouverneurs vom 2. September 1891, betreffend den Verkauf von Opium und gleichartigen Genussmitteln in Deutsch-Ostafrika," in *Austria: Archiv für Gesetzgebung und Statistik, XLIII. Jahrgang*, ed. Statistichen Departement im Kaiserlich-Königlichen Handelsministerium (Vienna: Kaiserlich-Königlichen Hof- und Staatsdruckerei, 1891), 514.

32. E. Wangermée, "Culture, vente, etc., du chanvre à fumer: Interdiction," *Bulletin Officiel de l'État Indépendant du Congo* 19 (February–March 1903): 36–38.

33. For instance, German East Africa's 25 percent *ad valorem* import tariff could not have generated meaningful revenue: Historical Section of the Foreign Service, *Tanganyika (German East Africa)*, Handbooks Prepared under the Direction of the Historical Section of the Foreign Office, no. 113 (London: Her Majesty's Stationery Office, 1920), 98.

34. E. Trivier, *Mon voyage au Continent Noir: La "Gironde" en Afrique* (Paris: Firmin-Didot and J. Rouam, 1891), 276.

35. D. C. Rankin, "Atrocities in the Kongo Free State," *The Independent* 52, no. 2670 (1 February 1900): 305.

36. Wangermée, "Culture, vente, etc., du chanvre à fumer."

37. Browne, "The Lado Enclave and Its Commercial Possibilities," 33.

38. R. Wingate, "The Hashish Ordinance 1907," in *Compte rendu de la session tenue à La Haye*, ed. Institut Colonial International (Brussels: Institut Colonial International, 1909), 415–18.

39. Governor-General of the Sudan, "The Contraband Goods Ordinance 1901," in *Ordinances Promulgated by the Governor-General of the Sudan* (Cairo: Al-Mokkattam, 1901), 62–64. Ḥashīsh smuggling was active in Sudan by 1914; supplies came from the Red Sea, either directly from Sudan's coastline or overland from Abyssinia. People also still grew cannabis locally: P. F. Martin, *The Sudan in Evolution: A Study of the Economic Financial and Administrative Conditions of the Anglo-Egyptian Sudan* (London: Constable, 1921), 105.

40. The decree allowed fiber production: J. Sibree, *Madagascar and Its People* (London: Religious Tract Society, 1870), 215; J. Sibree, *The Great African Island* (London: Trübner, 1880), 95.

41. R. Baron, "Jottings on Some of the Plants of Imerina," *Antananarivo Annual and Madagascar Magazine* 3 (1878): 109.

42. Merina royalty banned alcohol at the same time: J. F. A. Ajayi, ed., *General History of Africa, Volume 6: Africa in the Nineteenth Century until the 1880s* (Paris: United Nations Educational, Scientific and Cultural Organization, 1989), 442–43. Similarly, in 1921 the Congolese prophet Kimbangu banned cannabis, alcohol, and smoking as signs of spiritual backwardness: S. Asch, *L'église du prophète Kimbangu: De ses origines à son rôle actuel au Zaïre, 1921–1981* (Paris: Karthala, 1983).

43. This ban was justified in religious terms: J. Ohrwalder, *Ten Years' Captivity in the Mahdi's Camp: 1882–1892* (Leipzig: Heinemann and Balestier, 1893), 17.

44. M. Dinnerstein, "The American Zulu Mission in the Nineteenth Century: Clash over Customs," *Church History* 45, no. 2 (1976): 245–46; J. Tyler, *Forty Years among the Zulus* (Boston: Congregational Sunday-School and Publishing Society, 1891), 159.

45. Cannabis smoking provoked forty-six of sixty-eight excommunications from a missionary church in eastern Congo in 1907, four years into prohibition: N. R. Hunt, *A Colonial Lexicon: Of Birth Ritual, Medicalization, and Mobility in the Congo* (Durham, NC: Duke University Press, 1999), 55–56, 61.

46. Duvall, "Drug Laws, Bioprospecting, and the Agricultural Heritage of *Cannabis* in Africa."

47. Sibthorpe, quoted in C. Fyfe, "A. B. C. Sibthorpe: A Tribute," *History in Africa* 19 (1992): 341.

48. Protectorate of Sierra Leone, *Report by Her Majesty's Commissioner and Correspondence on the subject of the Insurrection in the Sierra Leone Protectorate 1898, Part I: Report and Correspondence* (London: Her Majesty's Stationery Office, 1899), 20, 25.

49. J. H. Mills, *Cannabis Britannica: Empire, Trade, and Prohibition, 1800–1928* (Oxford: Oxford University Press, 2003). Most laws that followed the 1912 convention restricted only opium, morphine, cocaine, "and similar drugs." The phrase "similar drugs" might have been construed to mean cannabis, but I have found no laws following the 1912

Convention that explicitly included cannabis: see C. Ilbert, "Review of Legislation, 1913" *Journal of the Society of Comparative Legislation* 15, series 2 (1915): i–xii, 1–181.

50. League of Nations, "No. 1845: International Convention, Adopted by the Second Opium Conference (League of Nations), and Protocol Relating Thereto, Signed at Geneva, February 19, 1925," in *League of Nations—Treaty Series* (Geneva: League of Nations, 1928): 329, 333.

51. Protectorate of Sierra Leone, *Dangerous Drugs Ordinance, No. 10 of 1926*, 1926, accessed 30 April 2018, https://www.sierralii.org/sl/legislation/act/2016/10.

52. E. Akyeampong, "Diaspora and Drug Trafficking in West Africa: A Case Study of Ghana," *African Affairs* 104, no. 416 (2005): 429–47. Akyeampong states that Sierra Leone added cannabis to its drug-control ordinances in 1920 but cites no source: Akyeampong, "Diaspora and Drug Trafficking in West Africa," 432. I have not identified a 1920 listing.

53. U.S. Bureau of Narcotics, *Traffic in Opium and Other Dangerous Drugs for the Year Ended December 31, 1934* (Washington, DC: U.S. Government Printing Office, 1935), 79.

54. Akyeampong, "Diaspora and Drug Trafficking in West Africa." Sailors were early traffickers in Brazil too, and their networks extended internationally. In 1934 a Brazilian boat brought 31 pounds of cannabis into Baltimore, Maryland: U.S. Bureau of Narcotics, *Traffic in Opium and Other Dangerous Drugs for the Year Ended December 31, 1934*, 42, 79; J. Pernambuco, "A maconha em Pernambuco," in *Novos estudos Afro-brasileiros: Trabalhos apresentados ao 1. Congresso Afro-brasileiro do Recife*, ed. A. Ramos (Rio de Janeiro: Civilização Brasileira, 1937), 190; J. R. da Costa Doria, "Os fumadores de maconha: Efeitos males do vicio," in *Proceedings of the Second Pan American Scientific Congress*, ed. G. L. Swiggett (Washington, DC: U.S. Government Printing Office, 1917): 154; D. Pierson, *O homem no vale do São Francisco*, vol. 2 (Rio de Janeiro: Ministério do Intérior, 1972), 97.

55. I exclude hashish, because the formal markets I will discuss below were for herbal material, not resin.

56. People also sold larger packets of leaves for the same price: R. O. Clarke, "Short Notice of the African Plant Diamba, Commonly Called Congo Tobacco," *Hooker's Journal of Botany* 3 (1851): 11.

57. The British monetary system was decimalized in 1971. In the pre-decimal system, one pound equaled 20 shillings or 240 pence or 480 half-pennies. Pre-decimal values were published in abbreviated forms, with "s" representing shillings and "d" representing pence; the pounds, shillings, and pence quantities were each followed by points. For example, a value of two pounds, ten shillings, and twelve-and-a-half pence was abbreviated as £2.10s.12½d. I use this form of abbreviation in these notes. Since the pre-decimal system will be unfamiliar to most readers, in the main text I provide decimal equivalents of pre-decimal values, which I provide in the notes. The decimal values are anachronistic, but useful in making the information legible to modern readers.

58. Clarke, "Short Notice of the African Plant Diamba," 10.

59. The historical farmers used fertilizer and irrigation. Height is less informative for yield than other factors, such as number of flowering tips. For yield estimates, see J. Cervantes, *Marijuana Outdoors: Guerrilla Growing* ([Sacramento, CA]: Van Patten, 2000);

E. Rosenthal, *Ed Rosenthal's Marijuana Grower's Handbook* (Oakland, CA: Quick American Archives, 2010).

60. The pre-decimal values for the range in this sentence are £1.5s. to £5.

61. R. F. Burton, *Explorations of the Highlands of Brazil*, vol. 1 (London: Tinsley Brothers, 1869), 276.

62. T. Simon, *The Brazilian Cambist's Help; Being a Ready Reckoner of Arbitrated Exchanges between Brazil, London, Paris, Hamburgh, and Lisbon* (London: Longmans, Green, Reader, and Dyer, 1869), 36.

63. £2.16s.8d. to £7.1s.8d.

64. Comte d'Estève, "Mémoire sur les finances de l'Égypte, depuis sa conquête par le sultan Selym I. er jusqu'à celle du général en chef Bonaparte," in *Description de l'Égypte*, ed. Commission des Sciences et des Artes d'Égypte (Paris: Impériale, 1809), 341.

65. J. P. Brown, *The Dervishes; or, Oriental Spiritualism* (London: Trübner, 1868), 308–12; E. A. W. Budge, *The Egyptian Sûdân: Its History and Monuments*, vol. 1 (London: Kegan Paul, Trench, Trübner, 1907), 222; W. Chambers and R. Chambers, "The Wakalahs, or Commercial Hotels of Egypt," *Chambers' Edinburgh Journal* 10, no. 258, new series (1848): 380.

66. Monsieur Rouyer, "Notice sur les médicaments usuels des Égyptiens," in *Description de l'Égypte*, ed. Commission des Sciences et des Artes d'Égypte (Paris: Imprimerie Impériale, 1809), 217–32.

67. L. Kozma, "Cannabis Prohibition in Egypt, 1880–1939: From Local Ban to League of Nations Diplomacy," *Middle Eastern Studies* 47, no. 3 (2011): 443–60.

68. Kozma, "Cannabis Prohibition in Egypt"; G. G. Nahas, "Hashish and Drug Abuse in Egypt during the 19th and 20th Centuries," *Bulletin of the New York Academy of Medicine* 61, no. 5 (1985): 428–44.

69. W. C. Mackenzie, "Hashish in Egypt," *Chemist and Druggist* 42 (29 July 1893): 183; "Pharmaceutical Trip in the Levant," *Chemist and Druggist* 36 (22 March 1890): 411–12.

70. C. S. Duvall, "Cannabis and Tobacco in Precolonial and Colonial Africa," in *Oxford Research Encyclopedia of African History*, ed. T. Spear (New York: Oxford University Press, 2017), accessed 24 April 2018, http://africanhistory. oxfordre. com/view/10.1093/acrefore/9780190277734.001.0001/acrefore-9780190277734-e-44.

71. Of the 1,703 cafés, European residents owned 22: E. A. W. Budge, ed., *Cook's Handbook for Egypt and the Sûdân*, 2d ed. (London: Thomas Cook and Son, 1906), 319.

72. Mackenzie, "Hashish in Egypt."

73. G. W. Herringham, "The Desert Coast Guard," *Cavalry Journal* 3, no. 12 (1908): 443–54.

74. The reported quantities were an average of four tons impounded of sixty-five total tons: Nahas, "Hashish and Drug Abuse in Egypt during the 19th and 20th Centuries," 432. Further, law enforcement did not seem to have significantly affected overall consumption. The 1919–24 estimated annual imports were only five tons less than what was estimated in 1907, seventy tons: A. Marie, "Note sur la folie haschichique," *Nouvelle Iconographie de la Salpêtrière* 20 (1907): 254.

75. H. de Monfried and I. Treat, *Pearls, Arms, and Hashish* (New York: Coward-McCann, 1930), 181.

76. Marie, "Note sur la folie haschichique," 253–54. See also Kozma, "Cannabis Prohibition in Egypt."

77. Monfried and Treat, *Pearls, Arms, and Hashish*, 180.

78. F. Bère, *Les tabacs* (Paris: Réunies, 1895), 243–44.

79. K. Afsahi and K. Mouna, "Cannabis dans le Rif central (Maroc): Construction d'un espace de déviance," EspacesTemps.net, 30 September 2014, accessed 28 August 2017, https://www. espacestemps.net/en/articles/cannabis-dans-le-rif-central-maroc-2.

80. P. Paquignon, "Le monopole du tabac au Maroc," *Revue du Monde Musulman* 5, no. 3 (1911): 501.

81. "Convention of Commerce and Navigation between Great Britain and Morocco, Signed, in the English and Arabic languages, at Tangier, December 9, 1856," in *A Complete Collection of the Treaties and Conventions, and Reciprocal Regulations, at Present Subsisting between Great Britain and Foreign Powers*, ed. L. Hertslet (London: Butterworths, 1859), 915–16.

82. L. Godard, *Description et histoire du Maroc* (Paris: Charles Tanera, 1860), 179.

83. A. Leared, *Morocco and the Moors* (London: Sampson Low, Marston, Searle, and Rivington, 1876).

84. D. T. de Cuevas, "Estudio general sobre geografía, usos agrícolas, historia política y mercantil, administración, estadística, comercio, y navegación del Bajalato de Larache . . . ," *Boletín de la Sociedad Geográfica de Madrid* 16, no. 1 (1884): 231–34.

85. P.-A. Chouvy, "Production de cannabis et de haschich au Maroc: Contexte et enjeux," *L'Espace Politique* 4, no. 1 (2008): art. 59.

86. L. Mercier, "Une opinion marocaine sur le monopole du tabac et du kif," *Archives Marocaines* 4 (1905): 154.

87. Afsahi and Mouna report that he allowed continued production in the Rif. The primary sources I have identified do not mention this exception, which was likely overlooked. See Afsahi and Mouna, "Cannabis dans le Rif central"; Paquignon, "Le monopole du tabac au Maroc," 494, 503; "Consul's Reports," *Chemist and Druggist* (30 July 1887): 125–26.

88. V. Piquet, *Le Maroc: Géographie, histoire, mise en valeur* (Paris: Armand Colin, 1917), 361.

89. "Dahir du 2 décembre 1922 (12 rebia II 1341) portant règlement sur l'importation, le commerce, la détention et l'usage des substances vénéneuses," *Bulletin Officiel de l'Empire Chérifien Protectorat de la République Française au Maroc* 12, no. 534 (1923): 57–64.

90. Chouvy, "Production de cannabis et de haschich au Maroc."

91. J. H. Dunant, *Notice sur la Régence de Tunis* (Geneva: Jules-Germaine Fick, 1858), 206; M. Morelet, "Les Maures de Constantine en 1840," *Mémoires de l'Académie des Sciences, Arts et Belles-Lettres de Dijon* 3, 3d series (1876): 275; A. Sebaut, *Dictionnaire de la législation tunisienne*, new ed. (Dijon, France: Sirodot, 1896), 584.

92. Sebaut, *Dictionnaire de la législation tunisienne*, 149.

93. "Décret beylical du 4 Djoumadi-el-Aoual 1308 (16 December 1890): Instituant une Direction des Monopoles chargée de la Régie des tabacs, des poudres et du sel," in *Journal des tribunaux français en Tunisie, 2e année: 1890*, ed. L. Bossu (Sousse, Tunisia: Imprimerie-Papeterie-Librairie Française, 1891), 333.

94. Dukerley, "Note sur les différences que présente avec le chanvre ordinaire et la variété de cette espèce connue en Algérie sous les noms de *kif* et de *tekrouri*." Indeed, when Tunisia displayed *takrūri* at a world's fair in 1883, it came from across the border: Société Franco-Africaine en Tunisie, ed., *Exposition Internationale and Coloniale d'Amsterdam 1883: Section Tunisienne, Catalogue* (Tunis: Française B. Borrel, 1885), 118.

95. In 1895, *kif, ḥashīsh*, and *shīra* imports were banned, but *takrūri* was not. *Shīra* was a name for hashish also recorded in what is now Syria. Tunisian imports came from Malta, although *shīra* was produced in the area of Constantine, Algeria, by 1921. See Sebaut, *Dictionnaire de la législation tunisienne*, 349. A. Pointière, *Les syndicats professionels* (Rochefory, France: Société Anonyme de l'Imprimerie Charles Thèze, 1906), 170; L. Livet, "Les fumeurs de Kif," *Bulletin de la Société Clinique de Médecine Mentale* 9 (17 January 1921): 40–45.

96. Visitors to Tunisia carried these packets out of the colony. In 1948, an old packet was found on a U.S. ship in Marseilles: United Nations Commission on Narcotic Drugs, *Summary of Illicit Transactions and Seizures*, vol. 3 (Lake Success, NY: United Nations Economic and Social Council, 1948), 51.

97. J.-L. de Lanessan, *La Tunisie*, 2d ed. (Paris: Challamel, 1918), 79.

98. L. Leclerc, *Kachef er-roumoûz (Révélation des énigmes) d'Abd er-Rezzaq ed-Djezaïry* (Paris: Baillière et Fils, and Leroux, 1874), 366–67.

99. Docteur Bertherand, "Mémoire sur le kif ou haschich en Algérie, au point de vue de la consommation, de l'influence sur la santé et de la réglementation administrative," *Revue des Sociétés Savantes* 3, 3d series (1878): 98–133. See also Monsieur Meilhon, "L'aliénation mentale chez les Arabes," *Annales Médico-Psychologiques* 3, 8th series (May 1896): 364–77.

100. "No. 10720: Décret rendant applicable à l'Algérie le décret du 14 septembre 1916 concernant l'importation, le commerce, la détention et l'usage des substances vénéneuses, notamment l'opium, la morphine, la cocaine," *Bulletin des Lois de la République Française, New Series* 9, nos. 193–216 (1917): 186; "Loi concernant l'importation, le commerce, la détention et l'usage des substances vénéneuses, notamment l'opium, la morphine, la cocaine," *Journal Officiel de la République Française* 48, no. 190 (1916): 6254.

101. Livet, "Les fumeurs de Kif."

102. J. C. Miller, *Way of Death: Merchant Capitalism and the Angolan Slave Trade, 1730–1839* (Madison: University of Wisconsin Press, 1988); D. B. Domingues da Silva, *The Atlantic Slave Trade from West Central Africa, 1780–1867* (Cambridge: Cambridge University Press, 2017).

103. A. Castilho, ed., *Exposition Universelle d'Anvers, Exposition Coloniale du Portugal: Catalogue Officiel* (Anvers, Belgium: Kockx, 1885), 109, 117, 171; "Productos de Angola," *Annaes do Conselho Ultramarino, Parte Não Official*, series 3 for 1862 (1868): 17–19; *Catalogue spécial de la section portugaise à l'Exposition Universelle de Paris en 1867* (Paris: Commission Impériale, 1867), 453; P. A. A. de Figueiredo, *Catalogue spécial de la section portugaise à l'Exposition Universelle de Paris en 1878* (Paris: A. Pougin, 1878), 316; Museu Colonial, "Exposição de productos tropicaes em Liverpool em setembro de 1907: Representação da Sociedade de Geographia de Lisboa," *Boletim da Sociedade de Geographia de Lisboa*, no. 12, 25th series (1907): 421.

104. C. de Almeida, "Generos coloniaes," advertisement, in *Novo almanach de lembranças Luso Brazileiro para o anno de 1884*, ed. A. X. Rodrigues Cordeiro (Lisbon: Lallement Frères, 1883), 189.

105. Mr. Lartigue, "Contributions à la géographie médicale: La lagune de Fernand-Vaz et le delta de l'Ogo-Wé," *Archives de Médecine Navale* 14 (1870): 175.

106. Daniell, "On the D'amba, or Dakka, of Southern Africa," 363–64; A. F. F. da Silva Porto, *Viagens e apontamentos de um portuense em África* (Lisbon: Divisão de Publicações e Biblioteca, Agência Geral das Colónias, [ca. 1885] 1942), 231; F. Welwitsch, "Apontamentos phyto-geographicos sobre a flora da Provincia de Angola na Africa equinocial servindo de relatorio preliminar ácerca da exploraçáo botanica da mesma provincia executada por ordem de Sua Magesta de Fidelissima," *Annaes do Conselho Ultramarino, Parte Não Official* 1 (1858): 547.

107. H. Capello and R. Ivens, *De Benguela as terras de Iácca*, vol. 2 (Lisbon: Imprensa Nacional, 1881), 259; H. A. Dias de Carvalho, *Expedição portugueza ao Muatiânvua: Descripção da viagem á Mussumba do Muatiânvua, Volume 2: Do Cuango ao Chicapa* (Lisbon: Imprensa Nacional, 1892), 50.

108. J. J. d'Almeida, "Na Provincia de Angola: Administração colonial debaixo do ponto de vista agricola," pt. 1, *Revista Agronómica* 2, no. 5 (1904): 143.

109. This is the high end of the range of dimensions Daniell suggests. The volume of these cones ranges from 824 cubic centimeters to 6,590 cubic centimeters: Daniell, "On the D'amba, or Dakka, of Southern Africa."

110. Jackson describes the packets as about two feet long but does not mention their diameter: J. R. Jackson, "On the Products of the Hemp Plant (*Cannabis Sativa*)," *The Technologist* 2 (1862): 177.

111. Monteiro, *Angola and the River Congo*, 61.

112. S. Lopes de Calheiros e Menezes, *Relatorio do Governador Geral da Provincia de Angola Sebastião Lopes de Calheiros e Menezes referido ao Ano do 1861* (Lisbon: Imprensa Nacional, 1867), 16, 21, 118, 203.

113. Tax rates ranged from 0 percent to 10 percent, depending on port and reporting period, and despite a flat 3 percent tax on declared value established in 1892: Ministerio dos Negocios da Marinha e Ultramar, *Pautas vigentes nas alfândegas das Provincias Ultramarinas Portuguezas: Documentos explicativos das pautas aduaneiros* (Lisbon: Imprensa Nacional, 1892), lxxv; H. A. da Silva Viola, *Guia Aduaneiro d'Angola e Congo* (Lisbon: Typographia de "A Editora," 1908), 152–53; G. A. de Brito Capello, "Providenciando sobre a fixação dos preços correntes dos generos coloniaes," in *Providencias publicadas pelo Commissario Regio a Provincia de Angola desde 18 de Junho até 15 de Fevereiro de 1897*, ed. Commissario Regio a Provincia de Angola (Lisbon: Imprensa National, 1897), 85–87.

114. Ministro d'Estado dos Negocios da Marinha e Ultramar, *Relatorio do Ministro e Secretario d'Estado dos Negocios da Marinha e Ultramar apresentado á Camara dos Senhores Deputados na Sessão Legislativa de 1898* (Lisbon: Imprensa Nacional, 1898), 201–2.

115. The 1899 data were published by a Belgian consul, not by Angolan authorities: Silva Viola, *Guia Aduaneiro d'Angola e Congo*, 152–53; J. Bribosia, "Consulat général de Belgique à Sainte-Croix de Ténériffe," in *Recueil consulaire contenant les rapports commerciaux des*

agents belges à l'étranger publié en execution de l'Arrêté royal du 13 novembre 1855, Tome 119: 1903, ed. Ministère des Affaires Étrangères, Belgium (Brussels: P. Weissenbruch, 1903): 274.

116. H. Chatelain and W. R. Summers, "Bantu Notes and Vocabularies, No. 1: The Language of the Bashi-Lange and Ba-Luba," *Journal of the American Geographical Society of New York* 25, no. 4 (1893): 527–28.

117. Ministro d'Estado dos Negocios da Marinha e Ultramar, *Relatorio do Ministro e Secretario d'Estado dos Negocios da Marinha e Ultramar apresentado á Camara dos Senhores Deputados na Sessão Legislativa de 1898*, 238–41. The reported tax revenue was 4$915 at an exchange rate of 4$504.11 per pound sterling: J. H. Norman, *A Reckoner of the Foreign and Colonial Exchanges between Seven Currency Intermediaries for the Traveller, Trader, and Financier* (London: Sampson Low, Marston, 1893), 84. The Angolan notation represents milréis followed, after the $ sign, by réis. Thus, one thousand réis, equal to one milréis, was written as 1$000.

118. Statistics initially included the category "*tabac en feuilles de Liamba*" (liamba-leaf tobacco), in which the "*de*" was probably an error for "*et*." The statistical category was later "*tabac en feuilles et Liamba*" (leaf tobacco and liamba). Reported Gabonese exports of leaf-tobacco-and-*liamba* likely consisted of only leaf tobacco: C. Cerisier, *Impressions coloniales (1868–1892): Étude comparative de colonisation* (Paris: Berger-Levrault, 1893), 267.

119. M. Iradier-Bulfy, *Africa: Viajes y trabajos de la Asociación Euskara, La Exploradora*, vol. 1 (Bilbão, Spain: Andres P.-Cardenal, 1901), 78; M. Iradier-Bulfy, *África: Fragmentos de un diario de viajes de exploración en la Zona de Corisco* (Madrid: Fortanet, 1878), 77; E. Jardin, "Aperçu sur la flore du Gabon avec quelques observations sur les plantes les plus importantes," *Bulletin de la Société Linnéenne de Normandie*, 4th series, vol. 4 (10 November 1890): 135–203, 179.

120. Iradier-Bulfy, *Africa* (1901), 94.

121. République Française, "Décret portant réglementation des Droits sur les Marchandises importées au Gabon," *Bulletin des Lois de la République Française, Series 29* 29 (1885): 585.

122. Gouvernement du Congo Français, "Arrêté promulguant la loi du 11 janvier 1892, relative au tariff général des Douanes et le décret du 29 novembre 1892, modifiant de tarif," *Bulletin Officiel Administratif du Congo Français* 1 (1893): 20; É. Loubert, "Congo français," *Archives Diplomatiques* 89, no. 1 (1904): 79–80.

123. Cerisier, *Impressions coloniales*, 280–85.

124. Import value from Gabon is from Cerisier, *Impressions coloniales*; the reported 118,147 francs converts to £4,684.7s.6¼d., based on 25.22 francs per pound. For Angola, published statistics were 112 kilograms of cannabis at 22$400; 115 kilograms of tobacco at 50$248. At an exchange of 21d. per milréis, the equivalent values are: cannabis, £1.19s.2¼d. (4¼d. per kilogram); tobacco, £4.7s.11¼d. (9¼d. per kilogram): see Administração Geral das Alfândegas, *Estatistica Geral das Alfândegas de Loanda, Benguella, Mossamedes e Ambriz nos annos de 1890 a 1894* (Lisbon: Imprensa Nacional, 1896), 211.

125. Exports valued at 182$000 were reported for 1891, from Luanda and Novo Redondo, but the exported weight was not reported. For 1892, 216 kilograms valued at 43$200 were exported. If the 1892 weight-to-value ratio is applied to 1891, this yields 910

kilograms. Taking the exchange of 1 milréis for 21 pence, the 1892 value is 4¼d.: see Administração Geral das Alfândegas, *Estatistica Geral das Alfândegas de Loanda, Benguella, Mossamedes e Ambriz nos annos de 1890 a 1894*, 23, 36.

126. The value was 4,694 francs. At 25.22 francs per pound, this makes 14¼d. pence per kilogram: see Cerisier, *Impressions coloniales*, 265; Norman, *A Reckoner of the Foreign and Colonial Exchanges between Seven Currency Intermediaries for the Traveller, Trader, and Financier*, 86.

127. M. Ferreira Ribeiro, *Relatorio ácerca do Serviço de Saude Publica na Provincia de S. Thomé e Principe no Anno de 1869* (Lisbon: Imprensa Nacional, 1871), 104, 258.

128. A. F. Moller, "Exploração botanica nas possessões Portuguezas," *Jornal de Horticultura Pratica* 17 (1886): 41; C. Ivens, "Consulat général de Belgique à Sainte-Croix de Ténériffe," in *Recueil consulaire contenant les rapports commerciaux des agents belges à l'étranger publié en execution de l'Arrêté royal du 13 novembre 1855, Tome 100: 1898*, ed. Ministère des Affaires Étrangères, Belgium (Brussels: P. Weissenbruch, 1898): 12; C. Ivens, "L'Angola méridional," *Société d'Études Coloniales (Belgium)* 5, no. 5 (1898): 233–69.

129. Bribosia, "Consulat général de Belgique à Sainte-Croix de Ténériffe," 274.

130. Ministerio da Marinha e Ultramar, *Doença do Somno: Relatorios enviados ao ministerio da marinha pela missão scientifica nomeada por portaria de 21 de fevereiro de 1901* (Lisbon: Libanio da Silva, 1901).

131. Moller, "Exploração botanica nas possessões Portuguezas," 41.

132. Ministério das Colónias, Portugal, "Portaria provincial proibindo, na provincia de Angola, o fornecimento a indigenas da *riamba*, ou *liamba*, por ter efeitos perniciosos semelhantes aos do ópio," in *Colecção da Legislação Colonial da República Portuguesa, 1913 (Janeiro a Dezembro)*, vol. 4 (Lisbon: Imprensa Nacional, 1918), 262.

133. Mattos e Silva, *Contribução o estudo da Região de Cabinda*, 263.

134. Ministério da Marinha e Colónias, Portugal, "Decreto, com fôrça de lei proibe a cultura, venda e importação de cânhamo indiano nas ilhas de S. Tomé e Principe, e o despacho aduaneiro de peixe sêco procedente da provincia de Angola, sem prévia inspecção sanitária," in *Colecção Oficial de Legislação Portuguesa: Ano de 1911, Primeiro semestre* (Lisbon: Imprensa Nacional, 1915), 694–95.

135. Ministère des Colonies, "Interdiction de la culture du chanvre et répression de son emploi comme stupéfiant en Afrique équatoriale française," *Journal Officiel de la République Française* 58, no. 207 (1926): 10017.

136. The 1918 law closed a loophole from 1916, eliminating uncertainty whether cannabis controls applied even to "natives": Présidence de la République, France, "Décret de 30 décembre 1916," *Journal Officiel de la République Française* 49, no. 3 (1917): 152; Présidence de la République, France, "Rapport et Décret de 5 March 1918," *Journal Officiel de la République Française* 50, no. 70 (1918): 2293–94.

137. Commissariat General du Gouvernment, "Circulaire au sujet des mesures à prendre contre l'usage et la diffusion du chanvre," *Bulletin Officiel Administratif des Possessions du Congo Français et Dépendances et du Moyen-Congo* (March 1907): 161–62.

138. Seguin, "Les hallucinations d'un fumeur de chanvre au Gabon."

139. These were "propaganda lessons" for administrators to use in teaching public health to colonial subjects: A. Ornelas and B. de Mesquita, *Relatorio da Missão Medica*

de Assistência aos Indígenas do Cuanza, República Portuguesa, Ministério das Colonias, Colecção de Relatórios, Estudos e Documentos Colonials, no. 24 (Lisbon: Agência Geral das Colónias, 1929), 62.

140. Export and import fees presumably went to the governments, but I have not found documentation.

141. The 1904 figure is questionable. The consul at Lourenço Marques (now Maputo, in southern Mozambique) reported that 35,183 pounds (about 17.5 tons) had been exported from that district. The consul at Mozambique town (northern Mozambique) reported that 110 tons had been exported from that district. The 110 tons exceeds the total reported from Lourenço Marques for 1904–13. I have found no other data from Mozambique town to assess whether the 110 tons represents a one-year event, an overestimate, or an error. See Mister Baldwin, *No. 3439 Annual Series: Diplomatic and Consular Reports. Portugal, Report for the Year 1904 on the Trade of Lourenço Marques* (London: Harrison and Sons, 1905), 42; Mister Greville, *No. 3422 Annual Series: Diplomatic and Consular Reports, Portugal, Report for the Year 1904 on the Trade and Commerce of the Consular District of Beira* (London: Harrison and Sons, 1905), 13–14. Additional trade statistics are in Mister Baldwin, *No. 3909 Annual Series: Diplomatic and Consular Reports, Portugal, Report for the Year 1906 on the Trade of Lourenço Marques* (London: Harrison and Sons, 1907), 31; Mister MacDonell, *No. 5558 Annual Series: Diplomatic and Consular Reports, Portugal, Report for the Year 1914 on the Trade and Commerce of Lourenço Marques and Other Portuguese Possessions in East Africa* (London: Harrison and Sons, 1916), 34; Mister Maugham, *No. 4881 Annual Series: Diplomatic and Consular Reports, Portugal, Report for the Year 1911 on the Trade of the Portuguese Possessions in East Africa* (London: Harrison and Sons, 1912), 21.

142. A. de Almeida de Eça, "Relatório de uma Comissão de serviço desempanhada no distrito de Moçambique," *Boletim de Agricultura*, nos. 7–9, 3d series (July–September 1915): 201, 209.

143. J. Burtt Davy, "Alien Plants Spontaneous in the Transvaal," in *Report of the South African Association for the Advancement of Science, Second Meeting Held at Johannesburg, April 1904* (Johannesburg: South African Association for the Advancement of Science, 1905), 275.

144. "South African News," *Chemist and Druggist* (31 December 1921): 39.

145. The figures are 129,000 kilograms in 1905 and 90 kilograms in 1910.

146. Almeida de Eça, "Relatório de uma Comissão de serviço desempanhada no distrito de Moçambique," 209.

147. Ministério das Colónias, Portugal, "Portaria provincial proibindo na colónia de Moçambique a importação, cultura, venda e consumo da planta conhecida cafrealmente por *bangue* ou *suruma*," in *Colecção da Legislação Colonial da República Portuguesa, 1914 (Janeiro a Dezembro)*, vol. 5 (Coimbra, Portugal: Imprensa da Universidade, 1918), 386.

148. E. Lupi, "A Região de Angoche," *Boletim da Sociedade de Geographia de Lisboa*, no. 8, 24th series (1906): 257; J. F. Elton, *Travels and Researches among the Lakes and Mountains of Eastern and Central Africa* (London: John Murray, 1879), 254; L. McLeod, *Travels in Eastern Africa*, vol. 2 (London: Hurst and Blackett, 1860), 301.

149. Elton, *Travels and Researches among the Lakes and Mountains of Eastern and Central Africa*, 254; "Companhia de Cultura e Comercio do Opio em Moçambique," advertisement, *Diario de Noticias [Lisbon]*, 17 November 1883, 4.

150. I have not located the text of Orange Free State's Ordinance No. 48 of 1903 (Dagga Prohibition Ordinance). The law's loophole was that it banned sales and use, not possession: Supreme Court of South Africa, "Rex v. Leeuw Chabalala," in *Reports of Cases Decided in the Supreme Court of South Africa (Orange Free State Provincial Division)*, ed. R. C. Streeten (Grahamstown, South Africa: African Book Company, 1911), 84.

151. Legal standardization was slow. In 1917, the Cape law formed the basis of a unified drug-control bill, though this did not become law until 1928, in the Medical, Dental and Pharmacy Act (No. 13 of 1928).

152. The 1899 amendment was influential but did not include either *dagga* or cannabis: "No. 7–1899: The Medical and Pharmacy Act Amendment Act," in *Acts of Parliament: Session of 1899, Being the Second Session of the Tenth Parliament*, ed. H. Tennant and E. M. Jackson (Cape Town: J. C. Juta, 1899): 4044–52.

153. "South African News," *Chemist and Druggist* 65 (3 December 1904): 897. This updates my 2016 paper, in which I stated that prohibition started 1922, a date I adopted from Chanock. The 1922 date is from a customs act, the full text of which I have been unable to locate: see Duvall, "Drug Laws, Bioprospecting, and the Agricultural Heritage of *Cannabis* in Africa"; M. Chanock, *Making of South African Legal Culture, 1902–1936: Fear, Favour, and Prejudice* (Cambridge: Cambridge University Press, 2001), 92–96.

154. Chanock, *Making of South African Legal Culture*, 92.

155. A. G. Stewart, "A Synopsis of a Report by G. A. Turner, M. B., D. P. H., on the Natives of Portuguese East Africa, South of Latitude 22°," *Proceedings of the Aberdeen University Anatomical and Anthropological Society* (1906–1908): 34–35.

156. Government of Natal, "Law No. 2, 1870: Law to Amend and Consolidate the Laws relating to the Introduction of Coolie Immigrants into this Colony, and to the Regulation and Government of such Coolie Immigrants," in *Natal Ordinances, Laws, and Proclamations, Volume 2: A.D. 1870–1878*, ed. C. F. Cadiz and R. Lyon (Pietermaritzburg, South Africa: William Watson, 1891), 752–73. German East Africa and German Southwest Africa also banned cannabis to control workers—specifically, colonial troops and other employees: Kaiserlichen Gouverneurs in Deutsch-Ostafrika, "Verordnung des kaiserlichen Gouverneurs vom 2. September 1891"; T. Seitz, "Sud-Ouest Africain Allemand. Importation, Culture, Commerce et Fumerie de Chanvre," *Recueil International de Législation Coloniale* 10, no. 3 (1912): 420.

157. Chanock, *Making of South African Legal Culture*, 92–96; C. J. G. Bourhill, "The Smoking of *Dagga* (Indian Hemp) among the Native Races of South Africa and the Resultant Evils," M.D. diss., School of Medicine, University of Edinburgh, 1913.

158. Before 1870, a church in Natal determined, "No member of this church is allowed to smoke wild hemp or tobacco": Tyler, *Forty Years among the Zulus*, 159.

159. D. Kidd, *Kafir Socialism and the Dawn of Individualism: An Introduction to the Study of the Native Problem* (London: Adam and Charles Black, 1908), 49.

160. J. Rebman, *Dictionary of the Kiniassa Language* (St. Chrischona, Switzerland: Church Missionary Society, 1877), 134; Government of the Colony of Natal, *Supplement*

to the Blue Book for the Colony of Natal: Departmental Reports, 1890–91 (Pietermaritzburg: P. Davis and Sons, 1892), B95.

161. Tyler, *Forty Years among the Zulus*, 123; Junod, H. A. (1912) *The Life of a South African Tribe. I. The Social Life* (Neuchatel, Switzerland: Attinger Frères), 314.

162. This quote is of a pharmacist who was paraphrasing a doctor's testimony; the pharmacist disagreed, believing instead that *dagga* "only causes [users] to sleep very heavily": "South African News," *Chemist and Druggist* (3 December 1904): 897.

163. Bourhill, "The Smoking of *Dagga*," 55; Sampson, "'Zeer grote liefhebbers van tobak,'" 6; Labor Commission of the Government of the Colony of the Cape of Good Hope, *Minutes of Evidence and Minutes of Proceedings, September–December 1893* (Cape Town: W. A. Richards and Sons, 1894), 356.

164. Puzzlingly, the 1925 convention does not specify *dagga*.

165. W. B. O'Shaughnessy, "Case of Tetanus, Cured by a Preparation of Hemp (the Cannabis Indica)," *Transactions of the Medical and Physical Society of Bengal* 8 (1839): 462–69.

166. Duvall, *Cannabis*, 135–38.

167. Indian Hemp Drugs Commission, *Report of the Indian Hemp Drugs Commission*.

168. A. Teodoro de Matos, ed., *O Tombo de Dio* (Lisbon: Comissão Nacional para as Comemorações dos Descobrimentos Portugueses, 1999), 99.

169. Mills, *Cannabis Britannica*.

170. Indian Hemp Drugs Commission, *Report of the Indian Hemp Drugs Commission*.

171. "Reviews and Literary Notes," *Chemist and Druggist* 41 (30 January 1892): 174–75.

172. In London, the term *gauza* was occasionally used. This cognate was associated with Bombay (now Mumbai), where most cannabis shipments were loaded, while *ganja* was associated with Calcutta (now Kolkata).

173. These descriptors may have suggested provenance to some people. In India, "brown" was associated with "Bengal ganja" (the favored type) and "green" with "Bombay" (which was disfavored): Indian Hemp Drugs Commission, *Report of the Indian Hemp Drugs Commission*, 96.

174. "Trade Report," *Chemist and Druggist* (18 June 1887): 754–57; "Trade Report," *Chemist and Druggist* (14 December 1889): 838–42; "Thursday's Drug Auctions," *Chemist and Druggist* (31 July 1909): 225–26.

175. "Trade Report" (18 June 1887), 199–202.

176. "Trade Report," *Chemist and Druggist* (2 October 1886): 470.

177. "Commercial Compendium," *Chemist and Druggist* (31 March 1925): 439–40.

178. "South African News," *Chemist and Druggist* (31 December 1921): 39.

179. Duvall, *Cannabis*, 138; S. Liet, *La philosophie absolue par le Docteur Mure* (Rio de Janeiro: L'Institute Homéopathique de Brésil, 1884), 3.

180. W. Manson, "A Proving of Indian Hemp," *Chemist and Druggist* (15 November 1883): 543–44; "Haschische-Eating," *Chemist and Druggist* (15 February 1870): 34–35.

181. Mills, *Cannabis Britannica*; J. H. Mills, *Cannabis Nation: Control and Consumption in Britain, 1928–2008* (Oxford: Oxford University Press, 2012).

182. D. Hooper, "Extract of Indian Hemp," *Chemist and Druggist* (4 August 1894): 207–8.

183. "Cannabis Indica," *Chemist and Druggist* (29 March 1902): 500. American imports were not recorded in London until 1917: "American Cannabis Indica," *Chemist and Druggist* (14 July 1917): 50.

184. National Wholesale Druggists Association, *Proceedings of the National Wholesale Druggists Association, 43rd Annual Meeting* (Minneapolis: The Association, 1917), 502.

185. Indian Hemp Drugs Commission, *Report of the Indian Hemp Drugs Commission*; W. Mair, "Indian Hemp: How It Is Grown and Prepared for Use in Medicine and as a Stimulant," *Chemist and Druggist* (30 July 1898): 166–68.

186. "Trade Report," *Chemist and Druggist* (31 May 1890): 745–48.

187. Mair, "Indian Hemp," 168; Hooper, "Extract of Indian Hemp."

188. "Commercial Compendium" (31 March 1925): 439–40.

189. A Pharmaceutical Resident, "Opium-Dealing in British Guiana," *Chemist and Druggist* 42 (28 January 1893): 120–21.

190. Historical consumers in Angola valued sticky, fragrant buds (Jackson, "On the Products of the Hemp Plant," 177), as do current marijuana aficionados.

191. Mair, "Indian Hemp."

192. Indian Hemp Drugs Commission, *Report of the Indian Hemp Drugs Commission*, 96.

193. Mair, "Indian Hemp."

194. G. Watt, "Dr. George Watt, C.I.E., on Ganja," *Chemist and Druggist* (19 February 1887): 225–26.

195. Mair, "Indian Hemp."

196. *Chur*, composed solely of flowers trimmed of seed leaves and separated from stems, is most similar to the "flowers" sold in present-day open markets.

197. E. M. Holmes, "Some of the Drug Exhibits at the Colonial and Indian Exhibition," *Pharmaceutical Journal and Transactions* 17 (20 November 1886): 419.

198. Watt, "Dr. George Watt, C.I.E., on Ganja."

199. "Commercial Compendium" (31 March 1925): 439–40. Just once did *Chemist and Druggist* mention a shipment destined for re-export: "Trade Report," *Chemist and Druggist* (1 June 1901): 901–4.

200. Watt, "Dr. George Watt, C.I.E., on Ganja."

201. A Pharmaceutical Resident, "Opium-Dealing in British Guiana"; T. Crossley Rayner, *The Laws of British Guiana*, vol. 5 (London: Waterlow and Sons, 1905), 73.

202. British Mauritius, Trinidad, and Guiana had import restrictions: R. J. Lechmere Guppy, *The Trinidad Official and Commercial Register* (Port-of-Spain, Trinidad: J. Wulff, n.d. [1882]), 63; C. W. Brebner, *New Handbook for the Indian Ocean, Arabian Sea and Bay of Bengal* (Mumbai: Times of India, 1898), 22. Dutch Guiana banned farming, sales, and unauthorized use: Governor of Surinam, "Ordinance of 17 February 1908, Tending inter alia to the Regulation of the Sale of Opium" (translation), in *Conference Internationale de l'Opium, La Haye, 1 décembre 1911–23 janvier 1912, Actes et documents, Tome 2: Documents* (The Hague: Imprimerie National, 1913), 147–55. Natal banned the plant drug specifically among Indian laborers: Government of Natal, "Law No. 2, 1870."

Jamaica, notably, was lax, by one account allowing "the indentured immigrant [to be] at full liberty to grow, manufacture and make use of the drug to his heart's content": J. H. Hart, *Trinidad: Annual Report on the Royal Botanic Gardens, and Their Work for 1888* (Port-of-Spain, Trinidad: Government Printing Office, 1889), 13.

203. A Pharmaceutical Resident, "Opium-Dealing in British Guiana."

204. Discounting happened in London, too, for uncertain reasons. A pharmaceutical trader in 1889 offered "seven bales of very stalky and dusty grey" herbal material at 2½ pence per pound, under the seller's original buying price of 4 pence: "Trade Report" (14 December 1889): 839.

205. The actual measures were ten grains of ganja and five grains of opium.

206. The stated price was 16s. per pound, or £1.15s.2½d. per kilogram: A. Sinclair, *In Tropical Lands: Recent Travels to the Sources of the Amazon, the West Indian Islands, and Ceylon* (Aberdeen, UK: D. Wyllie and Son, 1895), 130.

207. Hart, *Trinidad*, 13.

208. Sinclair, *In Tropical Lands*, 130; West India Royal Commission, *Report of the West India Royal Commission, Appendix C, Volume 2: Containing Parts II, III, IV, and V, Proceedings, Evidence, and Documents Relating to British Guiana, Barbados, Trinidad, and Tobago* (London: Eyre and Spottiswoode, 1897), 343.

209. West India Royal Commission, *Report of the West India Royal Commission*, 343.

210. "Commercial Compendium" (31 March 1925): 439–40; "The Cannabis-Indica Duty," *Chemist and Druggist* (28 February 1902): 71.

211. "Trade Report," *Chemist and Druggist* (21 July 1900): 112–16.

212. "Trade Report," *Chemist and Druggist* (6 April 1907): 528–30; Xrayser, "Observations and Reflections," *Chemist and Druggist* (10 November 1906): 715.

213. A Pharmaceutical Resident, "Opium-Dealing in British Guiana."

214. The non-decimal value was 1s.1d. I combine data from Guiana, Demerara, and Berbice. Published exchange rates for British Guiana were often not followed in the colony, which at various times used British, Dutch, Spanish, and U.S. currency, as well as local issues. The published data on *ganja* imports and exports used Spanish dollars as the monetary unit; the official exchange rate was 1 Spanish dollar (written 1$) to 4s.2d.: R. Chalmers, *A History of Currency in the British Colonies* (London: Eyre and Spottiswoode, 1893), 136.

215. P. Figyelmesy, "British Guiana," in *Commercial Relations of the United States with Foreign Countries during the Years 1882 and 1883, Volume 2: Africa, America, Asia, Australasia, and Polynesia* (Washington, DC: U.S. Government Printing Office, 1884), 280; D. G. Garraway, "Customs' Notice," *Official Gazette of British Guiana* 17 (27 May 1903): 1445–48.

216. "II. Suriname, Bijlage IJ, No. 30: Staat van den in- en doorvoer van het entrepot te Paramaribo," *Koloniaal Verslage* 5 (1895–96): 1–7; "II. Suriname, Bijlage T, No. 25: Staat van den invoer der Kolonie Suriname in 1894," *Koloniaal Verslage* 5 (1895–96): 1–7; Ministère des Affaires Étrangères, the Netherlands, *Conference Internationale de l'Opium, La Haye, 1 décembre 1911–23 janvier 1912, Actes et documents, Tome 2: Documents* (The Hague: Imprimerie National, 1913), 99.

217. Administração Geral das Alfândegas, *Estatística Geral das Alfândegas de Loanda, Benguella, Mossamedes e Ambriz nos annos de 1890 a 1894*, 14, 21, 23, 27, 30, 36, 41, 48, 50, 59–60, 71, 211.

218. G. Weigel, "Neues vom Drogenmarkt," *Pharmazeutische Zentralhalle für Deutschland* 49 (1908): 961.

219. British publications did not mention medicinal plant shortages, probably to conceal information during war. In 1914 and 1916, American pharmacists wrote about difficulties acquiring supplies from India and many other locations affected by the war: see "Increase in Cost of Drugs," *American Druggist and Pharmaceutical Record* 64 (April 1916): 55; "The European War and the Drug Trade," *American Druggist and Pharmaceutical Record* 62 (August 1914): 56–57.

220. Almeida de Eça, "Relatório de uma Comissão de serviço desempanhada no distrito de Moçambique," 201, 209.

221. "American Cannabis Indica" (14 July 1917): 50.

222. "Commercial Compendium" (31 March 1925): 439–40.

223. Angolan exporters were hindered because many British pharmacists were not sure what *liamba* was in 1884: "[In a Recent Report on the Commerce of Loanda]," *Pharmaceutical Journal and Transactions* 14, 3d series (31 May 1884): 976. Notably, however, some knew of Angolan cannabis as "liamber": "[Referring to the Subject of the Leaves]," *Pharmaceutical Journal and Transactions* 14, 3d series (21 June 1884): 1035. The spelling likely represents a Cockney accent, suggesting knowledge of the plant drug filtered to London via British sailors who had visited Central Africa. Recall from chapter 4 the sailor Robert Drury, whose Cockney accent was evident in his account of Madagascar's "jermaughler."

224. Duvall, *Cannabis*, 81–82.

225. "The Medical Activity of the American Hemp-Plant Cannabis Indica," *New York Medical Journal* 12 (1870): 439.

226. W. W. Stockberger, "Drug Plants under Cultivation," in *Farmers' Bulletin No. 663* (Washington, DC: U.S. Department of Agriculture, 1915), 19.

227. The rumormonger was a physician in Kentucky who also wrote, "Flowering tops have been smoked for years, [but] only recently has there been any concern about it": J. D. Reichard, "The Marihuana Problem," *Journal of the American Medical Association* 125, no. 8 (1944): 594–95.

228. Duvall, *Cannabis*, chap. 3.

229. "Trade Report," *Chemist and Druggist* (8 September 1888): 338–42.

230. "The Drug and Chemical Markets in 1907," *Chemist and Druggist* (28 December 1907): 977–80.

231. "Trade Report," *Chemist and Druggist* (4 November 1911): 60–63.

232. Bewley-Taylor et al., *The Rise and Decline of Cannabis Prohibition*; Mills, *Cannabis Britannica*.

233. "Poisons and Pharmacy Act, 1908: Poisons Schedule [as Amended by Orders in Council to April 3, 1925]," *Chemist and Druggist* (4 April 1925): 509.

234. "Commercial Compendium" (31 March 1925): 439–40.

235. Indian Hemp Drugs Commission, *Report of the Indian Hemp Drugs Commission*, 268.

236. Lanessan, *La Tunisie*, 79.

237. Indian Hemp Drugs Commission, *Report of the Indian Hemp Drugs Commission*, 35–36.

238. J. H. Lloyd, "Mental Diseases," in *A Handbook of Practical Treatment*, vol. 3, ed. J. H. Musser and A. O. J. Kelly (Philadelphia: W. B. Saunders, 1912): 1011.

239. J. R. Reynolds, "Therapeutical Uses and Toxic Effects of Cannabis Indica," *The Lancet* 68 (22 March 1890): 637–38.

240. A. de Saldanha da Gama, *Memoria sobre as colonias de Portugal: Situadas na costa occidental d'Afrique* (Paris: Casimir, 1839), 73; J. Barrow, *An Account of Travels into the Interior of Southern Africa in the Years 1797 and 1798* (London: T. Cadell Jr. and W. Davies, 1801), 408; C. A. Marques, *Dicionário histórico-geografico da Provincia do Maranhão* (Rio de Janeiro: Fon-Fon e Seleta, [1870] 1970), 517; W. Roxburgh, "Communication on the Culture, Properties, and Comparative Strength of Hemp, and Other Vegetable Fibres, the Growth of the East Indies," *Transactions of the Society Instituted at London, for the Encouragement of Arts, Manufactures, and Commerce* 22 (1804): 363–96. Notably, Dutch and Afrikaners in South Africa do not seem to have complained about the lack of hemp fiber production in South Africa. The Netherlands had a more vibrant hemp industry than Great Britain, and *dagga* wages were a valuable use of the plant for settlers.

241. Animal tests, and other available assays, were rejected as untrustworthy by American pharmacists in 1917: National Wholesale Druggists Association, *Proceedings of the National Wholesale Druggists Association*, 502–3.

242. E. M. Houghton and H. C. Hamilton, "A Pharmacological Study of Cannabis Americana (Cannabis Sativa)," in *Proceedings of the American Pharmaceutical Association at the Fifty-fifth Annual Meeting* (Baltimore: American Pharmaceutical Association, 1907): 445–46.

243. A. T. Weil, N. T. Zinberg, and J. M. Nelsen, "Clinical and Psychological Effects of Marihuana in Man," *Science* 162, no. 859 (1968): 1235.

244. Houghton and Hamilton, "A Pharmacological Study of Cannabis Americana."

245. See J. C. Scott, "Everyday Forms of Resistance," in *Everyday Forms of Peasant Resistance*, ed. F. D. Colburn (Armonk, NY: M. E. Sharpe, 1989), 3–33.

246. The added value for herbal material sold in pharmacies was the ostensibly expert quality control the business claimed to offer. The price was 10d. per pound: "Allen and Hanburys' Price Current," advertisement, *Chemist and Druggist* supp. (15 January 1884): 3–13.

247. E. Hahn and J. Holfert, *Spezialitäten und Geheimmittel: Ihre Herkunft und Zusammensetzung* (Berlin: Julius Springer, 1906), 41.

248. Customs departments in the United Kingdom and United States assumed that one thousand cigarettes weighed three pounds. Ads for Savar's Cubeb Cigarettes ran for decades with the same prices, including that given in the text. For smaller purchase quantities, the inferred retail value for cannabis increases; for twelve cigarettes purchased for 12 pence, the equivalent is £3 per kilogram. Actual retail value was higher, because cigarettes were fractionally cannabis.

249. For a photo of this card, see Duvall, *Cannabis*, 172.

1. A. Berriedale Keith, *The Belgian Congo and the Berlin Act* (Oxford: Clarendon, 1919), 195; N. R. Hunt, *A Colonial Lexicon: Of Birth Ritual, Medicalization, and Mobility in the Congo* (Durham, NC: Duke University Press, 1999), 56; O. Likaka, *Naming Colonialism: History and Collective Memory in the Congo, 1870–1960* (Madison: University of Wisconsin Press, 2009), 46; T. E. Reeve, *In Wembo Nyama's Land: A Story of the Thrilling Experiences in Establishing the Methodist Mission among the Atetela* (Nashville: Methodist Episcopal Church, 1921), 180.

2. R. Zurayk, "Should Farmers Just Say No?" *Journal of Agriculture, Food Systems, and Community Development* 4, no. 1 (2013): 11–14.

3. J. Bloomer, "Using a Political Ecology Framework to Examine Extra-legal Livelihood Strategies: A Lesotho-based Case Study of Cultivation of and Trade in Cannabis," *Journal of Political Ecology* 16 (2008): 49–69; T. Kepe, "Cannabis Sativa and Rural Livelihoods in South Africa: Politics of Cultivation, Trade and Value in Pondoland," *Development Southern Africa* 20, no. 5 (2003): 605–15; A. A. Laudati, "Out of the Shadows: Negotiations and Networks in the Cannabis Trade in Eastern Democratic Republic of Congo," in *Drugs in Africa: Histories and Ethnographies of Use*, ed. G. Klantschnig, N. Carrier, and C. Ambler (Gordonsville, NY: Palgrave Macmillan, 2014), 161–81.

4. J. H. Mills, *Cannabis Britannica: Empire, Trade, and Prohibition, 1800–1928* (Oxford: Oxford University Press, 2003); L. Kozma, "Cannabis Prohibition in Egypt, 1880–1939: From Local Ban to League of Nations Diplomacy," *Middle Eastern Studies* 47, no. 3 (2011): 443–60.

5. Natal's 1870 law specifically targeted an ethnic group, identified in the law's title: "Law No. 2, 1870, to Amend and Consolidate the Laws relating to the Introduction of Coolie Immigrants into This Colony." Other early laws simply banned the ethnically marked cannabis products *ganja, bhang,* and *charas*: T. Crossley Rayner, *The Laws of British Guiana*, vol. 5 (London: Waterlow and Sons, 1905), 73; Indian Hemp Drugs Commission, *Report of the Indian Hemp Drugs Commission, 1893–1894* (Simla, India: Government Central Printing Office, 1894), 429; Governor of Surinam, "Ordinance of 17 February 1908, Tending inter alia to the Regulation of the Sale of Opium" (translation), in *Conference Internationale de l'Opium, La Haye, 1 décembre 1911–23 janvier 1912, Actes et documents, Tome II: Documents* (The Hague: Imprimerie National, 1913): 147–55; Government of Natal, "Law No. 2, 1870: Law to Amend and Consolidate the Laws Relating to the Introduction of Coolie Immigrants into This Colony, and to the Regulation and Government of Such Coolie Immigrants," in *Natal Ordinances, Laws, and Proclamations, Volume 2: A.D. 1870–1878*, ed. C. F. Cadiz and R. Lyon (Pietermaritzburg, South Africa: William Watson, 1891), 752–73.

6. C. S. Duvall, "Drug Laws, Bioprospecting, and the Agricultural Heritage of *Cannabis* in Africa," *Space and Polity* 20, no. 1 (2016): 10–25.

7. D. Bewley-Taylor, T. Blickman, and M. Jelsma, *The Rise and Decline of Cannabis Prohibition* (Amsterdam: Transnational Institute, 2014).

8. Sinha writes, without citing sources, that independent states in the "Horn of Africa" challenged the SCND during its negotiation, which at the time would have meant Soma-

lia and Ethiopia: J. Sinha, *The History and Development of the Leading International Drug Control Conventions* (Ottawa: Parliamentary Research Branch, Library of Parliament, 2001), 19–20.

9. S. Ellis, "West Africa's International Drug Trade," *African Affairs* 108, no. 431 (2009): 171–96; G. Klantschnig, "Histories of Cannabis Use and Control in Nigeria, 1927–1967," in Klantschnig et al., *Drugs in Africa*, 69–88; C. Paterson, "Prohibition and Resistance: A Socio-political Exploration of the Changing Dynamics of the Southern African Cannabis Trade, circa 1850–the Present," M.A. thesis, Department of History, Rhodes University, Grahamstown, South Africa, 2009.

10. D. Borchardt, "$1 Billion In Marijuana Taxes Is Addictive to State Governors," Forbes.com, 11 April 2017, accessed 21 August 2017, https://www. forbes. com/sites/ debraborchardt/2017/04/11/1-billion-in-marijuana-taxes-is-addicting-to-state-governors/#2e5016382c3b.

11. C. Lochhead, "Nevada Marijuana Sales Blow Away Predictions in First Year," *Las Vegas Review-Journal*, 28 August 2018, accessed 31 August 2018, https://www.reviewjour-nal.com/news/pot-news/nevada-marijuana-sales-blow-away-projections-in-first-year/.

12. L. Degenhardt, C. Bucello, B. Calabria, P. Nelson, A. Roberts, W. Hall, M. T. Lynskey, and L. Wiessing, "What Data Are Available on the Extent of Illicit Drug Use and Dependence Globally?" *Drug and Alcohol Dependence* 117, nos. 2–3 (2011): 85–101; L. Degenhardt, W.-T. Chiu, N. Sampson, R. C. Kessler, J. C. Anthony, M. Angermeyer, R. Bruffaerts, G. de Girolamo, O. Gureje, Y. Huang, A. Karam, S. Kostyuchenko, J. P. Lepine, M. E. M. Mora, Y. Neumark, J. H. Ormel, A. Pinto-Meza, J. Posada-Villa, D. J. Stein, T. Takeshima, and J. E. Wells, "Toward a Global View of Alcohol, Tobacco, Cannabis, and Cocaine Use: Findings from the WHO World Mental Health Surveys," *PLoS Medicine* 5, no. 7 (2008): e141.

13. R. C. Clarke and M. D. Merlin, *Cannabis: Evolution and Ethnobotany* (Berkeley: University of California Press, 2013), 330.

14. This is folklore, not research. For instance, the quoted source also says, "A couple African countries that we can definitely say host many of these [Landraces] are Macato and Ghana." Macato is not on any map: B. Bluntman, "The Future of Sativas: African Strains," 28 March 2012, accessed 30 April 2018, https://www.marijuana.com/news/2012 /03/the-future-of-sativas-african-strains.

15. "Breeder and Seedbanks," Seedfinder.eu, n.d. [2015], accessed 21 August 2017, http://en.seedfinder.eu/database/breeder; J. Cervantes, "World's Greatest Seed Banks," High Times, 2002, accessed 21 August 2017, http://hightimes.com/read/worlds-greatest -seed-banks.

16. I regret that a cofounder of Strain Hunters, Franco Loja, died from malaria in January 2017 while on expedition in the DRC: "Cannabis World Mourns Untimely Death of Strain Hunter Franco Loja," High Times, 4 January 2017, accessed 21 August 2017, http:// hightimes.com/news/cannabis-world-mourns-untimely-death-of-strain-hunter-franco-loja.

17. "About SOA Seedbank," Seeds of Africa, 2013, accessed 21 August 2017, http://www .seeds-of-africa.com/about-soa-seedbank.

18. B. Breen, "Dr. Dope's Connection," Fast Company, 1 February 2004, accessed 21 August 2017, http://www.fastcompany.com/48172/dr-dopes-connection.

19. K. W. Hillig, "Genetic Evidence for Speciation in *Cannabis* (Cannabaceae)," *Genetic Resources and Crop Evolution* 52 (2005): 161–80; K. W. Hillig and P. G. Mahlberg, "A Chemotaxonomic Analysis of Cannabinoid Variation in *Cannabis* (Cannabaceae)," *American Journal of Botany* 91, no. 6 (2004): 966–75; J. Sawler, J. M. Stout, K. M. Gardner, D. Hudson, J. Vidmar, L. Butler, J. E. Page, and S. Myles, "The Genetic Structure of Marijuana and Hemp," *PLoS One* 10, no. 8 (2015): e0133292; S. L. Datwyler and G. D. Weiblen, "Genetic Variation in Hemp and Marijuana (*Cannabis Sativa* L.) According to Amplified Fragment Length Polymorphisms," *Journal of Forensic Sciences* 51, no. 2 (2006): 371–75.

20. "Who We Are," Biodiversity International, 2014, accessed 21 August 2017, http://www.bioversityinternational.org/about-us/who-we-are.

21. M. Pavelek and E. Lipman, *Report of a Working Group on Fibre Crops (Flax and Hemp)* (Velké Losiny, Czech Republic: European Cooperative Programme for Plant Genetic Resources and Biodiversity International, 2010), accessed 30 April 2018, http://www.ecpgr.cgiar.org/resources/ecpgr-publications/publication/report-of-a-working-group-on-fibre-crops-flax-and-hemp-2010.

22. See, e.g., the seed sources acknowledged in recent studies of cannabis genetics: Sawler et al., "The Genetic Structure of Marijuana and Hemp"; K. W. Hillig, "A Multivariate Analysis of Allozyme Variation in 93 *Cannabis* Accessions from the VIR Germplasm Collection," *Journal of Industrial Hemp* 9, no. 2 (2004): 5–22; K. W. Hillig, "A Combined Analysis of Agronomic Traits and Allozyme Allele Frequencies for 69 *Cannabis* Accessions," *Journal of Industrial Hemp* 10, no. 1 (2005): 17–30.

23. Scholars have also studied samples seized by police, but these do not include seeds and thus are not components of any biodiversity conservation initiatives. Scholarly studies that rely on commercial seed stock include: Hillig, "Genetic Evidence for Speciation in *Cannabis*"; Hillig and Mahlberg, "A Chemotaxonomic Analysis of Cannabinoid Variation in *Cannabis*"; Sawler et al., "The Genetic Structure of Marijuana and Hemp."

24. R. Bingham, "The Colorado Cannabis Business," BDS Analytics, n.d. [2016], accessed 21 August 2017, http://www.bdsanalytics.com/wp-content/uploads/2016/02/BDS_Analytics_Cannacon_Colorado.pdf.

25. During the fourth quarter of 2015, GSC was the tenth most valuable strain, with $1.5 million in sales: Bingham, "The Colorado Cannabis Business." Marijuana aficionados have known this strain as "Girl Scout Cookies," the name by which GSC entered open commerce sometime between 2010 and 2014. Girl Scouts of America, the youth organization, has challenged the "Girl Scout Cookies" strain name as trademark infringement. Consequently, marijuana merchants have shifted to the abbreviation: C. Sommers, "GSC: A Cookie by Any Other Name Would Smell as Dank," *Dope Magazine*, 5 April 2017, accessed 10 September 2018, https://www.dopemagazine.com/gsc-cookie-name-smell-dank/. More broadly, as marijuana moves out of a black market, trademark law has become a relevant consideration for the marijuana industry: B. McIver, "Are Your Strain Names Bait for a Lawsuit?," Cannabis Business Times, 11 July 2018, accessed 10 September 2018, http://www.cannabisbusinesstimes.com/article/are-your-strain-names-bait-for-a-lawsuit/; G. E. Temeles, C. Campbell, V. G. Norton, and A. Abelmann,

"IP Protection and the Cannabis Industry: Strategies and Trends," The Legal Intelligencer, 2 April 2018, accessed 10 September 2018, https://www.law.com/thelegalintelligencer/2018/04/02/ip-protection-and-the-cannabis-industry-strategies-and-trends/?slr eturn=20180810203059.

26. See the online catalogues of Sensi Seeds, https://sensiseeds.com/en, and Green House Seed Company, http://www.greenhouseseeds.nl/shop.

27. African News Agency, "Durban City Budget Embraces Radical Economic Transformation," The Citizen, 31 May 2017, accessed 21 August 2017, http://citizen.co.za/news /south-africa/1530157/durban-city-budget-embraces-radical-economic-transformation.

28. A. Nelson, "How Big Is the Marijuana Market?" CNBC.com, 19 April 2010, accessed 21 August 2017, https://www.cnbc.com/id/36179677; D. Borchardt, "Marijuana Sales Totaled $6.7 Billion in 2016," Forbes.com, 3 January 2017, accessed 21 August 2017, https://www. forbes.com/sites/debraborchardt/2017/01/03/marijuana-sales-totaled-6–7 -billion-in-2016/#1b4f283975e3.

29. See "List of Countries by GDP (Nominal)," Wikipedia.org, accessed 30 April 2018, https://en.wikipedia.org/wiki/List_of_countries_by_GDP_(nominal).

30. C. B. Thompson, "Alliance for a Green Revolution in Africa (AGRA): Advancing the Theft of African Genetic Wealth," Review of African Political Economy 39, no. 132 (2012): 345–50.

31. M. Cadogan, "Inside Views: The Legal Implications of Medical Marijuana as a Geographical Indication for Jamaica," Intellectual Property Watch, 2015, accessed 21 August 2017, http://www.ip-watch.org/2015/03/02/the-legal-implications-of-medicinal -marijuana-as-a-geographical-indication-for-jamaica.

32. M. Bouchard, G. Potter, and T. Decorte, eds., World Wide Weed: Global Trends in Cannabis Cultivation and Its Control (Farnham, UK: Ashgate, 2011); Zurayk, "Should Farmers Just Say No?"

33. R. Room, "Legalizing a Market for Cannabis for Pleasure: Colorado, Washington, Uruguay and Beyond," Addiction 109, no. 3 (2014): 345–51; International Narcotics Control Board, Report of the International Narcotics Control Board for 2014 (New York: United Nations, 2015), accessed 30 April 2018, https://www.incb.org/incb/en/publications /annual-reports/annual-report-2014.html.

34. Ministério das Colónias, Portugal, "Portaria provincial proibindo, na provincia de Angola, o fornecimento a indigenas da riamba, ou liamba, por ter efeitos perniciosos semelhantes aos do ópio," in Colecção da Legislação Colonial da República Portuguesa: 1913 (Janeiro a Dezembro), vol. 4 (Lisbon: Imprensa Nacional, 1918), 262.

35. Zurayk, "Should Farmers Just Say No?"; J. M. Blackwell, "The Costs and Consequences of U. S. Drug Prohibition for the Peoples of Developing Nations," Indiana International and Comparative Law Review 24, no. 3 (2014): 665–92; P.-A. Chouvy and L. Laniel, "Agricultural Drug Economies: Cause or Alternative to Intra-state conflicts?" Crime, Law, and Social Change 48 (2007): 133–50.

36. Kepe, "Cannabis Sativa and Rural Livelihoods in South Africa"; Bloomer, "Using a Political Ecology Framework to Examine Extra-legal Livelihood Strategies"; Laudati, "Out of the Shadows"; P. C. Pontes Fraga and J. A. Silva Iulianelli, "Plantios ilícitos de 'cannabis' no Brasil: Desigualdades, alternativa de renda e cultivo de compensação,"

Dilemas: Revista de Estudos de Conflito e Controle Social 4, no. 1 (2011): 11–39; L. Laniel, "Producing Cannabis in Africa South of the Sahara: A Review of OGD Findings in the 1990s," paper presented at the International Workshop on Drugs and Alcohol in Africa: Production, Distribution, Consumption, and Control, Oxford University, 2006, accessed 28 August 2017, http://laniel.free.fr/INDEXES/PapersIndex/CANNABIS _AFRICA_OXFORD/Cannabis_in_Africa_Oxford.htm; "Africa Expedition— Malawi," Green House Seed Company, 2010, accessed 16 August 2017, http://forums .strainhunters.com/index. html/expeditions/africa-expedition-malawi-r5.

37. United Nations Office on Drugs and Crime, *World Drug Report 2015* (New York: United Nations, 2015).

38. P.-A. Chouvy, "Production de cannabis et de haschich au Maroc: Contexte et enjeux," *L'Espace Politique* 4, no. 1 (2008): art. 59.

39. Laudati, "Out of the Shadows"; J. Buxton, *Drugs and Development: The Great Disconnect* (Singleton Park, UK: Global Drug Policy Observatory, 2015), accessed 17 September 2018, https://www.tni.org/en/publication/drugs-and-development-the -great-disconnect.

40. Kepe, "Cannabis Sativa and Rural Livelihoods in South Africa"; Zurayk, "Should Farmers Just Say No?"; Bloomer, "Using a Political Ecology Framework to Examine Extra-legal Livelihood Strategies." For example, in Zimbabwe, a license to grow cannabis for medicinal use costs US$50,000, which is certainly beyond the means of most people who currently grow in that country: T. Mukeredzi, "Zimbabwe's Medical Marijuana Future Uncertain," The Scientist, 12 September 2018, accessed 18 September 2018, https://www.the-scientist.com/news-opinion/ zimbabwes-medical-marijuana-future-uncertain-64785.

41. Laudati, "Out of the Shadows."

42. D. Baker, G. Pryce, G. Giovannoni, and A. J. Thompson, "The Therapeutic Potential of Cannabis," *Lancet Neurology* 2 (2003): 291.

43. C. S. Duvall, *Cannabis* (London: Reaktion, 2015), 186–87.

44. J. M. Bostwick, "Clinical Decisions, Option 1: Recommend the Medical Use of Marijuana," *New England Journal of Medicine* 368, no. 9 (2013): 866–67.

45. I thank my colleague John Carr for this phrase and concept.

46. N. D. Volkow, R. D. Baler, W. M. Compton, and S. R. B. Weiss, "Adverse Health Effects of Marijuana Use," *New England Journal of Medicine* 370, no. 23 (2014): 2219–27; W. Hall and L. Degenhardt, "The Adverse Health Effects of Chronic Cannabis Use," *Drug Testing and Analysis* 6 (2014): 39–45.

47. J. Herer, *The Emperor Wears No Clothes*, 12th ed. (Van Nuys, CA: Ah Ha, [1985] 2010).

48. Many authors in many journals appear to have taken material from *The Emperor Wears No Clothes* without citing it. I sincerely appreciate that the editors and author of the *Mayo Clinic Proceedings* cited their source: J. M. Bostwick, "Blurred Boundaries: The Therapeutics and Politics of Medical Marijuana," *Mayo Clinic Proceedings* 87, no. 2 (2012): 173.

49. V. Berridge, "Thinking in Time: Does Health Policy Need History as Evidence?" *The Lancet* 375 (6 March 2010): 798–99.

50. Mills, *Cannabis Britannica*; J. H. Mills, *Madness, Cannabis, and Colonialism: The "Native-Only" Lunatic Asylums of British India, 1857–1900* (New York: St. Martin's, 2000).

51. G. T. Carter, S. P. Javaher, M. H. V. Nguyen, S. Garret, and B. H. Carlini, "Rebranding Cannabis: The Next Generation of Chronic Pain Medicine?" *Pain Management* 5, no. 1 (2015): 13.

52. C. M. Lieberman and B. W. Lieberman, "Marihuana—A Medical Review," *New England Journal of Medicine* 284 (1971): 88–91. This pharmacopoeia is the *Běncǎo Jīng*, supposedly by the legendary Chinese Emperor Shénnóng.

53. Duvall, *Cannabis*, 33–36; G.-D. Lu and J. Needham, "A Contribution to the History of Chinese Dietetics," *Isis* 42, no. 1 (1951): 14.

54. P. Dioscorides, *De materia medica: Libri sex,* trans. Marcellus Vergilius (Florence: Iunta, 1518), 218.

55. T. Elby, "A Contemporary Guide to the Vedas: A Critical Survey of the Texts and Literature," *Religion Compass* 8 (2014): 130.

56. W. D. Whitney, *Atharva-Veda Samhita, Second Half: Books VIII to XIX, Indexes* (Cambridge, MA: Harvard University, 1905), book 8, hymn 8, verses 2–3, and book 11, hymn 6, verse 15.

57. G. J. Meulenbeld, "The Search for Clues to the Chronology of Sanskrit Medical Texts, as Illustrated by the History of *Bhanga* (Cannabis Sativa Linn.)," *Studien zur Indologie und Iranistik* 15 (1989): 64.

58. D. Friedman and O. Devinsky, "Cannabinoids in the Treatment of Epilepsy," *New England Journal of Medicine* 373, no. 11 (2015): 1048; W. R. Gowers, *Epilepsy and Other Chronic Convulsive Diseases: Their Causes, Symptoms, and Treatment* (London: J. and A. Churchill, 1881), 271–72.

59. Baker et al., "The Therapeutic Potential of Cannabis," 291; Carter et al., "Rebranding Cannabis," 13; D. I. Abrams and M. Guzman, "Cannabis in Cancer Care," *Clinical Pharmacology and Therapeutics* 97, no. 6 (2015): 575; R. D. Hosking and J. P. Zajicek, "Therapeutic Potential of Cannabis in Pain Medicine," *British Journal of Anaesthesia* 101, no. 1 (2008): 59.

60. S. H. Snyder, *Uses of Marijuana* (New York: Oxford University Press, 1971), 9.

61. Duvall, *Cannabis*, 186–87.

62. J. R. Reynolds, "Therapeutical Uses and Toxic Effects of Cannabis Indica," *The Lancet* 68 (22 March 1890): 637–38.

63. He qualified these sweeping statements. Regarding painful maladies, for instance, cannabis was "almost useless in sciatica, and in myodynia, whether in the neck, the thorax (pleurodynia), or the back (lumbago, sacralgia)."

64. A. M. Cooke, "Queen Victoria's Medical Household," *Medical History* 26 (1982): 307–20.

65. M. J. Eadie, "The Neurological Legacy of John Russell Reynolds (1828–1896)," *Journal of Clinical Neuroscience* 14 (2007): 311.

66. Berridge, "Thinking in Time."

67. M. Slavin, E. Barach, S. Farmer, R. Luba, and M. Earleywine, "Cannabis and Symptoms of PMS and PMDD," *Addiction Research and Theory* 25, no. 5 (2017): 384. These authors cite a pro-marijuana physician as evidence for the Victoria story: E. Russo,

"Cannabis Treatments in Obstetrics and Gynecology: A Historical Review," *Journal of Cannabis Therapeutics* 2, nos. 3–4 (2002): 5–35. For an example of the Victoria story in a formal medical training, see slide 18 in: J. M. David, "Medical Marijuana: The Evidence, the Law, and the New Guidelines," online presentation, St. Joseph's Hospital Health Center, Syracuse, NY, 2017, accessed 21 August 2017, https://www.sjhsyr.org/upload/docs/medicalEdu/46th/Saturday/2-Medical%20Marijuana.pdf.

68. Berridge, "Thinking in Time."

69. P. Sharpe and G. Smith, "Cannabis: Time for Scientific Evaluation of This Ancient Remedy?" *Anesthesia and Analgesia* 90, no. 2 (2000): 238.

70. None of the publications I've cited that link slaves and cannabis were obscure in nineteenth-century European science. Daniell's paper, as I stated in chapter 1, was in the leading *Pharmaceutical Journal*; Clarke's 1851 paper was in *Hooker's Journal of Botany*, an important periodical named for Joseph D. Hooker, a foremost British botanist. Du Chaillu's travelogues were widely read, as were many of the Portuguese sources that describe Angola. Monteiro's account of Angola was published in English. See W. F. Daniell, "On the D'amba, or Dakka, of Southern Africa," *Pharmaceutical Journal and Transactions* 9, no. 8 (1850): 363–65; P. B. Du Chaillu, *Explorations and Adventures in Equatorial Africa* (New York: Harper Brothers, 1861); J. J. Monteiro, *Angola and the River Congo*, vol. 2 (London: Macmillan, 1875); R. O. Clarke, "Short Notice of the African Plant Diamba, Commonly Called Congo Tobacco," *Hooker's Journal of Botany* 3 (1851): 9–11.

71. R. O. Clarke, "Observations on the Disease Lethargus: With Cases and Pathology," *London Medical Gazette* 26 (1839–40): 970–76.

72. Renner's paper provides a noteworthy description of conditions in commercial barracoons on Bunce Island, near Freetown ("crowded underground tunnels") and an account of the recollections of aged recaptives of the health conditions they experienced as enslaved children. Partly on the basis of Clarke's work, Renner argued that reports of sleeping sickness among slaves native to West Africa (not Central Africa) actually described beri-beri (thiamine deficiency): W. Renner, "Trypanosomiasis or Sleeping Sickness in Sierra Leone," *Journal of Tropical Medicine* 7 (1904): 349–50.

73. Renner, "Trypanosomiasis or Sleeping Sickness in Sierra Leone," 349. Thus, Sierra Leoneans may have been among the troops the Free State brought to bear on Kalamba Mukenge as his Bena Riamba movement crumbled.

74. Renner, "Trypanosomiasis or Sleeping Sickness in Sierra Leone."

75. Sara was a boy. This seems to have been his original, given name. He was found sick on a captured slave ship. He also suffered intestinal worms, which Clarke treated secondarily by administering turpentine against trypanosomiasis: Clarke, "Observations on the Disease Lethargus," 973.

76. R. O. Clarke, "Gold Coast, Enclosure No. 1: Medical Report for the Year 1858," in *The Reports Made for the Year 1858 to the Secretary of State Having the Department of the Colonies: The Past and Present State of Her Majesty's Colonial Possessions, Part II* (London: George Edward Eyre and William Spottiswoode, 1860), 29.

77. Perhaps cannabis might be useful in treating sleeping sickness? Several studies have shown that cannabis has pharmaceutical promise—and limitations—against trypanosomes:

J. L. Croxford, K. Wang, S. D. Miller, D. M. Engman, and K. M. Tyler, "Effects of Cannabinoid Treatment on Chagas Disease Pathogenesis: Balancing Inhibition of Parasite Invasion and Immunosuppression," *Cellular Microbiology* 7, no. 11 (2005): 1592–1602; A. J. Nok, S. Ibrahim, S. Arowosafe, I. Longdet, A. Ambrose, P. C. Onyenekwe, and C. Z. Whong, "The Trypanocidal Effect of Cannabis Sativa Constituents in Experimental Animal Trypanosomiasis," *Veterinary and Human Toxicology* 36, no. 6 (1994): 522–24; S. H. Abdelrahman, I. M. Mousa, S. M. E. Khojali, and A. A. Ismail, "Trypanocidal Effect of Cannabis Sativa on Experimental Camel Trypansomosis," *Research Journal of Medicinal Plants* 6, no. 3 (2012): 281–85.

78. R. O. Clarke, *Sierra Leone: A Description of the Manners and Customs of the Liberated Africans* (London: James Ridgway, 1843), 85.

79. R. O. Clarke, "Short Notes of the Prevailing Disease in the Colony of Sierra Leone," *Journal of the Royal Statistical Society* 19 (1853): 65. This publication offers a longer and more detailed description of the physical condition of recaptives than Clarke's earlier publication *Sierra Leone* (1843). Clarke was clearly affected by his observations, made principally in the late 1830s; "Short Notes of the Prevailing Disease in the Colony of Sierra Leone" is about illnesses seen at the colonial hospital among the general population. His description of recaptives was an aside.

80. Clarke, "Short Notice of the African Plant Diamba"; Clarke, *Sierra Leone*, 37.

81. Clarke, *Sierra Leone*, 37.

82. M. Singer, *Drugging the Poor: Legal and Illegal Drugs and Social Inequality* (Long Grove, IL: Waveland, 2008); S. R. Friedman, "Sociopharmacology of Drug Use: Initial Thoughts," *International Journal of Drug Policy* 13, no. 5 (2002): 341–47; A. Kalunta-Crumpton, "Introduction to Pan-African Issues in Drugs and Drug Control: An International Perspective," in *Pan-African Issues in Drugs and Drug Control: An International Perspective*, ed. A. Kalunta-Crumpton (New York: Routledge, 2015): 3–13; B. Alexander, *The Globalization of Addiction: A Study in Poverty of the Spirit* (New York: Oxford University Press, 2008).

83. R. Brunel, *Le monachisme errant dans l'Islam* (Paris: Maisonneuve and Larose, [1955] 2001).

84. L. Raynaud, *Étude sur l'hygiène et la médecine au Maroc suivie d'une notice sur la climatologie des principalese villes de l'empire* (Algiers: S. Léon, 1902), 109.

85. S. Galea and D. Vlahov, "Social Determinants and the Health of Drug Users: Socioeconomic Status, Homelessness, and Incarceration," *Public Health Reports* 117, supp. 1 (2002): S135–45; C. Spooner and K. Hetherington, "Social Determinants of Drug Use," technical report no 28, National Drug and Alcohol Research Centre, Sydney, 2004; K. E. Fothergill, M. E. Ensminger, K. Green, J. A. Robertson, and H. S. Juon, "Pathways to Adult Marijuana and Cocaine Use: A Prospective Study of African Americans from Age 6 to 42," *Journal of Health and Social Behavior* 50, no. 1 (2009): 65–81; K. J. Karriker-Jaffe, "Neighborhood Socioeconomic Status and Substance Use by U.S. Adults," *Drug and Alcohol Dependence* 133 (2013): 212–21; B. C. Haberstick, S. E. Young, J. S. Zeiger, J. M. Lessem, J. K. Hewitt, and C. J. Hopfer, "Prevalence and Correlates of Alcohol and Cannabis Use Disorders in the United States: Results from the National Longitudinal Study of Adolescent Health," *Drug and Alcohol Dependence* 136 (2014): 158–61.

86. B. Mirken, "Marijuana and the Media: Science, Propaganda, and Sloppy Reporting in the U.S. News Media," in *Pot Politics: Marijuana and the Costs of Prohibition*, ed. M. Earleywine (New York: Oxford University Press, 2007), 141–58; B. Stelter, "A Popular Plant Is Quietly Spreading across TV Screens," *New York Times*, 15 September 2009, C1; S. S. Davenport and J. P. Caulkins, "Evolution of the United States Marijuana Market in the Decade of Liberalization before Full Legalization," *Journal of Drug Issues* 46, no. 4 (2016): 411–27.

87. Friedman, "Sociopharmacology of Drug Use."

88. Cooke, "Queen Victoria's Medical Household."

89. P. G. Fine and M. J. Rosenfeld, "Cannabinoids for Neuropathic Pain," *Current Pain and Headache Reports* 18, no. 10 (2014): art. 451, 2.

90. R. A. Nicoll and B. E. Alger, "The Brain's Own Marijuana," *Scientific American* (December 2004): 70.

91. R. L. Pacula, B. Kilmer, A. C. Wagenaar, F. J. Chaloupka, and J. P. Caulkins, "Developing Public Health Regulations for Marijuana: Lessons from Alcohol and Tobacco," *American Journal of Public Health* 104, no. 6 (2014): 1021–28; T. S. Ghosh, M. Van Dyke, A. Maffey, E. Whitley, D. Erpelding, and L. Wolk, "Medical Marijuana's Public Health Lessons—Implications for Retail Marijuana in Colorado," *New England Journal of Medicine* 372 (2015): 991–93.

92. J. Fellner, *Decades of Disparity: Drug Arrests and Race in the United States* (New York: Human Rights Watch, 2009), accessed 30 April 2018, https://www.hrw.org/sites/default/files/reports/us0309web_1. pdf; H. G. Levine, "Global Drug Prohibition: Its Uses and Crises," *International Journal of Drug Policy* 14 (2003): 145–53; American Civil Liberties Union, *The War on Marijuana in Black and White* (New York: American Civil Liberties Union, 2013), accessed 30 April 2018, https://www.aclu.org/files/assets/aclu-the waronmarijuana-rel2.pdf.

93. I. Glasser, "American Drug Laws: The New Jim Crow," *Albany Law Review* 63, no. 3 (1999): 703–15; M. Alexander, *The New Jim Crow: Mass Incarceration in the Age of Colorblindness* (New York: New Press, 2010).

Index

henbane (*Hyoscyamus niger*), 81, 177
herders, 105, 168, 183, 202
Herer, Jack, 223
Herero (language), 60, 89
Hindi (language), 45, 55, 74, *77*, 78, 81, 86, 133, *134*, 136, 150, 160
Hindu Kush, 8, 47, 56, *75*
homosexuality, 135, 145, 296n44

indentured laborers, 31, 129, 160, 228; from Africa, *130*, 149, 164, 168, 180, 199; cannabis dispersal and, *82*, 150–51; cannabis use by, 29–30, 107, 150–51, 168; drug-control laws targeting, 107, 206, 216; from India, 107, 132–33, 150–51, 163–64; smoking pipes and, 150
India, 41, 62, *75*, 149, 170, 213, 219, 235n23; cannabis commerce and taxes in, 203, 205–6, 207, 209, 211–12; cannabis dispersal from, 56–57; cannabis evolution in Indian subcontinent, 46–47, 56; cannabis use by laborers in, 160, 214; cultural heritages of cannabis use in, 56–57, 103, 150, 153, 216–17; European and elite views of cannabis in, 167, 203, 160, 203, 211; Europeans in, 20, 22, 62, 85–86, 107, 212, 239n73; Indian laborers in overseas locations, 108, 132–33, 148, 149, 150–51, 205–6, 216, 242n119, 258n90; labor migration from, 45–46, *82*, 132, 163, 164; names for cannabis in, 56–57, 86, 253n26, 290n54, 293n92; non-pharmaceutical cannabis exports, 79, 81, 151, 205–6; psychoactive cannabis associated with, 35, 80, *103*, 207–8; role in global pharmaceutical market, 25, 188, 192, 199–200, 202–13; smoking pipes in, 58, 64, 150. *See also* South Asia (region)
Indian hemp: historical term for psychoactive cannabis, 20, 138, 149, 191, 202, 205, 207, 208, 224, 235n23; social construction of, 213
Indo-European language family, 40–42; names for cannabis in, 57, 252n15
Indonesia, 62, 74
intellectual property rights, 220–221. *See also* bioprospecting
International Opium Convention of 1912 (The Hague), 191
International Opium Convention of 1925 (Geneva), 8, 24, 184, 190, 202, 209, 210, 214, 216
Iran. *See* Persia
Islam: Islamic prohibitions of cannabis, 22, 96; portrayal in cannabis literature, 17–18, 22; Sufis, 96–100. *See also* Ḥeddawa brotherhood

Jamaica, *128*, 110, 141, 170, 17, 174, 213, 219, 220, 221; Africans in, 138, 139, 149, 164; cannabis use by laborers in, 25, 149, 160, 170–71, 327n202; cultural heritages of cannabis use in, 149–51, 155, 159–60, 221; Indian labor migration to, 45, 132–33, 149, 151, 327n202; labor migrants

from, 153, 299n213; names for cannabis in, 132, *134*, 139, 153; reggae music in, *4*, 150, 221. *See also* Caribbean region; Rastafarianism
Jula (language), 140, 142

Kambaata (language), 60
Kananga (Democratic Republic of the Congo), *73*, 114–15, 119, 284n42
Kanem-Bornu Empire, 84
Kanuri, Central (language), 60
Kanuri, Manga (language), 60
Kanyok (language), *77*, 91
Kenya, *26*, 76, 170
Kete (language), 91
Khmer (language), 58, 253n26
Khoisan (ethnolinguistic group), 13, 73, 74, 86–87, 88, 104, 108, 109, 165–66; Khoikhoi subgroup, 24, 177
kif (word), 31; connotations in cannabis commerce, 192, 194–95; connotations of cannabis use, 29, 97–100, 101–2, 174, 177, *195*, 196, 227; definition and etymology, 81–82; geography of use, *77*, 81–82
Kigiryama (language), 63
Kimbundu (language), 45, 105, 107, 127, 136, 137, 141, 143, 151
Kingsley, Mary, 20, 170, 175–76
Knox, Robert, 79
Kolbe, Peter, 20
Koongo (language), 138, 140, 143, 150, 151, 153, 155, 160
Krahô (language), 137, 142
Krio (language), *77*, 142
Kush, Kingdom of, 80
Kwango-to-Lualaba area (Central Africa): cannabis in, 91, 93, 105, 139, 167; geography of, *73*, 91, 112–15, 141; slavery and slave trading in, 130. *See also* Bena Riamba

labor underclasses, 10, 48, 49, 160–64, 227–28, 229. *See also* canoe paddlers; capitalism; farmers; *fellaḥin* (farmers in Egypt); herders; indentured laborers; miners; porters; prisoners; receptives; sailors; sex workers; slavery, chattel; slavery, wage; slaves; soldiers
Lake Chad basin, 59, 60, 73, 83, 84
Lake Tanganyika basin, *73*, 89, 91, 175. *See also* Malawi; Mozambique
Lala-Bisa (language), 89
Lamarck, Jean-Baptiste, 35, 38
Lancet, The (medical journal), 4, 222, 225
Lega (language), 103
Lemba (political-religious movement), 110–11
Leonotis species, 87
Lesotho, *26*, 86, 174, 217
Levant (region): early evidence for cannabis in, 18, 96; role in Orientalist thought, 19, 23–24, 71, 149;

cannabis fiber production in, 44, 208–9, 213; cannabis use by U.S. soldiers, 57, 127–28, 153, 174; current cannabis markets in, 30, 220; drug-law enforcement in, 5, 152, 218, 230; early evidence for *Cannabis indica* in, 44, 81–82, 154–55, 208–9; pharmaceutical cannabis market in, 208–9, *210*, 211, 213, 214; role in establishing international cannabis prohibition, 7–8, 209, 216; slavery and slave trading in, 129, 148, 151, 164; smoking pipes in, 57–58, *69*, 71

Uruguay, *128*; drug-control laws in, 217; names for cannabis in, *134*, 136

Venezuela, *128*, 151, 207
Victoria, Queen (United Kingdom), 6, 222, 224–25, 228
Vietnamese (language), 253n26
Vili (language), 60, 68, 155

Washington, George, 6, 228, 235n23
Winterbottom, Thomas, 182
Wissmann, Hermann von, 20, *21*, 22, 115, 118–22, 174, 280n5, 280n7, 283n27, 284n35, 284n42, 285n60
Wuzlam (language), 60

Xhosa (language), 60, 74

Yao (language), 60, *63*, 76, *77*, 89, 155
Yemen, 16, 56, 62, 100
yerba maté (*Ilex paraguarensis*), 135

Zambezi River basin, *73*, 267n121; cannabis biogeography and, 82, 86, 89–92; practices of cannabis use in, 79, 104, 109; smoking pipes in, 67–68
Zambia, *26*, 91, 93; names for cannabis in, 86, 89, 93; practices of cannabis use in, 106, 109, 124, 188; smoking pipes in, 58, 68, 73, 76
Zande (language and cultural group), 83, 84–85, 171
Zanzibar (Tanzania), 18, *26*, *73*, 78, 159, 312n74; cannabis commerce in, 79, 208, 209, *210*, 213; names for cannabis in, 78, 103
Zappo Zap (mercenaries), 114, 120, 123, 189
Zimbabwe, 24, *26*, 75, 76, 86, 87, 217
Zinacantán Tzotzil (language), 68, 257n84
Zulu: cultural group, 14, 29, 105, *106*, 107, 108, 124, 202; language, 78, *106*